KEEP TALKING

Keep Talking

An Invitation to Linguistic Anthropology

ERIC S. HENRY

UNIVERSITY OF TORONTO PRESS
Toronto Buffalo London

© University of Toronto Press 2025
Toronto Buffalo London
utppublishing.com
Printed in Canada

ISBN 978-1-4875-6370-7 (cloth)
ISBN 978-1-4875-6371-4 (paper)
ISBN 978-1-4875-6373-8 (EPUB)
ISBN 978-1-4875-6372-1 (PDF)

All rights reserved. The use of any part of this publication reproduced, transmitted in any form or by any means, electronic, mechanical, photocopying, recording, or otherwise, or stored in a retrieval system, without prior written consent of the publisher – or in the case of photocopying, a licence from Access Copyright, the Canadian Copyright Licensing Agency – is an infringement of the copyright law.

Library and Archives Canada Cataloguing in Publication

Title: Keep talking : an invitation to linguistic anthropology / Eric S. Henry.
Names: Henry, Eric S., author
Description: Includes bibliographical references and index.
Identifiers: Canadiana (print) 20250268914 | Canadiana (ebook) 20250268922 | ISBN 9781487563714 (paper) | ISBN 9781487563707 (cloth) | ISBN 9781487563738 (EPUB) | ISBN 9781487563721 (PDF)
Subjects: LCSH: Anthropological linguistics – Textbooks. | LCGFT: Textbooks.
Classification: LCC P35 .H46 2025 | DDC 306.44 – dc23

Cover design: Liz Harasymczuk
Cover image: iStock.com / Man_Half-tube

We welcome comments and suggestions regarding any aspect of our publications – please feel free to contact us at news@utorontopress.com or visit us at utppublishing.com.

Every effort has been made to contact copyright holders; in the event of an error or omission, please notify the publisher.

We wish to acknowledge the land on which the University of Toronto Press operates. This land is the traditional territory of the Wendat, the Anishnaabeg, the Haudenosaunee, the Métis, and the Mississaugas of the Credit First Nation.

University of Toronto Press acknowledges the financial support of the Government of Canada and the Ontario Arts Council, an agency of the Government of Ontario, for its publishing activities.

Funded by the Government of Canada
Financé par le gouvernement du Canada
Canada

ONTARIO ARTS COUNCIL
CONSEIL DES ARTS DE L'ONTARIO
an Ontario government agency
un organisme du gouvernement de l'Ontario

FSC www.fsc.org
MIX
Paper | Supporting responsible forestry
FSC® C016245

Brief Contents

List of Figures, Tables, and Boxes xi

Preface xv

1 Talking About Talk: Key Terms and Concepts 1
2 What Is Language? 25
3 Language Socialization 45
4 Linguistic Relativity 63
5 Indigenous Languages and Revitalization 84
6 Social Identity and Performativity 108
7 Language and Gender 124
8 Raciolinguistics 143
9 Multilingualism and Globalization 163
10 Orality and Literacy 186
11 Digital Language 204
12 Researching Language in Society 218

Notes 233

Glossary 237

References 247

Index 275

Contents

List of Figures, Tables, and Boxes xi

Preface xv

1 Talking About Talk: Key Terms and Concepts 1
  Anthropology 2
  Linguistics 7
  An Anthropology of Language 15
  Conclusion 22

2 What Is Language? 25
  Animal Communication 26
  Human Language 30
  Discourse 33
  Conclusion 42

3 Language Socialization 45
  Two Language Socialization Stories 47
  Social Orientation: From Language to Culture 51
  Ongoing Socialization: "Not Just Kid Stuff" 56
  Conclusion 59

4 Linguistic Relativity 63
  The Sapir–Whorf Hypothesis 64
  Language as Cultural Practice 73
  Conclusion 81

5 Indigenous Languages and Revitalization 84
Walking with Indigenous Languages 87
Language Endangerment 95
Language Revitalization 98
Conclusion 105

6 Social Identity and Performativity 108
Performativity 110
Enregisterment 117
Connecting Language and Identity 119
Conclusion 121

7 Language and Gender 124
From Women's Language to Gendered Language 126
Language and Masculinity 137
Conclusion 140

8 Raciolinguistics 143
What Is Race? 145
African American Language 150
Covert Racist Discourse 154
Encounters across Race and Language 156
Conclusion 160

9 Multilingualism and Globalization 163
Colonialism and Standardization 166
Multilingual Societies 169
Mixing Languages Together 180
Conclusion 183

10 Orality and Literacy 186
Spoken and Written Texts 187
Orality and Verbal Art 190
Literacy 195
Multiliteracies 200
Conclusion 201

11 Digital Language 204
New Communication Technologies 206
Interdiscursivity 209
Texting LOL! 211
Conclusion 215

12 Researching Language in Society 218
Ethics 218
Interviewing: Learning How to Ask, Learning How to Listen 221
Linguistic Landscape 223
Dialect Surveys 227
Conclusion 230

Notes 233

Glossary 237

References 247

Index 275

Figures, Tables, and Boxes

Figures

1.1 A spectrogram of the author saying the word "house" 9
1.2a IPA consonant chart 10
1.2b IPA vowel chart 10
1.3 The competence–performance distinction in language is common in other creative practices 13
1.4 Canada, an infographic 21
2.1 Sue Savage-Rumbaugh communicating with the bonobo Kanzi 27
2.2 Edward Sapir 31
2.3 Suspicion, xkcd.com 35
2.4 Erving Goffman 37
2.5 Motion event narratives 41
3.1 Language socialization event in Papua New Guinea 49
3.2 Lhamo's village labelled using the spatial terms of Tibetan 54
4.1 Forming the Mandarin Chinese word for cousin 69
5.1 George Hunt 85
5.2 Bilingual campus signs from the University of British Columbia Okanagan in English and Nsyilxcn 94
5.3 Youth participate in a workshop using virtual reality technologies to teach Indigenous languages at the University of Alberta 104
5.4 Super Shamou #1, a bilingual Inuktitut/English comic book based on the IBC television character 105
6.1 A stereotypical image of a loubard 119
7.1 Common symbols used for male and female 133
7.2 Illustration from *Canadian Business* magazine 134
8.1 Advertising for Yinglun Foreign Language Training School in Shenyang, China 145
8.2 Zora Neale Hurston 151

9.1 Sign outside a holistic animal store in Montreal 166
9.2 Data from the 2016 census on immigrant languages in Canada 172
9.3 Anti-Mubarak sign displayed during the Arab Spring protests in Egypt 176
10.1 Hindu mantra written in Sanskrit from 1829 189
10.2 An algyschyt (blessing-giver) makes an offering of food during an algys 202
11.1 Two tweets that share the same hashtag but are used for very different pragmatic effects 208
11.2 Two dating profiles created by the same person 211
12.1 Mural in Euskara from Deba, Spain 225
12.2 Location of signs on Saint Catherine Street in Montreal categorized by language 226

Tables

3.1 Language Socialization Practices in North America and Papua New Guinea 50
5.1 Evidentials in Nuu-chah-nulth 92
5.2 The Graded Intergenerational Disruption Scale (GIDS) 96
8.1 Racializing Discourses Surrounding Payday Muggings 150
8.2 Temporal Reference in AAL 153
10.1 Literacy Styles in Three Southeastern US Communities 198
12.1 Chart Recording Responses to a Dialect Survey 230

Boxes

1.1 About Me 3
1.2 The International Phonetic Alphabet 9
1.3 How Many Languages? 15
1.4 Research Spotlight: Alessandro Duranti 23
2.1 Multispecies Anthropology 29
2.2 Edward Sapir (1884–1939) 31
2.3 Design Features of Language 32
2.4 Language and Artificial Intelligence 36
2.5 Erving Goffman (1922–1982) 37
2.6 Are Sign Languages Real Languages? 39
2.7 Research Spotlight: Hanwool Choe 42
3.1 Space as a Social Construct 52
3.2 Multilingual Socialization 55
3.3 Socializing the Anthropologist 56
3.4 Research Spotlight: Mary Bucholtz 60
4.1 Tethering Language and Community Together 66
4.2 "No Retirement Savings? Perhaps It's Because of the Language You Speak" 72
4.3 Pirahã: The People with No Numbers 74

4.4 Absolute Spatial Reference in Sign Languages 80
4.5 Research Spotlight: Niclas Burenhult and Asifa Majid 82
5.1 George Hunt (1854–1933) 85
5.2 English is Weird! 88
5.3 Words for Snow 90
5.4 The Lessons of Conlangs 97
5.5 Rita Joe: I Lost My Talk 100
5.6 Research Spotlight: Joanne DiNova and Lila Pine 106
6.1 The Performativity of Coming Out 112
6.2 Shibboleths 114
6.3 Research Spotlight: Sabrina Billings 122
7.1 Drag Queens and Gender Performance 129
7.2 Transgender Voices 133
7.3 Eroticization of Women's Voices 136
7.4 The Social Functions of Gendered Discourse 137
7.5 Masculinity and Law Enforcement 139
7.6 Research Spotlight: Jie Yang 141
8.1 Racist Zombies! Racialization in Comedy 147
8.2 Ethnicity and the Tiger Mama 148
8.3 Zora Neale Hurston (1891–1960) 151
8.4 The Raciolinguistic Power of Mockery 155
8.5 The Ethics of Playing At Race 159
8.6 Research Spotlight: Steve Bialostok and Marcus Watson 160
9.1 Newfoundland English 164
9.2 Russian Colonialism in Ukraine 168
9.3 Acadian French 172
9.4 Should English Be the Official Language of the United States? 174
9.5 Is English a Creole? 179
9.6 Chiac 182
9.7 Research Spotlight: Patricia Lamarre 184
10.1 The Hindu Vedas as Oral Literature 188
10.2 Signifyin' in Black English 194
10.3 Love Letters 196
10.4 Research Spotlight: Jenanne Ferguson 201
11.1 Digital Speech Communities 205
11.2 Emoji 🤔 🧐 😆 213
11.3 Research Spotlight: Karen Pennesi 215
12.1 Ethics Case Studies 220
12.2 Research Spotlight: Lisa Schlegl and Sali Tagliamonte 231

Preface

This book, as the title says, is an *invitation* to linguistic anthropology. I cover a lot of ground, but linguistic anthropology is a broad field and includes a range of different perspectives, meaning it is impossible to address every topic, sub-topic, and sub-sub-topic. That would take a whole series of books, and trust me, they are already out there. But what I think is often lacking is a text that teaches you to *think* like a linguistic anthropologist, to look at language in a new light.

I came to linguistic anthropology the long way around. I started off as a socio-cultural anthropologist who got interested in linguistics rather than a linguist who got interested in culture. The people I talked to while I was doing research in China pushed the question of language on me – it was what *they* were interested in, what they wanted to know more about. I've followed that lead, and although they probably would not agree with half of what I say, it got me interested in this peculiar little sub-field of anthropology that asks us to listen – carefully, attentively, patiently – to what people say and how they say it.

I see linguistic anthropology as a dialogue, one that exists both among scholars and among our research partners, our students, and the public. If you are taking linguistic anthropology in a class, I am likely in conversation with the person teaching it. They will have their own interests, stories, and examples. They might even disagree with what I say in this book. That's a good thing; ask them about it. What gets them excited about language? One thing we all share – and I hope you will too – is a passion for words and language, a respect for difference, and an abiding curiosity about how we communicate with others.

No one can be an expert on an entire field, especially me. In fact, one of my delights in writing this book has been the experience of learning, of reading widely in my discipline and discovering the exciting stuff people are doing. I would like to thank the many people who have inspired and supported this work: my colleagues at Saint Mary's University, friends I've met through the LingAnthLing network and other scholars, and my students, who ask perceptive and challenging questions (even ones that stump me). It's hard to be an anthropologist and have a big ego (there are some, but they have to try really hard). So I invite you to read, to consider, to question, and to come to your own conclusions. That's really the heart of learning.

1 Talking About Talk: Key Terms and Concepts

Topics

- Anthropology and the culture concept
- The field of linguistics
- Key ideas in linguistic anthropology

We make ourselves through language. I mean that – you would not be who you are without the ability to use language. You would not be able to think beyond a rudimentary level of awareness. You would not be able to navigate complex relationships with others. You would not be able to acquire new skills or learn new ideas. As humans, everything we do, everything we know, everything we are is mediated through our language.

A lot of people think about language as just words for stuff. When we learn a new language, we spend hours memorizing new labels for things like trees, houses, rain, noses, and so on. But a nose is a nose, and whether you call it a *bizi* (Mandarin), *nez* (French), or *ihu* (Maori) does not really matter, right? I think it does. This textbook is both an introduction to the field of linguistic anthropology and an extended argument for that position. What language we use, how we speak it, and with whom we speak are all-important components of not just our lives but our identities. These are the building blocks through which we present ourselves to others, reflect on and develop our social relationships, and form the very foundation of our thinking and self-awareness.

All language is also social. It is something we do with others, one of the key ways we are tied into communities. "Hello" is not just a word of greeting; it is a powerful expression of commonality and a sense that you and I are people who *should* greet each other. That's true around the world, although the words will obviously differ: in China, I would often be greeted with *"ni chi le mei?"* meaning "have you eaten?" That implies that, if I hadn't, I'm the kind of person who should be invited in and fed. The exact cultural rules governing these kinds of exchanges and interactions vary from place to place, and if you have ever tried learning a new language you will know they often take years of study to get the hang of.

Language is therefore both a structured code of communication – composed of distinct sounds combined into larger units of words and then sentences – and a cultural system. It is not enough just to know the grammar of a language; if you want to get your ideas across to others, you will also have to know how loud to talk, what topics might be off limits, how to appeal to logic or tradition or common sense. You will have to know the cultural rules shaping the way you should talk. Think of language like a car: it has an engine, fuel system, axle, wheels, and so forth. Most people know the basics of how a car works. But if you want to drive successfully, you had better also know the rules of the road, like what a yellow light means or how to drive through a roundabout.

Language is the same. Linguists are like mechanics who understand what all the components are and how they work together. Anthropologists are more likely to study the social conventions and cultural dimensions of interaction. And a linguistic anthropologist is someone who tries to bring these two perspectives together, taking a more holistic approach to the way people talk. And just as driving in Britain has different rules than driving in Canada, the structure of every language and the social conventions for using it are also incredibly variable. Over a hundred years ago, the anthropologist Bronislaw Malinowski (1923, 306) observed, "the study of any language, spoken by a people who live under conditions different from our own and possess a different culture, must be carried out in conjunction with the study of their culture and of their environment." This is still true today, and it is a principle guiding research in linguistic anthropology. To start, though, we need to get a sense of the two parts of this field: anthropology on the one hand and linguistics on the other.

ANTHROPOLOGY

Most people think of anthropologists as scholars who study "other" humans. You know, exotic people who eat bizarre foods, practice strange rituals, and speak incomprehensible languages. The stereotype is so ingrained in our culture that one needs only see a picture of a person in a pith helmet and khaki shorts squatting next to someone in "tribal" dress to make the connection. These are all stereotypes, though, not just of anthropologists but also the people we study. They constitute what

Michel-Rolph Trouillot (2003) calls anthropology's "savage slot": the association between the academic discipline of anthropology and the non-Western – and by implication also backwards and undeveloped – world. Anthropologists always counter that it is far more common for us to study derivatives traders (Miyazaki 2013), roboticists (Robertson 2018), or even a Mardi Gras krewe in New Orleans (Radice 2021). Even when we do study people in far-flung locations, it is almost always with the understanding that those lives are integrated into a larger global system driven by colonialism and capitalism (Heller and McElhinny 2017). In its scope, contemporary anthropology is miles away from the study of predominantly simple or small-scale societies.

In North America, there is a tradition of what is called **four-field anthropology**, including archaeology, biological anthropology, sociocultural anthropology, and linguistic anthropology. All four fields study humans in some regard but approach the topic from different angles. Archaeologists are often associated with the study of the past but are more accurately said to be concerned with human material culture: the stuff we make, use, and leave behind. Biological anthropologists study humans as physical beings: the history, evolutionary development, and physiology of our species. Sociocultural anthropologists try to understand our social and cultural lives, how we adapt to a changing world and understand the similarities and differences between human groups. Finally, there is **linguistic anthropology**. Like the other branches of the discipline, linguistic anthropologists look at humans, but particularly at the role of language in framing, interpreting, and creating our social worlds. That may all sound a bit vague at this point, but what differentiates anthropology from other social sciences like sociology or psychology is a common approach to the idea of culture as an organizing principle of human society and interaction.

BOX 1.1 – ABOUT ME

I should take a moment to tell you a little about who I am and how I approach a lot of the questions raised in this book. I'm the product of fairly typical middle-class upbringing in southwestern Ontario. Both sides of my family arrived as immigrants to Canada from Northern Ireland. That fact reflects how I look and the language I grew up with.

In junior high school I started learning French, but I was not very good at it. Apologies to Madame Bolender, my high school French instructor, but the teaching strategies were pretty bad back in those days. I remember reciting countless verb conjugations and sentence patterns: *je suis, tu es, il est, elle est, nous somme, vous êtes, ils sont, elles sont.* I'm getting better, but my French needs a lot of work.

I studied anthropology in university because I liked history and thought archaeology was cool (I still do). But I moved more towards sociocultural anthropology over time. I taught English in a city called Shenyang in northeastern China for a few years, and that got me thinking about language and its social dimensions. I started learning Mandarin Chinese at a place called Liaoning University, and I also studied the local dialect called Dongbeihua. This dialect is interesting because most urban citizens speak it, but they also tend to look down on it. They see Standard Mandarin as the path to advancement and English as a language of global opportunity. I eventually wrote a book about the research I did there, so you will notice I refer to China and my work from time to time in this text.

Now I teach at a university in Halifax. All of these influences shape the ways I speak – my language, my accent, the words I use – and also the ways I study and think about language.

The Culture Concept

The modern discipline of anthropology finds its origins in the Enlightenment, a period of time in the seventeenth and eighteenth centuries when European intellectuals were grappling with questions such as the nature of humankind; questions that demanded comparison between the supposed pinnacle of civilization (Europe at the time) and the non-European others that inhabited the rest of the globe. Based on the reports of adventurers, soldiers, and missionaries, Enlightenment thinkers employed comparisons between themselves and the presumed "savages" of North America, Australia, and Africa to examine their own place in the world and the nature of human society. In time, the writings of travellers to distant lands were replaced by more empirical investigations, and anthropology emerged as an academic specialization by the late nineteenth century (Eriksen and Nielsen 2013; Liebersohn 2008).

Early definitions of **culture** in anthropology tended to focus on the various features of human groups around the world. In his book *Primitive Culture*, one of the first British anthropologists, Edward Tylor (1832–1917), defined culture as "that complex whole which includes knowledge, belief, art, morals, law, custom, and any other capabilities and habits acquired by man as a member of society" (Tylor 1874, 1). There are two things to note about Tylor's definition: first, it is all-encompassing. While popular notions of culture, even today, equate the idea with civility, art, taste, and aesthetics, Tylor included everything from law to religion to emotion. He even had a chapter on arithmetic! Anthropologists today generally retain this expansive approach, arguing that almost everything we do or think or even feel is mediated in some way by culture.

The second element of Tylor's definition, however, is the sense in which culture is separate and autonomous from the people themselves. Tylor's approach was to classify groups of people by their religious beliefs, agricultural tools, political structures, and so forth. And presumably, these were all shared by any particular group of people, so one could study Hawaiian culture or Persian culture and describe its features as a kind of self-contained homogeneous whole. As the discipline developed, however, anthropologists increasingly found such a definition wanting.

Talking about cultures as abstract units was a natural extension of colonialism: colonizers wanted to organize, study, and manage the groups of people (and languages) under their control (Errington 2008). Since many of these groups lived in rural agricultural areas, it was easier to isolate a village or a community as the object of study and treat the beliefs and practices of those people as uniform. And from there, it was easy to imagine the world as a collection of distinct societies, each with its own unique culture. Until the late twentieth century, the idea of culture in anthropology was understood as a totalizing, thoroughly integrated system of shared meanings and beliefs (Gupta and Ferguson 1997).

There are a few problems with this approach. First of all, think about what this means as we view more familiar collectivities. Is there a Canadian culture, for instance? Sure, we can talk about hockey and poutine and being polite. But I did not play hockey growing up – I can still barely skate – and I've also met some pretty rude Canadians. Does this mean we don't belong to a Canadian culture? If all of us subscribe to a shared set of cultural ideals, why doesn't everyone get along? Why do we have arguments, disputes, disagreements, and forms of social, economic, and political inequality? And are cultures really as discrete and totalizing as we sometimes imagine? My children are biracial: which culture do they belong to?

If not Tylor's view of culture as a totalizing and integrated system, then, what is culture? In the 1970s and 1980s, a French sociologist by the name of Pierre Bourdieu advanced a different interpretation of culture based around the idea of practice. Essentially, Bourdieu argued that culture was a way of "doing" rather than a set of beliefs. The term he used for this sense of doing was **habitus**, and it forms the basis for understanding our experiences and interpreting the actions of others. "One of the fundamental effects of the orchestration of habitus is the production of a commonsense world," and by doing things together with others, whether it be participating in religious festivals or just sharing a common language, we come to see others as belonging to the same group as us, united by shared understandings (Bourdieu 1977, 80). Culture is active; it requires effort. Our identities are not given ahead of time but crafted in the way we live in the world, while embedded within a range of institutional and political forces like colonialism or capitalism. In the end, culture is not something we *have*; it is something we *do*.

Consequently, each of the chapters in this textbook focuses on a particular kind of *doing*: doing gender, for instance, or doing ethnicity. When we talk, we are also *doing* language. We are not simply using labels for things like dogs and cars and hamburgers; we are using language to act in the world. We use it to persuade, or to incite anger, or to make someone feel guilty, or to put things in order, manage someone's expectations, or teach a class. The list is endless, and each of these requires a manner of control and deftness over our language. If we are making friends, we don't want to scare someone off; if we are managing employees, we don't want to make them feel resentful. Language is the key to threading all these social needles in our everyday cultural lives.

Let me give an example. Back when I was in graduate school, I was a teaching assistant for an introductory anthropology class and we had probably the worst final examination ever created. It was every student's nightmare: long, confusing questions with tiny boxes students were supposed to write essay responses in. A complete disaster. As the time limit approached and students, looking harried and shell-shocked, came to the front of the room to hand in their papers, one nearly broke into tears in fear that she would fail the class. In response, I said something like it would be okay, we would make sure the examination was graded fairly; if she had studied she would do well, and so on. After the student left, the other teaching assistant accepting papers at the front, who happened to be from China, turned to me and said, "Wah... I can't believe it. You really work hard to give the professor face."

Now what is going on here? Face is one of those ideas that has long been attributed to Chinese "culture" (in Tylor's sense), often defined as an individual's sense of their own prestige and social worth (Hwang 1987). Giving face to someone means working to protect their sense of social worth from things that might threaten it – such as being associated with a terrible final exam. Causing someone to lose face, on the other hand, is experienced as a kind of social assault, an attack on a person's status. So, was I acting Chinese in this case? No – I certainly was not thinking about protecting the professor's face, I just wanted to reassure the student. But my friend applied her own framework of understanding, rooted in her own cultural experiences, and interpreted my actions accordingly. Same situation, same action, different interpretations. Does every Chinese person act to always give people face? Absolutely not! But it is a common and shared framework for understanding and making sense of the actions of others. That is culture.

Contemporary anthropologists therefore reject broad statements like "Chinese culture is concerned with the idea of face," as if everyone was running around with the same ideas in their heads. Face might be an important feature of social life in China, but it is not culture on its own. Instead, culture is how people *use* concepts like face to understand the world around them. Face acts as an important shared framework for structuring a person's approach to social problems, and for evaluating the actions of others. Let's turn now to the field of linguistics and then see how this idea of culture as a way of doing is related to using language.

LINGUISTICS

When I tell people I'm a linguist (and I tell them that largely because they have never *heard* of a linguistic anthropologist before), one of the most common responses is to ask, "can you tell me why people always say things wrong?" Why do people say "my head is *literally* about to explode" when they should be saying "figuratively"? Or, why do people insist on using words like "ain't" and "kinda" in their sentences – isn't it, you know, kinda wrong? A lot of people think about questions like these when they think about language, but they are not in any way related to what linguists actually study.

Like the field of anthropology, **linguistics** – the study of language – is a fairly new academic discipline that developed during the late nineteenth and early twentieth centuries. Certainly, scholars and philosophers have long mulled over questions of language, but before this time the approach was very different to what is seen today in modern linguistics courses. Known as **philology**, the study of language in this early period was primarily concerned with interpreting and understanding canonical texts, primarily in literary languages (Momma 2013). In the philological tradition, scholars would describe and compare the forms of, for instance, Macedonian Greek in the Homeric verses of the *Illiad* to discover and describe its grammatical system. Most of what we think of today as English grammar – the set of rules for putting together a "correct" English sentence – derives from this tradition. In English, for instance, philology tells us that a definite article is used to modify a noun that specifies one of many possible examples, so that "*the* apple" refers to one particular apple when there are many potential others. To use a definite article with a proper name ("the Eric") is therefore an incorrect form of English. Linguists today call this approach to language **prescriptivism** because it is essentially telling us that there is one distinct, normative, and correct form of English, and prescribes that it is the one people should use.

Modern linguists, sociolinguists, linguistic ethnographers, and linguistic anthropologists, however, almost universally employ an approach to language known as **descriptivism**, meaning that we describe how people use language in practice. In other words, we are far more concerned with what people *actually* say than in how other people think they *should* say it. For linguistic anthropologists, that prescriptive rule about the definite article is interesting, not in telling us how English should be used, but in the ways that people actually "break" that rule all the time. Canadian singer Abel Tesfaye calls himself The Weeknd despite the prescriptive rule that definite articles should not be used with proper names. In casual speech, people might even omit the definite article or reduce the vowel so it comes out sounding more like "I'll eat d'apple." All of these "improper" uses of English (and even the "proper" uses too) tell us something about the speaker, their identity, and what that person is doing with their language.

Ferdinand de Saussure

This shift from prescriptive philology to descriptive linguistics is most often associated with the Swiss linguist Ferdinand de Saussure (1857–1913). The child of a relatively affluent family, Saussure had learned Latin, Greek, and Sanskrit by the age of 19, then graduated from the University of Leipzig in 1880. Although much of his early work was strictly within the philological tradition – Saussure was an expert in the vowel systems of Indo-European languages – towards the end of his life he aspired to create a general theory of language. At the University of Geneva, Saussure taught a class called Course in General Linguistics, although he only offered it three times; Saussure died from influenza at the relatively young age of 55. He never published the content of these lectures, and so after his death two of his students compiled their class notes and edited together a book also called *Course in General Linguistics* (Saussure 1959).

What was revolutionary about Saussure's approach was several key insights about the nature of language. First, he notes that every time we pronounce a word (let's say "house"), there are minute variations in tone, pitch, rhythm, and articulation within our vocal tracts. Linguists can actually see this graphically using what is called a spectrogram, a visual representation of sound frequencies emitted from a human vocal tract (Figure 1.1). Each spectrogram of a person saying "house" will be slightly different, and different speakers will have slightly different accents from others, such as the way Canadians often pronounce the vowel in "house" slightly higher than American speakers, an acoustic phenomenon known as **Canadian Raising** (Chambers 2006). And yet, we recognize each of these as examples of a single word: house. Despite all the variation in how people talk (which Saussure called ***parole***), there is an underlying linguistic system that all speakers of that language have in common (which he called ***langue***). *Langue* is the shared, psychological component of language, while *parole* is the physiological act of speaking.

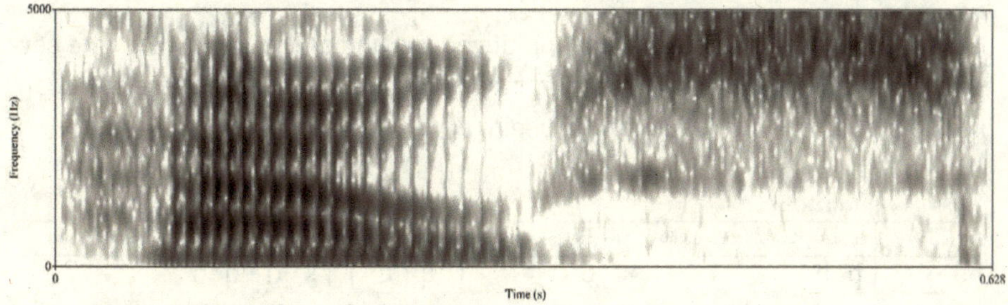

Figure 1.1 – A spectrogram of the author saying the word “house”

BOX 1.2 – THE INTERNATIONAL PHONETIC ALPHABET

English has notoriously bad spelling. Why do ‘ph’ and ‘f’ sound the same? Why does ‘ch’ sound like neither a ‘c’ or an ‘h’? Most of these issues came from the difficulty of adapting alphabets suited to Latin and Greek to an entirely different language, and the fact that much English spelling was standardized in the early seventeenth century when pronunciations were very different. As the linguist David Crystal (2014, 17) points out, the word “musician” – that we say as “myu-zi-shun” – would have been pronounced as “mu-zi-see-un” back in Shakespeare’s time, making the spelling a little more transparent.

Linguists need to deal with sounds in language, and those sounds are not always represented accurately by spelling. Nor does English spelling allow us to accurately represent the variety of sounds in other languages. The solution was the creation of the **International Phonetic Alphabet** (IPA) (Figures 1.2a and 1.2b). The IPA is a series of signs and notations that allow us to represent the full range of sounds in human languages. In this book, IPA notations will not be used frequently, but where they are they will be enclosed in slashes like this: /p/. Some of these look familiar: /f/ sounds like the ‘f’ sound in English (including ‘ph’ spellings as well). Others are a bit more exotic: the ‘sh’ sound looks like /ʃ/ and the vowel in the word ‘fun’ looks like /ʌ/. A trained linguist can look at the symbols /ænθɹəpɑlədʒ̃ɪ/ and easily see the word anthropology.

Two main charts, shown here, constitute the IPA. The consonant chart on the left is arranged into rows by type of sound (the quick release of air called a plosive in /p/ is different from the sustained flow, called a fricative, in /f/), and into columns by where the sound is produced in the mouth (/p/ at the lips, for instance, and /k/ at the roof of the mouth). The vowel chart is arranged like a cross-section of the mouth (facing left), so that the /i/ vowel in ‘sheep’ is produced high and at the front of the mouth, the /ɑ/ vowel in 'stop' produced low and at the back. There are several other markers that can be used to modify these symbols, but these two charts provide a good enough guide for the beginner.

CONSONANTS (PULMONIC)

	Bilabial	Labiodental	Dental	Alveolar	Postalveolar	Retroflex	Palatal	Velar	Uvular	Pharyngeal	Glottal
Plosive	p b			t d		ʈ ɖ	c ɟ	k ɡ	q ɢ		ʔ
Nasal	m	ɱ		n		ɳ	ɲ	ŋ	ɴ		
Trill	ʙ			r					ʀ		
Tap or Flap		ⱱ		ɾ		ɽ					
Fricative	ɸ β	f v	θ ð	s z	ʃ ʒ	ʂ ʐ	ç ʝ	x ɣ	χ ʁ	ħ ʕ	h ɦ
Lateral fricative				ɬ ɮ							
Approximant		ʋ		ɹ		ɻ	j	ɰ			
Lateral approximant				l		ɭ	ʎ	ʟ			

Symbols to the right in a cell are voiced, to the left are voiceless. Shaded areas denote articulations judged impossible.

(CC-BY-SA) 2020 IPA Typefaces: Doulos SIL (metatext); Doulos SIL, IPA Kiel, IPA LS Uni (symbols)

Figure 1.2a – IPA consonant chart

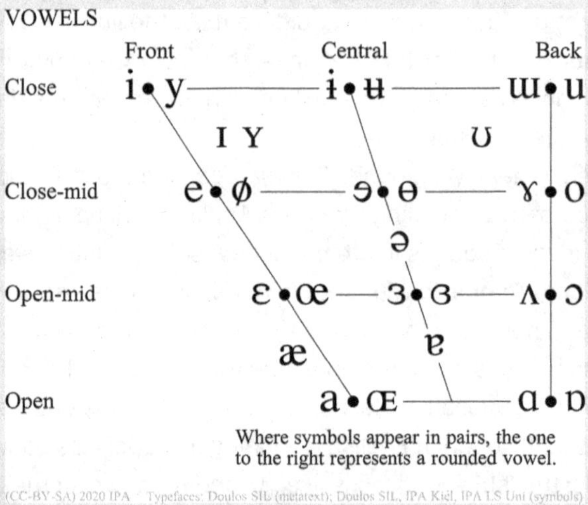

Figure 1.2b – IPA vowel chart

Source: Reproduced by permission of the International Phonetic Association

Second, Saussure proposed that the system of language is based on principles of opposition and contrast. A word can more properly be thought of as a **sign**, one that links a set of sounds or letters, which Saussure called the **signifier**, with a concept, the **signified**. The sounds /haʊs/ or the letters "house" are linked to the concept of a structure that people live in. That concept only gets its meaning, however, through contrasts with other concepts. In other words, the meaning of the word house is derived from its relation to other words (like cottage, apartment, and home), each with their own position within this system, rather than some fundamental quality of "house-ness" itself. A sign combines both of these aspects. The sounds of a language operate on similar principles – the recognition of the /t/ sound in English depends upon its contrast with /d/, /p/, /n/, and so on. That also means that the connection between any particular signifier and signified is fundamentally **arbitrary**: there is no natural link between the meaning of a word and how it sounds. For instance, there is no particular reason to label a tall, green, leafy thing with the word "tree." Any string of sounds will do, as we can see with words for tall, green, leafy things in other languages, like *arbre* in French or *cây* in Vietnamese. What is important is each sign's place within the overall system of meanings.

Third, language is always changing, and therefore the arrangement between components of the system is only ever temporary. Philology tended to trace the meaning of words over time (a **diachronic** approach), but Saussure believed that a true representation of a language comes from studying the complex relations between parts of the system at a given point of time (a **synchronic** approach). While the history of changes to a language are interesting in their own right, for Saussure it really does not matter where the word "house" comes from (the word is actually of Germanic origin), only what it means today.

The implications of Saussure's insights into the nature of linguistic systems were profound. Whereas philologists had imagined that language was just a way of expressing ideas (ideas that already exist in the mind independently of language), Saussure argued that our thought – our way of understanding and conceptualizing the world around us – is inherently linguistic (something we will come back to in Chapter 4 – Linguistic Relativity). Second, while philologists did not think much about language beyond the text they were studying, Saussure argued that language is an inherently *social* phenomenon, shifting and changing in response to the needs of a community of speakers. "For language is not complete in any speaker; it exists perfectly only within a collectivity" (Saussure 1959, 14).

Noam Chomsky

The next big paradigm shift in linguistics began in the 1960s with the work of Noam Chomsky (b. 1928), who fundamentally transformed the field of linguistics with his insights into the structure of language. While Saussure was primarily concerned with the meaning of words, Chomsky worked at the level of grammar. In particular, he was curious about how speakers of a language generate meaningful sentences – have we just memorized everything there is to say?

In 1957, the behavioural psychologist B.F. Skinner published *Verbal Behavior*, a landmark expression of his theory of language acquisition (Skinner 1957). In much the same way as a dog can be trained to sit or fetch a ball, Skinner believed that human children learn language through a process of training and reinforcement. Children see a stimulus (a red chair, for instance) and learn to formulate a response (the word "red"). Parents tell their child, "Don't say, 'he breaked the stick'; say, 'he broke the stick.'" Then, when children say, "he broke the stick," they receive positive reinforcement so that, over time, their linguistic system comes to resemble that of the previous generation. Chomsky's review of Skinner's book, however, demolished not only Skinner's argument, but his entire notion that behaviourism could explain language.

Chomsky borrows and extends Saussure's *langue/parole* distinction using the terms **competence** and **performance**. While Saussure's terminology was intended to capture the difference between the shared and individual elements of language, Chomsky argues that competence in a language is a product of each speaker understanding the underlying linguistic system, even if at an unconscious level. Look at two different sentences:

struggling artists can be a nuisance
marking papers can be a nuisance

At a surface level, these sentences appear very similar (Chomsky 1959, 54). But at a deeper, structural level, they are quite different: consider that you can say *struggling artists* are *a nuisance* but not **marking papers* are *a nuisance.*[1]

The intuitive, cognitive knowledge of language structure – knowing that one of these sentences is grammatical and the other ungrammatical, despite their surface similarity – is competence. Knowing that structure allows us to generate, from a few basic principles, an infinite variety of sentences (Chomsky 1965). This theory of language is therefore often called **generative grammar**. On the other hand, performance is the fragmentary and imperfect expression of that competence by any individual person, since we can never say every possible sentence in a language, and we often make mistakes when we speak. Performance is what we say and how we say it.

A good analogy here is the distinction, present in many forms of creative behaviour, between codes and their execution. A good musical score is a cohesive text demonstrating a profound understanding of harmony, genre, and the conventions of composition. It uses an exacting and detailed code to represent the placement and production of musical notes, allowing the generation of a nearly limitless variety of

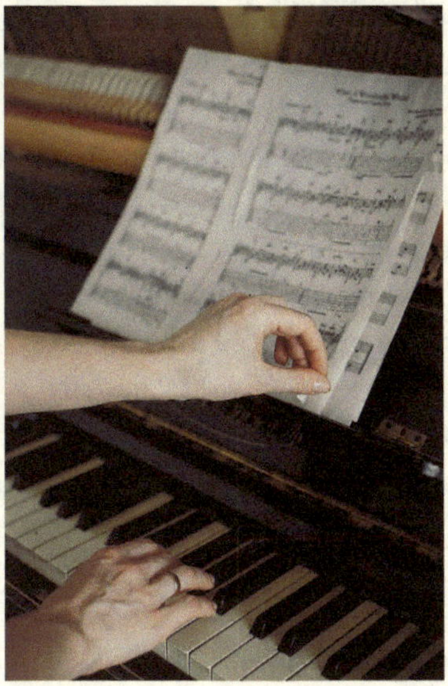

Figure 1.3 – The competence–performance distinction in language is common in other creative practices

musical compositions. However, a musician, even a good one, will never produce that idealized piece of music exactly in its intended form – in fact, part of the experience of hearing a good performer is that individual's interpretation of the music (Figure 1.3). Competence is to performance in language as the score is to its execution in music.

In his theoretical work, Chomsky downplayed the significance of performance in linguistic research, preferring to study the mental system itself rather than its messy realization in the act of speaking. "Linguistic theory," he wrote, "is concerned primarily with an ideal speaker-listener, in a completely homogeneous speech-community, who knows its language perfectly" (Chomsky 1965, 3). As we will learn, however, linguistic anthropologists see this as an oversimplification.

Levels of Linguistic Structure

Language is one of the most complex systems for encoding and conveying meaning between human beings. As such, linguists have developed a range of perspectives on this system, each with its own principles and theoretical models. Although anthropologists generally approach language from a more holistic perspective, it is still important to understand these different areas and how they relate to language as a whole.

1. **Phonology** – Sounds are the most fundamental unit of any spoken language.
   While **phonetics** studies how the human vocal tract produces sounds and how our

brains interpret them, phonology studies the use of sounds in human language to create meaning. As noted in the box on the IPA above, these sounds can be classified and organized into types (consonants and vowels, for instance), and the inventory of sounds (known as **phonemes**) that are used in one language will be different from those used in any other language.

2. **Morphology** – Sounds can be combined in sequence to create units of meaning. The phonemes /p/, /ɛ/, and /t/ come together to produce a **morpheme** "pet." Note that this is slightly different from the concept of a word, since "un-" and "-able" are also units of meaning in English; the word "unbelievable" is actually three morphemes strung together. Morphology is the study of the formation and structure of morphemes.
3. **Syntax** – When morphemes and words are strung together, they create larger structures such as sentences. Syntax describes the rules and principles through which meaningful sentences are generated in a language. For instance, a meaningful English sentence usually has a grammatical subject followed by a verb and then an object (*she drinks water*), and a different arrangement would make the sentence nonsensical (**drinks water she*).
4. **Semantics** – Understanding a sentence requires a person to decode the linguistic information they receive, and semantics is the study of how meaning is created and interpreted in a language. Sentences can often be ambiguous: does "a solitary bird" refer to a single bird, or to a species of bird that does not live in a flock? Semanticists examine how speakers interpret such ambiguities and process linguistic information.
5. **Pragmatics** – Language is social, and therefore social context plays a role in how people understand language. Putting the word "please" before a request in English is generally seen as making the request more polite. Similarly, French speakers have to choose between two second-person pronouns when addressing someone: *tu* (which is both singular and informal) and *vous* (which is plural and formal). Pragmatics studies this relationship between meaning and social context.

In North American universities, most linguists focus on the first three levels of linguistic structure: phonology, morphology, and syntax. These are, not coincidentally, the three levels that appear to be most objective – a linguist can generally test hypotheses and generate rules for language without worrying about the social context of the speaker. Linguistic anthropologists more generally pay attention to meaning and interaction, as constituted by semantics and pragmatics. This is not to say, however, that the first three levels are context-free. For example, linguistic anthropologist Norma Mendoza-Denton (2008) has studied Latina youth gangs in California high schools and argues that the phonetic realization of certain English words (the difference in pronunciation between "thing" and "ting") in certain morphological combinations (following some-, any-, or no-) is tied to shifting gang allegiances by the speakers.

As a discipline, linguistic anthropology lies at the intersection of these two fields of study: linguistics and anthropology. Obviously not everyone agrees on the exact ways in which they should be combined, but in general, linguistic anthropologists accept that the structured system of meaning we call language (the province of linguists) is deeply embedded in human culture (the province of anthropologists); therefore, language is a cultural system.

AN ANTHROPOLOGY OF LANGUAGE

If we want to study language as a cultural system, how do we do it? Most linguists can be said to study one or several languages; for instance, they look at the structure of French pronouns or Korean classifiers. When Chomsky described the "ideal speaker-listener," it was as part of an assumption that languages are perfectly shared (their words, grammar, and ways of speaking) among everyone who speaks that language. Linguistic anthropologists, in contrast, study specific groups of *speakers*.

BOX 1.3 – HOW MANY LANGUAGES?

Estimates of how many human languages are spoken in the world today vary greatly. *Ethnologue*, one of the most comprehensive sources on the world's languages, counted 7,151 as of 2022 (Eberhard, Sions, and Fennig 2022). However, some sources list more, others much less.

Uncertainty about the total number of languages comes from a range of factors. Many of the languages spoken in the world today are used by small communities of speakers, and documenting those languages takes time and resources. There are, quite simply, many languages that linguists do not know about.

Another issue lies in determining what separates one language from another. Consider that people from Denmark, Sweden, and Norway can more or less understand each other, despite speaking three "languages": Danish, Swedish, and Norwegian. On the other hand, many people refer to "dialects of Chinese" when in fact speakers of Mandarin and Cantonese cannot understand each other (just as an illustration, Mandarin Chinese has four tones while Cantonese has seven). Do we count the languages in these examples as separate languages? Or as the same?

Finally, the number of languages is rapidly shrinking as new technologies, forms of colonization, and economic pressures encourage people to shift to using national languages or global languages like English. Some linguists estimate that about half of the world's languages will disappear by the end of the twenty-first century (Anderson 2010).

When a linguist studies a language like Turkish or Icelandic, they often turn to texts with full sentences so that they can discern the syntax and morphology of the language. But a linguistic anthropologist, who studies the *doing* of Turkish or Icelandic, cannot rely on abstract sentences; you have to actually live with people speaking that language and see how they speak and what they do with it. The predominant method in both sociocultural anthropology and linguistic anthropology is therefore **ethnography**. Ethnography is a long-term method of engaging with a group of people, a kind of immersion into their cultural lives; some jokingly call it "deep hanging out." Most linguistic anthropologists do about a year of fieldwork as part of their graduate education, spending time with people, listening to how they talk, learning from them, asking questions, giving and receiving feedback on how we communicate. Social behaviour is complex and interconnected, making it difficult to comprehend. "Ethnography tries to do just that: describe the apparently messy and complex activities that make up social action, not to reduce their complexity but to describe and explain it" (Blommaert and Dong 2020, 12).

There are a few basic concepts we need to address in order to capture this social dimension of language, and they are ones that animate most linguistic anthropological research. These are the ideas of speech community, language ideology, and indexicality. In essence, they allow us to answer questions about who is talking, how they are talking, and what their language choices mean in context. Let's look at each of those in turn.

Speech Community

Linguistic anthropologists study groups of speakers because not everyone who speaks a language shares the same ideas about that language and how it should be used. For example, Tok Pisin is one of the national languages of Papua New Guinea, spoken by about four million people. In East Sepik province, Tok Pisin is largely replacing smaller local languages. The village of Gapun, studied by the linguistic anthropologist Don Kulick, is typical of this process: Tok Pisin is valued as a language of education, modernization, and economic development. Important leaders in the village speak Tok Pisin almost exclusively, while the local language Taiap is only used sporadically. Taiap is associated with family, tradition, and ritual, and thought to be best suited to women and children. As a result, almost everyone has shifted to speaking Tok Pisin, and Taiap words and phrases are gradually disappearing, to be replaced by those of the national language (Kulick 1992, 2019).

About a thousand kilometres away from Gapun is the village of Modawosi on the Trobriand Islands, just off the coast of Papua New Guinea. Here, most people can understand Tok Pisin and are able to speak the language, but Kilivila, the local language, is dominant and used for almost all everyday conversation. There is one exception though: Tok Pisin is used for *bisnis* (from the English word "business"). This includes politics, economic development, and relations with outsiders, but that's about it. People who speak Tok Pisin outside of such situations are considered pretentious and inauthentic, because Tok Pisin is associated with colonialism, outsider status, and economic exploitation (Michelle McCarthy, personal communication). One language, but two very different sets of ideas about how it should be used and what it represents.

Gapun and Modawosi are therefore considered two different speech communities. The standard definition of a **speech community** is "any human aggregate characterized by regular and frequent interaction by means of a shared body of verbal signs and set off from similar aggregates by significant differences in language usage" (Gumperz 1968, 43). Classically, this involved linguistic anthropologists looking at villages like these ones, or at other small groups of speakers who share a language with each other. But more recently, the complexity of speech communities has become apparent as people migrate around the world and new technologies mediate how we use language with each other (see Chapter 9 – Multilingualism and Globalization).

In my own work on language schools in China, the speech community of the city included lots of different people (local residents, migrants from other provinces, and foreigners) who used multiple languages (English, Mandarin, and the local dialect) in a range of different types of interactions (Henry 2021a). Despite this wide array of people and languages, most people broadly agreed on what it meant to speak them in any given situation. English is the language of global belonging and travel, Mandarin the language of school and work, and the local dialect the language of home and intimacy, and they used them accordingly. These common ideas and practices tied people together into a single speech community.

Speech communities are often defined geographically in terms of the location where a linguistic anthropologist does their research. But there are other ways to define a speech community too:

- **Occupation** – Charles Ferguson (1983) looked at sportscasters, arguing that the distinctive bare grammar and emphatic cadence ("He shoots! He scores!") transcends any individual sport. Sportscasters learn and employ this particular style to provide maximal information about the game in a punchy and exciting way for the audience. The conventionalization of sportscaster talk shows that its speakers not only share certain norms and rules for speaking, but also a certain enthusiasm about sports in general.
- **Generation** – Nancy Smith-Hefner (2007) has studied the emergence of a new language variety in Indonesia called *Bahasa gaul* that is used almost exclusively among young people. Borrowing from urban slang and foreign languages, *Bahasa gaul* is a casual language that youth use to differentiate themselves from the more formal, authoritarian, and hierarchical older generations.
- **Ethnicity** – Steve Bialostok and Marcus Watson (2022) explore the ways a group of Black men at a Midwestern community centre use a playful linguistic style called "talking shit" – characterized by vulgarity, insults, and humour – as a way of bonding together and imbuing their space with a shared African American experience, history, and identity.

Other possibilities include gender, religion, social class, or groups of people sharing self-ascribed interests and identities. This implies that people also belong to *multiple* speech communities, and that their language practices shift to match them as they navigate their lives (Morgan 2014). Some of these speech communities might overlap with the people close to them, while some do not. Different speech communities have different, and sometimes even competing, ideas about language – or even *languages*, since multilingual people can participate in a range of speech communities. Now let's think about how speech communities share *ideas* about language.

Language Ideology

In 2021, the *Oxford English Dictionary*, the self-described "definitive record of the English language," added the word "amirite," defining it as a colloquial interjection "used to invite agreement or to assert that one's previous statement is correct." Some people freaked out. A quick scroll through comments on Twitter and other social media channels reveals people exclaiming, "they're ruining English," "is nothing sacred?," and "just kill me now." Why? What's the big deal?

The issue here is our ideas about dictionaries, and in particular what function a dictionary performs. A lot of people treat a dictionary as a kind of authority on language; if a word is in the dictionary, it is in the language, and if a word is not in the dictionary, it isn't. Lexicographers, the people who actually compile dictionaries, see their role somewhat differently. For them, a dictionary is a record of the language as it is used over time: new words come in, old words become obsolete (Kirkness 2006). Echoing a distinction we made earlier, lexicographers are descriptivists while most of us think of dictionaries as prescriptive.

Speech communities are oriented towards common ideas and assumptions about language and how it is used: we call these **language ideologies**. Ideas about what a dictionary is – and by extension about language in general – are a good example. Other common language ideologies concern the nature of particular languages ("French is such a romantic language"), appropriate ways of speaking ("using the word 'like' all the time makes you sound like an idiot"), and stereotypes about groups of speakers ("women talk too much"). Note that none of these are objective statements; they are opinions and evaluations that masquerade as facts.

Linguistic anthropologists are interested in language ideologies because they shape how we use and interpret language. Think about the implications of a prescriptive approach to dictionaries. It implies that languages are defined by their words (and not their syntax or morphology or pragmatics) while prioritizing the written form of the language over the spoken as the definitive version. These words then appear to have relatively fixed meanings that are shared by all people who use that language (Seargeant 2011). That, in turn, serves to invalidate the creation of new words and meanings by the people who usually drive language change: youth. In other words, our very ideas about what a language is in the abstract – how it is defined, what purpose it serves, who has authority over it – are themselves ideological.

The concept of a language ideology is one we will return to throughout this book. For now, it is enough to say that language ideologies tend to reflect relations of power and serve certain political purposes. While these ideologies are usually explicitly about language, they are also implicitly about groups of speakers. For instance, we will see later how language ideologies that marginalize the speech of women and people of colour in the public sphere intersect with ideas about race and gender. Language ideology is therefore one of the key ways language links up with social structure (Woolard 2008).

Indexicality

So, speech communities are groups of people sharing similar speech practices and language ideologies. But if language ideologies tend to be relatively implicit, how do we make the connections between these ideologies and acts of speaking? To answer that, we need to consider some basic concepts in **semiotics**, the study of signs and meaning.

When Ferdinand de Saussure developed his new approach to language, he saw it as just one part of a larger system of meaning encompassing all manner of human activities. As we saw, each word in a language, for Saussure, was a sign that united a signifier and signified, or a pattern of sounds or letters with a concept. That is similar to how a symbol unites an object and a concept. A flag represents a country in much the same way that a word represents an idea. The philosopher Charles Sanders Peirce also developed an approach to understanding sign systems in the late nineteenth century that is still influential today. Although his approach to semiotics is intricate, one fundamental idea is that there are different types of signs.

- **Icon** – a sign in which the relationship between signifier and signified is based on a physical resemblance or likeness. Examples include portraits, maps, or diagrams (that resemble the thing being depicted); onomatopoeia (pronouncing the word "boom" resembles the sound of an explosion); and imitative gestures (flapping your hands to represent a bird).
- **Index** – a sign in which the relationship between signifier and signified is based on a logical or causal connection. Examples include how seeing smoke indicates the presence of fire, hearing thunder indicates lightning, and a fever indicates illness. A thermometer indicates the temperature and a clock indicates the time. When we point at something (with our *index* finger) we are creating an indexical sign relationship between our finger and the thing being pointed at.
- **Symbol** – a sign in which the relationship between signifier and signified is arbitrary and based on convention or culture. Symbols need to be *learned* to be understood. Examples include flags and logos, signalling systems like Morse code or traffic lights, and abstract forms of representation such as the alphabet. Most importantly for us, language itself is a symbolic system in which the link between signifier and signified is arbitrary.

If onomatopoeia is iconic and semantic meaning in language is symbolic, there does not appear to be much role for indexes in language. But linguists have noted that the relationship between speech and social context is deeply indexical (Silverstein 1976). Consider the pragmatics of politeness markers in English. In comparing the sentences "Can I get a drink?" and "May I please have a drink?," most people would agree that the second is more polite. If we hear the word "please" or a person replaces "can I" with "may I," we can say that it is indexing a situation in which politeness is desired or required.

In the 1990s, linguistic anthropologist Elinor Ochs (1992) pointed out that languages provide ways of indexing gender (bearing in mind that gender itself is a symbolic system that is learned and arbitrary) both directly – with words such as "she" or "mister"

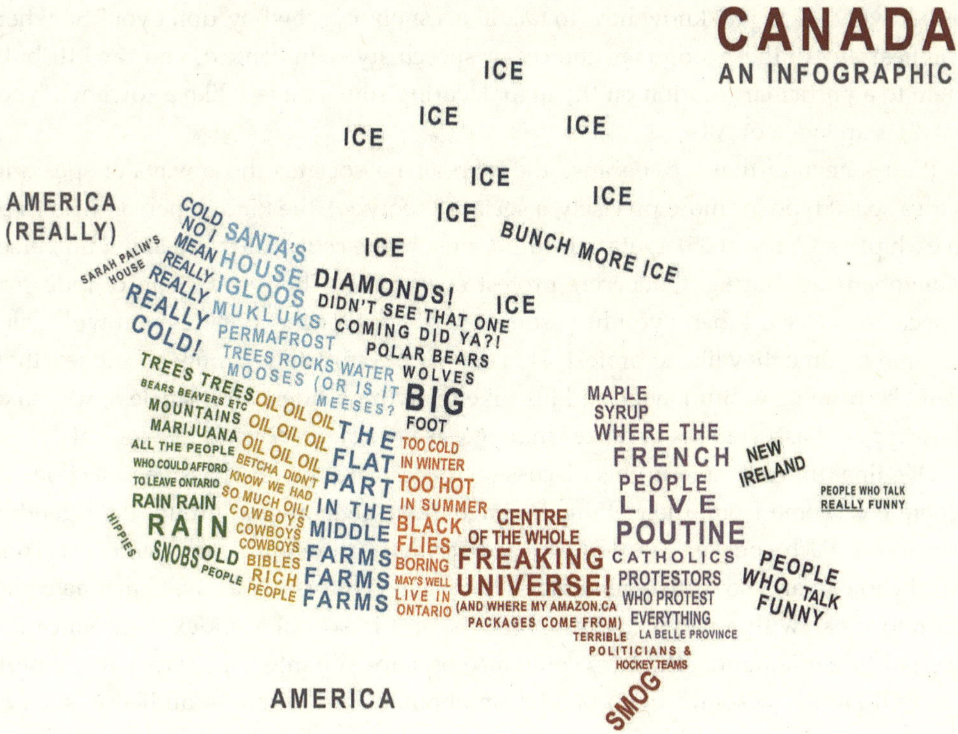

Figure 1.4 – Canada, an infographic

Source: Reproduced by permission of Kirstin Hepburn

or "brother" – and indirectly too. If we hear a higher pitched voice, it indexes a female speaker no matter the person's actual gender. If someone is loud and uses a lot of imperative commands, we take this to indicate a male speaker. Ochs argues that this kind of **indexicality** – sets of indexes that connect speech and social structure – does not demarcate men from women but rather creates a kind of "male voice" and "female voice" that is considered characteristic of each gender and, in turn, makes gender a social reality (see Chapter 7 – Language and Gender).

Since then, linguistic anthropologists have extended the notion of indexicality to include not just representations of gender, but of any kind of social status, category, or identity (Bucholtz and Hall 2005). You can see this in how we understand **dialects**, meaning regional varieties of a language. Figure 1.4 is a humorous map of Canada made using stereotypes of each region. Notice how many of these use language as a representation of the people living there. Quebecers speak French. Atlantic Canada has "people who talk funny" while Newfoundland has "people who talk really funny." The Northwest Territories is defined by Inuktitut words like *igloo* and *mukluk*, while the people in Alberta and British Columbia are labelled cowboys and snobs, respectively – and you know how to talk like a snob or a cowboy, don't you? So when you hear any of these language choices or speech styles in context, you can attribute them to a particular location on the map. Hearing someone talk like a cowboy ("yee-haw") is an index of Alberta.

It goes beyond that too, because the map also associates those ways of speaking with a social type (or more precisely, a social stereotype), the kind of person who lives in each place (Agha 2005). Ontarians think they're the centre of the freaking universe, Manitobans are boring, Quebecers protest everything. There is a chain of indexical associations at work here: you hear someone speak French, connect them with Quebec, and assume they like to protest. That could be completely wrong, of course – they could be from New Brunswick and just like really high tides. Nevertheless, we make these types of associations because language, as we noted above, is ideological.

One final thing to note in this discussion: people are not just passive reflections of where they come from, their ethnic heritage, their generational group, their gender, and so on. Each speaker can deploy a vast array of different speech styles, accents, word choices, and so forth – remember, language is a form of *doing*. Someone could learn to speak with a very standard French accent in school to index their education and political orientation. But they could also perhaps slip into a more casual and multilingual French to sound trendy and cosmopolitan for a different audience, such as hanging out in a pub with friends. People who can detect the differences between those two styles are able to make the indexical connections between those two identities because they have grown up in a common speech community and understand the language ideologies that shape it (Eckert 2019).

All these concepts therefore come together in the linguistic anthropological approach to language as a cultural system. We organize ourselves into speech communities with shared ideas about language, which allows us to pick up on the indexical cues people use to represent who they are to others. You can probably see now how language, for a linguistic anthropologist, is not just about grammar. It is about understanding speech as a form of action, of hearing and interpreting the choices people make as they are communicating, and then responding to them as we shape the course of our interactions through talk.

CONCLUSION

We started this chapter with the idea of culture, not as a set of attributes we have or beliefs we hold, but a shared framework of interpretation and patterned ways of doing things. One of those ways of doing is language. Although the structure of language is itself the topic of study for linguistics – and we discussed the various ways linguists approach language – understanding the integration of language into everyday social practices requires a nuanced perspective. Linguistic anthropologists have to understand how language works (which we will discuss in the next chapter) but also adopt an ethnographic approach to see what people do with it.

I realize this chapter introduces a lot of new terms and ideas; it's hard to avoid that when introducing a new field of study. And we still have 11 more chapters to go! Even if things aren't totally clear yet, we will come back to all of these ideas throughout the book. They have become fundamental to the discipline and show up in almost all the topics linguistic anthropologists discuss.

For now, pay attention to the ways people are using language around you and ask questions about it: why are they talking that way? What ideologies structure the ways we all use language? How are speakers using language to index parts of their identity? Students sometimes think that these ideas are only relevant during "important" events, like big speeches or national news stories. That's not true; you can apply them to simple moments and everyday conversations, like when one of your colleagues says you're giving a professor face, or when someone rolls their eyes at a new word in the dictionary. Once you start thinking like a linguistic anthropologist, it's hard to stop.

BOX 1.4 – RESEARCH SPOTLIGHT: ALESSANDRO DURANTI

Duranti, Alessandro. 2003. "Language as Culture in U.S. Anthropology: Three Paradigms." *Current Anthropology* 44 (3): 321–450.

You have just read a very quick survey of a very big field, with brief introductions to a lot of important underlying concepts in how we approach language. It's not easy to condense over one hundred years of thinking about the social life of language down to a few thousand words. Fortunately, some scholars have taken a step back and written overviews of the field, both where it has come from and, from their perspective, where it is going.

Alessandro Duranti is an anthropologist at the University of California Los Angeles who has done linguistic fieldwork in Samoa, particularly political speech events where he focuses on how speakers assign intention and agency to others (see Duranti 1994). He has also written several compilations of important research and essays in the field. In this article he argues that linguistic anthropology has gone through three important paradigm shifts. The first one roughly coincides with our discussion of philology and Saussure above, the second with Chomsky and the development of the speech community as an organizing concept, and the third with everything since.

Eighty pages seems like a lot, but Duranti's argument is only part of the article. The rest is comments from other scholars in the field and then Duranti's responses; those give a bit more context to what he is saying and offer some gentle critique. Duranti was very prescient in understanding where the field was going, and his analysis is still relevant even though it is more than 20 years old. The article is also valuable for its list of references. A lot of classic studies that linguistic anthropologists based their ideas on can be found here.

Discussion

1. You read a bit about me in this chapter. What about you? What languages do you use? How has your background and your experiences shaped the way you speak? A lot of times people will say their speech isn't special or that they don't have an accent, but an accent is just the unique phonological patterns of your speech. So think a bit about where you come from and the people in your life who have influenced your language – you might be surprised.
2. A lot of the research you will read about in this textbook is published in scholarly journals. Linguistic anthropologists publish their research in a wide range of those, but some of the more common ones you will see in the references are the *Journal of Linguistic Anthropology*, *Language in Society*, and *Language & Communication*. Have a look at the website for one of these journals. Click on the most recent issue and read through the article abstracts. What do you see? Where in the world is the research being done? How do you think the research topics connect to the concepts in this chapter?
3. If someone handed you a blank map of your country, like the one in Figure 1.4, how would you fill in the different regions with types of talk? Do this as a group; what is common among your maps, and what is different?
4. This chapter discusses the difference between *descriptivism* and *prescriptivism*. What are your language peeves? Come on, we all have them, even me. Do you get steamed by supermarket lines labelled "12 items or less" (shouldn't it be "12 items or fewer") or look down on people who end sentences with a preposition (are they hard to deal *with*)? Why do they make you cringe? The thing about language peeves is that they are often ideological, tied into our views about "proper" ways of using language by people we think are not following the "rules." Think about the reasons your peeves get to you: is it something about the language itself, or something about the speakers?

2

What Is Language?

Topics

- Animal communication as a closed system
- Human language as an open system
- The meaning of discourse
- Characteristics of sign languages

Growing up, I had a dog that loved going for walks. If I took his leash down off its peg, he would start to scamper and jump. Eventually, he learned to recognize the word "walk," and when someone said the word – whether asking my dog "Do you want to go for a walk?" or just in passing, such as "I'll walk to school" – my dog would also start to scamper and jump. Sometimes we did not want the dog to know we were talking about a walk, so we would spell it out: "Do you have time to take the dog for a w-a-l-k?" But my dog soon figured that one out too, and saying "w-a-l-k" would also make him scamper and jump. My dog was therefore able to recognize sequences of sounds that come together to form units of meaning, and to associate those units of meaning with a particular activity. So, can we say that my dog was learning a language?

Pets and other animals communicate in a multitude of ways. Dogs growl to intimidate, cats meow with pleasure, birds chirp their presence to each other. Psychologists, biologists, linguists, and anthropologists have all long wondered about the relation between the ways animals communicate and the ways humans communicate. Is language just a more fleshed-out version of dog barks and whale song? Or is there something categorically different about human speech?

These questions are also closely connected to speculation over the origins of language. Where did language come from? At what point did grunts and squeals become words and sentences? We still do not know when exactly language emerged; speech leaves no trace in the prehistoric record (until there is a writing system – see Chapter 10 – Orality and Literacy). Some scholars have argued that archaic *Homo sapiens* possessed the required cognitive capabilities and vocal apparatus to use language as early as 100,000 years ago (Dubreuil and Henshilwood 2013). However, since language is fundamentally symbolic – making one thing, like a word, stand in for something else, like an object – most researchers argue that language must have emerged at the same time as other symbolic elements of human culture, such as burials and artistic expression (Tattersall 2018). There is definitive evidence of design elements on material artefacts that are clearly not functional, such as carved lines, shapes used as decoration, and painted ornamentation, beginning about 50,000 years ago. But did language appear all at once, or was there a series of stages in its development? The evidence is not conclusive, but understanding how animals communicate can shed light on the development of human language.

ANIMAL COMMUNICATION

If you have ever seen inside a beehive, you have probably witnessed a waggle dance. When European honeybees return from foraging, they move over the honeycomb in a distinctive pattern in order to communicate the location of the food source to other bees (Schürch et al. 2019). First, they move in a straight line, vibrating their bodies, and then circle back to the beginning. They waggle again, and then circle back to the beginning the other way, forming a figure eight. Biologists have been able to decode the information in this dance. The duration of the waggle corresponds to the distance of the food source, roughly 1.5 seconds of waggling for each kilometre. The angle of the waggle line indicates the direction in relation to the position of the sun: straight up tells other bees the food source is directly towards the sun, while moving at an angle translates to a similar angle from the sun's direction. Just think about that: the dancing bee translates distance into duration and an angle in the horizontal plane (flying to the flowers) into an angle in the vertical plane (waggling in the hive). Other bees observe this dance and translate the information back into distance and horizontal direction. That is some fairly complex information for bees to communicate to each other.

Similarly sophisticated signalling behaviours have been studied in wild vervet monkeys. Vervet monkeys live in social groups that inhabit semi-arid savanna terrain dotted with forests. Four different predators commonly eat vervet monkeys in this environment: leopards, eagles, pythons, and baboons. When a monkey sees one of these animals, it lets out a distinct alarm call, a different one for each type of predator.

Figure 2.1 – Sue Savage-Rumbaugh communicating with the bonobo Kanzi using a visual symbol board
Source: William Calvin, Creative Commons BY-SA 4.0

Each call also leads to different responses. For instance, hearing the leopard alarm call prompts other monkeys to race up into the trees, since leopards usually attack them on the ground, but an eagle alarm call would lead them to hide in bushes, since eagles attack from the air (Seyfarth, Cheney, and Marler 1980). Vervet monkeys therefore created a series of associations between one type of predator and one type of call and have learned how to respond to each type; in other words, each type of call has a different meaning in a semantic sense.

Perhaps the most intriguing research on animal communication has been the attempts, starting in the 1960s, to teach human language to great apes such as the chimpanzee Washoe and the gorilla Koko (Figure 2.1). At first, they were taught spoken languages, rather unsuccessfully, but later, psychologists shifted to using American Sign Language (ASL) or visual symbols (called lexigrams) that the apes could touch. Initially these experiments appeared to have great success: the apes were able to understand and use hundreds of signs (132 signs for Washoe, 1,000 lexigrams for a bonobo named Kanzi) (Gardner and Gardner 1975; Segerdahl, Fields, and Savage-Rumbaugh 2005, 215). Even more exciting was the apparent ability of various apes to combine signs together. Washoe, not having learned a sign for swan before, combined the ASL signs for *water* and *bird* together when seeing one (Fouts 1975). Lana, a chimpanzee, learned to combine lexigrams such as *please machine give apple* (in that specific order) to receive a treat from a computer console. In other words, the apes were apparently taking advantage of a rudimentary form of syntax to develop novel sentences.

More recently, however, researchers have become skeptical of these experiments. Ape hands are not as dextrous as those of humans, and so there was sometimes ambiguity around which exact sign a gorilla like Koko could be making; research assistants on these projects required a substantial amount of training to be able to "interpret" what the apes were apparently communicating. Lana's success in obtaining an apple depended upon a great deal of random trial and error before she eventually discovered the patterns of symbols that would award an apple. Herbert Terrace, one of the psychologists who designed such an ape language-learning experiment but eventually concluded none of the findings were valid, has stated that "Unlike human children, who use words to name things in conversational exchanges, chimpanzees only used signs to request or earn rewards. Slow-motion analyses of videotapes and films confirmed that most of the subject chimpanzees' utterances were prompted by their teachers" (2019, 71). The academic consensus is now that, while the apes in these studies demonstrated tremendous abilities in memorization and learning by being able to semantically associate hand signs or lexigrams with objects or actions, their overall ability to combine these signs syntactically was quite limited (Slocombe and Scott-Phillips 2017).

Research on animal communication continues in many fields, but most linguists argue that the systems of communication used by animals – such as the bees, monkeys, and apes discussed above – are qualitatively different from those of human language. Despite the sophisticated ability of many animals to encode and transmit information, some basic elements of any human language appear to be lacking in the examples noted above:

- Negation, or the ability to say, "Let's *not* go for a walk today," or "I have *not* just seen an eagle."
- Asking questions, like "When will we go for a walk?" or "What colour was the leopard?"
- Quoting others, such as, "The queen told me, 'Go out there and gather some honey.'"
- Talking about things that are not immediately present or happening at that time, such as going for a walk tomorrow, or the leopard attack that happened yesterday.
- Combining information together (through the syntactic processes of recursion and comparison), such as saying "The leopard with the big spots is faster than the one with the small spots."

Perhaps most important is the way in which animal communication systems are relatively fixed while human language is able to generate novel messages. Bees are limited in what *type* of information they can communicate. Waggle dances communicate distance and direction but nothing else. Bees cannot indicate the colour of the flowers or landmarks to follow, or even ask why they all have to serve the queen bee anyway. Vervet monkeys can communicate what type of predator is approaching, but not from which direction or how far away it is. If a new predator were to arrive (let's say, a crocodile), a new alarm call might develop over time, but only through evolutionary processes rather than active and conscious discussion of the monkeys together. In other words, animal communication systems are **closed systems** that are limited in scope. All human languages, however, can be adapted to new types of information and new situations. We can discuss new topics, invent new words, and imagine new circumstances or scenarios. Human languages are infinitely creative and are therefore **open systems**.

BOX 2.1 – MULTISPECIES ANTHROPOLOGY

Even if animals cannot use human language, our lives are entangled with them. A fascinating trend in recent anthropological research has been a focus on the "more than human" in what is often called **multispecies ethnography**: a description of "how a multitude of organisms' livelihoods shape and are shaped by political, economic, and cultural forces" (Kirksey and Helmreich 2010, 545). Crucially, this often includes communication across species boundaries.

One important example of this is Eduardo Kohn's (2007) article "How Dogs Dream: Amazonian Natures and the Politics of Transspecies Engagement." Kohn describes the ways that the Avíla Runa, living in Ecuador's Upper Amazon, engage with their dogs, treating them as both non-human creatures *and* sentient others. When they speak to dogs, the Runa adopt a specialized third-person grammatical construction ("it will not bite the master") likely borrowed from Spanish. This allows the Avíla Runa to communicate with dogs, but in ways that are different from how they talk to other humans. The aim of this talk is to socialize the dogs into appropriate forms of behaviour, such as hunting, and away from inappropriate forms of behaviour, such as barking loudly. They also listen to their dogs and interpret what dogs are dreaming about, adopting the dog's subjectivity and imagining what it must be feeling and experiencing.

Kohn argues that most of our descriptions of animals are human-centred – we typically cannot help but see our own perspective on things. But as we grapple with a world wracked by climate change and species extinction, an anthropology of the non-human helps us appreciate the ways we are intertwined with those animals in a broader ecological structure.

HUMAN LANGUAGE

This distinction between closed and open systems of communication leads most linguists to consider human language as qualitatively different from animal communication rather than just an improved version of it with more words and a few grammatical rules. One of the reasons for this is that human languages are not qualitatively different from each other in the sense that that there are no better or worse languages. If human languages just added complexity as they evolved, we would expect ancient languages (like Babylonian, Latin, or Sanskrit) to be simpler than modern languages. But that is not the case at all. Ancient languages might not have all the vocabulary relevant to a conversation today, but with a little ingenuity we could discuss artificial intelligence or electric vehicles in any of these languages (and remember, English did not have words for any of those things a thousand years ago either). All human languages are equally capable of communicating any information.

Let's test this: here is a sentence that is unique, does not refer to any real situation, and requires sophisticated ideas and grammatical processes to communicate to someone else.

The unicorn picnic starts at noon.

Can we use other human languages to communicate this information? Of course we can! Even basic translation software can render this sentence very easily in another language like Mandarin Chinese.

qilin	*de*	*yecan*	*shi*	*zhongwu*	*kaishi*
unicorn	[possessive]	outdoor-meal	is	noon	begin

Note how the Mandarin word for "picnic" is a combination of the words for "outdoor" and "meal," but the meaning here is still perfectly clear. We can even render this sentence in an invented language, like Klingon from the television show *Star Trek*:

DungluQ	*tagh*	*wa' pu'*	*Sargh rorgh*	*'unwat megh*[1]
Noon	starts	one-horned	Sargh-fantastical	basket-lunch

Klingon employs a different word order from English, and the closest thing to a horse on the Klingon homeworld is an animal called a Sargh. Admittedly, Klingons do not go on many picnics, but you can still successfully communicate the meaning of this sentence to anyone who speaks Klingon. There is, however, no conceivable way we could put this into dog barks, bee dances, monkey calls, or whale song. Could you even explain something as abstract as a mythological creature in an animal communication system? A key difference between animal communication and human language is therefore something we call **translatability**: anything said in one human language can be translated into any other language.

BOX 2.2 – EDWARD SAPIR (1884–1939)

Figure 2.2 – Edward Sapir

Edward Sapir studied philology at Columbia University as an undergraduate and developed a fascination with languages. Despite focusing on German in his early studies, Sapir shifted to the description of Indigenous North American languages in his doctorate, studying under the pioneering twentieth-century anthropologist Franz Boas (Darnell 1990). While Boas was certainly interested in languages, it was almost always with a view to disrupting conventional views of biological determinism prevalent at the time – he took pains to show, for instance, that language was not related to a person's biological race (Boas 1911).

Sapir, on the other hand, grounded his work in the detailed study of particular languages, notably Paiute, Nuu-chah-nulth, and Takelma. Doing so allowed him to make compelling arguments about the history of and relationships among Indigenous languages. He also used the richly complex grammatical structures of these languages to counter claims that they were simple or undeveloped. He argued that every language is functionally equivalent; each is capable of expressing the full range of human thought. "We know of no people," he proclaimed, "that is not possessed of a fully developed language" (1921, 22). Balanced against this idea of the universality of language, however, was also the incredible diversity of linguistic patterns. "Every language has its special method or methods of binding words into a larger unity," and these can take a near-infinite number of forms (1921, 116). Dispelling the very idea of "primitive" languages while highlighting the many different ways languages are structured is therefore Sapir's enduring contribution to the field of linguistic anthropology.

Now, the idea of translatability does not mean that everything has a word-for-word translation. Klingon does not have a word for "unicorn," so in the example above it is rendered as "one-horned fantastical Sargh." German has the word *schadenfreude* for the pleasure derived from witnessing the misfortune of others. In Inuktitut, there is a wonderful word, ᐃᒃᑦᓱᐊᕐᐳᒃ or *iktsuarpok*, that describes the feeling of anticipation while waiting for a person's arrival, leading to one going outside periodically to look for them. Examples such as these are often termed "words in language X that are untranslatable into language Y," but of course we just did translate them into English – it just takes a bit more explaining while the other language has a single pithy word for that concept. Even if languages are perfectly translatable, that does not mean they will always express concepts in the same way – this is a point we will come back to in Chapter 4 – Linguistic Relativity.

There are a lot of other features that all human languages share. In the 1960s, the linguistic anthropologist Charles Hockett tried to systematize these into a list of **design features** (Hockett 1963). Some of these are shared with other animals (since animal communication systems do vary in levels of complexity), while others are unique to human language. Taken together, however, these design features represent a dynamic and complex system of meaning creation that all human languages exhibit. As John Leavitt writes, "every human language has a distinctive multilevelled architecture in which some tens of non-signifying elements (phonemes) combine to produce some thousands of signs (morphemes), which combine in turn to generate a potentially infinite number of phrases and sentences" (2011, 4).

BOX 2.3 – DESIGN FEATURES OF LANGUAGE

Charles Hockett's list of design features changed several times over his career as he worked on and refined the concepts. But one of the most commonly used lists is below:

1. Vocal-Auditory Channel – The primary mode of language use is through speech and hearing.
2. Broadcast Transmission and Directional Reception – Speech propagates in all directions, but humans can detect which direction it is coming from.
3. Rapid Fading – Speech is transitory and disappears after the speaker has stopped talking.
4. Interchangeability – A person can repeat any message they hear in their language and, in turn, can understand any message they speak.
5. Total Feedback – People can hear what they are saying as they speak, and can therefore control and modify the message while speaking.
6. Specialization – Speech is not a by-product of other biological functions but only used for communication.
7. Semanticity – Specific combinations of sounds are associated with specific objects or ideas; they have meaning.

8. Arbitrariness – With only a few exceptions, the sound pattern of a word does not relate to what it means; there is no logical connection between the sound of the word "cat" and a feline or between the same animal and the words *chat* (French), *gato* (Spanish), or *kissa* (Finnish).
9. Discreteness – A single sound change (from "dog" to "hog") changes the meaning of a word; each sound is also distinct, so that there is no sound that is halfway between d and h, it is only either one or the other.
10. Displacement – Language can refer to things that are not physically present; they can be far away, in the past or future, or even imaginary.
11. Productivity – As an open system, there is no limit to the information or ideas that can be communicated through language; speakers can create novel words, sentences, or even new ways of speaking.
12. Cultural Transmission – Although the capacity for language is biological, humans learn one particular language from birth in a social and cultural setting.
13. Duality of Patterning – Sentences are made by combining strings of meaningful units (words) that are themselves composed of strings of meaningless units (sounds).

Some of these features are shared with other animals. Cricket chirps are also subject to rapid fading, for instance, and dogs are capable of semanticity (or knowing the relationship between a word like "walk" and a particular activity). Features 8–13, however, are almost entirely unique to human language. These features give human language its power for infinite creativity and openness, and highlight its embedding within systems of culture.

DISCOURSE

So far, we have established what we might think of as the mechanics of language, the structure and features that make language unique to human beings. But we also need to consider the humans themselves and add this social dimension to our model of language. While pure linguists might look at the form of a sentence on its own (examining the sounds produced, or its syntactic rules), linguistic anthropologists almost always examine the use of language within its surrounding **social context**. Talk is never used in the abstract, but always entangled with people (their purposes, goals, relationships) and places (its location, setting, and the events that inform it). As Marjorie Goodwin (2008, 5–6) writes in her book *The Hidden Life of Girls*, "In order for any human beings to coordinate their behavior with that of their coparticipants, in the midst of talk they must display to one another what they are doing and how they expect others to coordinate their talk with them." To illustrate these ideas, Goodwin offers a conversation she recorded:

EMI: We have it today.
RON: We play soccer every day. = okay?
MIGUEL: It's more boys than girls.
EMI: ***So?*** Your point?
RON: This is ***our field***.
EMI: It's ***not*** your field. Did you pay for it? ***No***.
  Your name is not written on this land.
KATHY: ***Mine*** is. K-A-T-H-Y! ((writing in the dirt))

This conversation is recorded using a method of **transcription** – that is, a way of representing actual speech in text – that highlights elements such as emphasis (bolded, italicized text) and the lack of a pause between two phrases (the "=" sign).

Goodwin points out that merely possessing a grammatical knowledge of English is not enough to make sense of this conversation. One needs to know something about the *setting*. For instance, this conversation took place on a school soccer field, and it is a place that two groups of people are fighting over in terms of who it belongs to. Note the several references to this field in the course of the conversation and the way in which Kathy even inscribes her name on it to make it "hers." We also need to know who the *participants* in this conversation are: the boys usually play soccer during the lunch hour, but on this occasion the girls got there first. Ron and Miguel are boys trying to take the soccer field back from Emi and Kathy, who are the girls claiming it for themselves. Finally, note that this conversation is not abstract, but a form of action with discrete *goals*: both groups want to use the soccer field, and both employ strategies to claim it as their own.[2]

This conversation is not just a recitation of words either; there are prosodic features at play in communication. **Prosody** (also called paralanguage) encompasses the non-linguistic elements of speech, including intonation, tempo, volume, and pitch. When Kathy reacts to Emi's assertion that the boys' names are not written on the field, she uses her finger to draw hers in the dirt while putting emphasis on the word "mine." Those words are also accompanied by facial expressions, gestures, and physical interactions between the speakers. Our communication does not rely on language alone but is **multimodal**, involving a range of physical and acoustic inputs that affect how participants interpret the situation.

As we can see, the language used here is inseparable from the setting, the participants, and their respective goals. Linguistic anthropologists argue that language is always embedded in this kind of social context and describe such talk in context as **discourse**. Furthermore, discourse is a fundamental feature of all human language usage but is in every case culturally specific. The exact methods of signalling to another person that you are angry and want to have an argument, or that you are just teasing and do not want your words to be taken seriously, vary from group to group, speech community to speech community. Discourse contexts are therefore only readily understood by people who are familiar with underlying cultural frameworks and language ideologies.

Talking Like a Human

Technology has progressed to the point that computers now have a basic ability to respond appropriately to both text and speech, closely approximating the ways that humans communicate with each other. You can ask a smart speaker for the weather or direct your phone to tell you a joke. A great deal of online customer service, for instance, is now managed by **natural language processing** software that can respond to inquiries, make suggestions, and solve problems while adhering to norms of politeness and topic appropriateness (Figure 2.3). Nevertheless, computer scientists have not yet achieved communication that feels distinctly "human." In 1950, the British mathematician (and designer of early computing machines) Alan Turing proposed what has come to be known as the Turing Test: a person sits in an isolation room with a keyboard and a display and can communicate with two other individuals by typing questions and answers (Turing 1950). Can a machine advance to the point, he asks us, that the person cannot identify which of these is a machine and which is a human being?

There has been significant argument within linguistics, philosophy, and computer science about what it would mean for a computer to "think" and how we would engage with such forms of artificial intelligence. To date, however, no computer has been able to fool a human despite the increasing sophistication of chatbots and other software. The question for linguistic anthropologists is: why is human language so tough for a machine to crack? Or, to turn the question around, what is it about language that makes us human (Kockelman 2013)?

Figure 2.3 – Suspicion, xkcd.com

Source: Randall Munroe, https://xkcd.com/632. Creative Commons BY-NC 2.5

BOX 2.4 – LANGUAGE AND ARTIFICIAL INTELLIGENCE

In 2022, researchers at OpenAI launched an artificial intelligence (AI) chatbot called ChatGPT that was trained on a 500-billion-word corpus of text taken from web pages and published books. A group of human trainers then provided additional feedback to the AI to fine-tune its responses. The goal was to mimic human writing and conversation, and many commentators have been struck by ChatGPT's ability to create cogent prose in response to detailed instructions (such as "write an essay about the history of linguistics"). These abilities raise important questions around language, academic honesty, and what role AI will play in future society.

ChatGPT is not perfect. Sometimes it makes factual errors, especially in response to questions that are syntactically complex. ChatGPT works by calculating the frequency with which words and phrases are located in close proximity in its massive database, but it is unable to differentiate fiction and non-fiction, serious writing from comedic, and so forth. It can therefore sometimes offer bad information in an utterly confident writing style.

Some scholars have pointed out that, beyond its linguistic capabilities, ChatGPT raises important cultural issues. In a detailed blog post, digital culture scholar Jill Walker Rettberg (2022) noted several biases in its training data. Despite possessing multilingual abilities, Rettberg argues that ChatGPT is monocultural, "trained on English-language texts, with the cultural biases and values embedded in them, and then *aligned* with the values of a fairly small group of US-based contractors." The software therefore sometimes reproduces the biases and stereotypes – ethnic, racial, gender, and so forth – found in its data.

Of course, ChatGPT and other AI-powered writing tools are also designed to learn based on human inputs. As the feedback from more diverse groups of users is incorporated into its models, Rettberg argues that it is training itself to be aligned ever more closely with our social and cultural values. For good or for worse, AI language programs are here to stay.

Consider a fairly ordinary example of discourse that points to just how sophisticated humans are in processing the nuances of language in use. In 2017, Mark Hamill (the actor who played Luke Skywalker in the *Star Wars* films), posted a sound bite to Twitter of himself reading President Donald Trump's New Year's greeting, in character as The Joker from *Batman: The Animated Series*:

> Happy New Year to all, including to my many enemies and those who have fought me and lost so badly they just don't know what to do. Love!

The soundbite was widely circulated on the internet as a humorous take on the president's tweet, but there are some fascinating discursive elements at play. Here we have a person's words being said by another person in the voice of someone else entirely. A human can figure out the joke immediately, while an artificial intelligence cannot understand the utterance in its context.

The sociologist Erving Goffman, who was a keen observer of conversational interactions, argued that while most people tend to think of a "speaker" as a singular person, in practice people play a variety of roles as they speak. For instance, we know that when politicians speak publicly, they are usually reading from a text either prepared by, or co-written with, one of their staff. Or think about a public relations specialist speaking "for" a company. Goffman (1981) therefore argued that the concept of a "speaker" can be broken down into several different roles:

1. **Animator** – the person physically forming the words and uttering them for others
2. **Author** – the person who has selected the ideas that will be expressed and chosen the words to express them
3. **Principal** – the person whose position or identity is represented through the speech.

In other words, the animator is the voice box, the one forming the words, but the author is the one who wrote the words or planned out what the animator will say. The principal is the one who takes on a social role through the act of speaking and stands behind the ideas being articulated. We can apply this framework to Hamill's speech: Donald Trump authored the words, Mark Hamill animated them, but it is The Joker (with his evil disposition and sinister voice) who is the principal. Goffman argues that from a young age, children learn implicitly to understand these different roles in their own talk and the talk of others; all human language users have this in common. It is the root of common discourse features such as sarcasm, joking, quoting others, and reflecting on our own language usage itself. Discourse is therefore the most social, most human dimension of language.

BOX 2.5 – ERVING GOFFMAN (1922–1982)

Although a sociologist by training, Goffman has been remembered as "an outsider, a brilliant maverick, a one of a kind genius" (Manning 1992, 1). Born in Mannville, Manitoba, Goffman's family later moved to Winnipeg, where he

Figure 2.4 – Erving Goffman

attended high school and university before attending the University of Toronto and University of Chicago for his graduate work. For a year and a half he lived on Unst, a remote part of the Shetland Islands in the United Kingdom, and studied how people interacted (Goffman 1953). Goffman was interested in the mostly unspoken rules that govern interaction: who could interrupt someone else? Where and when could they do so? How did people show embarrassment or frustration? How did people criticize or praise others? As a result, he paid a great deal of attention to how people talked and the subtext of their words.

Although he did later serve as president of the American Sociology Association, at the time his work had limited impact on the overall field. The 1950s were the heyday of structuralism in sociology. Theorists analysed societies as organic wholes, with each social class, institution, or system contributing to its maintenance. Goffman instead turned his attention to hospitals and asylums, gamblers and con artists; his areas of interest were both eclectic and quirky. It is very hard to pin Goffman down as belonging to a major school of thought or contributing to some overarching social theory.

However, Goffman's keen eye for detail and his in-depth understanding of the role of culture in shaping human action and interpretation has subsequently endeared him to generations of linguistic anthropologists (his work has inspired some of my own writing on language use in China). In the field of sociology too there has been some resurgent interest in his approaches. Unfortunately, Goffman passed away at the age of 60, leaving much of his work unfinished, but many of the ideas covered in this textbook can, directly or indirectly, be traced back to him.

Sign Languages in Nicaragua

One criticism of Hockett's design features, described above, is their almost complete reliance on speech as the medium of language, which ignores written language and perpetuates the misconception that sign languages are not *real* languages but just collections of gestures. In fact, however, all of the unique features of human language (arbitrariness, discreteness, displacement, etc.) are also present in sign languages like ASL. This shows that language comes naturally to us, no matter whether we are speaking it or signing it. As we saw in Chapter 1, almost all of our social existence is mediated by language. And where humans do not have access to a pre-existing language, they can invent it together. Evidence for this comes from a unique case study derived from sign language development in Nicaragua.

BOX 2.6 – ARE SIGN LANGUAGES REAL LANGUAGES?

The easy answer is: of course they are! A **sign language** refers to any language performed in three-dimensional space using movements of the body rather than speech. Most sign languages are used in Deaf communities around the world. They are very different from the non-Deaf languages used in the same community. American Sign Language (ASL) is not English done with hands; in fact, sign languages used in Britain, Ireland, and North America are all different despite the common use of English. There are hundreds of distinct sign languages used around the globe today. Glottolog, an online catalogue of the world's languages, has entries on 139 different sign languages, but this probably underestimates that number significantly – and of course, counting sign languages is just as difficult as counting spoken languages (Hammarström et al. 2022; Woll, Sutton-Spence, and Elton 2004).

Although some people might think sign languages are comprised of just gestures, like nodding one's head or beckoning someone with a curled finger, they are far more complex than this. Some signs in ASL for instance, are indeed iconic – they resemble the object or action they are meant to indicate. The sign for "book" involves folding one's hands open as though opening a book. Nevertheless, the vast majority of signs in ASL exhibit the feature of arbitrariness. The sign for "home" is made by holding one's fingers and thumb together and then touching first the corner of the mouth and then again farther back on the cheek. And just as with spoken languages, different sign languages have different signs for the same object or concept.

The complexity of sign languages goes far beyond their vocabulary, however; they possess all of the design features and syntax of other human languages. A comprehensive example of this is provided by Shaylee Mansfield, a Deaf American YouTuber. One of her videos, a narration of *'Twas the Night Before Christmas*, was analysed in an article by the linguist Arika Okrent (2015), who points out the sophisticated way Shaylee performs role shifts. In sign languages, role shifting is a strategy of switching from the signer's perspective to those of others (much like quoting another, which is a universal feature of human language). In her narration, for instance, Shaylee uses her facial expression to take on the role of the sleeping children and their "visions of sugar plums" before shifting to the role of the father as he hears a clatter from the lawn. This type of grammatical structure in ASL is certainly different from spoken languages, but it demonstrates the many ways humans can use their linguistic capacity to communicate fluently.

Nicaragua, a country in Central America, was under a military dictatorship from the 1920s until 1979. During this time, the underfunded education system was not able to provide for the needs of Deaf[3] children; they usually grew up isolated from other Deaf people, unable to speak Spanish or to learn a sign language that would allow communication with a wider community (Senghas 2003). After the revolution that overthrew the regime, several educational reforms were undertaken, including the development of centralized schooling for Deaf students. At the time, the predominant educational model for the Deaf was to encourage oral abilities based on lip-reading and speech rather than signing. Educators quickly became frustrated, however, at the students' reliance on **homesigns** – idiosyncratic gestures Deaf children in hearing households develop to make their needs and intentions known – as a crutch at the expense of spoken Spanish.

When linguists brought in to help develop a Deaf curriculum arrived at the school, they realized that the system of signs being used was much more complex than originally thought. As students taught their homesigns to each other, they also began to develop a simple syntax. A raised eyebrow combined with a sign, for instance, marked that sign as the topic of a sentence (Kegl, Senghas, and Coppola 1999). Each year, new children entered the school and were taught this emerging sign language by older children, and over time this sign system developed into a full-fledged language, now called *Idioma de Señas Nicaragüense* (Nicaraguan Sign Language or NSL).

To track the development of this sign language, and to show that it is a language and not some simple form of gestural communication, the linguist Ann Senghas and her colleagues designed a scientific experiment (Senghas, Kita, and Özyürek 2004). They took 30 Deaf NSL signers and divided them into three cohorts according to age. They also used 10 non-Deaf Spanish speakers as a control group. All were shown a cartoon and then asked to narrate the events of the cartoon to another person while the researchers videotaped them and recorded their gestures. Specifically, the researchers were looking for how participants narrated motions, such as a ball rolling down a hill. Motion contains two distinct elements: the manner of movement (rolling) and the path or direction (downhill). There are two possibilities for illustrating motion to others visually. First, they could illustrate the manner and path simultaneously, using a finger to trace out how the ball rolled. The second possibility was to separate manner and path and show them sequentially (Figure 2.5). The results were clear: the non-Deaf Spanish speakers used simultaneous gestures exclusively. Older students used simultaneous gestures most of the time, with a few sequential ones. The younger students predominantly used sequential gestures.

Senghas and her colleagues argue that the sequential narrations are more linguistic, while the simultaneous ones are simple iconic gestures. Why? Think about what dividing the motion into manner and path allows a signer to do. With a simultaneous

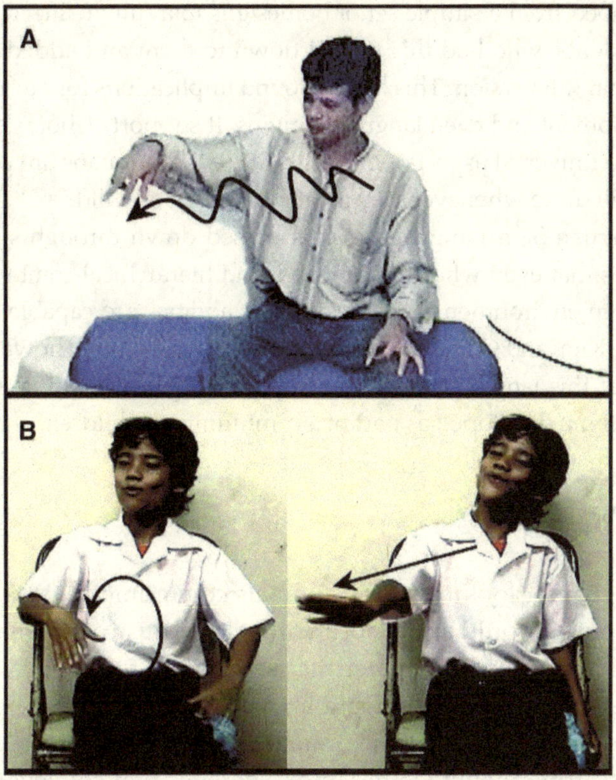

Figure 2.5 – Motion event narratives, where (A) shows manner and path illustrated simultaneously, and (B) shows manner and path illustrated sequentially

Source: Reproduced by permission from Senghas, Kita, and Özyürek (2004)

narration, all the person can do is show how the ball moved. But a sequential one allows the combination of various signs. The ball could be rolling, bouncing, spinning, sliding, twirling, shaking, or pulsing. In turn, it could be moving right, left, up, down, at an angle, towards you, away from you, around you, through you, and so forth. Many of these possibilities would be difficult to convey iconically, but separating the signs permits a nearly limitless amount of information to be communicated when combined in sequence. Adding other signs into the sequence – a noun or adverb, for instance – allows the signer to convey even more information: "the stone rolled down the hill quickly." In other words, the signers demonstrated in their gestures the qualities of discreteness and productivity that are part of Hockett's design features.

It seems paradoxical, but the younger NSL signers were more proficient than their older peers. Shouldn't the older children be more knowledgeable? Senghas and her colleagues argue that NSL developed over time. Each cohort that graduated from school left with the version of the language they had learned to that point. Over several years, that language developed from a simple set of homesigns to a fully realized language; it was the younger students, who had this passed down to them and added to it themselves, that possessed that full version. This has profound implications for our understanding of language development and even language origins. It supports Chomsky's idea that language taps into a universal aspect of our cognition – that humans are primed to acquire language and will do so whenever they are exposed to it as children. "The rapid restructuring of Nicaraguan Sign Language as it is passed down through successive cohorts of learners shows that even where discreteness and hierarchical combination are absent from the language environment, human learning abilities are capable of creating them anew" (Senghas, Kita, and Özyürek 2004, 1782). At the same time, however, the researchers point out that this language does not simply emerge in isolation. Language is also inherently *social*; NSL developed as part of a community of children.

CONCLUSION

We started this chapter looking at how animals communicate. Was my dog talking to me? Most linguists would argue no, and that is because of the many components of language discussed in this chapter that are unique to humans. Because of our cognitive powers of representation and abstraction, we can very easily make one thing (a group of sounds, for instance) stand in for something else (an object or an action) and then string them together into a sentence that conveys the information to someone else. The power of language is in openness, its ability to create an infinite number of new sentences with no limits on the types of information that can be communicated.

But more than its structural form, it is the human quality of language that makes it so powerful: the ways we can shift among stances and roles, signal our intentions about how our words should be interpreted (or ignored altogether), or layer our voices with those of others. We can joke, be serious, and tell stories. We can imagine worlds beyond possibility, and through the near-magic of language – and the shared norms of a speech community – make them understandable to others. However, it is the specific qualities of *particular* languages and how they shape those practices that we turn to next.

BOX 2.7 – RESEARCH SPOTLIGHT: HANWOOL CHOE

Choe, Hanwool. 2019. "Eating Together Multimodally: Collaborative Eating in *Mukbang*, a Korean Livestream of Eating." *Language in Society* 48 (2): 171–208.

A true theory of language needs to account for not only basic words and sentences, but all of the complicated multimodal interactions that we engage in – that's what is encompassed by the idea of discourse discussed above. In this article, Hanwool Choe from the University of Hong Kong looks at *mukbang*, an online phenomenon where young Koreans livestream themselves eating. Choe says this is something like "food porn": the host consumes a range of gustatory delights while slurping or chewing loudly for an adoring audience. Viewers get to enjoy a meal vicariously through the host, but can also chat with them about the food, connecting everyone together into a digital community. We will have more to say about online communication in Chapter 11 – Digital Language, but here Choe is concerned with how viewers and hosts communicate with each other during the broadcast.

Choe argues that *mukbang* are joint productions between the host and the audience, looking in particular at one broadcast by the streamer Changhyun. Viewers are frequently invited, through chat, to direct which foods he will eat ("What do you want me to eat first?") and how ("Do you want me to dip?"). Here, Changhyun takes on a passive stance that Choe calls puppeteering, almost as if the viewers were controlling his actions. But as host, he also takes a more active role with the audience, sometimes holding the food up to the camera and asking them to imagine eating it with him. The words are combined with actions, eye gaze, hand gestures, eating sounds, and exclamations to draw his viewers into the experience.

Choe draws upon a concept in linguistic anthropology known as **footing**, which refers to a person's social position or stance within a conversation (see Agha 2005). If you are trying to comfort or soothe someone, your conversational footing is different than if you are trying to coerce them or convince them – it affects the language choices you make and how you interact with others. In this example, Changhyun constantly changes footing from active to passive. When one of his viewers sends him 1,004 star balloons (an online currency used on the streaming platform), Changhyun changes footing again, making a prayer gesture and taking on the role of a preacher with the word "Hallelujah!"

Notice how Choe's analysis addresses the various participants and their goals in this interaction, all shaped by the textual dynamics of the online setting. To understand what Changhyun and his audience are doing, one needs to understand the unspoken rules, expectations, and speech dynamics of this online environment – a good illustration of discourse in all its complexity.

Discussion

1. New research on animal communication is published every day, showing some of the sophisticated ways animals communicate – do a quick search for recent studies. Is the way the authors describe what the animals are doing accurate (think about words like "dialect" or "speech community" when they discuss their results)? Are there any examples you think might actually qualify as human language?
2. If you or anyone in your class speaks a second language, find out about those terms or ideas that are hard to translate. One that I noticed in China was the term *wanr*, which literally means "play." The difference is that in English play is limited to certain types of games and associated especially with the activities of children. In Mandarin *wanr* encompasses a wider range of activities, including things that adults do for fun, like going shopping or singing karaoke. What terms give you trouble in translation?
3. Transcription may seem a relatively transparent process, but it actually takes linguistic anthropologists years of practice to transcribe conversations accurately and completely. Just listen to some people talking and note the kinds of overlaps in speech, tempo changes, emphasis, and so on that are included in transcribed conversations. Try transcribing a minute or so of natural conversation, either from an online video or in person – identify the contextual information that Goodwin was discussing (setting, participants, goals) and think about how the speakers accomplish what they want in a conversation.
4. There are a lot of ASL online resources and apps to help people pick up the language. Have a look around online and see what you can find. Go through some of the signs and think about those design features of language – how many of these are iconic gestures, and how many demonstrate that feature of arbitrariness in their design?

3 Language Socialization

Topics

- Developing communicative competence
- Comparing language socialization practices
- The things we are socialized to
- Socialization as a lifelong practice

In Vietnam, 15-month-old Em is visiting her neighbour Minh's home with her mother. As they move to leave, Em's mother tells her in Vietnamese, "Perform *ạ* to Minh before we go back. *Ạ* to Minh." *Ạ* is a simplification of the Vietnamese respect particle *dạ*, which is used to show deference to others. Minh nods towards Em and encourages her, saying "Go *ạ*… *ạ*, *ạ*," stretching out the sound for her. As they watch, Em bows her head and intones, "*ạ*." Her mother then directs Em to do the same for Minh's wife Vi before they turn to go.

Linguistic anthropologist Merav Shohet observed this and many other instances of cultural instruction during her field research. Shohet (2021) argues that the Vietnamese practice of *hy sinh*, or "sacrifice," is performed through actions taken by younger generations towards elder ones: bowing, making offerings, and using respectful language. Here, Em's mother directs her how to show respect to elders by bowing and saying the correct word, and the neighbour helps her by modelling the term for Em several times before she says it herself. Adults, in turn, light incense, bow, and address elders with appropriate respect, while elders similarly prostrate themselves before family altars to pay respect to their ancestors.

The teaching given to Em is therefore about more than just saying the right words; it combines cultural instruction (how to bow) with language instruction (what to say). Em is being taught how to talk respectfully at the same time she is being taught respect, which "initiates children into a social and emotional order based on hierarchy and expectations of asymmetrical reciprocity that later implicates the ancestors as well as the living" (Shohet 2021, 90). In time, the acts of respect she performs towards her elders will become as naturalized for her as speaking her language. She is being taught, in other words, how to be Vietnamese.

In Chapter 1, we discussed the idea of a speech community as a group of people with shared ideas and attitudes about language and how to use it. But that raises the question: where do these ideas come from? Obviously, people don't just come up with such attitudes on their own. Anthropologists have long understood that culture is not just handed to or absorbed by each succeeding generation – it needs to be taught.

From the moment they are born, infants are surrounded by sounds, including the sounds of people talking. One of the most fascinating parts of our cognitive development as humans is the child's ability to understand that those sounds are not just random noise (they have communicative intent), perceive and categorize them into a system (the inventory of different sounds in a language), discover that those sounds combine into units of meaning, and finally grasp that those units can be arranged sequentially, following a range of grammatical rules, to create sentences (Lust 2006). This is the essence of Noam Chomsky's idea of competence: each child, without any explicit instruction from others, independently invents the idea of language before the age of two. This process of learning language as a cognitive system is known as **language acquisition**.

Because the ability to develop competence is universal among humans, most linguists argue that we have an innate capacity for language. But the development of language requires input – exposure to language – during the period when a child's brain is primed to acquire language. Children have a high degree of plasticity in their brains compared to adults, meaning that the synaptic networks of neurons have not yet stabilized. As we age, however, those neural pathways become less malleable. From birth to about the age of six is the time known as the **critical period** for language acquisition (Herschensohn 2007). After that window, acquiring full competence in a language becomes increasingly difficult.

Children do not, however, just absorb language from their surroundings like a sponge. During the acquisition process, other people – parents, siblings, caregivers, neighbours, and so forth – are involved in shaping and guiding their language learning. As the story of Em above makes clear, this is a cultural process. Learning and internalizing cultural patterns of behaviour is termed socialization. Linguistic anthropologists have argued that, because socialization practices are mediated through language, and because cultural ways of speaking are themselves the product of socialization, we should call this **language socialization**. As Elinor Ochs and Bambi Schieffelin (1984, 277) write:

1. The process of acquiring language is deeply affected by the process of becoming a competent member of society.
2. The process of becoming a competent member of society is realized to a large extent through language.

Acquiring culture and acquiring language are processes that are therefore entwined and interdependent.

Imagine a child who has perfectly acquired the phonological and grammatical structure of a language, but none of the cultural rules behind it. The child would not know how to ask for things politely, what topics are off limits, how loud to speak, how to tease someone, and when they should not speak at all. They would use slang with parents and formal words with friends. The skill of knowing how to use language appropriately in any given context is also part of learning a language.

Dell Hymes (1972) calls this knowledge of the sociocultural rules governing how language should be used **communicative competence**. The term competence here might be confusing because we have already encountered it in regards to Chomsky's theories of language in Chapter 1, but Hymes uses it in a very different way. Competence, for Chomsky, is the mental template of language structure, one that is encompassed by the idea of language acquisition discussed above. For Chomsky, performance is simply the ways we manifest this underlying structure in our speech; indeed, its significance is as the source of evidence about competence rather than as an example of cultural patterns of language. Chomsky's ideas of performance would include *how* people talk, but not the cultural ideas or frameworks – like respect in Vietnamese – that explain *why* they talk that way. With the idea of communicative competence, Hymes critiques this lack of attention to cultural knowledge of language in Chomsky's theory. Language socialization is therefore a practice of acquiring both grammatical competence in language and communicative competence in how it is used in a socially acceptable way.

TWO LANGUAGE SOCIALIZATION STORIES

Let's look at two contrasting methods of language socialization, one that might feel relatively normal and familiar (white middle-class North American households)[1] and one that might feel a little different (a group of people called the Kaluli, who live in the southern highlands of Papua New Guinea). These widely varying practices were explored by linguistic anthropologists Elinor Ochs and Bambi Schieffelin (1984) to illustrate language socialization processes. From the outset, it is important to note that both these language socialization methods are successful; children develop into mature and capable members of society with the full range of language abilities, knowledge of genres and styles, and customs of use. From an anthropological perspective, neither one of these should be considered the natural or obvious approach to things.

Most infants born into white middle-class North American families are raised in single-family households. Although on average they have two parents and possibly one or two siblings, infants primarily interact with a single caregiver, usually the mother. When adults speak to an infant, they tend to orient the child face-to-face so that interactions are dyadic, with only one speaker at a time. Adults also engage in a kind of speech play, talking to the infant as though they are a conversational partner (greeting them, asking questions) and frequently interpreting the sounds infants make as intentional responses. This type of interaction is called a **protoconversation**. In the following example, Ellen is playing with her nine-month-old child Peggy, who has a rattle in her hand:

ELLEN: Can I have the rattle?
PEGGY: Aaaaah! [Pulls rattle away from Ellen]
ELLEN: Does that mean no?
Peggy, you little stinker.

(Yingling 2004, 65)

Here we can see Ellen talk to Peggy as if she were fully capable of articulating her intentions and responses, filling in any communicative gaps herself. This strategy is called **child-raising**. Meanwhile, adults adopt a grammatically simplified speech style – with exaggerated pitch differences, lengthened vowels, and diminutive suffixes – called babytalk or child-directed speech (Soderstrom 2007). Ochs and Schieffelin term this strategy **self-lowering**.

Ochs and Schieffelin argue that the features described above are part of an overall strategy of accommodation. Adults make special arrangements for children by removing perceived dangers in the house, creating spaces with toys and small furniture, preparing special foods, and arranging schedules for the child's feeding and sleeping. Collaborative activities or competitive play often focus on the child's success, letting them put the last block on top of the tower or allowing them to win in a play fight. The adults adapting themselves to the perceived verbal abilities of children is just one element of this general pattern (Ochs and Schieffelin 1984).

Compare this child's experience growing up to one raised by the Kaluli of Papua New Guinea. The first obvious difference is that infants are part of a wide network of extended family and neighbours. Women often sit in groups as they work, and the child is typically seated facing out towards the group (Figure 3.1). Rather than

Figure 3.1 – Language socialization event in Papua New Guinea. The child on the left is the anthropologist's daughter

Source: Image courtesy of Marty Zelenietz

dyadic one-to-one conversations, children are exposed to multiple people speaking at once.

Kaluli mothers and other adults rarely talk to babies or create protoconversations with them. Their babblings are not treated as attempts to communicate, and there are no efforts to interpret what they might be saying or to address them directly. Older children and siblings will greet and talk to infants, and when they do the mother will pick the child up and respond in a distinctive high-pitched nasalized voice, essentially voicing the child's response on their behalf. When doing so, the mother does not simplify or moderate her speech in any way – she responds as a fully developed older child would (Schieffelin 1990).

Once the child begins to talk (notably, after the child says the words "mother" and "breast"), Kaluli parents actively begin to teach their child how to speak. They model what the child should say, followed by the imperative phrase *ɛlɛma,* meaning "say it like that." These conversations look like this:

> [Osolowa is cooking bananas with her daughter Mɛli, age two, when her husband Degelɛ enters the house. Mɛli starts teasing her father that she won't give him any of the bananas.]

DEGELƆ: Think about it!

OSOLOWA: [to Mɛli] You don't – I won't give you! – *ɛlɛma*

MƐLI: I won't give you!

DEGELƆ: You think about it! I usually give.
OSOLOWA: [to Mɛli] Think about it yourself! – *ɛlɛma*
MƐLI: Think about it yourself!

(Schieffelin 1990, 95)

Even though Mɛli is just teasing her father, Osolowa models how to refuse his request for food that she does not want to share. One of the key goals for Kaluli parents is to encourage their children to be assertive. Children may start out by whining or begging others for the things they want, but these utterances are corrected with the *ɛlɛma* routine to ask for things directly, to say why they deserve what they are asking for.

There's a reason for this: Kaluli talk about infants as soft. The foods they eat are mushy, their bodies are tender, they have "no understanding" of the world around them. Growing up is a process of "hardening." A mature person is "hard": their bodies are strong, they use "hard words" that are purposeful and convincing. To this end, the goal of language socialization is to teach children how to be "hard" too, to "say something powerful to get what you want but to say it without destroying social relationships" (Schieffelin 1990, 90).

Obviously, the ways that children are taught to talk in white middle-class North American homes and Papuan Kaluli homes are very different. We can see these compared in Table 3.1. A parent in one culture might look at the practices in the other in shock; how can you not look at your child in the face and talk to them? Or, from the other direction, why on Earth would you use cutesy silly language when talking to your child? In this sense, language socialization practices reveal cultural ideologies of childhood. Notice how Em, the Vietnamese girl in the first example above, is not taught the word for respect (*dạ*) but an explicitly simplified version of it (*ạ*). Shohet's informants explained that children need an easy way to say the word because they are not yet capable of using the adult version – which is another way of saying Vietnamese children are not capable of being adults (Shohet 2021). North American parents frequently, on the other hand, treat their children as if they are communicatively

Table 3.1 – Language Socialization Practices in North America and Papua New Guinea

	White middle-class North America	Kaluli, Papua New Guinea
Participant structure	Dyadic interactions	Multi-party interactions
Discourse features	• Infants addressed directly • Child-raising (addressing child as a competent speaker) • Self-lowering (adjusting speech to child's presumed level)	• Infants rarely addressed directly • Parents use a distinctive high-pitched voice to speak for the child • Parents model appropriate speech for child ("ɛlɛma")
Developmental framework	Accommodation (parents adapt themselves to children)	Hardening (children become socially and physically mature)

already adults who can maturely voice their needs and desires (as my son's kindergarten teacher often says, "use your words!"). Yet both these sets of practices have the same goal: producing a person who is capable, competent, and able to live a happy and productive life. Both of them are also successful, in that the children grow up knowing the language fluently and develop communicative competence.

SOCIAL ORIENTATION: FROM LANGUAGE TO CULTURE

Kaluli children, as we have seen, are socialized to become "hard." But there are many cultural patterns that children become socialized to through learning a language. Parents and caregivers often use language as a way to point children towards idealized ways of acting or being. It is also the way in which our shared frameworks for interpreting and understanding the world around us are formed (see Chapter 4 – Linguistic Relativity). Although by no means exhaustive, here are a few examples of socialization from the research literature that show how different cultural patterns are produced in new generations of speakers.

Ideology

In Chapter 1, we discussed language ideologies as coherent sets of beliefs people have about language, and such ideologies are reproduced in the speech community through socialization practices. Martin Guardado (2009), for instance, has looked at a Spanish-speaking Boy Scout troop in Vancouver called El Grupo Scout Vistas. Although the parents and children were all fluent in English, the troop differed from others in that it focused on using Spanish during its activities and inculcating pride in the boys' Latin American heritage.

In a speech welcoming new members, one active parent addressed the troop in Spanish:

> I would like all of us to maintain that practice of talking to them – they speak English perfectly like all of you but I would like you to always speak to them to always speak Spanish because it's part of what distinguishes us from others. All right? (Guardado 2009, 113–14).

This type of explicit valorization of Spanish was accompanied by other efforts to make it the dominant language of the troop, such as giving instructions or doing activities in Spanish. This reinforces the ideology that makes Spanish a key element of Latin American heritage (as the parent said, it "distinguishes us from others"), but also recognizes the dominance of English outside the confines of the troop itself.

Guardado observed many instances where the children actively made choices to speak Spanish despite not being able to express themselves fluently. In attempting to maintain their language, he argues that the parents and leaders of El Grupo Scout Vistas created a setting where ideologies about the value and distinctiveness of Spanish within Canada could be taught to the younger generation.

Space

We can also move beyond strictly linguistic phenomena and see how children are socialized to other cultural patterns through language as well, such as how we orient ourselves and move through the world. Shannon Ward (2022) has examined how Tibetan children learn to navigate their lived social space through play. The Tibetan dialect studied by Ward has a complex way of discussing spatial relations. There are words for both near (*"di*) and far (*gen*), like in English. But the language also has a word for somewhere far from the speaker but near to the listener (*"de*) and includes adverbs that label places as above (*jar*), below (*mar*), or level (*har*) with the speaker.

BOX 3.1 – SPACE AS A SOCIAL CONSTRUCT

There's a famous quote by the French philosopher Henri Lefebvre (1991, 26): "(Social) space is a (social) product." What he means by this is that space is not simply empty nature; it is the product of controlled and intentional human activity. Think about all the work, for instance, that goes into maintaining a city park or a nature preserve. We are always embedded within landscapes that have been shaped and organized by our actions. Even something as natural as a glacier is imbued with social meaning as a token of nature's power or a symptom of climate change (Howe and Boyer 2024).

Anthropologists have long paid attention to the ways people understand the spaces around them, and language is a powerful tool for organizing that experience. For instance, although East and West Germany unified in 1990, the separate histories of capitalism and socialism mean that these places are experienced very differently even today. The former East Germany still lags behind the West economically, but its citizens also recall the past as a time of cooperation and solidarity. These disparate emotions and associations are evoked when East Germans refer to their former state as "here" and the former West Germany as "over there" (Davidson 2007).

> In my own research on urban China (Henry 2021a), I looked at how different spaces are imbued with values: old socialist apartment blocks were described as being "backwards" or stuck in the past in comparison to gleaming new housing developments. People expected different ways of speaking in these different neighbourhoods. The local northeastern dialect is considered normal in old areas, but English is indicative of modern ones. Language socialization is therefore an important process in teaching us how to experience the spaces we inhabit.

When children are playing, adults often use such words to focus their attention on people, places, and objects around them. In one interaction, four-year-old Lhamo employed these spatial terms to describe how one infant, Tashi, was looking at another, Yangkyi:

LHAMO: Tashi is looking ***over there*** (*gen*) [at Yangkyi]…
When she [pointing to Yangkyi] is a year old, she'll be called "older sister" (*atɕ*^{h}*i*)
When ***this*** (^{n}*di*) one [pointing to Tashi] is a year old, he'll be called "older brother" (*awu*)
(Ward 2022, 470)

Lhamo combines these near and far location words with the appropriate kinship terms that Tashi and Yangkyi will use with each other to chart out their respective relationships. Later, when Lhamo was outside looking for dandelions to pick, she used spatial words to label areas of the village as "here," "up there," and "over there" (Figure 3.2). As Ward notes, Tibetan provides "grammatical resources for locating social relationships in the course of face-to-face interaction and emplacing these relationships in the village homeland" (2022, 481). In effect, Lhamo was learning a particular way to navigate the social and physical environments around her through these types of instructional episodes.

Gender

Other forms of socialization are less explicitly about teaching language; children passively take lessons about the nature of the social world just by listening. Elinor Ochs and Carolyn Taylor (1992) argue that everyday household communication is a key means for teaching children gender norms (see Chapter 7 – Language and Gender). They recorded family dinner conversations in several American middle-class households. In one, the father (Patrick) has just been served a roast for dinner by his wife (Molly) while their two children eat. He first praises Molly for following

Figure 3.2 – Lhamo's village labelled using the spatial terms of Tibetan
Source: Reproduced by permission from Ward (2022)

his advice on how long to cook the meat. After he tastes it, the following exchange takes place:

> PATRICK: So you cooked it about the length that I said?
> MOLLY: Yeah a little bit longer maybe
> PATRICK: So you cooked it about the *length* but not to the degree on the thermometer – which – perhaps indicates that the thermometer…
> MOLLY: This is perfect
> PATRICK: that the thermometer is off
> MOLLY: Maybe?
>
> (Ochs and Taylor 1992, 331)

In this brief exchange, Ochs and Taylor argue that Patrick positions himself as the voice of authority: he is the one who knows how long a roast takes to cook, and he is the one who will judge Molly's success in cooking it. After tasting the meat, Patrick asks Molly questions that problematize her actions, and despite Molly proclaiming that the roast is perfect, she eventually ends her evaluation on an uncertain tone ("Maybe?").

Taking this conversation as but one example of many others they recorded, Ochs and Taylor argue that they constitute a "father knows best" dynamic common to the household: the father observes and arbitrates the actions and decisions of the other family members (Ochs and Taylor 1995). Often the mother would recruit the children into this narrative structure by introducing events in their lives ("You wanna tell Daddy what happened to you today?"), reaffirming the central role of the father. Children are socialized to gender roles and norms as they observe these interactions between their parents and are then encouraged to participate in them as well.

Whether it is common language ideologies, cultural patterns of organizing space, or prevailing gender roles, we come to grasp these concepts through the process of language socialization. As we saw Ochs and Schieffelin point out earlier in this chapter, the kinds of "language lessons" we receive from adults are never simply about teaching words and sentences themselves, but about how to become a particular kind of speaker and a particular kind of person. It is through language that societies reproduce themselves.

BOX 3.2 – MULTILINGUAL SOCIALIZATION

Lots of people grow up in households that use more than one language, and research has shown that children not only quickly learn to identify and use these separate languages but are also socialized to important norms of use. For instance, in one study of an English–Chinese multilingual family living in Japan, the father spoke predominantly English and the mother predominantly Mandarin to their two-year-old child Xiaoxiao (Quay 2008). She also attended a Japanese-language preschool. Xiaoxiao picked up all of these languages quite quickly and even understood who to address them to. For instance, unlike her parents, Xiaoxiao used mostly Japanese that she was learning in preschool, but would mix in Mandarin when talking to her mother and English when talking to her father.

Moreover, children rapidly pick up on adult language ideologies when speaking, as linguist Juyoung Song found when studying the socialization of a Korean family living in the United States. Five-year-old Yongho, who had only been exposed to English for a year through school, shifted between different voices and personas when using the two languages. In Korean, he would adopt a soft, pleading tone appropriate to deferential Korean speech practices. But if that did not work, he would switch into a more assertive tone in English, often raising his voice to get what he wanted. These practices echoed beliefs his mother articulated about the authoritative nature of English (Song 2019).

A lot of the families I met in China were worried that learning English would confuse their child as to what word to use for various things around them. But these studies show that, far from being bewildered by language, young children not only can acquire multiple languages fluently, they are also socialized to the interactional norms governing their use.

ONGOING SOCIALIZATION: "NOT JUST KID STUFF"

One key difference between language acquisition and language socialization is that once children are past the critical period, their language acquisition is effectively over. Certainly, we continue to learn new words and speech styles as we get older, but that intuitive knowledge of a language's grammar is very difficult to develop afterwards. Although linguists often debate whether a second-language learner can become as fluent as a native speaker (White and Genesee 1996), for most people, languages acquired after the critical period do not feel as natural as those learned during it (my Mandarin will certainly never be as good as a native speaker's). Socialization, on the other hand, is not confined to childhood and continues throughout a person's lifetime.

You've probably seen this yourself. Any time you start a new job, become part of a new social group, or enter a new cultural setting, one of the first things you have to do is learn new words and new ways of talking. When I started my job as a professor, we had an orientation day where staff from various campus offices made presentations about their areas of responsibility. Even the word for this process, "onboarding," was something we had to learn from Human Resources. We were told about budget codes and research-related course releases. And just as with child language socialization, we were being instructed about the cultural norms of this new speech community. The language, for instance, was highly technical and bureaucratic, which is kind of what we were expected to become too. Now, whenever I propose a new course or a new initiative, I am conditioned to immediately consider which budget allocation will pay for it and how it aligns with different strategic initiatives at my university. Through this exposure to new forms of language, professors are socialized to think in terms of institutional goals and resources, knowledge creation, and research excellence – it's maddening sometimes! Let's look at a few examples of adult language socialization.

BOX 3.3 – SOCIALIZING THE ANTHROPOLOGIST

Anthropologists, of course, often experience ongoing language socialization when we do fieldwork in a different language. It is one thing to know what a word means, and something entirely different to know how it is used in a culturally appropriate manner. There's a common joke that anthropologists are often treated like children because both groups are in the process of being socialized; the mistakes we make when speaking often provide opportunities for people to teach us how we ought to talk (Riley 2009). When Elise Berman was doing fieldwork in the Marshall Islands, she became acquainted with the concept of *āliklik*, which is generally translated into English as "shame" (Berman 2019). *Āliklik* is the feeling that spurs people to act appropriately, particularly in terms of sharing; when someone asks you for something, it is *āliklik* that stops you from refusing.

Berman knew all this at a theoretical level, but when a friend suggested they go to the next village and buy a soda – a treat not available where she was living – the question was how she could do so without having to buy one for everyone. To avoid feeling shame, Marshallese find ways to stop people asking in the first place. One can avoid answering questions like "Why are you going there?" by keeping silent, lying about the true purpose of the trip, or giving an obviously exaggerated answer. "This trip quickly socialized me into the numerous forms of indirection that adults employ to avoid giving to each other" (Berman 2019, 63). Over time, Berman had to learn to use all of these verbal strategies as a way to hold on to things without feeling ashamed.

Baristas

A barista is that fantastic cafe worker who makes your morning coffee. One thing baristas need to do – and they undergo extensive training to do so – is translate a customer's order ("I want a medium latte with no caffeine and make it with skim milk") into an efficient code ("decaf grande skinny latte") that can be spoken to other baristas who will then make the drink precisely. However, this barista code sometimes comes into conflict with customer stances and attitudes. The spoken code used at places like the ever-popular Starbucks is not just about efficiency, but about developing a distinct linguistic style. "Part of Starbucks' branding strategy," writes linguistic anthropologist Paul Manning, "relies on the idea that customers do not just want coffee, they want 'distinction'" (Manning 2008, 106). So a lot of customers attempt to adopt this style of ordering as well because it allows them to associate themselves with the elitism and sophistication of a luxury brand (Gaudio 2003).

Manning then looked at what are called "stupid customer of the week" stories posted online, in which baristas complain about interactions they have had at work. A significant number of these stories are about language, either customers who refuse to allow baristas to translate their orders ("I said a 'medium,' not a 'grande'") or, even worse, people who *think* they know how to order but do not. The real power of these stories, Manning argues, is to draw baristas into a shared social world oriented towards common tasks and experiences, a group of people who actually know how to make a proper cappuccino.

Bureaucrats

This incorporation of people into a shared social world through language is something that linguistic anthropologist Don Brenneis – whose remark about socialization being more than "kid stuff" starts out this section – also found when he was tasked with reviewing graduate student fellowship applications for the National Science Foundation (NSF) in the United States. In an article reflecting on the experience, Brenneis (1994) describes the linguistic and bureaucratic processes that whittle hundreds of applications down to the dozens that will be funded. Each application, consisting of pages of documents and transcripts, is read and assigned a numerical score by reviewers; but not all reviewers agree on those scores.

From the beginning, the NSF officers promote the idea of objectivity and fairness: each file should be judged by the same criteria as any other. But how does one compare a student with high grades and a bad proposal to someone with a great proposal and bad grades? Or one with a standard methodology to one that promises groundbreaking results? When reviewers disagree on a file, they have to verbally work out their differences and come to a compromise. The training that NSF reviewers undergo, the ways in which they learn to quickly evaluate different types of applications, and the ways in which they quickly and efficiently negotiate differences (because there are only so many hours to complete the whole process) are part of an emergent consensus in their speech community around the ideas of "quality" and "excellence." Summing up his experience, and recalling here our ideas about socialization as a way of *doing*, Brenneis writes, "Instead of becoming a bureaucrat, one learns, with striking rapidity, to do bureaucratic things" (1994, 33).

Lawyers

Finally, there is the fascinating work done by Elizabeth Mertz (2007) in American law schools. Mertz studied first-year contracts classes in eight law schools across the United States to learn about how language is used in law. But what she found more interesting was how law professors use language to socialize students into a legal mindset. Lawyers are supposed to act a certain way, talk a certain way and, more importantly, think a certain way about the world around them. Lawyers need to be analytical, dispassionate, and conversant with a wide range of authoritative texts and concepts that shape the law and its interpretation. Law school is what teaches them that.

Law school education in the United States typically employs a dialogic teaching style known as the Socratic method. Rather than simply imparting information, law school professors call on individual students during lectures and ask a series of probing questions to test their knowledge and focus attention on particular elements of a case.

PROFESSOR: Well, let's go back to Mr. H. What is the good involved in the transaction?

MR. H: I would say that it… service.

PROFESSOR: Is there a good in that transaction? Is Article 2 applicable at all? Come on now, I don't want to… Yes or no.

MR. H: No, it's not.

PROFESSOR: Is that a "no" that you believe in, or is that a "no" that you're just wimping out? [Class laughter] Are you sure?

MR. H: I am sure. I would say that it is "no" –

PROFESSOR: – No. No good in that transaction. UCC, no. Common law, yes.

(Mertz 2007, 90)

In this particular exchange, the professor calls on Mr. H (and students were always addressed formally) and asks him to determine whether a particular contract involved goods or services (which would dictate the applicability of the Uniform Commercial Code or common law, respectively). Although on its surface the dialogue seems somewhat light-hearted, even satirical, Mertz argues that there is an underlying adversarial style, with the professor demanding clear, committed answers from the student that conform to the genre of legal discourse. This, of course, models what lawyers must do in a courtroom, where they spar with an opposing legal counsel and can win their case through a superior knowledge of law and legal precedent.

The goal, however, is not just to get students to talk like lawyers, but also to *think* like lawyers. These exchanges direct students away from social causes or personal opinions. Discussions of fairness, ethics, or the impacts of race, social class, and gender on particular cases are abandoned in favour of a singular interpretation: what does the law say? Doing so socializes the students into a particular mindset where doctrine, statutes and legal codes reign supreme.

CONCLUSION

Before they can study in a Canadian university, foreign students have to take a language test to prove that they have an adequate level of English. In China, I watched many classes and interviewed many teachers that prepare students to take these tests, and one of the things that struck me time and again was just how little actual language instruction went on. The emphasis, instead, was on how to frame the answer, how to put it together. As one Chinese teacher explained it to me, in conversations with those in authority, Chinese people tend to respond to questions with short, direct answers: "You don't have to tell why you think that. You just tell the conclusions" (Henry 2021b, 113). But these oral language tests require students to expand their responses into long narratives which will serve, in turn, to demonstrate their English abilities to the examiner. So if an examiner asks the student, "Tell me about what you did last night," the answer "Nothing special," while perfectly appropriate in Mandarin, will lead to them failing the test in English. Constructing more extended narrative responses is what the students were being taught to do in their classes, not new English words. In the meantime, when I talked to the language examiners, they often bemoaned unimaginative students who simply gave direct answers to their question prompts.

How to respond to a question is a fundamental part of communicative competence and, as we have seen here, the strategies for doing so are shaped during the language socialization process. The syntax of question formation is a key part of language acquisition, but it is inseparable from the cultural knowledge of how to ask and answer those questions. This chapter has repeatedly stressed the entanglement of linguistic and cultural knowledge; the linguistic anthropologist Michael Agar goes so far as to say that the use of one term always implies the other, for which he coins the admittedly clunky word **languaculture**. "Language, in all its varieties, in all the ways it appears in everyday life, builds a world of meanings… Language fills the spaces between us with sound; culture forges the human connection through them. Culture is in language, and language is loaded with culture" (Agar 1994, 28). This precept that language and culture are entwined, itself a product of the socialization process, will be a recurrent theme throughout this book.

BOX 3.4 – RESEARCH SPOTLIGHT: MARY BUCHOLTZ

Bucholtz, Mary, Elena Skapoulli, Brendan Barnwell, and Jung-Eun Janie Lee. 2011. "Entextualized Humor in the Formation of Scientist Identities among U.S. Undergraduates." *Anthropology & Education Quarterly* 42 (3): 177–92.

Here's a joke: "So there are these two neutrons. They're walking along. They bump into each other. So this guy was like 'Hey, I think you have one of my electrons.' So the other guy goes, 'Are you sure?' He says, 'Yeah, positive.'" Morrisse, a student, told this joke to his friends while working together in a calculus seminar for science majors at an American university. They responded with a bit of sarcastic mock approval, but it was also clear that science jokes like this one were instrumental in creating close ties among the students.

In this article, Mary Bucholtz and her colleagues are interested in the ways that that students come to identify themselves as "scientists in the making" (Morrisse can't be a scientist yet, they tell us, otherwise he would have known neutrons do not contain electrons). In other words, how do students orient themselves towards the values and practices of scientists? Humour, they found, is one key way in which the students claimed such an affiliation, but also how they were socialized to science. Scientists value displays of esoteric knowledge, nerdy pursuits, and academic collaboration – which may not be quite so valued outside of science – and so these jokes served to reinforce those ideals among the students.

One of the key terms they use here is **entextualization**, which refers to borrowing pre-existing chunks of language (like jokes) and planting them within a new discourse context. They argue that this allows us to index the values of one piece of discourse without having to explain it to others every time: we can quote a famous line from a movie, for instance, and people will know what we are referring to without having to describe the plot. Jokes are therefore perfect for offering information to others about our beliefs, stances, and attitudes without having to state them explicitly.

When we think about the idea of becoming a scientist, it is usually in terms of learning math and the scientific method. The work of Bucholtz and colleagues points to how language practices such as jokes socialize people into these identities, and how socialization is therefore a process that occurs throughout our lives.

Discussion

1. Every culture has its own way of talking to babies. We discussed protoconversations above, where adults engage prelinguistic children in conversation, but there are many other aspects of babytalk we could identify (like calling it a "doggie" rather than a "dog"). When you talk to babies, how do you do it? What kinds of cultural lessons do you think are being conveyed to the child?
2. As I said above, you have probably experienced language socialization yourself when you started a new job or took on a new role. When I worked in a fast-food restaurant (ages ago), part of our training was in being polite, speaking clearly, and not provoking conflict with customers: I was being socialized to the idea that "the customer is always right." What kinds of training have you received, and what types of cultural lessons (about how to work, how to act, or how to approach problems) were you being taught?
3. In his book *Language Shock*, Michael Agar discusses an article in *The Washington Post* about the 1991 Mount Pleasant riot in Washington, DC, that happened

after a police officer shot a Salvadoran man. The article recommended teaching Spanish to police officers to allow more effective communication with the Latino community. "The *Post*, and most everybody else, assumes that language instruction would solve the problem. The *Post*, and most everybody else, is wrong" (Agar 1994, 15). Using what we've learned about language socialization, why would Agar argue that just learning Spanish would not help ease tensions in this community? What else would the police force need to do?

4. Have you ever learned a second (or third, or fourth) language? Learning a new language is also a socialization process, a way of entering a new cultural world through language. Just remembering a list of words for different things will not make you communicatively competent. What have you learned about communicating appropriately in the language you are learning?

4

Linguistic Relativity

Topics

- The relation between language and cognition
- The Sapir–Whorf hypothesis
- Critiques of linguistic relativity
- Linguistic relativity and language practices

Victor Klemperer (1881–1960), a linguist and German Jewish convert to Christianity, lived and taught in Dresden during the 1930s and 1940s. He witnessed the rise to power of Hitler's Third Reich and the disaster of the Second World War, during which he kept a diary detailing his observations about changes in the German language, often through the influence of the Nazi Party and a complicit media. For instance, before the Nazis, the German word *fanatisch* (fanatical) had overwhelmingly negative connotations. Someone who was fanatical was threatening and vulgar, with an unthinking devotion to self and socially harmful ideas. Under the Nazis, however, *fanatisch* gradually took on positive connotations of courage and devotion, especially to the state and the fascist cause: "On the anniversary of the day the Nazis came to power, there wasn't a single newspaper article, message of congratulation, or address to some army unit or other organization, which didn't include a 'fanatical vow (*fanatisches Gelöbnis*)' or 'fanatical declaration (*fanatisches Bekenntnis*),' or which didn't affirm its 'fanatical belief (*fanatischen Glauben*)' in the everlasting life of Hitler's Reich" (Klemperer 2013, 62). Klemperer called such changes "language that thinks and writes for you." A similar concern with language animates George Orwell's dystopian novel *Nineteen Eighty-Four* (1949), in which a totalitarian state – the "Big Brother" that watches over the novel's characters – develops and mandates the use of "Newspeak." This limited and highly regimented language serves to curtail critical thinking and dissent among its speakers.

Another view of the power of language is offered in the 2016 science fiction film *Arrival*. Two scientists – Ian, a physicist, and Louise, a linguist – are tasked with learning how to communicate with a seven-limbed alien species that has arrived on Earth. As they work on untangling the "Heptapod" writing system, which appears as swirly circular inkblots, they begin to realize the language is non-linear: rather than a sequence of words, each inkblot is a holistic depiction of a thought. This prompts Ian to bring up the relationship between language and cognition with Louise.

> IAN: You know I was doing some reading about this idea that if you immerse yourself into a foreign language that you can actually re-wire your brain.
>
> LOUISE: Yeah, the Sapir–Whorf hypothesis. It's the theory that the language you speak determines how you think.

Before long, Louise is experiencing past, present, and future simultaneously due to her exposure to the Heptapod language.

So what is the Sapir–Whorf hypothesis? Does language really determine how you think: limiting our thought as with Newspeak, or opening it up as with Heptapod? If I learn another language, do I experience the world differently? These are big questions that, aside from linguistics, also impact philosophy and psychology. There is, however, significant opposition to the idea that the language we speak affects us in any but a most superficial way, particularly within formal linguistic approaches that analyse phonology or syntax. Nevertheless, most linguistic anthropologists do argue that, because language is an inherently cultural phenomenon and culture is both a way of doing *and* a way of thinking, our language and our thinking are linked in important ways. This is the idea of **linguistic relativity.** In this chapter we look at the complex and intriguing relationships between language and thought, hopefully clearing out many of the misconceptions along the way.

THE SAPIR–WHORF HYPOTHESIS

Linguists have long recognized that languages are not simply objective descriptions of reality; they encapsulate a perspective on the world around us. The nineteenth-century linguist Wilhelm von Humboldt proposed that because languages link sounds with ideas, language is itself the very foundation of thought: "Just as no concept is possible without language, so also there can be no object for the mind, since it is only through the concept, of course, that anything external acquires full being for consciousness…

and since a like subjectivity also affects language in the same nation, there resides in every language a characteristic *world-view*"(Humboldt 1988, 59–60). As we saw in Chapter 1, early anthropologists had an abiding interest in how the varieties of human experience were expressed through languages. Franz Boas hinted that this diversity has implications for how we think. Surveying the many ways different languages would express the same idea, he concludes, "when we consider for a moment what this implies, it will be recognized that in each language only a part of the complete concept that we have in mind is expressed, and that each language has a peculiar tendency to select this or that aspect of the mental image which is conveyed by the expression of the thought" (Boas 1911, 43).

This kind of off-hand observation was later addressed more directly by Boas's student Edward Sapir. Language, he argued, is our way of apprehending and interpreting the world around us. For instance, he asks us to think of a stone falling to the ground. In English we would say "the stone falls," but in languages like French and German we would need to specify the stone's grammatical gender. Anishinaabemowin obliges the speaker to specify that the stone is an inanimate object, while in Kwak'wala one must state whether the stone is visible to the speaker or not, and near to the speaker or far away. In other words, the means of expressing even a simple physical movement are not universal but *relative* to each particular language (Sapir 1924). That has implications for how we perceive the world around us. "Human beings do not live in the objective world alone, nor alone in the world of social activity as ordinarily understood, but are very much at the mercy of the particular language which has become the medium of expression for their society… The fact of the matter is that the 'real world' is to a large extent unconsciously built up on the language habits of the group" (Sapir 1929b, 209). Our culture, Sapir argues, constitutes an "unconscious pattern" that highlights some things and takes others for granted, a pattern expressed through the culture's language (Sapir 1929a).

It was Sapir's student Benjamin Lee Whorf, however, who took Sapir's general idea and ran with it. Whorf was not an academic linguist; for most of his life he worked as an inspector for the Hartford Fire Insurance Company. Despite a background in chemistry, Whorf became interested in linguistics and spent his free time in the Hartford public library translating Aztec texts and proposing new approaches to deciphering the Mayan writing system.[1] In 1931, Whorf took Edward Sapir's class at Yale and was heavily influenced by his thinking. He started looking for specific examples of this connection between the form of a language and patterns of thought.

Interestingly, it was in his work as a fire inspector that Whorf found evidence of how language shapes the way we think. A chemical factory stored empty gasoline drums in an area where workers were frequently hanging around on their breaks. The workers would toss their cigarette butts, and when one landed near the drums the remaining vapour inside ignited and started a fire. Now, what started the fire? Sure, it was a worker carelessly tossing a cigarette, but why was the worker careless around gasoline drums? Whorf posits that language itself was the issue. No one was being careful because the drums were *empty* and thus, as Whorf argues, semantically interpreted as inert and not dangerous. The linguistic definition of a situation had more influence on people's actions than its physical reality (Whorf 1956, 135).

In the 1930s, Whorf began a study of Hopi, an Indigenous language spoken in the southwestern United States. Here, he found a language that was structurally very different from English and other related languages (which for convenience and comparative purposes he termed "standard average European"). English, for instance, allows the pluralization of both abstract and concrete nouns: we can talk about "five days" in the same way we talk about "five people." Syntactically, English therefore treats time as a quantity of things (minutes, days, years) that can be objectively counted, arranged, saved, spent, and so on. In Hopi, pluralization only affects concrete objects, not abstract entities like time. Additionally, English differentiates past, present, and future grammatically; Hopi does not, but rather uses various morphemes to indicate whether events are reported, expected, or customary. Many of these morphemes function as descriptors that specify the duration, tendency, and intensity of something (Whorf 1956).

These differences lead, argues Whorf, to different "thought worlds" for speakers of English and Hopi languages. If English is a language of "things" (both real and imagined) that can be counted and arranged, Hopi is more concerned with experience. "Events are expressed mainly as outlines, colors, movements, and other perceptive reports" (Whorf 1956, 147). Whorf even proposes that a more accurate translation of the word "event" in Hopi would be "eventing," capturing its sense of coming-into-being. And these are not simply different ways of processing the world around us; they lead to different patterns of culture. Because a day is more of an experiential artefact than a unit of time, in Hopi culture there is a tremendous emphasis on preparation, diligence, and envisioning proper outcomes. Everything from speech to agriculture to ritual reflects the idea of quietly building intensity for success.

BOX 4.1 – TETHERING LANGUAGE AND COMMUNITY TOGETHER

Despite the innovative way Whorf turned scholarly attention to the role of language in structuring our social worlds, his research was the product of a different era in the discipline. Scholars in Whorf's time were far more apt to study Indigenous languages for what "they" could tell "us," rather than collaborating with Indigenous communities and addressing the most pressing social issues, such as language change and revitalization.

In this context, linguistic anthropologist Hannah McElgunn (2021, 435) has called for linguistic anthropologists to resist the study of language that has become "untethered, like loose threads," from its speech communities. For Hopi today, language is more than just a means of communication; it is an important form of cultural knowledge and wisdom in its own right. She describes the many ways her Hopi interlocutors nudged her into thinking about their culture, their language, and her own relation to these in new ways.

Listening to Hopi today and understanding the role language plays in a continued sense of history, community, and identity helps us understand Hopi as an enduring presence rather than a historical artefact (Bernardini et al. 2021). Leigh Kuwanwisiwma, a Hopi scholar and elder, put it this way in understanding the significance of the past: "We start from here, don't we? We live here. From there, we remember where we came from to arrive here" (McElgunn 2021, 434).

Whorf's outline of the effects of Hopi grammar on the thought worlds and cultural patterns of Hopi people has been tremendously influential. It captures a common sense that *how* we say something matters to some degree more than *what* we say. To call it the **Sapir–Whorf hypothesis**, however, is a bit of a misnomer, since Sapir and Whorf never collaborated on a formal statement of it, and it was never actually proposed as a testable hypothesis (Hill and Mannheim 1992, 386). Still, over the years there have been several attempts to systematize Whorf's insights into a more formal set of propositions (Brown and Lenneberg 1954; Kay and Kempton 1984), which would look something like this:

1. Language is a way of categorizing and classifying the world.
2. No two languages do this in exactly the same way.
3. Therefore, our view of the world is built upon the structures of our language and our habits of speaking.

Classifying the World

Much anthropological research in the 1950s and 1960s was therefore expended on documenting *how* various languages classify the world, an approach known as **ethnosemantics**. Charles Frake (1970, 435) described the task for anthropologists not as "getting words for things" but "finding the 'things' that go with the words." Just because we can refer to "trees" in English does not mean that they are a natural category, clearly differentiated from other plants like bushes or grasses. Other languages may classify things differently. One of the most compelling areas where what we take as "natural" turns out to be very cultural is systems of colour.

How many colours are there? The answer depends on the language. Colour is, by itself, just the visual perception of various wavelengths of light with no discrete divisions within the spectrum. Nevertheless, people who speak the same language will generally identify the same number of colours in a rainbow with a consistent set of words. In an early paper on this topic, Harold Conklin (1955) studied an Indigenous Filipino group called the Hanunóo who had only four main colour terms (the ʔ symbol below represents a phoneme called a glottal stop, which is a quick closure of the vocal cords – it's the sound in the middle of "uh-oh"):

bīru black (along with blue, purple, and any dark shade)
lagtiʔ white (along with any light shade)
raraʔ red
latuy green

This does not mean the Hanunóo could not perceive other colours, but they simply labelled what we call blue as a type of black. They also imposed a kind of value system on these colour distinctions: *latuy* holds connotations of lushness and freshness, like recently cut bamboo, while *raraʔ* implies dryness and desiccation.

Building on this work, the cognitive anthropologists Paul Berlin and Brent Kay (1969) collected colour-naming data from 20 different languages around the world. They performed an experiment where they presented people with a large set of colour chips and asked them to name them in their language. They were looking for what they called "basic colour terms" (words like red and blue, but not types of red, such as scarlet or crimson). Then they asked people to pick out the best example of each term. What they found is that languages vary greatly in the number of colour terms: some only have words for white, black, and red. Others have over 12, like Russian, which has a system very similar to English but also distinguishes light blue (*goluboy*) from dark blue (*siniy*). The interesting twist was that most languages agree on a particular hue that we can identify as red, one we can identify as blue (where there is a word for that in a language), yellow, and so forth. In other words, the "reddest" red is nearly always the same in all the languages they looked at, the greenest green, bluest blue, and so forth. Additionally, colours appear to be added to languages in a particular order: first comes white and black, then red, then yellow and green, and so on. They found no languages, for instance, that have a word for pink but no word for red.

Cousin Term		Sibling Term
tang (cousin on father's side)	+	*di* (younger male)
biao (cousin on mother's side)		*ge* (older male)
		mei (younger female)
		jie (older female)

Figure 4.1 – Forming the Mandarin Chinese word for cousin

Another area that demonstrates the varying ways languages classify is kinship. In English, the word "cousin" describes the child of a parent's sibling, but many cultures differentiate types of cousins: they have a separate term for parallel-cousins, who are the children of siblings of the same sex (your father's brother's child or mother's sister's child) and for cross-cousins, who are the children of siblings of opposite sex (your father's sister's child or mother's brother's child) (Fox 1967). In lineal descent systems, where membership in an extended family group like a clan is a product of descent either through one's mother or father, different terms for parallel- and cross-cousins differentiates relatives who are members of one's clan from relatives who are not.

I encountered a very different kinship system myself when I went to China. Mandarin Chinese speakers differentiate cousins on the father's side from cousins on the mother's side, but then combine this with sibling terms that indicate whether the cousin is older or younger than the speaker, male or female. The system for figuring out what to call your cousin looks like what you see in Figure 4.1.

So an older male cousin on your mother's side is your *biaoge* while a younger female cousin on your father's side is your *tangmei*. There are also different words for each uncle and aunt, depending on side of family, age, biological relation or in-marrying relative, and so forth; it is an incredibly complex system and one that took me years to get a handle on. However, it is not a fixed system and was undergoing continuous changes. When I first went to China, the one-child policy – which restricted families to a single child – had been in effect for about 30 years. I would talk to people and constantly be hearing about their sister or brother. I thought that I had stumbled upon a household defying the state's family planning rules! But it turns out, instead, that people were dropping the cousin word and referring to biological cousins as siblings to account for the closer relations among cousins now that siblings were rare. Linguistic classification systems are therefore flexible and open to change.

Evaluating the Sapir–Whorf Hypothesis

What does all this mean for the Sapir–Whorf hypothesis? First of all, it is clear that languages categorize and that different languages do so differently. But does this mean that speakers of different languages *think* differently? That's where there is considerable disagreement. In psychology, there has been a lot of research on the impacts of different languages on cognition (Bohnemeyer 2020). Remember the distinction between two shades of blue in Russian? In one experiment, Russian speakers and English speakers were both given the same task: when given a choice of three colour chips, pick out the one that was a different shade than the others (Winawer et al. 2007). In general, Russian speakers were able to more quickly discriminate between light and dark shades of blue than between similar shades of blue, while English speakers had no such advantage.

In another study, psychologists compared how speakers of varying languages described events (Bylund, Athanasopoulos, and Oostendorp 2013). In the experiment, they showed participants video clips of events in progress, such as a woman walking towards a car, and asked "what happened?" They compared whether the answers given had an endpoint ("a woman is walking to a car") or no endpoint ("a woman is walking"). Speakers of English, an aspect language that requires *-ing* for ongoing motion, tended to include an endpoint less often than speakers of Swedish and Afrikaans, two languages where aspect is optional. The researchers argue that this occurs because grammatical aspect focuses the speaker's attention on what is going on at the moment, while lack of grammatical aspect provides a big-picture perspective.

Although most linguistic anthropologists may find such research intriguing, it is rarely considered compelling. Both the number of participants and purported cognitive effects of language are often quite small – in the study of Russian blue colour discrimination, they only tested 50 people, and the mean differences under various conditions were usually in the order of 200 milliseconds. Moreover, although the Russian speakers (most of whom were actually Russian–English bilinguals) were able to discriminate light/dark blue differences faster than similar shades, it was actually the English speakers who were faster overall. Their times for light/dark and similar shades were fairly equal – the authors hypothesize that English speakers might have been faster because they are more familiar with the computers used in the study, but that seems like a stretch. The Afrikaans speakers in the second study used endpoints only 16 per cent more often than English speakers. In addition to these methodological problems, it is not clear what the significance of these effects are for the larger questions Whorf was considering, such as whether the *experience* of time is different for Hopi and English speakers or even how to go about measuring that.

We can also consider some rather obvious issues with the idea that language determines how we think: if we do not have a shared framework for perceiving the world, how is translation possible (and recall that translatability is a fundamental feature of human languages)? What about people who are bilingual – do they switch back and forth between different mindsets every time they switch languages? These kinds of criticisms have led some scholars to propose two separate versions of the Sapir–Whorf hypothesis: a strong version in which language structures and determines our way of thinking, and a weak version in which specific language structures may influence our patterns of thought, guiding us to think in some ways but not leaving us "at the mercy of a particular language," to use Sapir's words (Ardener 2007, 164; Lucy 1992). Nevertheless, many scholars have countered that the strong version is most certainly wrong, and the weak version is so generic as to be untestable (Pinker 2007).

The linguist John McWhorter (2014, xviii) goes so far as to call the Sapir–Whorf hypothesis a hoax, arguing that "the whole notion that how someone's language works determines, in any significant way, how they see the world is utterly incoherent, and even dangerous." McWhorter lays out a series of very specific objections to the Sapir–Whorf hypothesis, a few of which are:

- Linguistic features are not a product of cultural features. Many languages mark evidentiality in their grammar (the source of knowledge for a speaker's statement), but this does not mean that members of those cultures are any more skeptical or wary of the source of a person's knowledge.
- Cultural features are not a product of linguistic features. Mandarin Chinese does not mark gender in its grammar (like "he" and "she" in English), but this does not imply that gender plays any less of a role in Chinese culture or that gender in China is more egalitarian.
- Cultural features, such as warfare or pacificism, cannot even be conclusively correlated with particular linguistic features. Cultures with similar features (e.g., hierarchy) do not always share linguistic features (e.g., respect registers). In similar fashion, very dissimilar cultures (English and Indonesian, for instance) often share common linguistic features: both describe time metaphorically in terms of length (long or short) while other languages, like Spanish and Greek, describe time metaphorically in terms of size (big or small).

Most of all, McWhorter objects to the idea that language *limits* our thoughts in some way: that Hopi do not understand the notion of time, or that Russians cannot save for their retirement. As a result, McWhorter, like many other formalist linguists (those who work on questions of syntax, morphology, and phonology) downplay the importance of culture on language.[2]

BOX 4.2 – "NO RETIREMENT SAVINGS? PERHAPS IT'S BECAUSE OF THE LANGUAGE YOU SPEAK"

That's from a headline (Berreby 2012) reporting on research by the economist Keith Chen (2013) that correlates the presence of future tense marking in a language ("I *will* do it") with a tendency not to save for the future. Chen argues that "grammatically separating the future and the present leads speakers to disassociate the future from the present. This would make the future feel more distant, and since saving involves current costs for future rewards, would make saving harder" (Chen 2013, 691). Chen provides a wealth of statistical and mathematical analysis, comparing speakers of different languages within nine separate countries to support his claim. Speakers of languages with future tense marking, such as Russian and Tamil, saved less than speakers of languages with no future tense marking, such as Mandarin and Yoruba. So, has he found proof of the Sapir–Whorf hypothesis?

While it is certainly possible, there are a lot of assumptions built into Chen's model. Linguists have pointed out that while English does mark future tense, it does not do so consistently ("I *am* having bananas tomorrow" is also a future-oriented sentence). And typical analyses of Whorfian effects usually posit that the presence of a linguistic feature *heightens* its salience rather than lessening it, so use of the future tense conceivably should make people notice it *more* rather than less.

The more critical issue for anthropologists, however, is the elimination of any role for culture in Chen's analysis. China has a notoriously high household savings rate, but is this because Mandarin Chinese does not have future tense marking? Or because the lineage organization of Chinese households traditionally meant that most families were also corporate entities requiring significant capital accumulation and redistribution (Gates 1996)? Linguistic anthropologists are therefore very cautious about making extravagant claims about language determinism based on correlations between linguistic and social features, seeking instead to understand how language, culture, and thought are interconnected.

One of the key problems in the debate outlined here is that – as stated above – Whorf never conceived of his work as a formal hypothesis, but many scholars treat it as if he did (Enfield 2015; Leavitt 2011, 169). His reflections on Hopi, for instance, are often reduced to the idea that Hopi does not have any way of expressing time and, therefore, finding examples of temporal reference in Hopi disproves his thesis

(Malotki 1983). Whorf (1956, 217) himself did not argue that Hopi could not comprehend time, only that the language tended to "distinguish among momentary, continued, and repeated occurrences" rather than treat time as a linear progression.[3] Berlin and Kay (1969) saw their study of colour classification (described above) as invalidating the Sapir–Whorf hypothesis because it showed there are *some* constraints on how people organize the colour spectrum rather than it being completely random, which, again, is not something Whorf himself argued (Saunders 2000). A more significant problem for us, though, is how Whorf's critics and interpreters often rely upon a rather static notion of culture.

By listing cultural features such as aggression, hierarchy, or skepticism, for instance, McWhorter implicitly subscribes to a notion of culture as sets of attributes that people have. As I have stressed before, culture is something we do, a particular way of interpreting and acting in the world. The structures of a language neither determine how we think nor mimic the essence of a culture because culture is itself a process, not a thing. Whorf realized this when he discussed the influence of language on our "habits of thought" rather than on perception or cognition. As the example of Chinese kinship classification discussed above also shows, these connections between language and culture are also not fixed but responsive to each other. Linguistic anthropologists have therefore largely abandoned the Sapir–Whorf hypothesis as a testable proposition and moved on to a more nuanced version of linguistic relativity, one that sees the relationship between language, culture, and thought as a dynamic and interactive process.

LANGUAGE AS CULTURAL PRACTICE

Language is patterned (what we hear is not just arbitrary squeaky noises) and so is culture (how we act is not random). A core idea of linguistic anthropology is that these patternings reflect each other. Within this understanding, language is not the source of our culture or what shapes our cognition, nor is culture the origin of our patterns of language. Instead, the diversity of human languages offers each speech community a different set of tools for interpreting the social and physical world – things like social relationships, objects, space, intentions, and so forth. Rather than just listing categories and taking those as representative of some kind of cognitive system, this approach highlights the active role people take in creating shared understandings of what is going on around them. Linguistic anthropologists have therefore largely moved away from using *words* as the unit of analysis in linguistic relativity and instead turned to forms of language *practice*.

BOX 4.3 – PIRAHÃ: THE PEOPLE WITH NO NUMBERS

In 2005, linguist Daniel Everett published a provocative article that challenged numerous orthodoxies in linguistics. Based on research in the Brazilian Amazon, Everett (2005) described a language, Pirahã, that has no words for numbers, quantities, or counting; no words for colour; and very few pronouns or verb tenses. But his most explosive claim was that Pirahã lacks recursion, a form of syntactic embedding such as "Larry thinks that Alice said he was tall," where Alice's opinion of Larry's height is embedded in a larger sentence of what Larry thinks. That might seem like the least consequential of Everett's findings, but recursion is a fundamental principle of Chomsky's generative grammar; documenting a language that lacks this feature challenged the foundations of modern linguistics and led to highly acrimonious debate.

In a review article of the controversy, Janet Chernela (2023) argues that the controversy over Everett's description of Pirahã grammar may be overblown. There is actually no universally accepted definition of recursion in linguistics, and languages can embed information in multiple ways. Many of the features Everett finds lacking in Pirahã are also absent in other Amazonian languages, while his methodology of recording elicitation sessions with Pirahã speakers neglects the social dimension of discourse. Other aspects of Everett's article, however, such as the lack of numeration, have been confirmed by subsequent research.

Proponents of a strict linguistic determinism posit that having no numbers constrains Pirahã speakers in their ability to perceive or conceptualize quantities larger than what can tabulated on one's fingers (Gordon 2003). This is a classic formulation of the Sapir–Whorf hypothesis. The cognitive theorist Steven Pinker has countered, however, that the lack of numeracy probably has other causes. "It can't be a coincidence that the Pirahã language just happens to lack big number words (unlike the English language) and the Pirahã speakers just happen to hunt and gather in remote stone-age villages (unlike English speakers). A more plausible interpretation is that the lifestyle, history, and culture of a technologically underdeveloped hunter-gatherer people will cause it to lack both number words and numerical reasoning" (Pinker 2007, 139).

Although he intends it as a refutation of linguistic relativity, if we were to drop Pinker's patronizing tone towards a dynamic Indigenous society, his statement is actually in agreement with how many linguistic anthropologists think about the concept. Rather than language causing us to think in certain ways, linguistic relativity is about the interrelation of linguistic and cultural patterns, which is clearly demonstrated in the Pirahã case.

Here's an example: in China there is a great deal of what I would call "relationship talk." There are long-standing ideas going back to Confucius about the proper relations between people: between parents and children, for instance, or between emperors and subjects. The word for relationship is *guanxi*, but it goes far beyond just the idea of a connection. *Guanxi* implies a host of deeply ethical rights and obligations between people, forged and maintained through the back-and-forth flow of favours, gifts, and communal meals (Kipnis 1997; Yang 1994). Success in life is considered to be dependent upon successfully managing all the ties you have to various other people. Someone with good *guanxi* has a wide network of contacts they can use to get things done in a highly bureaucratic system. Through *guanxi* people find a good job, place their child in a top school, get around government regulations, and meet potential marriage partners.

So people use the word *guanxi* a lot. People would ask me rhetorically, "what is our relationship?" before going ahead and defining its exact terms – for instance, as an in-marrying male to the eldest woman in my wife's lineage generation, I was *jiefu* to other relatives. This meant I was expected to take on the proper role in relation to them, like paying for meals at family gatherings. But it goes beyond just the presence of the word *guanxi* in conversation. The crux of a Chinese wedding is not the wife saying "I do" to her husband, but when she addresses her new husband's parents with the appropriate kinship term. Similarly, Susan Blum (1997) notes a common socialization practice in China when children are introduced to new people. The parent usually begins by coaching the child on how to address the person, such as "say *laoye* (paternal grandfather)" or "call her *gugu* (father's elder sister)," and the child murmurs the relationship term to the addressed person's approval. This articulates the nature of the social bond between them, subordinates the younger to the elder (as the child is the one naming the relative appropriately), and defines how they should act and speak to each other in the future.

We have, then, a particular cultural pattern surrounding ideas of kinship and relationship, and an accompanying linguistic pattern around the classification of relatives and how children are taught to navigate these relationships through speech. Even when the exact kinship terms themselves are changing (as we saw above in "cousins" becoming "siblings"), there is a manifest language ideology in which calling a person by the correct name brings the relationship into being. But this kind of patterning is very hard to demonstrate experimentally in the way psychologists study things like colour classification.

Linguistic anthropologists are more apt to look for the ways in which cultural practices and language practices are interrelated and how they reinforce and reflect each other. This also implicates how we think. Since languages organize the world differently (through the kinds of classificatory schemes we discussed above), they offer different ways of interpreting or framing the actions and words of others. When I pick up the tab for a meal in China, for instance, it is filtered through that framework of relationships I discussed above, which would be different if I was doing so here in Canada. It is the way in which language acts as a shared framework organizing our cultural interpretations that is the core of contemporary approaches to linguistic relativity. Some of those approaches are outlined below.

Metaphor

Language is not simply a set of words or labels, but a meaning-making system in its own right (Kockelman 2010; Mertz and Parmentier 1985). Our ways of comprehending reality are mediated by the kinds of semiotic relationships we discussed in Chapter 1 (icons, indexes, and symbols). One of the most powerful ways we create meaning is through **metaphor** – making one thing stand in for another thing – and, of course, languages vary in the ways they use metaphor.

We usually associate metaphor with literature and poetry, but in many ways metaphor is at the heart of our thinking. In a highly original collaboration, the linguist George Lakoff and philosopher Mark Johnson argued that many metaphors are so prevalent and unconscious that, despite their particularity, they take on the form of universal truths (Lakoff and Johnson 1980). How do we talk about an argument, for instance? In English we often say that there are two *sides,* and that one person *won* the argument while another *lost*. They did so by *attacking* the other person's ideas, which might have been so *indefensible* they were all *shot down*. Notice how talking about arguments draws extensively on the language of war. That is not just a figure of speech: we literally experience an argument as a battle between two positions, with a winner and a loser. What if, they propose, we talked about arguments as a dance? Two people might disagree, but they could also be partners in a choreographed giving and taking.

Other metaphors are more basic. Lakoff and Johnson point out, for instance, that in English we typically associate positive things with "up" and negative things with "down." A sad person is feeling *down* while happiness is expressed as *rising* spirits. We *fall* ill but wake *up*. Someone who is rich is *upper* class while criminal behaviour is described as *low* or *underhanded*. There is no objective reason to conceive social class or health through an up–down metaphorical framework, but these expressions are so baked into our understanding of the world that they become naturalized. Our language and our culture are therefore essential to how we give coherence to our experience and perception. "Cultural assumptions, values, and attitudes are not a conceptual overlay which we may or may not place upon experience as we choose. It would be more correct to say that all experience is cultural through and through, that we experience our 'world' in such a way that our culture is already present in the very experience itself" (Lakoff and Johnson 1980, 57).

A key area of research in linguistic relativity has therefore been to understand the metaphors that structure our understanding of reality. Some examples of these are:

- **Reproduction** – All animals begin their lives as an embryo, formed from the fertilization of two gametes, a sperm and an egg. These gametes are simply haploid cells, but the language used in introductory biology textbooks to describe the process of reproduction is illustrative of a metaphorical process that attributes femininity to eggs and masculinity to sperm. Eggs *drift* down the fallopian tube, while sperm embark on an *arduous* journey. Eggs are *dormant*, while sperm are on a *mission*. Despite research that shows fertilization to be an interactive process (with the egg chemically binding the sperm to its surface), these textbooks narrate a story of active sperm seeking out and penetrating a passive egg. Emily Martin (1991) argues that this story of fertilization not only reinforces dominant Western gender norms, but also influences the ways biologists study human reproduction. The idea that it is the sperm which actively burrows into a receptive egg was only revised after an accidental discovery – had biologists drawn upon a more interactive metaphor for reproduction, this reciprocal creation of the embryo might have been identified earlier.
- **Food** – "Food plays a dynamic role in the way people think of themselves and others" (Ohnuki-Tierney 1993, 3). Emiko Ohnuki-Tierney has looked at the way that rice has come to represent the Japanese nation as a whole. Consuming rice establishes and nurtures social relationships among family and friends. Every meal should include at least a token bowl of cooked rice on the table, and the expression "to eat cold rice" (*hiyameshi o kuu*) signifies a lack of social ties or the comfort of family. The prefix *wa-*, representing a sense of Japaneseness, is often paired with rice-related terms (*washoku* for Japanese cuisine, and *washi* for Japanese rice paper). People therefore talk about *our* rice and *our* rice paddies in ways that associate them with Japanese identity. But in recent years Japanese rice consumption declined significantly, to the point that economic policies were instituted by the government to preserve the industry. The Japanese government spent ¥1.5 trillion on financial support for rice farmers between 2008 and 2010, equal to about Can$14.4 billion (Takahashi 2012). Such tremendous financial investment is felt necessary, Ohnuki-Tierney argues, because of rice's symbolic importance to Japanese identity.
- **Nuclear weapons** – In research at Livermore National Laboratory, one of only three nuclear weapons development laboratories in the United States, anthropologist Hugh Gusterson listened extensively to how scientists talked about nuclear weapons and the processes of detonating them during tests.

> One thing that struck him was the prevalence of birth metaphors in talk about weapons. Going all the way back to the first nuclear explosion, the Trinity test of 1945 was called Oppenheimer's *baby* (after the director of the Manhattan Project) and housed in a *cradle* suspended above the ground. The bomb dropped on Hiroshima was *Little Boy*, and physicist Edward Teller announced the success of the Ivy Mike test with the message "It's a *boy*" (a dud would have been a "*girl*"). The source of the plutonium in bombs is a *breeder reactor* while ICBMs are stored in *cribs* connected to control panels by *umbilical cords* (Gusterson 1996, 162). Even though the scientists and engineers laughed off the significance of these metaphors, they are ubiquitous within the nuclear defence industry. Gusterson argues that power of this metaphor is in transforming dangerous and unpredictable weapons into reliable technologies that people (especially the scientists themselves) can control. After spending a year studying the defence industry in the United States, feminist scholar Carol Cohn similarly argued that the technostrategic discourse of "clean strikes" and "collateral damage" allows defence intellectuals to distance themselves from the horrors of nuclear war. Of her own experience, she wrote, "Learning to speak the language of defense analysts is not a conscious, cold-blooded decision to ignore the effects of nuclear weapons on real live human beings, to ignore the sensory, the emotional experience, the human impact. It is simply learning a new language, but by the time you are through, the content of what you can talk about is monumentally different, as is the perspective from which you speak" (Cohn 1987, 705).

In each of these examples, we can see the ways that dominant linguistic metaphors shape how people understand and respond to various issues. Metaphors provide a kind of conceptual framework for interpretation and are shared among members of a speech community. This makes them not only a key element of social belonging, but also guides our thought in certain directions while ignoring others.

Context

Another fruitful area of research in linguistic relativity is the role of language in referring to context, the social, cultural, and physical settings in which our conversations take place. The way this is expressed is called **deixis**: words and phrases that are relative to the setting of a conversation, such as pronouns ("I" and "you"), demonstratives ("here" and "there"), and temporal terms ("now" and "soon"). The meaning of these terms is not fixed; who "I" refers to depends upon who is speaking. Through deixis, people indicate the participants in a conversation, relationships with each other, where things are located, and when events are happening.

For example, some languages, like Korean, have elaborate honorific repertoires. There are several different second-person pronouns used in Korean (equivalent to "you" in English) depending upon whether one is speaking to a child (*ne*), a subordinate (*caney*), a lover (*caki*), a spouse (*tangsin*), and so on. In formal settings, Korean speakers tend to avoid pronouns altogether and address other people with their title or rank (Brown 2011, 41). The use of pronoun in each case is, however, not always readily transparent, and choosing among the various options allows people to position themselves in various ways in respect to others: as a parent or lover or subordinate. We can therefore think of honorifics as a tool in Korean of deferring to others (Agha 2007, 316). In other languages, acts of respect and deference are encoded in different ways.

Deixis also allows us to refer to the environment in the ways we describe and label the space around us. Context-dependent expressions like "here," "there," "above," "next to," and so forth allow us to refer to various areas and locations. We might assume that since we all share the same three-dimensional space, languages would all have relatively similar systems of **spatial deixis**, but there is actually a great deal of variation. William Hanks's study of Yucatec Maya reveals a complex system that involves a base deictic term (such as "here" or "there") with an affix that indicates relative proximity. This combination allows complex spatial reasoning in a very efficient linguistic form. In one example, a woman was watering her plants and then called out to her children in Yucatec Maya, "Here comes the water!" as she jokingly tried to spray them. The woman combined the base term "here" with the distant affix to indicate to the children that the water was coming, but that they had time to run. If she had meant to surprise them with the water, she would have used the proximate affix (Hanks 2005, 204). On this basis, Hanks argues that the ways Yucatec Maya speakers analyse space – and the people and objects within it – are demonstrably different from other languages.

Even basic directional terms vary across languages. Most languages (including English) employ a system called **relative spatial reference**, where positions are identified relative to the speaker using terms such as "right," "left," and "behind." Which direction is "left" depends upon which direction you are facing. In Tzeltal, another Mayan language spoken in Mexico, people use what is called **absolute spatial reference**. In this system, directions are fixed around the speaker's position rather than relative to them. The land in this area generally slopes downwards from south to north, and so anything south of the speaker is labelled "uphill" and anything north of the speaker "downhill" (with another term for "transverse" between these two directions). When a woman wanted to ask her husband which tap in the house they were staying in was for hot water, she asked "is it this one uphillward?" meaning the more southerly one. As another Tzeltal Mayan speaker was guiding some anthropologists through a village, he naturally told them, "We're dropping downward here toward the uphill" meaning they were descending southward (Brown and Levinson 1993). Another example of absolute spatial reference is Guugu Yimithirr, an Australian aboriginal language spoken in northern Queensland. Rather than using words such as "left" or "right," speakers of Guugu Yimithirr refer to cardinal directions equivalent to north, south, east, and west. So in speaking to another person, you would point out "the bottle north of you" or say "get in the east side of the boat" (Haviland 1998; Levinson 1997). Consequently, speakers of languages with absolute spatial reference are profoundly attentive to spatial orientation at all times.

BOX 4.4 – ABSOLUTE SPATIAL REFERENCE IN SIGN LANGUAGES

A substantial number of people around the world use sign languages. Like several of the other languages discussed here, many of these, including American Sign Language (ASL), use a system of absolute spatial reference.

Pronouns in ASL can take two forms: a signer can literally point to the person or thing being indicated or, if not physically present, they can associate that person or thing with a location in their signing space (Liddell 2003). By gesturing back to that spot, creating what is called a token, the signer can refer to it again.

When referring to places, the signer can therefore just point towards it, or they can establish a token in the geographical direction of the location. If a signer were in Ottawa and referring to Montreal, they would set the token in the righthand portion of their signing space, implying east, but if they were in Halifax they would set the token in the lefthand portion, implying west. If a signer wanted to communicate "In Canada, there are many maple trees," they could gloss it in ASL as: "CANADA-across (topicalized) maple tree(s) have (nod)." In this instance, the token for "CANADA-across" would sweep left to right in Vancouver and right to left in Halifax.

Another example comes from Kata Kolok, a sign language used in Bali. Kata Kolok also uses absolute spatial reference by pointing to locations, but signers can also create a kind of overhead diagram in their signing space where cardinal directions are transposed onto a two-dimensional plane and narrated in reference to the already-established absolute direction (De Vos 2014). Sign languages, therefore, offer many alternative ways that people can communicate orientation and direction to those found in English.

Recently, linguistic anthropologists have begun to extend the scope of linguistic relativity to new areas such as **social deixis**, or the ways we encode the roles and relationships of conversational participants. Jack Sidnell and Nick Enfield (2012) look at how several different languages manage the act of agreeing with someone after you have been corrected (as in, "No, it's that one" followed by "Oh, I get it" in English). Finnish speakers repeat back what they originally said, but with an inverted word order, while Lao speakers employ a sentence-final particle *lèq* that accepts the other person's assertion as fact. These differing strategies produce differing pragmatic effects: in the Finnish case, it highlights the different perspective being offered to the speaker, while the Lao case introduces a sense of finality. Languages therefore differ in how they perform such actions and their resulting social impacts. Despite over a hundred years of anthropological scrutiny of the cognitive effects of language variation, much work remains to be done.

CONCLUSION

There is an incredible amount of diversity in the world's languages, from the sounds used to how concepts like temporality or space or encoded in them. Linguistic relativity posits that these differences are not just random but *consequential* for the speakers of those varying languages, that they shape our shared frameworks of understanding. In the same way that different tools lead to different actions (a hammer and a glue gun both stick two pieces of wood together, but in different ways), the tools of language provide us with multiple perspectives on the world around us.

In this chapter we have charted a long history of how linguistic anthropologists have approached this topic, from looking at classificatory schemes of colour and kinship to grappling with how those classifications organize our experience. Along the way we've also had to deal with some of the more extravagant claims about how language forces us to think one way or another or prevents us from understanding something: linguists sometimes talk about a "no word for X" cliché in which the lack of a word in a language implies people can't comprehend it. Those cases, I've argued, usually fail to grasp an anthropological view of culture.

Linguistic relativity, on the other hand, begins with the idea that language is socially embedded. As the primary tool we have for organizing, framing, discussing, and interpreting the world around us, the structures of our language and our cultural practices are complementary. We have seen how metaphors shape our understanding of physical and social processes, and how language organizes the expression of spatial, social, and temporal relationships. Grammar, in this view, is less about rules for stringing words together; it is the framework we use to figure out the world around us, what other people are doing, how we should react, and how to put all of these ideas into words.

BOX 4.5 – RESEARCH SPOTLIGHT: NICLAS BURENHULT AND ASIFA MAJID

Burenhult, Niclas, and Asifa Majid. 2011. "Olfaction in Aslian Ideology and Language." *The Senses and Society* 6 (1): 19–29.

We're bad at smell, especially compared to other animals like dogs or bears. But with our stereoscopic vision and upright bipedalism (enabling a greater elevation for our eyes), humans seem to be natural seers. That's why vision is often touted as the primary among all our senses. Just as with forms of spatial deixis and colour classification, however, languages have different ways of organizing smell, which many scholars argue can impact the ways we interpret the environment around us. In this article, Burenhult and Majid examine the sense vocabulary of a language spoken by the Jahai ethnic minority of Malaysia and argue that smell plays a prominent role.

The religious system of the Jahai is dominated by Karɛy, a powerful spirit that nurtures the forest and monitors the behaviour of humans. The Jahai practise a complex set of taboos meant to avoid attracting Karɛy's attention and disapproval. One thing Karɛy is said to hate is bad smells, so people abstain from laughing while bathing or washing different types of animal meat together so that he is not drawn to the water and offended by its odour.

The Jahai language has at least a dozen basic smell terms (like the basic colour terms discussed above), including specific words for the smell of roasted food, stinging smells like gasoline, rotting smells, and the smell of blood. There are several different words covering what English speakers would describe collectively as fragrant, but the majority of these smell terms relate to offensive odours (especially where Karɛy is concerned). People are therefore often focused on what types of smells exist around them and find ways to obscure the presence of unpleasant smells from Karɛy's awareness, such as by preparing pungent foods indoors or at night when Karɛy sleeps.

This is a very approachable article that blends descriptions of taboos and religious beliefs with the smell lexicon that shapes Jahai life. It also shows the great variety of human experience, varying even in the ways sense is organized. The Jahai "provide compelling evidence that basic odor vocabularies can be tremendously sophisticated and show that speakers of these languages are able to represent and cognize about odors robustly and effectively" (Burenhult and Majid 2011, 26).

Discussion

1. Speaking Mandarin, for me, has a different feel than speaking English. For instance, politeness words are not usually used in informal speech, and the topic of sentences are generally prioritized rather than the subject (so if you are talking

about a book you like, you generally don't say it as "I like this book" but "this book, I like"). As a group, consider the classificatory and linguistic differences between English and other languages you are familiar with. How do those differences affect the ways you speak and think?

2. Have you noticed differences when you read things from 30 or 40 years ago? The person on an airplane pointing to the exits was called a stewardess, not a flight attendant. People rarely used the singular they (as in "each person should turn their phone off"), and no one introduced themselves with the words "my pronouns are…" Given what we know about linguistic relativity, why do you think these changes have happened? What else is likely to change in the future?
3. That film *Arrival*, where we have to find a way to communicate with aliens, is actually a scenario many scientists have considered (for instance, see Vakoch and Punske 2023). Without a common shared humanity, how would we communicate? Would aliens even recognize what we are doing – making sounds and gesturing wildly – as an attempt to communicate? Think about all the basic things you would need to teach an alien about human language before you could start to bridge that gap.
4. We looked at metaphor as one of the key elements that structures human cognition. Some of the other metaphors Lakoff and Johnson (1980) discuss are the idea that the future is in front of us and the past behind, that theories are like buildings (they need a good *foundation*), and time is like money. What other metaphors structure our experience? How do we talk about love or health or work in ways that shape our understandings of these concepts?

5

Indigenous Languages and Revitalization

Topics

- Indigenous languages and linguistic anthropology
- What are the characteristics of Indigenous languages?
- Why languages become endangered
- Revitalization of endangered languages

In 2024, Sol Mamakwa rose in the Ontario provincial legislature and spoke in his native Anishininiimowin language, also known as Oji-Cree. It was the first time that a language other than French or English had been officially recorded in the chamber. Mamakwa's speech, which required changes to the legislature's rules of procedure, was hailed as a historic event by the premier and other legislators. Afterwards, Mamakwa told reporters, "We receive strength in speaking our language. It is like a healing medicine as we stand together to continue fighting for our rights as First Nations people." To understand the significance of Mamakwa's speech, and how it gives him and his community strength, we need to learn about Indigenous languages and what has happened to them since the time of contact with Europeans.

I am not Indigenous, and I do not claim to speak any more than a few words in an Indigenous language. Nevertheless, this is an important topic to highlight in any linguistic anthropology textbook, for a variety of reasons. One of those is the crucial role Indigenous languages have played in the disciplinary history of linguistic anthropology, which in many ways was founded on their study. From Boas and Sapir to a host of other early scholars, Indigenous languages provided the data upon which more general theories of language were created (Leonard 2021; Meek 2017). Although there were exceptions, some of which we will discuss below, the value of Indigenous languages was often configured rhetorically in terms of what *they* could tell *us* about language – and "us" very explicitly did not include Indigenous peoples themselves, but rather Western academic linguists.

BOX 5.1 – GEORGE HUNT (1854–1933)

Figure 5.1 – George Hunt

Many early anthropologists, including Franz Boas, employed Indigenous people in the field to supplement their own research. One such person was George Hunt, the son of a Hudson's Bay Company clerk and a Tsimshian woman. Hunt travelled extensively throughout the Canadian northwest, serving as a translator and artefact collector for various ethnological surveys. He met Franz Boas in 1888 and, since he was married to a Kwakwa̱ka̱'wakw woman, was hired to assemble a collection of their texts and artefacts.

We might think of Hunt as nothing more than an agent of Boas's own ethnographic interests, but a careful examination of their long-standing relationship and communications reveals Hunt took an active role in choosing what data to collect and how Boas should interpret it (Bruchac 2018; Jacknis 2019). Boas worked mainly with the goal of preserving and recording "traditional" Indigenous cultures, but Hunt chose to collect contemporary objects that people made everyday use of, even if they had adopted European materials in their construction (he also ensured people were duly compensated for those artefacts). He took a keen interest in Kwakwa̱ka̱'wakw medicine and shamanism, forwarding his findings to Boas, and photographed rituals, costumes, and dances to create a record for the community (Glass 2009).

Hunt's own vision of Indigenous cultures is embedded in his collection of Kwak'wala language texts such as legends, oral histories, and folklore. Hunt was careful to record where he had heard a myth and who had told it to him in order to acknowledge the speech of elders. While Boas removed any spoken English from these stories, Hunt recorded the complex interplay of languages in Kwakwa̱ka̱'wakw speech (Bauman and Briggs 1990a). In other words, he disagreed with Boas on what makes a narrative "authentic" and asserted his own interpretation of its meaning.

At a Kwakwa̱ka̱'wakw feast in 1897, Hunt read out a letter written to him by Boas. "My friend, George Hunt, will read this to you... It is good that you should have a box in which your laws and your stories are kept" (Jacknis 2019, 247). That "box" was a record of Kwakwa̱ka̱'wakw culture and Kwak'wala language that persists to this day thanks to efforts of Indigenous fieldworkers like George Hunt.

Beyond just disciplinary interests, however, there are other reasons to put a spotlight on Indigenous languages. They are, as illustrated by Mamakwa's speech above, one way of recognizing the historic inequalities experienced by Indigenous communities that, quite literally, often wrote them completely out of history (Groat and Anderson 2021). Many national policies – in both Canada and other colonial states – were adopted with the explicit goal of eradicating Indigenous languages and assimilating their speakers into the nation state (Haque and Patrick 2015). The residential schooling system in Canada, for example, took Indigenous children from their families and forced them into centralized boarding schools, with the explicit goal, in the words of one of its architects, to "cause them to forget their customs, habits & language of their ancestors" (Truth and Reconciliation Commission 2015a, 159). Speakers of Indigenous languages today still face discrimination and stigma for using their languages in schools or in public.

To focus global attention on such issues, the United Nations declared 2022–2032 to be the International Decade of Indigenous Languages, recognizing "the urgent need to preserve, revitalize and promote indigenous languages" (United Nations 2020). There are, nevertheless, significant challenges to meeting that goal. Most Indigenous languages spoken in Canada today are considered endangered. Later in this chapter we will look at the idea of endangerment, but just as a point of comparison, the 2021 Canadian census reported that 31,628,570 people can speak English conversationally. In contrast, only 237,420 can speak an Indigenous language. The most widely spoken of those, Inuktitut, has 42,795 speakers while a range of others – such as Ililimowin, Gwich'in, Kaska, Cayuga, and Squamish – have less than 500 speakers each (Statistics Canada 2023a). That does not mean these languages are doomed to extinction, and we will look later at revitalization efforts being undertaken to expand the number of speakers. The absolute numbers of people who are conversational in an Indigenous language grew substantially between 1991 and 2016, reflecting the number of people learning them as a second language in either the home or school.

But as Indigenous scholars point out, the issue is about far more than language alone. "Languages do not exist in a vacuum and languages do not simply 'die' of natural causes" (Chiblow and Meighan 2022, 208). Indigenous languages are embedded within complex cultural, moral, and material universes: the lands, peoples, and nations to which they belong. As the Mojave language activist Natalie Diaz writes, "To lose a language is to lose many things other than vocabulary. To lose a language is also to lose the body, the bodies of our ancestors and of our futures... When a word is silenced, what happens to the bodies who spoke it? What happens to the bodies once carried in those erased words?" (McCarty et al. 2018, 163). This has prompted calls for new frameworks for inclusion and recognition in the academic study of Indigenous languages. One of these frameworks is **reconciliation**, which the Truth and Reconciliation Commission, part of the official inquiry into the residential school system in Canada, defines as "a process of healing of relationships that requires public truth sharing, apology, and commemoration that acknowledge and redress past harms" (Truth and Reconciliation Commission 2015c, 3). Reconciliation includes the recognition of treaty rights, repudiation of past harms, and intentional progress towards justice (Blackburn 2007). Specifically in terms of language, reconciliation requires the recognition of Indigenous communities' rights to, and sovereignty over, their languages, extending to how these languages are identified, studied, protected, and taught (Craft and Regan 2020; Sterzuk and Fayant 2016).

Another important framework is that of **decolonization**. If the Canadian state, along with its policies and institutions, is premised upon the colonial imposition of settler outsiders on Indigenous peoples, then decolonization is the ambitious process of dismantling those structures (Battiste 2013; Sium, Desai, and Ritskes 2012; Todd 2016; Tuck and Yang 2012). The goal, in the words of Adam Gaudry and Danielle Lorenz (2018, 224), is to "transform existing institutions, to remake colonial structures in a new image." Doing so not only requires bringing Indigenous people into the academy, but also reconfiguring the very ideas of a university, a discipline, and a language. As just one example, Wesley Leonard (2021) imagines a linguistic anthropology that engages with Indigenous knowledge systems, collaborates with Indigenous speakers and communities as co-authors of knowledge, and embeds language within a shared Indigenous moral universe rather than an objective scientific one (see also Absolon 2011). Most linguistic anthropologists who work with Indigenous communities have taken both reconciliation and decolonization as worthy goals to work towards while also acknowledging the long road ahead.

WALKING WITH INDIGENOUS LANGUAGES

In a study of Kaska language revitalization in the Yukon, Barbra Meek (2010, x) uses the metaphor of "walking with a language" to refer to the experience of learning and speaking that develops over time. Being surrounded by a language's sounds, growing familiar with its forms and cadences, and turning the unfamiliar into something customary and normal is a key part of linguistic anthropological fieldwork. From the perspective of an outsider, it is easy to look at Indigenous languages as exotic, full of strange sounds and grammatical quirks. But for Indigenous peoples, these *are* their languages, not peculiar but natural and routine. Looking at some of the characteristics of these languages can help develop that sense of normalcy for non-speakers.

BOX 5.2 – ENGLISH IS WEIRD!

It is common for English to be used as *the* template for understanding what a language is. Most linguists, after all, teach and publish in English, so it is a familiar language for students to use in drawing syntax trees or discussing phonology. Languages like Khmer, Yoruba, or Malayalam may feel, in comparison, a little strange if not outright exotic. It helps, though, to reverse that perspective; to normalize Indigenous languages, we can make the parallel move of highlighting what is strange and uncommon about English.

Think of the following characteristics of English that are actually fairly rare among the world's languages:

- Dental fricatives – These are the 'th' sounds in English. There are two of them, /θ/ and /ð/, which you can hear in the words "thing" and "there," respectively (the second one vibrates the vocal cords, the first one does not). Only about 7 per cent of the world's languages use these consonants.
- No reduplication rule – In about 85 per cent of the world's languages, repeating a word or part of a word changes the meaning of a sentence. In Finnish, repeating a word connotes a sense of being the genuine or real thing: ruoka means food, but ruokaruoka is "foodfood" and implies a hearty, healthy meal. Although English speakers sometimes repeat an adjective for emphasis ("It's a hot hot day"), this is not a generalizable grammatical rule (you can't say "that's a comfortable comfortable chair").
- Obligatory subject pronouns – Most languages allow you to omit a pronoun when the listener can infer them from context. In Japanese, you can say *ocha-o katteita yo*, which means "was buying tea," and you do not need to include "he" or "she." In English, you have to specify who was buying tea to make the sentence grammatical. Only about 12 per cent of the world's languages require a speaker to include a pronoun.
- Interrogative word order – If you want to change a declarative sentence into a question in Polish, you add *czy* at the beginning. So "*ona pije wodę*" means "she

is drinking water" while "*czy ona pije wodę*" means "is she drinking water?" Unlike 98 per cent of the world's languages, English forms questions by changing the word order from "she is" to "is she."

This is not to argue that English is somehow special – all languages include some features that are rare. The point is to stop us from thinking of English as "normal" and see it as just one of the many languages around the world.

All of the features above are drawn from the World Atlas of Language Structures (find it online at https://wals.info/), which maps out the distribution of hundreds of linguistic features in the world's languages (Dryer and Haspelmath 2013). Some of those can be quite technical, but you can have a look around to see which features of the languages you speak are shared with others.

The first thing to note is their diversity. Most European languages belong to a single **language family**, a group of languages that share a common ancestor. In Europe's case it is Indo-European, a family that includes languages stretching from South Asia all the way to Iceland. Members of Indo-European include Hindi, Pashto, Kurdish, Greek, Latin, Russian, German, Welsh, and English, among dozens of others. In Canada alone, however, there are eight distinct Indigenous language families: Inuit, Na-Dene, Algonquian, Iroquoian, Siouan, Salishan, Wakashan, and Tsimshianic. In addition, Haida and Kutenai are considered **language isolates**, meaning languages that do not appear to be related to any others (Euskara, also known as Basque, is an example of a language isolate from Europe). Within these Indigenous language families are over 60 distinct languages (Canadian Language Museum 2019; Mithun 1999). Nevertheless, despite their tremendous variety, there are some features that are relatively common – although by no means universal – in North American Indigenous languages.

Polysynthesis

Many Indigenous languages in Canada exhibit a complex morphological structure known as **polysynthesis**. Usually beginning with a root verb, words are composed by adding suffixes and prefixes to the verb that modify its meaning (Mithun 1999). Look at the following Inuktitut word for instance: *aquttunnarniaqpit* (Will you be able to drive?).[1]

aqut-	drive
-tunnaq-	able to do something
-niaq-	[near future tense]
-pit	question [second-person subject form]

That is quite a lot of information to be packed into one word. None of these suffixes can be used independently of the verb (just like you cannot say *-ing* or *-ily* in English and expect people to know what you mean), so in many ways each "word" in Inuktitut can be equivalent to a sentence in English.

BOX 5.3 – WORDS FOR SNOW

In his 1911 *Handbook of American Indian Languages*, Franz Boas gave examples of different words for "snow" in Inuktitut, the language of the Baffin Island Inuit he studied in the 1880s. "Here we find one word, *aput*, expressing snow on the ground; another one, *qana*, falling snow; a third one, *piqsirpoq*, drifting snow; and a fourth one, *qimuqsuq*, a snowdrift" (1911, 25–6).[2] And with that, a thousand memes were born.

You have probably heard the factoid at some point that northern peoples have 50 (or 500, or 5,000!) words for snow, often used as an illustration that languages put tremendous emphasis on whatever is important to the people who speak them. So just how many "Eskimo" words for snow are there? To answer that, we have to clear up a few misconceptions. First of all, the peoples living in communities throughout the Arctic, from Alaska to Greenland, call themselves Inuit, and they speak a range of different languages and dialects over this vast geographic area (Dorais 2010). Second, Inuktut languages are polysynthetic and so create words – which act more like sentences in non-polysynthetic languages – through attaching strings of morphemes to root verbs.

In a famous article, linguistic anthropologist Laura Martin (1986) traced the history of claims about the numerous words for snow to several textbooks in the 1950s and 1960s by authors with little knowledge of Inuktitut grammar and some overly ambitious ideas about what this plethora of snow words signified for human psychology. She argues that the ever-inflating number of Inuktitut snow words in those sources merely served to exoticize Inuit people. Grammatically, though, it is equivalent to asking how many "sentences for snow" there are in English.

However, even if the idea of "words" is wrong here, recent analyses have been more kind to Boas's original findings. Inuit are keen observers of their environment, and Inuktitut does have very sophisticated and complex terminologies for snow and ice. These include dozens of terms for types of snow, patterns of snowfall, snow formations, and so forth. Although these terms are built through affixes in a polysynthetic manner, "each represents a meaningful and clearly distinguishable phenomenon to indigenous speakers" (Krupnik and Müller-Wille 2010, 391). Knowledge of

Inuktitut snow terminology can also help Inuit track and understand the effects of climate change on their environment. This case shows the benefits of working with expert Indigenous knowledge-keepers who have preserved this linguistic heritage and know just how many "words" they have for something.

Many of these prefixes and suffixes describe quality and manner of actions and movements. This feature gives Indigenous languages a very different feel than Indo-European ones. Doug Smith, who along with Bernie Francis developed the standard orthography for Mi'kmaw, describes the "verb-like quality of Mi'kmaw in that it reflects the Mi'kmaw world view where the world is perceived primarily as flow or as flux, movement as opposed to the Indo-European noun-centered languages which objectify the world; they turn the world into objects which can then be analyzed" (Sable and Francis 2012, 30). In an example of the linguistic relativity we discussed in Chapter 4, he argues that Mi'kmaw speakers are always sensitive to the interconnectedness and movement of the world around them.

Another good example is provided by Siksiká, the language spoken by the Niitsitapi or Blackfoot people of the North American plains. The polysynthetic nature of Siksiká means that words referring to people are always marked by their relationships to others along with the social and physical worlds around them. "English concepts such as 'person' or 'individual' do not evoke the experiential connections to the sacred that the *Siksikaitsipowahsin* equivalents do" (Bastien 2004, 128). Speaking Siksiká is therefore to always be aware of connections to others, to one's culture, and to the land. It imbues the act of speech with a sacred quality, a "spiritual process that originates in an organic holistic world" (2004, 132).

Evidentiality

Imagine that you meet one of your neighbours on the street. She advises you, "Watch out! There's a rabid dog on the loose." How does she know this? From her utterance, we have no way of knowing. She could, if she chose, modify her sentence to provide more information, saying one of the following:

1. I saw a rabid dog loose in the area.
2. I heard on the news that there's a rabid dog loose in the area.
3. Someone was bitten by a rabid dog. It's probably still on the loose.

In the first sentence, the speaker is indicating she knows this information through personal observation, in the second that the information was told to her by someone

Table 5.1 – Evidentials in Nuu-chah-nulth

mĩƛaa-waʔiš	I heard it's raining.
mĩƛaa-qač̓a	It must be raining.
mĩƛaa-matak-ʔiš	Maybe it's raining.
mĩƛaa-k̓uk-ʔiš	It looks like it's raining.
mĩƛaa-ʔiš naʔaat	It sounds like it's raining.

else, and in the third that she is making an inference based on available information. The ways a language indicates the source of knowledge being expressed is called **evidentiality** (Aikhenvald 2004; San Roque 2019). English speakers do this by providing additional clauses in a sentence in order to specify where the information came from. Other languages, among them many North American Indigenous languages, actually build evidentiality into their syntax.

We have already seen how many of Canada's Indigenous languages are polysynthetic, and one type of morpheme affixed to verbs is an **evidential**. Take the word *mĩƛaawaʔiš* from Nuu-chah-nulth, an Indigenous language spoken on the west coast of Vancouver Island (Waldie 2012). The word can be broken down into the following morphemes: *mĩƛ-*, means "rain," *-aa-* is a long vowel that indicates the continuous aspect (equivalent to *-ing* in English), and *-waʔiš* is an evidential indicating that the knowledge was heard from another person. In sum, this word means "I heard it's raining." Note that *-waʔiš* is not a word on its own; it can only be used to modify a verb. Evidentials are obligatory in declarative sentences; a Nuu-chah-ulth speaker must include an evidential for the sentence to be grammatical.[3] Other evidentials mark the difference between being told, inferring, supposing, observing, and directly hearing evidence of the knowledge the speaker is communicating (Table 5.1).

The centrality of evidentiality to a language like Nuu-chah-nulth is not simply a grammatical feature but impacts cultural attitudes and ideologies towards personhood and subjectivity. Janis Nuckolls (2008) has argued, for instance, that obligatory use of evidentials in the Pastaza Quichua language of Ecuador supports a principle of **perspectivism**, the idea that our perceptions of others are dependent upon our perspective, as humans, animals, or spirits. Essentially, Amazonian myths and legends emphasize the idea that animals and humans are not categorically different kinds of creatures, but reflections of each other. What from a human perspective is animal blood is, from a jaguar's perspective, delicious beer; what from a human perspective is a muddy hole is, from a tapir's perspective, a ceremonial house (Viveiros de Castro 1998).

Pastaza Quichua speakers employ several evidentials that indicate whether statements are made from their own perspective or by taking that of another person. Reflecting our discussion in Chapter 4 – Linguistic Relativity, Nuckolls therefore suggests that Western scientific understandings of the world that separate an objective truth from subjective experience are not strictly relevant: all experience is mediated through someone's perspective. Instead, Pastaza Quichua speakers are "extremely preoccupied with the aesthetic and emotional significance of their experience, rather than with the merely verifiable 'facts' of experience" (1993, 236).

Land and Place-Making

Indigenous languages are, as we have seen, embedded in physical, cultural, and moral landscapes. They are not simply systems of words and grammatical relations disconnected from any particular people or history; Indigenous languages are inescapably tied to a sense of place. When linguistic anthropologist Andie Palmer was driving through the landscape of central British Columbia, her Secwepemc interlocutors consistently drew her attention to various places through the use of stories. As her host Angela George would explain:

> This is a place too.
> They call it *Nukláwt*.
> That's where we get
> wild rhubarb in the spring time.
>
> (Palmer 2005, 106)

Whether it is trailheads leading to fishing grounds or places suffused with memories, Secwepemc elders ground their experience in the lands that have sustained them: "The strings of anecdotes in each participant's repertoire may be seen as comprising a personal map of the landscape travelled. All such narratives acquaint those present who are less familiar with that part of the territory with the resources to be found there; personal and ancestral knowledge of the land is thereby pooled among groups of hunters or gatherers. The result is a shared cognitive map of the area, where personal experience becomes group experience" (Palmer 2005, 116).

In eastern Canada, language similarly mediates between the landscape and the Mi'kmaw people. Prominent rocks and other distinctive features act as waypoints in the wilderness but are also incorporated into the human world of kinship. "These rock formations were honorifically referred to as Kukumijinu ('our Grandmother') or Kniskamijinu ('our Grandfather') and commonly have legends associated with them... Mi'kmaq travelling by these sites would offer punk, tobacco or other offerings in respect and supplication, as if to an honoured relative" (Sable and Francis 2012, 43). Crucially, these landmarks belong to the grammatical category of animate nouns and are addressed using a first-person plural inclusive pronoun (essentially "we, all of us"). Like other relatives, they are thought to guide and protect the people under their care.

Figure 5.2 – Bilingual campus signs from the University of British Columbia Okanagan in English and Nsyilxcn

Source: Image courtesy of Christine Schreyer

Both these examples show us that, in many Indigenous communities, language is itself a spiritual experience, connecting people to the land and their ancestors. Keith Basso, who conducted decades of research with the Western Apache of Arizona, illustrates this connection. While out with two men on a hot day in the desert, participating in a project to record Apache place names, Basso was trying to pronounce the name of a small bog but could not get it right. Ready to give up in frustration, Basso was admonished by an Apache elder: "Our ancestors made this name. They made it just as it is. They made it for a reason. *They spoke it first, a long time ago*" (Basso 1996, 10). In other words, the elder was counselling Basso that place names are never just words, but the speech of Apache ancestors.

The desert landscape Basso travelled through that day is replete with such names. "Water Lies with Mud in an Open Container" (*goshtł'ish tú bił sikąné*) is the name of that bog, while a group of tall boulders is called "Scattered Rocks Stand Erect" (*tséé naadadn'áhá*). Other names commemorate events, such as "Widows Pause for Breath" (*'istaa hadaanáyołé*), where three sisters mourned their husbands who had died in a raid. Each of these places has stories attached to it, and in conversation Apache speakers can employ a strategy of "speaking with names"; naming the place evokes the story and the moral lesson the listener should take from it. "By virtue of their role as spatial anchors in traditional Apache narratives, place names can be made to represent the narratives themselves, summarizing them, as it were, and condensing into compact form their essential moral truths" (Basso 1996, 101). If we compare this to conventional Western notions of nature as essentially timeless, unmoving, and inert, Indigenous languages instead place the speaker within vibrant landscapes filled with the voices, histories, and spirits of a multitude of others (Figure 5.2).

LANGUAGE ENDANGERMENT

Sometime around the twenty-fourth century BC, Sargon the Great, King of the Akkadians, swept out of the north and conquered the mighty city of Sumer. At the time of this conquest, Sumerian was one of the most prominent languages of Mesopotamia, the basis for clay tablet cuneiform writing, and the language of hymns and literature throughout the region. The Akkadians spoke a very different language, a member of the Semitic family and an ancestor of modern Arabic. For a time, Akkadian rulers and scribes valued bilingual proficiency in both the Sumerian and Akkadian languages, but then their own empire fell, first to Amorites and then to Elamites. By the middle of the second millennium BC, Sumerian disappears from the historical record (Ostler 2005, 38–55). Sumerian is the first documented instance of language death.

Sumerian may have been the first recorded language extinction, but it has definitely not been the last. Although languages are always in a state of change, some rising to prominence while others die out or develop into new forms, global conditions currently seem ripe for a significant percentage of the world's languages to go extinct by the end of this century (Krauss 1992; Nettle and Romaine 2000). Linguist K. David Harrison estimates the world loses one language about every 10 days (Harrison 2007, 5). Whether in the popular press or academic research, stories abound of the last speaker of a language dying and, as a result, taking their language with them. The bulk of these are languages spoken in small-scale societies, often by Indigenous peoples, but endangerment affects languages all around the world. There is a poignant sense of loss in reading such stories, and linguistic anthropologists are generally troubled by the steady decline of linguistic diversity.

In the words of linguist David Crystal, "a language dies when nobody speaks it any more" (Crystal 2000, 1). Although true, this is a deceptively simple statement and reflects a gradual social process made up of individual and collective decisions about language. **Language shift** is the gradual change in the balance of languages in a speech community, typically as a local language is replaced by a national or global language. The root cause is usually a difference in the prestige of the two languages that leads to popular ideologies about their differing utility and importance. The minority language undergoes a process of **language endangerment** as fewer people speak it and, in turn, young people begin to acquire the dominant language. Eventually only elderly speakers remain and, once they pass, the language is said to pass with them, a situation called **language death**.

Table 5.2 – The Graded Intergenerational Disruption Scale (GIDS)

Stage	Description
8	The only remaining speakers of the language are elderly
7	Adults know the language, but children are not learning it
6	All generations know the language, but it is mainly used in the home
5	The language has a written form that is widely used
4	The language is taught in schools
3	The language is used at work within a region
2	The language is used in media and government within a region
1	The language is used in all domains at a national or international level

Source: Adapted from Fishman (1991)

There are many ways of measuring or quantifying language endangerment. One of the first was the Graded Intergenerational Disruption Scale (GIDS) developed by the linguist Joshua Fishman (1991). This is an eight-point scale that uses a range of language status and population indicators to assess the relative health or endangerment of a language (Table 5.2). Fishman also ties each stage to differing revitalization strategies – at Stage 6, for instance, he advocates for integrating language use into extra-curricular and community activities so that children begin using it with each other.

Other scholars have built upon or expanded Fishman's scale (Bradley and Bradley 2019, 14–37), but all tend to cluster around three main elements of language shift:

1. **A reduction in the number of speakers**
   The fullest measure of fluency is developed when people acquire their language during the critical period of childhood (see Chapter 3 – Language Socialization). Perhaps the most important measure of a language's vitality is whether it is being passed on to children, a factor known as **intergenerational transmission**. No matter how important or prestigious a language is, or how many speakers it has, the language is threatened if children are not learning it. And speakers do not live forever; the elders of a community, who learned the language before the process of language shift began in earnest, are likely to speak it most fluently. Once they pass, the opportunity to transmit it to a new generation is also lost. Endangered languages are typically those with dwindling numbers of speakers as people age and children grow up without learning the language.
2. **A reduction in the language's domains of use**
   Languages become associated with particular **domains** in multilingual societies, a term that refers to commonly recognized settings, participants, and topics of conversation. These domains can include settings such as schools, workplaces,

courts, ceremonial occasions, the home, and so forth. Language shift entails the gradual reduction of the number of domains in which the endangered language is used. In Corsica, for instance, Alexandra Jaffe has documented how people on this Mediterranean island shifted from Corsican to French. When Corsica became a territory of France in the eighteenth century, the language of governance and public administration switched to French, followed later by language in the legal system, education, and print media. Corsican remained the language of the home and of the rural countryside. "The minority language (Corsican) is perceived to be the language of the heart and of the hearth, of the warm and informal context of social relations in the village (the symbolic core of Corsican culture), while French commands the domain of the formal, the authoritative, the instrumental and the intellectual" (Jaffe 1999, 19–20). In general, minority languages become limited to the private sphere and dominant languages take over the public sphere. Endangered languages become more restricted over time in terms of where and when they are used.

BOX 5.4 – THE LESSONS OF CONLANGS

For many years now, University of British Columbia Okanagan linguistic anthropologist Christine Schreyer has been studying created languages (also known as **conlangs**, from the words "constructed language"). These include languages such as Klingon from *Star Trek* and Na'vi from the *Avatar* film series. In fact, she has become so fascinated with them that she was actually tasked with constructing her own; she created Kryptonian and Atlantean for DC Comics movies and two dialects of Beama for the adventure film *Alpha*. She has also studied language revitalization efforts for Tlingit (spoken in northwestern Canada) and Kala (spoken in Papua New Guinea).

Schreyer's research on conlangs examines the ways in which communities of fans sustain invented languages, and what lessons these might have, in turn, for endangered language communities. There are many similarities between these two groups: the communities are both generally small in number; most speakers are learning the languages later in life; and the languages themselves typically lack official status. But conlang communities are often more adept at promoting the prestige of their languages through new forms of technology and media, such as public performances of Klingon opera or the numerous websites dedicated to learning these languages. "One way that endangered language communities can emulate the language planning of created language communities is by incorporating 'the cool factor' into their own curriculum and documentation efforts" (Schreyer 2018, 414). In turn, conlangs are mainly textual, offering few opportunities for fans to speak them outside of conventions or other events. They lack the explicit link to cultural practices that make

Indigenous languages so meaningful to their communities. Although the goals of language maintenance and political realities faced by these communities may not always be similar, Schreyer nevertheless thinks learners of both Klingon and Tlingit have a lot to learn from each other.

3. **A reduction in knowledge of the language**
   Not everyone shares the same depth of knowledge of a language. When you start learning a language as an adult, you begin with simple words and grammatical structures ("here is the library") and gradually begin to incorporate more complex syntax such as conditionals ("it would be shame if the library were to burn down") or syntactic nominalization ("the library's acquisition of new books is essential"). As communities shift from one language to another, those complex syntactic formations become less common, breadth of vocabulary shrinks, and the knowledge acquired of the language by the next generation is, consequently, restricted. They become what linguist Nancy Dorian terms **semi-speakers** (Dorian 1977).

   The reduction of knowledge about a language is tied to the restriction in domains of use described above. The shift to another language in areas of politics, for instance, leads to less knowledge of formal or elaborate forms of political speech. The loss of cultural practices such as traditional healing or craft production often entails the loss of entire lexical categories related to those practices (Nettle and Romaine 2000, 56–62). Even speakers who may have at one time been fluent can forget complex forms of the language if they are not used regularly. The end result of this process may be the retention of only a set of stock phrases or speech formulae that are employed in ritual settings.

The process of language shift may appear irresistible at times, and indeed many nations – through the implementation of language standardization policies – actively promote dominant languages at the expense of minority ones (Roche 2022). If all language did was to act as a conduit of information between one speaker and another, having only one language in the world would probably make a whole lot of sense. But one of the themes we have discussed in this book is the idea that language encompasses far more than this utilitarian purpose. As the very term "speech community" implies, languages are ways of connecting with the people around us, to our culture.

LANGUAGE REVITALIZATION

So do we accept that some languages will simply pass out of history? For most speakers of a language, that is an uncomfortable proposition and one that is often countered through **language revitalization**. This is a process of halting the decline of a language and reversing language shift within a speech community. "As a reaction to a history of oppression and forced assimilation, language revitalization movements are seen by speech communities as paths to healing, justice, and empowerment" (Hinton, Huss, and Roche 2018, xxii). Linguistic anthropologists can play an important role in such movements.

If the loss of a language is seen in a reduction of speakers, domains of use, and knowledge about a language, revitalization aims to address each of those. This takes the form of:

1. **Teaching the language to new speakers and passing it on to children**
   Most revitalization efforts have the goal of re-establishing intergenerational transmission of the language. Ideally this would take place in the home, but at larger scales it requires the development of heritage language and language immersion programs in schools. Barbra Meek (2010), for instance, did research at an Indigenous elementary school in the Yukon. Students were exposed to the Kaska language on an everyday basis, while elders and fluent community members were often brought in to converse with the children. The school also incorporated cultural activities such as moose hide tanning and drumming.

   Meek found that students began to incorporate Kaska into their speech, often spontaneously using Kaska words with teachers and peers. Nevertheless, there were significant challenges. Kaska was mainly taught as an oral language, and English as a more prestigious written language (see Chapter 10 – Orality and Literacy). The Kaska that was taught to students was often simplified, dominated by routine phrases such as greetings. "Once Kaska class was over, the presence of the Kaska language within the school environment diminished to little or none" (Meek 2010, 86). One of the major challenges of revitalization is that, unlike home environments, the regimented nature of classroom interactions makes it a poor setting for the acquisition of language fluency (see also Perley 2011). Other revitalization projects include teaching the language to older children and adults as part of heritage language programs.
2. **Revalorizing the language and including it in multiple domains**
   Another necessary condition for the revitalization of languages is the expansion of domains in which they are used; a language limited to the home will rarely be used outside it, and the importance attached to that language is diminished in the community. In China, for instance, Uradyn Bulag (2003) argues that a key reason for the decline of the Mongolian language has been the state's reclassification of Mongols in China from an autonomous "nationality" to a de-territorialized "ethnic group," thus relegating their language to the domain of heritage and tradition.

Changing the trajectory of language loss requires changing not only the value of a language within the community, but also at higher levels of governance. The practices, regulations, and actions taken by states, communities, and institutions towards language are called **language policy and planning** and can alter the status of languages within the speech community (Lo Bianco 2010). Linguistic anthropologists often study the ways that states and institutions can support language revitalization efforts.

Many scholars point out that the endangerment of Indigenous languages in Canada stems from a language policy that recognizes English and French as the only official languages (McCarty 2016). Language is such a fundamental component of cultural identity that some have even proposed understanding language choice as a fundamental human right (Phillipson and Skutnabb-Kangas 1995). To ensure such rights, however, requires coordinated efforts at multiple social levels to maintain the vitality of Indigenous languages. In an overview of language revitalization efforts for Kanien'keha (also known as Mohawk), Grace Gomashie (2019) notes that the participation of community leadership, tribal elders, educators, and students is required for success. Nevertheless, revitalization necessitates widespread investments in curriculum design, pedagogical materials, and media production, along with recognition of the language within a range of public and institutional settings, to be effective.

BOX 5.5 – RITA JOE: I LOST MY TALK

Mi'kmaw poet Rita Joe (1932–2007) was sent to the Shubenacadie Residential School in Nova Scotia when she was 10 years old. Up to that point she had mainly spoken the Mi'kmaw language, but at the school the nuns who served as teachers forbade speaking anything but English (Joe 1996). Children who used their native language were beaten, had their mouths washed out with soap, or were locked in their rooms for days at a time. Moreover, many children were taken to the school against their parents' wishes and were forbidden from returning home to see their families, even on holidays. The Truth and Reconciliation Commission (2015b) recorded numerous reports of physical and sexual abuse against children attending the school. The effect of the residential schooling system, at Shubenacadie and across Canada, was to take away the language of an entire generation of Indigenous children. Rita Joe's poem "I Lost My Talk" powerfully illustrates the personal and collective impact of the school and other discriminatory language policies.

> I lost my talk
> The talk you took away.
> When I was a little girl
> At Shubenacadie school.
> You snatched it away:
> I speak like you
> I think like you
> I create like you
> The scrambled ballad, about my word.
> Two ways I talk
> Both ways I say,
> Your way is more powerful.
> So gently I offer my hand and ask,
> Let me find my talk
> So I can teach you about me.

3. **Documenting the language**
For most early linguistic anthropologists, working on Indigenous languages meant collecting texts such as myths, narratives, and oral histories. Boas and many other anthropologists shared an assumption that Indigenous languages were on the brink of disappearing forever, and thus engaged in a program of **salvage ethnography**, making a record of cultures and languages before they disappeared. Today, many linguists continue to do fieldwork in order to document endangered languages: recording texts, developing an inventory of vocabulary, and writing a grammar of the language (Newman and Ratliff 2001). These texts are often combined with photographs, audio, and video recordings. The goal is to be systematic enough that a near-complete record of the language exists, both for the community of speakers and for academic linguists who study language variation.

But rather than just archival documents of dead languages, such texts can play a significant role in language revitalization activities. They are particularly useful for languages that have become dormant; Wesley Leonard (2008) uses the term **sleeping languages** to describe languages that are no longer actively used but have sufficient documentation that they can be reclaimed later by their communities. When Gordon Marsh, one of Boas's students, collected stories in the Chiwere language from fluent elders in the 1930s, he probably had no idea that they would find a second life in Chiwere language textbooks decades later (Schwartz 2019).

Emergent Vitalities

So far, we have been using terms like language death and language extinction unproblematically, and it is worth thinking a little about the implications of these metaphors. When talking about language loss, it is hard not to compare a language to a biological organism – one that is born, connected to others genealogically, and may eventually die. Recently, though, many anthropologists have pointed out the shortcomings of such rhetoric and related comparisons of languages to natural resources or cultural treasures (Duchêne and Heller 2007). Using these terms to discuss language loss obscures the choices individual people make about what languages to speak. "By encouraging us to think in terms of ecosystems rather than political systems, comparisons of endangered languages to endangered species obscure the simple realization that *language death is anything but a natural phenomenon*. It is, on the contrary, a profoundly social phenomenon… Languages die because people stop speaking them" (Kulick 2019, 25–6). Jane Hill, in turn, warns us that the discourse of language death – in which linguists talk about the *value* of languages or of *our* responsibility to preserve them – alienates those languages from their communities. "Community language workers, speakers, and other members of local groups are both participants and overhearers in a global conversation about language endangerment in which the voices of academics and policymakers are especially prominent" (Hill 2002, 119).

Consider the impact these discourses have on Indigenous communities. In the northern Mexican community of El Mayor, at the mouth of the Colorado River, Shaylih Muehlmann listened to a radio report about the death of 71-year-old Adelia, calling her one of the last speakers of Cucapá. Adelia's son Cruz countered that his mother was so much more: a storyteller, a singer, and an expert fisher. Limiting Adelia's status to that of a speaker of a dying language obscures a range of other ways of belonging in the community – Cucapá often tied their own identity to the practice of fishing, the main subsistence activity, rather than language fluency. It has even had a negative impact on the Cucapá people themselves, as some authorities now claim that, without the language, the Cucapá have ceased to exist (Muehlmann 2012).

Likewise, Daria Boltokova (2017) argues that the ways we measure language endangerment may actually serve to harm language vitality. Think of the term "semi-speaker," discussed above: in the Dene community Boltokova studied, using the term semi-speaker to describe young language learners who are also proficient in English delegitimizes their speech. Focusing solely on "pure" language users "masks the emergence of new forms of language use that fall between established categories of 'safe' and 'endangered' linguistic practices" (Boltokova 2017, 23). Meanwhile, in the city of São Gabriel in the Brazilian Amazon, Sarah Shulist has documented how Indigenous identities are linked to distinctive languages. But the city's multilingual urban environment, where families often speak multiple languages together, would seem to call the Indigeneity of its residents into question. "Given that language revitalization movements are self-conscious efforts to resist assimilation and assert the value of Indigenous cultural practices, they often make use of rhetoric and symbolic practices that reiterate assumptions about urbanization as assimilation" (Shulist 2018, 21).

In response to these complicated entanglements of peoples, nations, communities, and languages, many anthropologists now argue that language "revitalization" is too narrow a term, creating policies that address language teaching and documentation but missing the cultural context. Instead, **language reclamation** refers to "a larger effort by a community to claim its right to speak a language and to set associated goals in response to community needs and perspectives" (Leonard 2012, 359). It explicitly addresses the social factors that lead to language shift, empowering communities to take control of their languages. The whole idea of saving languages without addressing the needs and interests of its speakers and custodians is what Bernard Perley (2012), an Indigenous linguistic anthropologist, terms "zombie linguistics" – severed from their communities, the languages are but empty shells (see also Davis 2017). In response, he proposes we come to appreciate **emergent vitalities**, the many ways Indigenous communities engage with and sustain their languages, often in very creative fashions. In his home community of Tobique First Nation, for instance, an English-language television series was dubbed into Maliseet in a project that involved producers, elders, and a range of Maliseet speakers. "Institutions and experts may offer formal structures and attendant expectations, but the life of the language is best witnessed when speakers use it to create new relationships" (Perley 2012, 143). Similarly, Allyson Lynch has designed a program for teaching Indigenous languages through the use of virtual reality technologies. With the participation of fluent elders, young people were invited to explore an application that wove together cultural teachings and Siksiká language instruction (Figure 5.3). Lynch shows that technology can offer emergent opportunities to make language more immersive and interactive, while still being rooted in Indigenous knowledge practices.

Other vitalities are apparent in the development of the Inuit Broadcasting Corporation (IBC), the first Indigenous-language television network in North America that delivers Inuktitut-language content across the northern territory of Nunavut (Pasch 2010). Started in the 1980s, today IBC broadcasts everything from soap operas and children's programs to cooking shows. In one episode of *Niqitsiat*, for instance, the hosts Rebecca and Susie show their audience how to cook caribou head and fish casserole, narrating the entire process in Inuktitut (with English subtitles). Many of their dishes are not traditionally Inuit – their casserole has pasta noodles and parmesan

Figure 5.3 – Youth participate in a workshop using virtual reality technologies to teach Indigenous languages at the University of Alberta

Source: Image courtesy of Allyson Lynch

Figure 5.4 – Super Shamou #1, a bilingual Inuktitut/English comic book based on the IBC television character

Source: Reproduced by permission of the Inuit Broadcasting Corporation

cheese – but reflect how people are living and cooking in northern communities today. IBC also created a program about an Inuit superhero, Super Shamou, who flies across the tundra dispensing lessons to children in Inuktitut on friendship and healthy living (Stern 2014; see Figure 5.4). The innovative use of Inuktitut in these media created for Inuit communities shows one pathway to revitalization that is rooted in the emergent vitality of the language and its speakers.

CONCLUSION

Through the examples offered in this chapter, our attention has been drawn to what makes Indigenous languages distinctive, why many are now endangered, and how the conditions for restoring them can be created. That last question is addressed to all of us – me, you the reader, Indigenous and non-Indigenous alike. Reconciliation and decolonization are not easy processes – in fact, they are intentionally discomfiting because they require a reconsideration of underlying structures of power. Joining in that process requires patience, honesty, and a willingness to listen, actions that are necessary for establishing a more just and equitable society. Linguistic anthropology has never been an objective science that simply reports on what is out there – the discipline has a long history of activism and advocacy, particularly for communities that struggle to find a voice through their own language. Doing so is a crucial component of our collective task of restoring Indigenous communities to a state of autonomy and self-determination.

As disciplines, both linguistics and anthropology were born out of the nineteenth and twentieth centuries' experiments with rationalism and liberalism. Some of the unintended consequences, as we have seen, are to sever the connections between languages and peoples and between languages and the land. What can be done to restore them? What might an Indigenous linguistics look like? What might an Indigenous anthropology look like? These are questions that Indigenous people challenge us to ask.

BOX 5.6 – RESEARCH SPOTLIGHT: JOANNE DINOVA AND LILA PINE

DiNova, Joanne, and Lila Pine. 2015. "Sight Unseen: Imag(in)ing Indigeneity in English." *AlterNative: An International Journal of Indigenous Peoples* 11 (4): 363–75.

As we saw with Rita Joe's poem "I Lost My Talk," language loss and a shift to using English can act as an alienating experience for Indigenous peoples. In this article, the authors explore the nature of that experience while highlighting the importance of listening to Indigenous voices. The journal *AlterNative* often publishes research that takes the form of a dialogue, and in this piece DiNova and Pine – students and speakers of Anishinaabemowin and Mi'kmaw, respectively – take turns narrating their own perspectives and discussing ways of "restoring Indigeneity in language" (DiNova and Pine 2015, 364). This starts with an observation from a Métis elder that the English language has no mother: as an overly objective and abstract system, it has lost its connection to the land and the spirit. They ask how that relationship could be brought back into English.

Rather than turning to the past, however, the authors identify digital technologies and new media as tools for language revitalization. They point to the vitalities inherent in the #SpeakMikmaq campaign, Indigenous-language apps, and online dictionaries as ways Indigenous people can reclaim their languages in the twenty-first century. Pine, in particular, uses a range of visualization tools to make language tangible for the public. More than anything, however, they recognize that although English is the first language of many Indigenous people today, this does not compromise their identity. Given the tremendous variety of English dialects and speech patterns, there is room for an English that has the mother put back into it.

Discussion

1. Academia sometimes thrives on debates, on disagreements over how best to interpret data and understand the world around us. We discussed Perley's (2012) idea that a linguistics that privileges languages over speech communities is a zombie linguistics. Australian linguist Josh Nash (2013) has countered that field linguists are not solely interested in documentation and have transcended the colonial legacies of the past. Read through these articles and Perley's (2013) rejoinder to Nash's critique – what do you think? What role does colonialism and racism play in language endangerment today, and what responsibilities do linguists and linguistic anthropologists have to the communities we work with?
2. The ways in which Indigenous languages are bound to the lands in which they are spoken has led to the development of several mapping projects. One of these, the Mi'kmaw digital atlas (https://placenames.mapdev.ca/), records the names for hundreds of locations throughout my province of Nova Scotia. Have a look through this resource or another digital atlas of Indigenous place names – what do you find? What types of knowledge are preserved about the landscape through these names?
3. In 2016, many news outlets reported on a Grade 8 student in Cape Dorset, Nunavut, who was disciplined for speaking Inuktitut, his native language, at school. Teachers were concerned that students not speaking English could be secretly bullying others. Most Indigenous leaders were outraged but not surprised by this episode, considering the many ways that Indigenous languages have been marginalized. Nunavut MLA Paul Okalik responded, "All teachers should be told that the language of Inuktitut should be promoted – not stopped." Think about the underlying ideologies of this situation – what are the impacts of such policies on Indigenous speech communities?
4. Endangered languages are often silent outside their speech communities, barely recognized by the nations and dominant languages surrounding them. What endangered languages are spoken in your community, province, or state? What would be the most effective strategies in helping to revitalize them (bearing in mind that such efforts should always be done in partnership with the speech communities themselves)?

6

Social Identity and Performativity

Topics

- Language as a form of social action
- The nature of identity
- Assigning values to patterns of speech

In the 1960s, a linguist by the name of William Labov noticed that a lot of people on the island of Martha's Vineyard, off the coast of Massachusetts, pronounced the vowel diphthong /aɪ/ (in words like price, right, and knife) in a more central position of the mouth than mainlanders – the word "right" would sound a bit more like "rawht." But not everyone was doing it; rural fishermen were more likely to do it than urban townsfolk, and younger people more likely to do it than older. Instead of anything to do with the language itself, Labov (1963) argued that this variation was a product of socioeconomic changes happening on the island. Families that had been on Martha's Vineyard for generations were gradually being pushed out by wealthy mainlanders buying up the land for summer homes. The centralization of /aɪ/ was most likely to be found in groups of people who opposed the influence of these rich newcomers. Moreover, the centralized vowel appeared to have emerged many years before and was gradually becoming stronger in younger generations, especially those that had resisted the pull of opportunities on the mainland. "It is apparent that the immediate meaning of this phonetic feature is 'Vineyarder'" (Labov 1963, 304).

Labov's paper on this topic diverged greatly from previous analyses, which often attributed language change to physiological or environmental influences. For Labov, language variation is a social phenomenon. In this and other research, he asserts that language differences – like the centralization of /aɪ/ – may crop up randomly in various speech communities, but their maintenance and preservation is socially motivated. In collaboration with scholars such as Dell Hymes, John Gumperz and Susan Ervin-Tripp (some of whom we have discussed already), Labov founded a new field of inquiry called **sociolinguistics**, which studies the social dimensions of language in use.

Sociolinguistics is what you might call a cognate field to linguistic anthropology. Sociolinguists and linguistic anthropologists do tend to have different approaches; the former discipline is usually a bit more quantitative and attentive to discrete phonological or syntactic differences, the latter more ethnographic and interpretive. Nevertheless, these fields of study overlap considerably, and both draw upon insights from the other (Gumperz and Cook-Gumperz 2008). They also share an overarching concern with questions of how language is used in establishing a sense of identity.

Penelope Eckert (2012) argues that there have been three waves of research on questions of language and identity in sociolinguistics.

1. The first wave (1960s and 1970s) linked language variation to social categories. For example, people of higher social class tend to use more formal language, while lower-class people typically use informal language. Ethnicity and gender are also important categories that appear to structure linguistic differences between groups of people. During this period, sociolinguists attempted to find linguistic variables that had some kind of correlation to social status or identity. Peter Trudgill (1972), for instance, found that in Norwich, England, women tended to use standard pronunciations more often than men, who instead used regional pronunciations with greater frequency. He attributed the difference to men's greater affinity for a working-class identity than women.
2. The second wave (1980s and 1990s) was more ethnographic in nature, and it showed that linguistic repertoires are not simply determined by social categories. In her own study of a Detroit high school in the 1980s, for instance, Eckert (1989) found that students tended to congregate in two distinct social groups called the Jocks and the Burnouts. The Jocks wore current fashions, participated in student government, and attended pep rallies and athletic events; many went on to higher education. The Burnouts, on the other hand, rejected the social norms of school. They smoked, wore heavy makeup and ripped clothing, and often skipped classes. They were more likely to go on to vocational school. What Eckert discovered was that linguistic variables in student talk were far more dependent upon the social group (Jock or Burnout) than on the person's social class or ethnicity: a white middle-class Jock and a white middle-class Burnout could sound remarkably different. Eckert therefore concluded that language is not just a reflection of

variables like social class, but that people could choose the groups that mattered to them.

3. The third wave (2000s and beyond) reversed the arrow of causality. Whereas both first- and second-wave studies accepted social categories as primary (such as middle class, or Jock, or female), third-wave studies came to see speech as an active process, where people draw upon the full range of stylistic resources available in the speech community to navigate a variety of identities throughout their lives. Or perhaps we should say it is an *interactive* process, since assertions of identity through language are always measured and judged by an audience – is this person really who they sound like, or are they just putting on an act? "The principal move in the third wave then was from a view of variation as a reflection of social identities and categories to the linguistic practice in which speakers place themselves in the social landscape through stylistic practice" (Eckert 2012, 93–4).

Research in linguistic anthropology may not always have been explicitly doing so, but due to its ethnographic nature – and sensitivity to what people were *doing* with language – it often shared the same analytical framework as the third wave from the beginning. Nevertheless, most of the scholarly work being done today accepts the third-wave idea of language as an active system for crafting social identity. The communicative meaning of our speech, the messages we are trying to get across to others, is always layered with social meaning as well about who we are or who we want to be. This chapter provides an overview of how we do that and gives some examples of the ways people use language to position themselves within an ever-changing social field.

PERFORMATIVITY

To chart this shift in our understanding from language reflecting who we are to language as a form of social practice, we need a little background on the philosophy of language. Until the early twentieth century, the field was largely an analytical enterprise. Scholars such as Bertrand Russell – working in a tradition that goes back to the European Enlightenment – were concerned with the factuality of language: what is the relationship between language and truth? Russell saw language as akin to a mathematical equation wherein each word combines with those that came before it to encode objective propositions about the world. For instance, Russell (1940, 37) diagrams the sentence "Brutus killed Caesar" as "there are occurrences x, P, y, such that x is a member of *ß*," and so on; pretty complicated stuff. But Russell also acknowledged that language could be messy and ambiguous; if used incorrectly, language confuses and obfuscates factual information. The key was to structure linguistic expression as a logical system. You can imagine that Russell's approach implies a certain prescriptive view of language, in that there are right ways and wrong ways to communicate this information to others.

However, along with Saussure's structural approach to language and meaning (discussed in Chapter 1), other theorists began advancing an alternative point of view that challenged this logical, objective approach to expression and instead saw language as inseparable from the people speaking it. The Soviet linguist Valentin Vološinov,[1] writing in the 1920s, argued that language is ideological. "A sign does not simply exist as a part of reality – it reflects and refracts another reality" (1986, 10). The "truth" of any logical proposition, he asserts, is not universal – like Russell's sentence equations – but a social construct related to things like social class or political orientation. The philosopher Ludwig Wittgenstein (1958), likewise, rejected Russell's positivism in favour of the idea that language is like a game, as speakers negotiate meaning together in the delicate dance of everyday talk.[2]

It was within this intellectual milieu that the philosopher J.L. Austin published a book called *How to Do Things with Words* (1962). Rather than language being an instrument of description, Austin looked at language as a social activity. A sentence like "I bet you five bucks it is going to rain tomorrow" does not just *describe* a bet between two people, it is itself an *act* of betting. When two people proclaim "I do" in a wedding, they become married, or when a juror announces "not guilty" in a courtroom, the accused person goes free. Austin calls sentences such as these, where saying something is also doing something, **performatives**, and what the sentence actually does is called the **speech act**.

Austin then divides a speech act into three parts:

- **Locution** – This is the performative itself, the words that the speaker utters.
- **Illocution** – This is the action that the words perform, such as betting, congratulating, announcing, appointing, and so forth.
- **Perlocution** – Every action has consequences, and the perlocution is the social effect of the act on the speaker and listeners.

Let's go back to that example of "I bet you five bucks it is going to rain tomorrow." Obviously, the locution is the sentence itself, the words as they are uttered. The illocution, what this performative accomplishes, is the establishment of a bet between two people. The perlocution is the result of this action, namely that tomorrow one person will be five dollars richer and the other five dollars poorer depending on the weather. Austin's approach here is to highlight the social impact of our speech rather than its objective truth. If you promise to drive me to work but then do not show up, you still made a *promise* – it's just that you failed to carry it out. Like Vološinov and Wittgenstein, Austin was therefore less concerned with how language describes our reality and more with how we negotiate meaning.

BOX 6.1 – THE PERFORMATIVITY OF COMING OUT

Coming out, the public declaration of an alternative sexual or gender identity, is both a highly significant and potentially stressful event in the lives of many people. Saying something like "I'm gay" or "I'm trans" allows someone to openly reconcile their public life with their private desires, and people who have come out often report a sense of liberation from feelings of shame and uncertainty (Davies 2014). "Coming out narratives are largely about coming to *be*, and they are stories worth telling because of the challenges inherent in coming to embrace a contested identity. These stories all describe how speakers came to understand their feelings of otherness in relation to normative constructs of gender and sexuality, and how this understanding came to be realized socially as an identity" (Zimman 2009, 71). That's a lot of work for just a few short words, but it can also be nerve-wracking not knowing how friends and family will react.

In a popular YouTube video posted in 2011, Randy Phillips, an airman in the United States Air Force stationed in Germany, phoned his father.

RANDY: Can I tell ya something?
FATHER: Yeah
RANDY: Will you love me, period?
FATHER: Yes
RANDY: Like, you'll- you'll always love me, as long as I'm a-
FATHER: Of course
RANDY: Dad, I'm gay...
FATHER: Okay
RANDY: Like, always have been, I've known since forever

The call ends with Randy's father affirming he still loves him.

Austin's model of the speech act reveals to us something of why Phillips would be so nervous coming out to his father. The locution is the relatively simple "I'm gay," and the illocution is just the act of revealing this information to his father. But imagine the perlocutionary consequences. His family must now readjust their image of him: conventional expectations of him marrying a nice girlfriend and having biological children with her will have to be abandoned. Their perspectives of themselves will also change. "Straight mothers and fathers may find that on their sons' and daughters' coming out, they can no longer claim simply to be 'parents'; instead, they become 'the parents of lesbians and gay men'" (Fields 2001, 165). Despite the ring of truth in terms of his revealing his identity, the words "I'm gay" did nothing less than upend his entire social world. Saying them takes a lot of courage!

There is, so far, one problem in this analysis: our words do not always accomplish what they say. During a wedding rehearsal, a prospective bride and groom may say "I do," but they are not immediately married. Outside the courtroom, a person proclaiming someone "not guilty" does not have any force of law. Austin therefore proposes that, to be effective, a performative must also meet certain criteria called **felicity conditions**. "I do" must be spoken in the context of a wedding, in front of an officiant, and not as part of a movie or play or in jest. These are, in other words, the social constraints on our speech as action. But this also means that speakers can play around with language – we can intentionally violate these conditions to say something without *really* saying it, like when we are being sarcastic (Goffman 1983).

Austin's approach has been tremendously influential. Although he largely confined himself to particular words and their attendant actions (such as promising, betting, and nominating), subsequent work in philosophy and linguistic anthropology has pointed to the ways that all speech is in some sense performative (Kulick 2003). In a highly influential book called *Gender Trouble*, the philosopher Judith Butler argues that gender identities such as male and female do not exist as natural categories. They are, instead, produced within a social field that incorporates pre-existing ideas of masculinity and femininity. When a doctor announces to a new mother "it's a girl," the performative statement activates a range of perlocutionary effects that will have considerable sway over "her" life – everything from what colour her room will be painted to what university major she will be encouraged to choose. "The appearance of an abiding substance or gendered self… is thus produced by the regulation of attributes along culturally established lines of coherence" (Butler 2007, 33). This is not to say our gender is determined by the statements of others – in our language and behaviour we also identify ourselves to others as particular kinds of gendered beings. Our gendered identities are produced through the ways we talk because we share a cultural framework with already-established ideas about how men and women *should* talk (see Chapter 7 – Language and Gender). The key point in all of this is that we make choices when we speak, and those choices have social implications. Whether it is pitch, vocabulary, pronunciation, or selecting among different dialects and languages, they affect how our words are understood and interpreted by different audiences.

BOX 6.2 – SHIBBOLETHS

Have you ever been far away from home, heard someone talk, and just known they come from the same place you do? Some language choices allow us to plug people into a social geography, identifying where they are from based on how they talk. It is often an accent, but there are also particular phrases or words that act as a kind of test of someone's membership in a community: these are called **shibboleths**.

The term comes from an account in the biblical book of Judges, where an invading army of Ephraimites was defeated in battle by the Gileadites. As the invaders tried to retreat across the River Jordan, the Gileadites asked anyone approaching a simple question: say the word "shibboleth." The Ephraimite language did not feature a voiceless postalveolar fricative that we write today as *sh* and so would respond "sibboleth." As the Bible says, "and there fell at that time of the Ephraimites forty and two thousand" (Judg. 12:6).

Shibboleths today may start as quirks of local pronunciation, but they often take on a broader role as a way of affirming in-group membership and, therefore, a sense of belonging. According to a popular meme, for instance, if you pronounce Toronto as *CHRAWNna* your "pulse sounds like the TTC chimes and you piss Steamwhistle," referring to the local transit agency and beer, respectively. Other shibboleths are phrases like the Bostonian "pahk the car in Hahvahd Yahd" (Metcalf 2000, 66), which reflects local pronunciation patterns.

In her study of "Pittsburghese," Barbara Johnstone argues that emblems of local identity, like calling the local football team "the Stillers" instead of Steelers, may have originated with the dialects of Scots-Irish immigrants who originally settled the area. But many older Pittsburghers did not see their speech as distinct and different. It was only when that speech became tied to a local social identity and promoted through material artefacts like T-shirts and coffee mugs printed with words like *dahntahn* (downtown) and *yinz* (you-plural). As she writes, "Pittsburghers teach each other about Pittsburghese as they talk to each other; as they tell stories; as they perform on and listen to the radio; and as they write, read, and react to newspapers and magazines" (Johnstone 2015, 109). Shibboleths, in other words, are the reflexive products of local identity.

Social Identity

Just as our understanding of language has shifted from a passive reflection of the world to a means of acting in it, so too has our conception of identity changed. **Identity** is a notoriously difficult term to define because it is rooted in a Western philosophical tradition that posits an autonomous unitary "self" aware of its own thoughts and actions: think of Descartes's famous phrase "I think therefore I am." Other cultural and philosophical traditions define the self in more relational terms, as a person embedded within multiple networks of kinship, nation, clan, caste, and so forth (Carrithers, Collins, and Lukes 1985; Morris 1994). Sometimes these relations may be complementary, at other times in conflict. At its core, however, the idea of identity implies a sense of social positioning, a feeling of where one belongs in the social fabric based on similarities and differences with other people (Sökefeld 1999).

Early anthropologists tended to focus on identity as a relatively fixed attribute. In her 1934 book *Patterns of Culture*, anthropologist Ruth Benedict wrote, "The life-history of the individual is first and foremost an accommodation to the patterns and standards traditionally handed down in his community. From the moment of his birth the customs into which he is born shape his experience and behaviour. By the time he can talk, he is the little creature of his culture, and by the time he is grown and able to take part in its activities, its habits are his habits, its beliefs his beliefs, its impossibilities his impossibilities" (1934, 2–3). Who you are, in other words, is what your culture says you are. But more recent work, especially in linguistic anthropology, tends to see ideas of self and identity as both *multiple* and *constructed* in interaction with others. For instance, in the 1950s Erving Goffman advanced the idea that how we act in public is very different from how we act in private. Borrowing a metaphor from theatre, he described these as **frontstage** and **backstage**. Our identity is different in each: in frontstage settings we often perform a version of ourselves for public consumption, but in backstage settings we can be relatively informal and emphasize solidarity with others. Importantly, Goffman argues that our backstage persona is no more natural or authentic than our frontstage one – in both, we are acting out a particular character for others based on social expectations (Goffman 1959). We do not possess a single unitary identity, but shift among a multiplicity of them as we move through our lives.

Sociolinguists and linguistic anthropologists have also looked at the ways these various identities are constructed. Deborah Schiffrin (1996), for example, has analysed narratives offered by middle-class Jewish American mothers. In these stories, the women discussed their relationships with their families, such as disagreements, conflicts, and resolutions. Jan, for instance, narrated a fight with her daughter over whether she should date non-Jewish men. Jan shifted, in her telling, among various stances during the narrative, sometimes as an open-minded and permissive mother, at other times as someone more critical and pragmatic than her daughter. These varying stances, entwined in the story Jan was telling to Schiffrin, were inseparable parts of her own personality. "We are continually locating and relocating ourselves, defining and redefining ourselves and our worlds: telling a story about a personal experience is merely another example of a process that pervades our ways of speaking, acting, and being in the world" (Schiffrin 1996, 200). In this sense, Schiffrin calls stories "self-portraits" in that they represent who we are to others.

In 1995, Alessandro Duranti (2006) followed Walter Capps, a candidate for the United States House of Representatives, on the campaign trail. To impress voters, politicians need to craft a cohesive identity, a story of who they are and why they should be elected. Duranti was therefore interested in how Capps narrated his life story, putting forward an image of the ideal political candidate for voters. In the back and forth of political debates, Capps made strategic use of his biography to identify himself as someone "not from Washington" (in other words, a political outsider) and an "independent" (who resisted party influence), while his opponents used that same personal history to argue that he was offering "politics as usual." The very ambiguity of these terms allowed candidates to position themselves in a crowded political field in different ways, but always with the goal of creating a coherent identity of who they were and why they were running for office. The goal was to construct an identity of "the kind of person that they want the voters to know and believe in" (Duranti 2006, 492) – otherwise they would not get elected.

The narrative examples provided by Schiffrin and Duranti show us that identity is neither unitary nor predetermined. We can be a mother, a professor, Black, a good golfer, a fan of superhero movies, and so forth all at the same time; and these identities are crafted through complex linguistic interactions with others, such as the stories told above. A good summary of the insights developed by linguistic anthropologists towards identity is offered by Mary Bucholtz and Kira Hall (2005). They argue that identity has the following characteristics:

1. **Emergent** – Identity is not predetermined by our culture or social position but is the outcome of linguistic and cultural practices, including speech acts that bring these identities into being.
2. **Positional** – Identity is not simply a bundle of attributes (gender, race, sexuality, religion, etc.) but a set of roles we take on. These could be momentary, like narrator or joke-teller, or they could be more enduring, like Christian or lesbian. These positions, however, are neither mutually exclusive nor absolute.
3. **Indexical** – We take on these roles by employing language forms that are linked to them, often in relatively indirect ways – this is the concept of indexicality we have discussed several times. "Assertive" language comes to index the male gender, or the use of English in China comes to index a cosmopolitan identity.
4. **Relational** – The identities we take on acquire their meaning in relation to other available identities within the social field. To take on the position of a woman is to also *not* take on the position of a man, and to use language that indexes a Black

identity is to also explicitly be not white. This is not to say that gender or race are binary categories, but that any identity position is framed in relation to other possible positions.

5. **Partial** – No identity is totalizing or completely coherent, nor are we completely defined by the various stances we take on. During the course of our interactions we may shift roles and positions several times, taking up a multiplicity of identities or, in turn, having them thrust upon us.

ENREGISTERMENT

To summarize so far, we have outlined a few fundamental ideas, including that language is a form of social action and that our identities are crafted through language. But there is one piece left of the puzzle: how is it that something like a centralized vowel comes to represent the identity of Vineyarders on Martha's Vineyard, as in the example from William Labov's research discussed above? There's no logical reason this particular phonological feature should do so. What is it about certain patterns of language that allow us to perform identities?

A lot of the linguistic features that we recognize as being indexical of an identity are fairly random. At the beginning of this chapter, for instance, we talked about the ways that upper-class speakers tend to be more formal and lower-class speakers more informal. That appears to make sense on the surface – rich people are stuck up and poor people pretty relaxed, right? But if you think about it, what does avoiding contractions or using strict grammar have to do with social class? Could we not just define formality as "the types of language used more often by upper class speakers" rather than by its form (Irvine 1979)? A similar thing happens when we describe certain devalued accents as "coarse" or "rough": that has nothing to do with the language itself, only our social interpretation of it.

Linguistic anthropologist Asif Agha (2007) uses the term **register** to refer to any socially recognized pattern of language. This can include a regional accent, gendered language, or professional discourse like legal register or medical register (note how we associate each of these registers with a particular identity). He argues that to be socially meaningful, a register needs to undergo a process of **enregisterment** through which its indexical values are established. Once this is done, hearing the pattern evokes the identity of the speaker, and speakers can draw upon the register to make claims to various identities.

You've probably heard of Received Pronunciation (RP) in the United Kingdom, sometimes called the Queen's English. It is considered the most prestigious accent, associated with the aristocracy, the upper class, and higher education. While there are many regional varieties of British English, RP is considered the national standard. Phonologically it is characterized by things like the differentiation between long and short vowels – why many British speakers pronounce the word dance as "dawnce" – and not pronouncing the /r/ sound after vowels – so that "farther" and "father" sound the same. But like the idea of formality, we have to ask why these particular pronunciations connote sophistication and class.

Agha charts out the history of RP, which has its origins in the variety of English spoken in southeastern England in the sixteenth century, a region that includes the capital city of London and the universities of Oxford and Cambridge. Over the next few hundred years, various writers, scholars, and educators created treatises on oratory and elocution, making specific reference to this dialect. At the same time, waves of European nationalism were creating a sense of distinct *peoples*, like "the British," and RP was recruited into the development of British nationalism. RP became a socially recognizable pattern, the "right" way to speak. Handbooks educated the populace on the value of speech for signalling "good breeding and good education" to others, and adoption of RP became a passport to social mobility within British society (Agha 2007, 210). Authors like Charles Dickens populated their novels with wealthy, educated, and "gentlemanly" characters who used RP. Agha argues that all of these discourses about RP worked together, gradually teaching the populace about the desirability and status of RP, even if many could not speak it themselves. Enregisterment is therefore the social process through which particular language patterns, or registers, become indexical of particular identities.

In the west African country of Côte d'Ivoire, especially in the capital city of Abidjan, people talk about a new urban street language called *nouchi*, a blend of English, French, and Dioula. The register emerged in the 1990s during a time of student demonstrations and political activism and then spread through the hip-hop music scene. Nouchi is a slangy, trendy way of speaking, a clear example of what Dutch sociolinguist Jan Blommaert (2015) calls "cool language," meaning a register where the point is showing off rather than communicating information. Nouchi is far more than just a collection of words; it is an attitude. Speaking nouchi identifies someone as streetwise, tough, and confident – it evokes images of the urban gangster and the modern *bluffeur*, someone who eats lavishly and dresses fashionably, even if they don't actually have any money (Newell 2012).

How did that happen? When it first became popular, articles in magazines and newspapers taught the vocabulary to urban youth with words like *glôglô* (gangster territory) and *bizness* (the illicit economy). It became associated with the *logobi* dance style modelled on street fighting and flashy poses. Nouchi showed up in comic strips in the mouths of characters drawn as physically tough, muscled, and intimidating (Figure 6.1). As many Ivoirians explained, a nouchi struts rather than walks, fists balled up and

Figure 6.1 – A stereotypical image of a loubard (a particular type of nouchi)

Source: Image courtesy of Sasha Newell

ready to fight: "even if they are talking to the president," claimed one, "*nouchi* will not change their attitude… They always show confidence in the art of the bluff" (Newell 2012, 38). Like RP, nouchi was therefore gradually enregistered with distinct values as it spread through music, pop culture, and media. As people learned what nouchi is, they also learned what it represents and associated it with an identity; the *bluffeur* is nouchi and nouchi is the *bluffeur*.

CONNECTING LANGUAGE AND IDENTITY

The last step ties it all together – there is some kind of language difference, it gets attached to some kind of identity through a process of enregisterment, and then people can use language performatively to invoke that identity. Whether other people accept that identity is dependent upon whether the speaker satisfies the felicity conditions of the speech act; a nouchi without swagger, for instance, is no nouchi at all.

A lot of social science research in other fields tends to associate identity with affirmative statements such as "I am Canadian" or "I am a local." That allows scholars to use larger-scale quantitative data, like survey or census questions, to chart out belonging. But most linguistic anthropologists point to ethnography as the only way to connect the individual performativity of identity with larger social processes like enregisterment. You have to be "in the mix" of all these speech acts and interactions to see how they really work.

I also want to stress that identity is not just a feeling or some kind of ephemeral affectation; it can have very real consequences for people's lives. Jan Blommaert, whom we discussed above, has studied the refugee process in Belgium. In evaluating applications for political asylum, authorities analyse the narratives offered by asylum seekers and evaluate whether they are legitimate refugees from their home countries or opportunists attempting to take advantage of others; in other words, are they good refugees or bad refugees? Like the politician Walter Capps, the refugees offer narratives of their life histories during the application process, including stories of why they chose to leave their home countries.

> HABIBA: So Somalia is starting war nineteen ninety one, so until ninety one to ninety five I was in Somalia and wa- and I have four children at that time and um… My husband comes from uh north Somalia and I south Somalia is fighting north at- at south is fighting, so my- my husband and my children have no safety for their lives.
>
> (Blommaert 2001, 424)

In this extract, Habiba struggles to communicate her story in her second language of English but puts forward a narrative of her journey from the war in Somalia to Belgium. Habiba thus uses performative speech to align herself with the identity of a "good" refugee fleeing war. When Blommaert looked at the interviewers' reports, however, many used these narratives as evidence that asylum seekers were not who they claimed to be. "Inconsistencies in the stories are a major cause for refusing refugee status to asylum seekers… ranging from contradictions between two versions of the story over not remembering names, places or dates, and superficial or incomplete knowledge of things assumed to be known to people from one country (e.g. the name of the president, names of towns and cities, etc.) can all serve as cause for refusal" (Blommaert 2001, 436). One asylum seeker was refused entry because she could not answer questions about the surname of her childhood friend or the date she fled her home. These are, fundamentally, conflicts over identity, over whether the asylum seeker is legitimate or not.

A similar example is provided in Alejandro Paz's research on the children of undocumented migrants living in Israel (Paz 2016). Although many of these youths had been in Israel for years – they were enrolled in school and spoke Hebrew fluently – their parents' non-citizen status left them at risk of deportation at any time. Paz studied how these young people, in collaboration with Israeli immigration activists, actively adopt a strategy of speaking like a citizen; in other words, identifying as truly Israeli.

Eight-year-old Wendy was born in Israel to a Ghanaian mother, and therefore at risk of being deported with her family to Ghana. Activists made a case for her to stay in Israel by highlighting her orientation towards Israeli values, making her "Israeli in every way," according to the media. Newspaper reports described her as speaking without an accent, using Hebrew slang, and most telling of all, speaking to her parents and teachers with *chutzpa,* an audacious and obstinate speaking style that is considered distinctively Jewish (Paz 2016, 24). In this instance, describing how Wendy talked back to her mother as *chutzpa* turns the phrase into a performative token of Wendy's successful assimilation of Israeli cultural values. Whether Wendy would face deportation or not was therefore dependent upon the success of speech acts that justified her presence within the Israeli state.

CONCLUSION

From centralized diphthongs to a child's confrontational *chutzpa,* this chapter has looked at the ways people adopt, assert, and manage their identities through language. Remember that the word is intentionally plural – we are not a singular individual but shift among multiple stances and positions in our lives. Those identities are also brought into being and communicated to others through our language, in the form of speech acts. In addition to the delivery of factual information to others, this is an essential feature of what language can do: as Erving Goffman (1959, 160) put it over 60 years ago, "The role of expression is conveying impressions of the self." We have also seen how these identities may be received, interpreted, and sometimes contested by others. In many ways, the performative framework of language – where words call our identities into being – lies at the core of who we are.

Notice how the choices people make about their ways of speaking in this chapter are significant. Choosing one language over another, one word over another, one style over another can have tremendous import because those choices reflect different varieties of language enregistered with social value. If I want to talk snooty, all I need are some snooty academic words; and the only reason those words index a snooty identity is because of social conventions that identify certain types of words with certain types of people. In the following chapters we will explore some specific types of identity that are the product of speech acts (such as gender and race) to demonstrate just how powerful this perspective is within the field of linguistic anthropology.

BOX 6.3 – RESEARCH SPOTLIGHT: SABRINA BILLINGS

Billings, Sabrina. 2009. "Speaking Beauties: Linguistic Posturing, Language Inequality, and the Construction of a Tanzanian Beauty Queen." *Language in Society* 38 (5): 581–606.

Nargis Mohammed, on stage under bright lights in a flowing gown, is asked what should be done to remove poverty in Tanzania:

> MOHAMMED: If we empower our people with capital services, soc- eh social c- social services, human services, we have no doubt to fight, we have no- sorry, sorry, sorry.
>
> (Billings 2009, 597)

At this point, the audience erupts in shouts and laughter. It was, unfortunately, the end of Mohammed's dream of being crowned Miss Tanzania in 2003 – she placed third instead. We can see how Nargis struggled putting together her answer, particularly because she is not a native speaker of English. And yet, before the question was asked, she was given the choice to answer in either English or Kiswahili, the national language of Tanzania. Why did she choose English?

Billings, a lecturer in anthropology at Dartmouth College, spent years studying Tanzanian beauty pageants. These are high-stakes contests that draw women from across the country. A win will secure a woman fame, money, and opportunity for years, which is especially attractive in uncertain economic times. But unlike Western beauty pageants, Tanzanian ones have much more vocal audiences who evaluate a contestant's speaking, either applauding her performance or laughing her off stage.

In this article, Billings differentiates between what she calls implicit and explicit language ideologies: explicit ideologies are those that people affirm in public, but implicit ones are left unsaid despite still guiding people's actions. Explicitly, everyone from judges to contestants told Billings that the choice of whether a contestant answered questions in English or Kiswahili did not matter ("the score is the same"), but implicitly, people give more weight to an English answer – almost all the winners answered in English. The trick for pageant contestants, especially for those from rural areas, is to speak in a way that convinces audiences – who are not native English speakers either – that they know English fluently, even if they don't speak it well. This is done through poise and confidence.

In identity terms, Tanzanian pageant contestants use language – and the all-important choice of *which* language to answer questions in – to craft identities for themselves as educated, sophisticated, elite women: as beauty queens. The wealth of examples Billings provides, and the sensitivity she shows towards the lived dilemmas contestants face, make this a valuable article for understanding contemporary approaches to identity in linguistic anthropology.

Discussion

1. "I'm sorry if you were offended." That kind of phrase constitutes what is often called a non-apology; on the surface, it looks like an apology but fails at the illocutionary level. There is a wealth of public examples of non-apologies, from Bryan Adams retracting a rant about people he characterized as "virus making greedy bastards" at the start of the COVID-19 pandemic to Bill Clinton admitting that "mistakes were made" in response to a fundraising scandal. Find a few of these and examine them: what makes them fail as apologies? Here, Austin's notion of felicity conditions – the requirements for making a speech act effective – can show us what the general criteria are for a successful apology.
2. Late night talk show host Seth Meyers once created a fake trailer for a movie called *Boston Accent*. "You all know me. I'm not just a cop. I'm a fadder, I'm a son, and above all, I'm from Bahstun." He then goes on to perform all the accents of different Bostonians, from the Harvard-educated on down to the street punk who calls everyone "bro." For all of them, that peculiar of pronunciation of "Boston" acts as a shibboleth – something that signals a local identity to others. What types of shibboleths, like a local word or local pronunciation, do you know?
3. What are your identities? How is each evoked as you shift from one to another? Keeping in mind the idea that our identities are both multiple and constructed, think about the clothes you put on, the way you hold yourself, or how your language changes in each instance. Talk these over in a group and see if they are consistent with or different than other people's experiences.
4. Register differences are meaningful because they are socially recognizable – even if you can't use medical register like a doctor, you can probably identify it and maybe even mimic it just from watching movies and television. The reverse is also true: older people, the kinds who write movies and television shows for instance, really don't understand the register of young people although they can mimic some of it. Watch clips of young people talking in movies and television. What do the writers get right, and what do they get wrong?

7

Language and Gender

Topics

- The "nature" of gender
- Gendered communication differences
- Gender in cross-cultural perspective
- Language and masculinity

A popular 1990s relationship advice book, *Men Are from Mars, Women Are from Venus* (Gray 1992), posited that many of the problems men and women experience in their relationships are not due to differing values or points of view, but to gender-specific communication strategies. For instance, the book tells us that when a problem arises, men automatically begin offering solutions. When a woman complains that her job leaves her with no time to herself, a man advises her to quit and find a job that is less stressful. Women, on the other hand, experience intimacy through sharing and relating their problems to others. "So many times a woman just wants to share her feelings about her day, and her husband, thinking he is helping, interrupts her by offering a steady flow of solutions to her problems. He has no idea why she isn't pleased" (Gray 1992, 16).

At first glance, this type of scenario appears to make a whole lot of sense, especially within a North American cultural context. Who hasn't thought that someone of another gender just does not understand their point? Or seems to approach conversations with very different goals and expectations? A lot of people would therefore agree that men and women talk differently. We often hear that women talk more than men, that they speak more collaboratively, and talk more about emotions and feelings (Cameron 2006).

Just ask a group of people which gender gossips more, and they are almost sure to answer women. One popular explanation for this is that during our prehistoric past men had to be silent while out hunting game, while women were free to chat as they gathered food (Joseph 2000). As many anthropologists have shown, however, these are fundamentally sexist ideas that have no basis in either hunter-gatherer social practices (male hunters are often really good at storytelling) or genetics (there is no sex-based gene controlling how much or how little someone talks) (Everett 2012, 70; Rosaldo 1986). Rather, these are arguments that rely on stereotypes of the ancient past in order to explain – and some might say justify – our gendered stereotypes of today (Slocum 1975).

Do women really gossip more than men? It depends quite a bit on how you define gossip. In one famous paper, the linguist Deborah Cameron (1997) discusses a conversation between five men that was recorded by one of her students. In it, the men discuss another guy in their class, whom they characterize as "gay":

> BRYAN: He wore shorts again, by the way, it's like 42 degrees out
> he wore shorts again [laugher].
> It's like a Speedo, he wears a Speedo to class.
> He's got incredibly skinny legs you know?
> ED: You know like those shorts women volleyball players wear? It's like those.
> It's like French cut spandex.
> BRYAN: You know what's even more ridiculous?
> When you wear those shorts and like a parka on.
>
> (adapted from Cameron 1997, 53)

Cameron's student argued that the boisterous back and forth between the men, with each trying to interrupt and surpass the other, was a stereotypically male conversational style. But Cameron also noticed that this exchange contains many of the characteristics of ostensibly female conversational styles too, such as the repetition of "you know" as a mark of solidarity. The men, in other words, were gossiping. Cameron argues that there is no clear distinction between male and female speech. Instead, "what is important in gendering talk is the 'performative gender work' the talk is doing; its role in constituting people as gendered subjects" (1997, 59). We position ourselves as gendered individuals (men, or women, or non-binary) through our talk, rather than our gender defining how we talk.

This leads us to an important point about the nature of **gender**. A clear assumption in discussions of how men and women talk differently is that there is a binary distinction between men and women. This is not the case at all. At the biological level, there are a host of chromosomal, hormonal, and genital conditions that lead to many people expressing physical characteristics of both sexes; not everyone can be easily sorted into distinct "male" and "female" categories (Fausto-Sterling 2012). Moreover, at a practical level we often base our interactions with others on a surface observation of gendered characteristics: we *read* gender just by looking at people, then treat them accordingly as male or female.

When Mary Bucholtz was doing linguistic research in an American high school, she once caught a student glancing at her from across the classroom. The student was wearing jeans and a T-shirt. No jewellery or makeup. The student had long hair, but both male and female classmates had long hair. "It was only when Ms. Stein introduced me to the class and the teenager turned fully toward me, caught my eye, and smiled broadly that the ambiguity was resolved. With a clear view of her face, I could see that the friendly student was a girl" (Bucholtz 2011, 139).

Note Bucholtz's almost palpable sense of relief, almost as if now she had all the information she needed to be able to engage with this person. We make a range of gendered associations about people based on their appearance, clothing, posture, and so forth. None of this, of course, has anything to do with their biology.

An important corollary to this idea of reading gender is that patterns of gender are not straightforward or instinctive; we also *perform* our own gender through a range of practices such as clothing, hairstyle, makeup, bodily comportment, and especially language (see Chapter 6 – Social Identity and Performativity). As the French feminist Simone de Beauvoir famously remarked, "One is not born, but rather one becomes, woman" (2011, 283). Gender can also be expressed in a multitude of ways that do not conform to the standard male/female binary, including travesti in Brazil, Two-Spirit in North America, hijra in India, kathoey in Thailand, fa'afafine in Samoa, and many others.

In this chapter we look at the complicated role sex and gender play in language. We will start with the recognition, beginning in the 1970s, that language itself is gendered and how that initially cast attention on how women use language differently from men. Before long, linguistic anthropologists began to point out that gender (and gender differences in language) vary cross-culturally. At the same time, scholars started to recognize that gender is not just about women: all people do the kind of "performative gender work" Cameron mentioned above, including men, genderqueer and transgender people, and so on. But let's go back and start with how people came to realize that language is not a gender-neutral system.

FROM WOMEN'S LANGUAGE TO GENDERED LANGUAGE

Until the 1970s very few scholars had paid much attention to the relationship between gender and language. That decade, however, saw both the growth of the feminist movement and more women becoming prominent within the field of linguistics. One of those was Robin Lakoff at the University of California, Berkeley, who published a short book in 1975 entitled *Language and Woman's Place*. It leads with the phrase, "Language uses us as much as we use language" (1975, 1). Lakoff's book considered how dominant gender ideologies shaped the ways women talked at the time. Some of the characteristic features of women's speech that she pointed out are:

- Hedges and fillers – phrases like "sort of" and "you know" that soften the impact of declarative statements
- Tag questions – confirmation-seeking questions at the end of statements, such as "That looks nice, doesn't it?" or "Cold in here, isn't it?"
- Euphemism – using words like "fudge" or "goodness" instead of swearing
- Lexical choices – use of specific colour terminology like "mauve" or "lavender," or feminized adjectives like "divine" or "lovely"
- Compound requests – asking "Could you please close the door?" instead of just saying "Close the door"
- Uptalk – a rising intonation on statements or responses such as "Dinner will be ready at seven" or "I can finish that by tomorrow" so that they sound like questions

There are many others that Lakoff cites; the fact that some of them feel very outdated also speaks to how rapidly language can change (for instance, Lakoff remarks that the phrase, "she is a professional" intrinsically leads people to consider the woman a sex worker). At the same time, however, Lakoff asks us to consider how the features of speech noted above reflect the roles, authority, and equality of women in society. The pragmatic effect of hedges, tag questions, compound requests, and so forth, Lakoff argues, is to minimize the force of women's speech and relegate them to the roles of polite helper and quiet supporter; to be "ladylike" rather than independent social actors (Lakoff 1975). While women could choose not to adopt these speech patterns, they risked being labelled as socially inappropriate and nonconforming. Later researchers have called Lakoff's approach to language and gender the **dominance model** because it shows the ways in which society uses language to control and subordinate women.

The idea that women employ discourse features that are distinct from those used by men was taken further – and popularized to a wider audience – by the linguist Deborah Tannen in her book *You Just Don't Understand* (1990). Her argument was that women not only use different discourse features, but that the opposing conversational styles of men and women are a source of misunderstanding between the genders. You can see an echo of this in the *Men Are from Mars, Women Are from Venus* book cited at the beginning of this chapter. Using numerous anecdotes of the differences between how men and women communicate – such as the idea that men gather to talk about sports, while women gossip with each other – Tannen argues that children are socialized to gendered norms of conversation at a young age. These conversational norms are markedly different: men, she argues, prioritize negotiating status and maintaining it in a conversation, while women prioritize creating meaningful connections with each other.

The labels Tannen gives to these different styles are **rapport-talk** and **report-talk**. "For most women, the language of conversation is primarily a language of rapport: a way of establishing connections and negotiating relationships. Emphasis is placed on displaying similarities and matching experiences." Men, on the contrary, talk in ways meant to preserve their independence and maintain their social status. "This is done by exhibiting knowledge and skill, and by holding center stage through verbal performance such as story-telling, joking, or imparting information. From childhood, men learn to use talking as a way to get and keep attention" (Tannen 1990, 77).

Nevertheless, people assume that their own gendered conversational norms are universal, and so Tannen contends that men and women rarely realize the differences between the genders. "Because men and women are regarding the landscape from contrasting vantage points, the same scene can appear very different to them, and they often have opposite interpretations of the same action" (Tannen 1990, 38). In contrast to Lakoff, Tannen argues for a **difference model** in which men and women are socialized to different communication styles.

Subsequent research on gender and communication has raised several issues with both Lakoff's and Tannen's models. A few of these are:

- Both presume a binary system of gender which, as we have discussed, oversimplifies the issue.
- Men and women do not necessarily have inherently different approaches to talk, nor do women all share the same communicative inferences and strategies with other women (and men with other men). Can we really presume that people in same-sex relationships *never* misunderstand each other?
- The features of "women's talk" are extrapolated from a very specific racial, geographic, and class setting; it might be more accurate to call this white middle-class North American women's talk.

One further issue with Tannen's work is that she tends to overlook any measure of inequality in gendered relationships; men and women are just different, according to her, and power does not play a role. That goes against years of feminist research on the status of women.

Both of these models therefore appear to oversimplify the relationship between language and gender. If not dominance or difference, how then do we understand the meaning of gendered forms of talk? More recent approaches to gender highlight Judith Butler's idea of performativity (Meyerhoff and Ehrlich 2019). In other words, rather than presuming that men and women are clearly different and then examining the different ways they talk, linguistic anthropologists today look at how we categorize different ways of speaking as masculine or feminine – and the implications for how those categories are ideologically structured – while understanding that everyone is capable of using all of these gendered styles.

BOX 7.1 – DRAG QUEENS AND GENDER PERFORMANCE

One reason that scholars now discuss gender as a kind of performance is because, well, for some groups of people that is the whole point. A good example of this is drag queens. Using clothing, wigs, makeup, and language, drag queens are men who craft an image of exaggerated femininity in public performances. One of the fascinating features of drag is that the performers are not necessarily trying to pass as women. They intentionally mimic the pitch, prosody, and features of women's style as described by Lakoff above. But they do so in an intentionally campy way (blending tacky extravagance with gay-inspired styles) to essentially wink at the audience, never letting them forget it is a man talking.

Rusty Barrett (2017) studied African American drag queens in Houston, describing the predominantly feminine style of their performances. They used standard pronunciations, feminine adjectives, and correct grammar. But at times, a masculine voice might be thrown in for dramatic or humorous effect. In one performance, Barrett shows how the drag queen begins in a high-pitched feminine voice at the start of her show, drops into a masculine voice to swear, and shifts into a Black pronunciation when she jokes about having razor bumps (the ingrown hairs caused by shaving).

Barrett argues that the feminine voice used by drag queens therefore also has racial and class dimensions: it is a stereotypically white women's voice being performed by Black male drag queens. "The white-woman style is used to create specific personas and shifting identities throughout the course of a performance, often interrogating hegemonic assumptions about race and class" (Barrett 2017, 48). The point is not to pass for a white woman, but to highlight the very instability of the gender and racial identities being performed.

For instance, in North America, masculine speech styles (which are not just used by men) are often employed in situations of dominance and hierarchy. Feminine speech styles (which are, again, not just used by women) are used when people want to be helpful and supportive. At the same time, however, these gendered speech styles are not given equal importance: in most cultures, feminine speech styles are seen as less sophisticated, less authoritative, less important than masculine ones.

Gendered Communication in Cross-Cultural Perspective

An important counterpoint to both models noted above are the ways gendered communication is structured in other languages and speech communities around the world. It is simply not the case that women's language is always characterized by hedging or tag questions or passive constructions. In a study of gendered language in Madagascar, for instance, Elinor Ochs discovered that it was men who were expected to be polite and indirect in their speech, while women were characterized as assertive and confrontational. When a man and woman flagged down a car, it was the woman who would step forward to ask for a ride. It was the women who haggled loudly in the market, women who took the lead in disputes. In one case, when a group of boys playing ball damaged a newly painted house, the male owner gently admonished them. But the next day he returned with his wife, who angrily criticized the boys, their parents, and anyone else who would listen. "It was not a shocking encounter as it came from the wife and not the landlord himself. Such a display of anger is permissible, perhaps even appropriate, because it is initiated by a woman" (Keenan 1974, 138).

Men, on the other hand, are expected to be properly demure, passive, and quiet. When men do speak, it is often in a formal, ceremonial style known as *kabary*. This type of speech relies upon elaborate politeness formulae, indirect allusion, and excessive deference. Ochs offers the following translation of a *kabary* performance as an example: "When I ask for the guilt and blame to be lifted from me (for standing here before you), I am not an originator of words but a preserver only of tradition, a successor to my father by accident. And not only this, I am like a small cricket, not master of the tall plant or able to perch on the tip of the tall plant like the *sopanga* cricket, but my destiny is to stay on the ground because I am like the *tsimbotry* cricket, an orphan with no ancestors…" (Kennan 1974, 135). Not exactly the commanding aggressive language that Lakoff and Tannen thought natural to men.

Consider also women's speech styles analysed by Don Kulick in his research in Gapun, Papua New Guinea. If men were, like in Madagascar, expected to remain polite and reserved, women could often be quite vocal in their anger. The epitome of this is a verbal performance known as a *kros*, an epic barrage of "feminine" swearing and invective. Kulick offers the following example from a woman named Sake after she put her foot through the rotting floorboards of her house and turned on her husband: "It's your shame. If you'd been a man, you would have built a house for your wife. You stink stink you stink like an outhouse. If I'd married a man, you would have built me a good house. You're a rubbish man" (Kulick 1993, 527). Again, like in Ochs's example, belligerent language is thought to come naturally to women. Kulick also notes that Sake's *kros* is deliberately loud; her dissatisfaction is broadcast beyond her home and throughout the village, thus adding social stigma to her husband's actions and exhorting him to better perform his role.

Nevertheless, in both of these settings, it is the male speech style that is highly valued. In Madagascar, *kabary* is an elite and highly prized form of communication. Similarly, for the Gapun villagers that Kulick studied, conflicts *should* be resolved through negotiation, compromise, and with goodwill between both parties (Kulick 1993). That process often marginalizes and silences women; a *kros* essentially elevates a woman's voice until it cannot be ignored, but significantly in a way that men perceive as driven by anger and emotion rather than reason and logic. Sake also speaks mainly in the local Taiap language (and its highly expressive vocabulary) while men are more likely to adopt the national language of Tok Pisin.

Although we are often prompted to consider gender as a "natural" construct, with men, driven by their testosterone and violent competition with others, being aggressive and powerful while women are focused more on collaboration and intimacy, these examples highlight the variability of gender identity over time and space. Nevertheless, there is a disturbing tendency for women's talk to be devalued in the public sphere, a dynamic that has been pointed out repeatedly by feminist scholars. As Susan Gal argues, "the strongest form of power may well be the ability to define social reality, to impose visions of the world. And such visions are inscribed in language and, most important, enacted in interaction" (Gal 1995, 178). Gender, as we will see next, is therefore but one more form of power hiding in plain sight.

The Problem of Women's Voices

"The problem of young women's voices is gaining new cultural visibility," writes one author. What is that problem? A "guttural growl at the back of the throat, as a Valley girl might sound if she had been shouting herself hoarse at a rave all night. The less charitable refer to it privately as painfully nasal, and to young women in conversation sounding like ducks quacking." Yikes! Not only are these women squandering their valuable time on all-night dance parties, but their voices apparently sound trivial, insecure, and annoying. You might be asking yourself which sexist commentator was rolling out such stereotypes this time. Would you be surprised to learn it is feminist author Naomi Wolf writing in a major newspaper (Wolf 2015)? Wolf's alarm with women's voices – which she claims are relegating a generation of women to irrelevance – shows us that concerns about gendered language are not just the province of a few male chauvinists being overly fussy; language is part of the broader social construct of gender.

Deborah Cameron (1995) has pointed to the many ways in which our everyday speech is critically examined and regulated, a process she calls **verbal hygiene**. We are admonished to use "good English" in school; our teachers point out our grammar mistakes in writing; we are teased if we pronounce something incorrectly or sometimes even make fun of someone's accent. All these practices act as social interventions in the way we talk, attempts to bring our language in line with some prescribed standard. Cameron argues that feminine speech styles, like the one identified by Wolf above, are quite often the target of such efforts.

To see how this occurs, let's turn first to a discussion of **markedness**. The concept comes from formalist approaches to syntax: a linguistic form is marked when it is distinguished in some way from the norm, or unmarked form. For instance, in English many nouns are marked for plurality and verbs marked for tense:

house (singular)	houses (plural)
finish (present)	finished (past)

The addition of the -s on the end of the word therefore marks the plural and -ed marks the past tense. Similar features mark English verbs as passive (was bitten), or mark pronouns as possessive (their). In more anthropological terms, however, we can say that **marked** forms of language are noticeable; they are different or stand out in some way. **Unmarked** forms of language are generally considered normal and pass without much notice.

English marks many words for gender: an actor is a person who acts, but an actress is specifically a woman who acts. Feminist scholars have pointed out that the male term is often the default term, a decidedly unmarked one that encompasses anyone, while the female term draws attention specifically to the gender of the person. Common depictions of gender on signs, for instance, use an unmarked representation of a human body for men, but women are marked by the addition of feminine clothing (Figure 7.1). Markedness therefore frequently indexes gender. It goes even further than specific words and images; we have been socialized to gender ideologies that manifest themselves in our assumptions about words and speech. Gendered pronouns like "he" and "she" or address terms like "mister" and "madam" are forms of **direct indexicality** – they clearly refer to a gendered person. But far more common are forms of **indirect indexicality** (Ochs 1992). This occurs when we associate the *way* a person talks with a particular gender, such as using any of the forms Robin Lakoff discussed above. A higher pitch indirectly indexes femininity, while assertive talk indirectly indexes masculinity. Think about the implications of this for how we understand and interpret gender and language. A lot of the times when we discuss *language* prescriptively, we are implicating gender indirectly.

Figure 7.1 – Common symbols used for male and female

BOX 7.2 – TRANSGENDER VOICES

Despite a marked bias towards linguistic research on cisgender people (meaning those whose gender identity matches that assigned to them at birth), the growing public recognition of transgender people complicates this picture. For instance, one of the most salient differences between masculine and feminine voices is pitch, with men having lower-pitched voices than women. Lal Zimman (2018) has noted how this presents particular difficulties for transgender people, who are often prescribed speech therapy to bring their existing voice into alignment with their new gender identity while transitioning. There is often tremendous social pressure for people to sound like the gender they appear to be.

But the pitch of transgender voices also has important implications for our study of gender itself. Whereas many scholars believe that gender is deterministic (that our gender at birth determines our voice) and others believe gender is constructed (that we are socialized to our voices through childhood experiences), Zimman argues that trans people (who may have been raised as one gender but successfully transition to another) challenge this overly simplistic picture. Gendered voices "do not always bundle together in normative ways. As is the case with sociolinguistic style more generally, speakers have the ability to combine and recombine stylistic variables in ways that reflect and constitute their complex, intersectional identities" (Zimman 2018). In other words, our understanding of gender as a social process owes a lot to the transgender experience.

Figure 7.2 – Illustration from *Canadian Business* magazine

Source: Reproduced by permission of Peter Arkle

Take vocal fry, for instance – that is the "guttural growl" that had Wolf rolling her eyes (Figure 7.2). You may not recognize the term, but you would probably recognize the sound. Also called creaky voice, **vocal fry** is a distinct low-pitched vibration of the larynx during speech. Think Britney Spears singing "Oops, I did it again" or Kim Kardashian's "you know!" Although sometimes treated as a speech pathology, vocal fry is more of a cultural style adopted by its users. Originally popularized by rap and hip-hop artists in the 1990s, today it is more likely to be associated with the speech of young women (Mendoza-Denton 2011; Yuasa 2010). Many people respond to this vocal phenomenon with disdain: they call it distracting, hard to understand, and even infantilizing (Chao and Bursten 2021). In psychological experiments where people were asked to rate their impressions of different voices, those with vocal fry were rated lower on scales of trustworthiness, competence, and even attractiveness than those without; they were even judged to be less employable (Anderson et al. 2014). The question here is: why?

In order to answer that, it might help to look at a parallel example. In nineteenth-century Japan, universal education was promoted by the state as a distinctly modernizing strategy. This gave birth to a new social type: the *jogakusei* or "schoolgirl" (Inoue 2006). Whereas women were previously bound to the traditional role of wife and mother, education opened up not only opportunities for social advancement but also a new feminine ethos. Schoolgirls abandoned old styles of dress and hairstyle in favour of European ones, and very quickly they developed a new way of talking called *teyo dawa* speech. This new style added sounds with no grammatical content, notably *teyo* and *dawa,* to the end of words, giving them a distinctive pronunciation and feeling. You can see a similarity to the non-standard use of "like" in young people's speech today, as in "That's, like, so cool" (Tagliamonte 2005).

Newspaper articles began to appear in Japan at this time, often written by male intellectuals, decrying the way young women were talking. They urged parents and teachers to criticize this vulgar language and encouraged young women to model traditional morals, behaviours, and speech styles. As Japanese writer Ozaki Koyo wrote in a popular magazine, "Thoughtful ladies must not let a beautiful jewel become damaged or a polished mirror become clouded by using such language" (quoted in Inoue 2006, 58).

Miyako Inoue notes that this linguistic style emerged during a time of intense cultural transformation in Japan: the end of the isolationist imperial period and the emergence of a modern nation. There were acute social anxieties about the loss of tradition, moral decay, and deterioration of social class divisions. These narratives were therefore "symptomatic of a sense of moral panic over social unrest and the collapse of the traditional social order. The commentators felt – or (perhaps more appropriately) 'heard' through their auditory senses – social change coming, not from the top, but from the bottom of society" (Inoue 2006, 59). Such anxieties were displaced onto women, and *teyo dawa* speech simply became a convenient symptom of the fears elite males had for the future of Japanese society.

Ironically, by the 1980s *teyo dawa* speech had become synonymous with traditional Japanese femininity. But as women entered the traditionally male professional workplace and greater attention was paid to gender equality, Japanese women began to abandon *teyo dawa* speech as old-fashioned, overly formal, and meek (Inoue 2006;

Okamoto 1995). Of course, that set off a new round of commentary about the loss of traditional Japanese femininity.

Laura Miller (2008) found a similar dynamic in the development of the *kogal* aesthetic among Japanese women in the 1990s. Kogal style included the adoption of baggy socks, dyed hair, exaggerated makeup, and deliberate tackiness, but also new forms of speech. These included intensifiers like *maji* ("seriously") and *meccha* ("awesomely"). They mixed Japanese with alphabetic letters (such as *chô SW*, meaning "super bad personality"), clipped long words down to new slang phrases (*mendoi* as a short form for *mendokusai* or "pain in the ass") or created new words by adding verb markers to nouns (*uni-ru* means "screwing your face up to look like a sea urchin," a popular pose for kogals during photographs).

Kogals were the target of intense media fascination in the 1990s. They were at once hyper-sexualized but also, like schoolgirls a century earlier, symptomatic of moral decay in Japanese society. "The media's angst over the Kogal is really a battle over the redefinition of the female body display, sexuality, and selfhood" (Miller 2008, 242). Applying this insight to the contemporary debate about vocal fry, we can deduce that concern over this acoustic phenomenon has less to do with women not being understood or sounding ignorant, and more to do with social control. Since vocal fry is associated with lower job prospects, women are told to change the way they talk; no one suggests that the people discriminating against them change their own behaviour. The regulation of women's voices by those with power and authority is therefore just a part of a broader attempt to regulate their bodies, their sexuality, and their virtue.

BOX 7.3 – EROTICIZATION OF WOMEN'S VOICES

In Laura Miller's example, kogals were both eroticized and disparaged in the media. That is a common dynamic in commentaries on women's speech, where femininity is often associated with male desire. Kira Hall's (1995) research on telephone fantasy line operators shows how women often exploit and even commercialize that desire. In the pre-internet era of the 1990s, a lot of men turned to phone sex lines where they could listen to racy stories or talk explicitly about their sexual fantasies with women, paying a standard rate for each minute they were on the line. The operators who catered to these fantasies therefore had to craft personae and performances that would keep their clients on the phone as long as possible.

Hall describes how the operators adapted their speech to idealized notions of womanhood and femininity. For instance, operators would speak in a soft, breathy voice, employ the types of complex colour terminology Robin Lakoff identified (saying their lingerie was "charcoal-coloured" rather than black) and would employ highly feminized adjectives and intensifiers (like "lusty imagination" or "great little halter top"). Doing so tended to stretch out their performances, but also appealed to their listeners by "producing a language that adheres to a popular male perception of what women's speech should be: flowery, inviting and supportive" (Hall 1995, 201).

The catch, of course, was that these fantasies were all staged. Most of the phone sex operators, often highly educated women, were just trying to make a decent living in tough economic circumstances. And not all of them were women either: one of Hall's informants was Andy, a Latino male who posed as a straight woman for his callers. All the operators recognized the contrived nature of their interactions and the irony of selling their oppressed femininity back to a captive audience of men. As one woman noted, she was not doing phone sex but "*auditory improvisational theatre on the theme of eros*" (Hall 1995, 204).

LANGUAGE AND MASCULINITY

You could be forgiven, at this point, for thinking that the study of gender is really just the study of women. That's how markedness works; you notice the marked category first. But it would be a mistake to limit our investigation to only one gender. Consequently, in recent years, there has been significant attention paid to language and masculinity to complement the research on women we have examined so far. One of the key insights from this work is the understanding that while femininity may be marked, masculinity – which, again, is often perceived as normative and natural – is just as much a performative and linguistic construct. This is particularly important when many aspects of toxic masculinity ("locker room talk" about women, for instance) are positioned as customary and acceptable in popular discourse.

BOX 7.4 – THE SOCIAL FUNCTIONS OF GENDERED DISCOURSE

We have discussed how various forms of speech act as indirect indexes of gender, but linguists also recognize that they do much more than that. People speak that way for a reason! It just so happens that many gendered forms of talk have a conversational purpose: helping others interpret our intentions, creating empathy, securing a turn to talk, and so forth. Let's look at two, one from a study of women, and one from a study of men.

Uptalk: "I'm really stressin' about it?"

Uptalk is a stressed intonation rise in sentences that are not actually questions and, like vocal fry, is frequently evident in the speech of young women. Although often evaluated as hesitant and unassertive, linguist Cynthia McLemore (1991) found numerous conversational purposes for uptalk when she studied speech in a Texas sorority.

In one example, a sorority member addressed a group of her sisters about a controversy in the house [uptalk is in bold]:

"I KNOW that I always tried to do a pretty good **job** of bein' dis**creet** about it? An' I think that it's **up** to people to be really disc**reet**?"

Here the speaker is trying to elicit confirmation and agreement from her audience, and uses uptalk extensively to do so. The women in McLemore's study also used uptalk when they wanted to secure a turn to speak, gain approval, or assert consensus about a topic.

One final purpose for uptalk was to make requests feel less confrontational:

"We have a rush event this **Thursday**? And everyone needs to **be there**?"

Women joining the sorority (called pledges) were socialized into these patterns by more senior members. McLemore also noticed that uptalk was used less frequently outside the sorority house than within, especially when addressing men. Therefore, uptalk was about more than just phrasing statements as questions. It made the women feel involved with the sorority, part of a collective, and developed a sense of sisterhood with each other.

Bro-talk: "Dude, this class is soooo boring."

When Scott Kiesling (2004) asked his students to collect information on "dude," he found that while everyone used the word, it was predominantly found in speech between men, especially as a greeting ("Hey dude" or "What's up dude?"). In other contexts, it was used to signal that the speaker was teasing ("Dude, that's just not cool") or to make statements less direct ("Dude, turn signal!").

However, dude's most important function was to establish a conversational stance of what Kiesling calls "cool solidarity," a sense of friendship and affinity with others, but in an aloof and casual manner. When one man was talking about his love of a particular drinking game, another responded:

"Everybody plays that damn game, dude."

This shows the speaker's agreement with the statement, but in a relatively nonchalant and detached manner.

Kiesling argues that cool solidarity is important for young men because there is a contradiction in contemporary Western heterosexual identity. Guys want to have close friendships with other guys, but homosexuality is often treated as a non-masculine, taboo status. The contemporary discourses of masculinity "simultaneously demand masculine solidarity, strict heterosexuality, and nonconformity" (Kiesling 2004, 282). "Dude" lets guys be close, but not too close.

Along with other terms like "bro" and "man," dude allows young men to navigate these complicated social requirements. It also shows that, far from being the natural form of identity, masculine heterosexuality requires purposeful and diligent performance to pull off.

Masculinity is more than just the domain of people who identify as male. "Men and masculinities," writes the linguist Scott Kiesling (2007, 655), "are different things, and while they are connected, all things that men do are not masculine, and all things masculine are not necessarily done by men." Men who do not speak in a stereotypically manly way can find themselves being ridiculed, marginalized, and derided as "gay" no matter their actual sexual orientation. In other words, men are also subjected to forms of verbal hygiene if their speech practices fall outside a normative range of acceptable behaviours and features.

Masculinity therefore does not exist in a vacuum; it is critically linked to the idea of heterosexuality as the norm. Discourse among men can often highlight a presumably shared heterosexual desire. Donald Trump's infamous Hollywood Access tape, in which he was recorded on a bus boasting of his attempts to sexually assault women, shows the role such discourse plays in male bonding: "You know I'm automatically attracted to beautiful – I just start kissing them. It's like a magnet. Just kiss. I don't even wait. [laughter from other men] And when you're a star they let you do it. You can do anything." Deborah Cameron notes how Trump uses this boasting with his audience of other men to forge relations between them. "Like the sharing of secrets, the sharing of transgressive desires, acts and words is a token of intimacy and trust. It says, 'I am showing that I trust you by saying things, and using words, that I wouldn't want the whole world to hear'" (Cameron 2016). The role of women here (as objects of heterosexual desire) is secondary to the interpersonal function of the banter that elicits laughter and tacit agreement from the other men participating in the conversation (Coates 2013). And it is also that objectification of women that reinforces the sexual inequality of society.

BOX 7.5 – MASCULINITY AND LAW ENFORCEMENT

The circulation of gendered ideologies of masculinity, particularly in relation to various professions, can serve to exclude women from established networks that are dominated by men and make their entrance into such social worlds more difficult. One area where this is apparent is in the field of policing, which, although open to both men and women, perpetuates discourses that centre on the physicality and toughness required to do the job.

Bonnie McElhinny, a linguistic anthropologist at the University of Toronto, collected stories told by police officers in Pittsburgh about times when they used physical force. Such narratives of policing, offered by both male and female officers, promote a view of society as rooted in conflict and violence (McElhinny 2003). One way of dealing with such conflict was to adopt a professional, no-nonsense, tough-talk demeanour. Female police officers reported deliberately avoiding the display of emotions (such as by smiling). One female officer named Cissy described how she reacted to a situation in which people were not cooperating with her. "It was funny cause they would see two females come down in the car and it was like, 'We're not afraid of you' so you kinda had to get real hard-nosed with them at first" (McElhinny 2003, 273). In her telling, Cissy and her partner aggressively confronted the women, who then realized "those girls are CRA:zy" and became more deferential. Female police officers thus often feel obliged to accommodate themselves to masculine behaviours and speech styles as part of their professional identity.

The construction of masculinity through language does not in itself constitute a negative or anti-feminist performance; in many contexts it can act as a way to deal with feelings of isolation and alienation. Darren Byler (2021), for instance, writes about the experiences of Muslim Uyghur men living in western China. Over the past decade, this group has come under increasing surveillance and control by the Chinese state, with over a million interned in "re-education camps." Those that remain have difficulty finding jobs or social stability; they are always under threat of being investigated and detained. This leads to feelings of extreme insecurity and dispossession, especially among men who are more likely to migrate for labour and be cut off from ties to their home villages. To survive, they must assimilate not only to Chinese cultural norms (by shaving their beards and avoiding religious activity), but also to the use of Mandarin Chinese in urban spaces.

As Byler shows, one of the ways that young Uyghur men contest this challenge to their masculinity is through storytelling in the Uyghur language, both in mediatized form (through novels) and in friendships with other men. Narratives of avoiding police violence or shared cultural traditions create a sense of camaraderie among the men, who recognize their own experiences in the stories of others. Through stories told in the Uyghur language, their sense of vulnerability disappeared and allowed them to feel empowered and secure, if only for a little while (Byler 2021).

CONCLUSION

For just $2,595 the American Management Association (AMA) offers a two-day Assertiveness Training for Women in Business seminar. You can learn how to speak with confidence, respond to criticism, and say "no" without hesitation. As their website notes, "With these skills, women can feel secure that they are sending the right signals that elicit the right responses. They will help you command respect while being respectful and handle almost any situation you're likely to encounter without seeming overbearing" (AMA 2023).

Underlying the description of AMA's workshop are a number of assumptions. Presumably without the benefit of this seminar, women will be unable to send the right signals, be unable to say "no," and be perceived as both unsure and overbearing at the same time! The association offers no complementary seminar for men, which implies that these qualities come naturally to them – who needs to be taught what you know by instinct, right?

By now you should be able to realize that these ideas about women's language are really ideologies about gender. They are pervasive, not just in our own societies but around the world, and they shape how we perceive, understand, and interact with the variously gendered individuals we encounter everyday. So, the next time someone rolls their eyes about women gossiping or shakes their heads at those guys talking about sports, remember that these are not neutral interpretations of communicative behaviour. They are laden with values, stereotypes, and ideologies which we recognize and perform as we present ourselves to the outside world in some distinctively gendered way.

BOX 7.6 – RESEARCH SPOTLIGHT: JIE YANG

Yang, Jie. 2007. "Zuiqian 'Deficient Mouth': Discourse, Gender and Domestic Violence." *Gender and Language* 1 (1): 107–18.

What is the source of gendered violence? That is an incredibly pressing concern, especially in China where reported rates of domestic violence have increased almost 1,700 per cent in recent years! In this article, Jie Yang tries to connect the broader social causes of violence (such as poverty and gender discrimination) with an analysis of language ideologies surrounding how women in China speak. Yang focuses here on one particular gendered language ideology, the idea of *zuiqian*, which can be translated as "deficient mouth" but connotes a sense of someone who cannot control their tongue, who speaks out of turn or without care.

A professor of anthropology at Simon Fraser University, Yang studies how everyday power in China is applied through the ways people use language, examining such diverse fields as the beauty industry and psychotherapy. This article is rich in ethnographic detail, and she interviews both battered women and members of women's organizations who are meant to support them. It might help to understand some concepts before reading the article, such as **metapragmatic discourse** – this simply describes how people assess the speech of others, such as commentary on how people should speak or, in this case, what kind of talk might prompt men to beat their partners. Yang also employs the terms anatamo-politics and biopolitics; these are a little advanced for our purposes but basically refer to the ways a state attempts to regulate and manage the bodies of its citizens (through public health initiatives or quarantine policies, for instance). Understanding the theory is not, however, essential to understanding her argument.

The discourse of *zuiqian* in China, which tries to explain domestic violence as a product of how some women talk (too much, too loudly, or about topics that are too trivial), places the responsibility for that violence squarely on the woman's shoulders. As one female leader told a worker suffering violence at home: "Don't argue with him. Don't complain." Women, in other words, were told to first regulate the ways they talk in order for them to be deserving of support from social and legal institutions. As Yang writes, "When a talking mouth becomes a modality to regulate women, the politics of gender is then played out in biological terms" (Yang 2007, 111).

Discussion

1. Proponents of sex differences in language frequently point to biology: the brains of men and women are just wired differently. Men's brains tend to be bigger, have more higher ratios of white to grey matter, greater intercerebral connectivity, and so forth. A recent review of neuroscientific research, however, finds that nearly all of these differences are merely a product of men's larger average body size. "Rather," the authors write, "a picture is emerging not of two brain types nor even a continuous gradient from masculine to feminine, but of a multidimensional 'mosaic' of countless brain attributes that differ in unique patterns across all individuals" (Eliot et al. 2021, 690). So why do we consistently find claims about differences between the male and female brain (that presumably make men better at reading maps and women at reading people)? What is the attraction of a biological explanation for gendered differences in language?
2. Elinor Ochs famously wrote, "Gender ideologies are socialized, sustained, and transformed through talk, particularly through verbal practices that recur innumerable times in the lives of members of social groups" (Ochs 1992, 146). Think about how the people around you talk: what kinds of gender ideologies are created through the ways they interact?
3. One of the things we have learned in this chapter (and in others) is that gender ideologies can be communicated in subtle ways that, on the surface, have nothing to do with language. Have you ever been told to "calm down"? Who said it to you and in what context? On the other hand, who among you has been told to "man up," and how is that phrase used in context?
4. In the 2023 NCAA women's basketball championship final, the LSU Tigers beat the Iowa Hawkeyes 102 to 85. But that victory was overshadowed by reporting of how Tigers forward Angela Reese waved her hand in a "you can't see me" gesture while trash-talking Hawkeyes guard Caitlin Clark. Reese was attacked over social media as "classless" and not acting "gracious" in her victory. Clark stepped up to defend Reese, saying that men always trash talk other players and women should be able to do the same. What role did gender play in this incident? Based on what you've learned in this chapter, why are female athletes held to a higher standard of decorum than men?

8

Raciolinguistics

Topics

- Race and ethnicity as social constructed categories
- African American Language
- Covert racist discourse
- Interethnic communication

Over 50 years ago, the Afro-Caribbean intellectual Frantz Fanon pointed out an equivalence between language and race: "The Negro of the Antilles will be proportionately whiter – that is, he will come closer to being a real human being – in direct ratio to his mastery of the French language… A man who has a language consequently possesses the world expressed and implied by that language" (Fanon 1967, 18). Born a French citizen in the colony of Martinique, Fanon nevertheless always felt ambivalent about his language and his status as a Black man speaking it. This quote therefore points to his own fractured sense of identity. On the one hand, his ability to speak French gave him access to French society, but on the other, as a Black man, he would never be fully accepted.

In a similar vein, Cécile B. Vigouroux (2017) has charted the circulation of the phrase *y'a bon* in France (roughly "there's good") as a reflection of the alleged deficiencies of African speakers of French. *Y'a bon* is from a fictitious variety of French fabricated in the 1930s to facilitate communication between French officers and African soldiers recruited into the army – its derogatory nature is perfectly captured by its name, Petit Nègre. The attempt probably confused the soldiers more than anything, but over time the variety was popularized in France through children's media like the Tintin comic books, popular novels, travelogues, and even advertisements. The popular chocolate drink brand Banania featured an African soldier on its packaging exclaiming "y'a bon" until the 1960s. These pervasive representations in French popular culture have contributed to enduring language ideologies that characterize French as a refined language and portray African speakers, regardless of their actual proficiency, as linguistically and culturally inferior.

"Language," writes linguistic anthropologist Mary Bucholtz, "is often overlooked as an analytic concern in research on race, yet it is nonetheless central to how race is culturally understood" (2011, 5). There are two elements of race entwined together in these examples. First, certain linguistic forms index certain racial identities. *Y'a bon* in French points us towards a Black identity, no matter the actual race of the person speaking it. In Fanon's quote above, French is a white language despite Fanon's own status as a Black man, and many features of language can point a listener towards assuming a Black or Latino or Asian identity for the speaker based on what they hear. Forms of speech such as accent, vocabulary, syntax, and so forth act as emblems of racial categories and therefore slot speakers into one of a variety of racialized types. In a very real sense, we *hear* race in ways that are similar to how we *see* race (Rosa 2019).

Second, the inverse of this is also true: certain racialized bodies are associated with certain languages, to the point they appear to become natural properties of them. We expect people to speak a certain way based on phenotypic features like their skin colour. See how, for instance, this advertising billboard uses racialized bodies to represent the language it is marketing: the mostly white bodies actively index the authenticity of the language being taught (Figure 8.1). Many people of colour who grew up in English-speaking countries have also heard someone offer them the supposed compliment of "you speak English so well," a phrase that calls out their skin colour while questioning their status as legitimate speakers of English. Recalling our discussion of markedness in Chapter 7 – Language and Gender, we can see how a phrase like this marks fluent English as unexpected or surprising due to someone's physical appearance.

Another example can be found in a 2007 comment by Senator Joe Biden (later US President) when he was contesting Barack Obama for the Democratic nomination. Of his opponent, he said, "I mean, you got the first mainstream African American who is articulate and bright and clean and a nice-looking guy." Although likely intended as a compliment, use of the word "articulate" also marks Obama's race through language (Alim and Smitherman 2012). As journalist Lynette Clemetson (2007) explained in *The New York Times*, "When whites use the word in reference to blacks, it often carries a subtext of amazement, even bewilderment… it suggests that the recipient of the 'compliment' is notably different from other black people."

Figure 8.1 – Advertising for Yinglun Foreign Language Training School in Shenyang, China
Source: Photograph by Eric Henry

Clearly language is entangled with race in a multitude of complex ways. **Raciolinguistics** is a scholarly approach that attempts to destabilize common ideologies around language and race. As Jonathan Rosa and Nelson Flores (2017, 622) write in an article outlining this perspective, "Rather than taking for granted existing categories for parsing and classifying race and language, we seek to understand how and why these categories have been co-naturalized in particular societal contexts, and to imagine their denaturalization as part of a broader structural project of contesting white supremacy on a global scale."

This chapter therefore challenges all of us to examine our assumptions and ideologies about race as they manifest themselves in and through language.

WHAT IS RACE?

People have always recognized the physical differences of others, particularly when travel or population movements brought new groups into contact. But the idea of distinct, structured, and most notably *hierarchical* differences among human groups centred around biological distinctiveness is actually a fairly recent invention. "Scientific racism and the folk ideology that informed it had their beginnings in the age of European expansion, when exposure to greater degrees of human physical and cultural variation increased dramatically" (Harrison 1995, 51). In fact, anthropology played a role in this: as a science of human diversity, many early anthropologists were interested in attributing social differences to biological origins. Anthropologists measured bones, analysed faces, and filled skulls with sand to calculate brain capacity, but could find no diagnostic that reliably sorted a person into one race or another; in fact, they were so bad at finding correlations that many just fudged the numbers until they found what they were looking for (Gould 1981). It was only in the early twentieth century with Franz Boas's (1940) pioneering critique of scientific racism that anthropology as a discipline began to gradually abandon such a position.

Yet, we have become accustomed to thinking we can find race in our genes. Commercial ancestry tests tell us we're 23 per cent African or 11 per cent Chinese. But race just doesn't work that way (these tests look at the percentage of similarity between your DNA and a reference sample, but the similarities may be due to a range of factors other than ancestry). Indigenous scholar Kim TallBear (2013, 518) argues this perspective "informs research questions and methods that sort and delineate peoples into *genetic populations* in ways that oversimplify entanglements of biology and peoplehood." Ultimately, the genetic diversity *within* human groups is far greater than the average differences *between* groups; at a genetic level, race just doesn't make sense (Fuentes 2012; Marks 2017).

Race is therefore not about biology, but about the ways our perceived biological differences are interpreted at a social level. Whether your heritage is from Africa or New Guinea, you are positioned as Black within the racial dynamics of white North American society, while groups that might once have been considered non-white or problematic in the past – in 1924 the United States restricted immigration from countries such as Italy, Russia, Spain, and Poland – have been assimilated to whiteness today (Ignatiev 1995; Ngai 2004). Racial categories are also not universal, but instead expressed in different ways across the world; ideas about race in China are markedly different from ideas about race in Canada (Dikötter 2015). This is all to say that what *appears* on its surface to be a relatively straightforward classification (such as when you are asked to list your "race" on a census) is actually ambiguous and fraught with histories of colonialism, exploitation, and marginalization (Alim, Rickford, and Ball 2016; Reyes and Lo 2009).

Racialization and Ethnicization

Linguistic anthropologists generally do not accept race as an objective fact but rather as an ongoing and emergent social process, which turns our attention to how race is an identity *produced* in interaction with others. Sociologists Michael Omi and Howard Winant (1986) put forward the concept of **racialization** in the 1980s to describe how racial categories are projected onto various groups of people. Linguistic anthropologist Bonnie Urciuoli (1996) extended this idea to the realm of language. In particular, she looked at Puerto Ricans in the United States, who are often negatively portrayed as poor, uneducated, and resistant to assimilation. These values were then transplanted to evaluations of their language: the continued use of Spanish was interpreted as stubbornness, but whenever they spoke English, it was called broken or unintelligible. "Racializing discourses equate language difference with disorder, with images of illiterate foreigners flooding the United States and refusing to speak English or hordes of the underclass speaking an accented English with 'broken' grammar and 'mixed' vocabulary" (Urciuoli 1996, 18). In other words, people became stereotyped by their language, and their language indexed social stereotypes.

BOX 8.1 – RACIST ZOMBIES! RACIALIZATION IN COMEDY

Keegan-Michael Key and Jordan Peele are a sketch comedy team who often address issues of race and racialization. In one of their sketches, two men are trapped in a zombie apocalypse, and their route to safety must take them through a crowd of wandering zombies. "We gotta go through 'em," says Peele, "Just stay together, keep moving, and don't get bit." But as they race through the mass of zombies, they start to realize something is off: none of the zombies seem interested in biting them. As Peele reaches out to one, she jerks backwards. Some zombies in a car lock their doors, and a family of zombies pull their daughter back from her targets. Did you guess that Key and Peele are Black?

To understand racialization, we have to ask ourselves: at what point did this sketch go from two men running away from zombies to two *Black* men running away from zombies? The answer lies in the reactions and interactions between the groups. In other words, Key and Peele were racialized through the actions of the zombies towards them that slotted them into the category of Black men.

All ends well, however, as Key and Peele find another group of Black folks hosting a barbecue in their backyard ("these racist zombies are leaving us alone!") and join the party.

Another way that we often talk about the differences among human populations is through the term ethnicity. If race is a way of classifying people based on perceived biological differences, **ethnicity** is a way of classifying people on the basis of perceived cultural differences. This would presumably eliminate the kinds of racial prejudice outlined above, but even here, ethnicity represents an ideological process. In the 1960s, anthropologist Frederik Barth (1969) argued that ethnicity is also not an objective category but an identity that social groups perform in order to differentiate themselves from others. Urciuoli contrasts the process of racialization with a parallel one of **ethnicization** – this describes how ethnic categories are projected onto various groups of people based on such things as language and cultural practices. But if racialization highlights disorderly forms of social difference, ethnicization offers an apparently benign alternative. "In ethnic discourses, cultural difference is safe, ordered, a contribution to nation-state offered by striving immigrants making their way up the ladder of class mobility" (Urciuoli 1996, 16). Ethnicization includes cultural festivals, folk traditions, and traditional costumes – it is the celebration of heritage but in a way that does not threaten the status quo. Ethnicization is also dependent, Urciuoli argues, on communities managing their linguistic difference and people learning to speak in an unmarked fashion.

BOX 8.2 – ETHNICITY AND THE TIGER MAMA

In 2011, Yale law professor Amy Chua published *Battle Hymn of the Tiger Mother*, which begins, "A lot of people wonder how Chinese parents raise such stereotypically successful kids. They wonder what these parents do to produce so many math whizzes and music prodigies, what it's like inside the family and whether they could do it too" (2011, 3). Chua then goes on to describe a strict regime of parenting in which schoolwork always comes first, an A– is a bad grade, and children should never be praised in public. Has this cultural pattern of parenting been responsible for the status of Asians as a "model minority"?

The idea that Asians are naturally good at math and science is actually a harmful stereotype that places extreme pressures on many students of Asian heritage (Bucholtz 2009). It also ignores the role that economic factors, such as class, have in social mobility. Amy Chua's daughter secured a clerkship with a Supreme Court Justice – but was this a result of Chua's parenting practices, or the fact that she and her husband are both law professors at Yale? The Tiger Mama phenomenon is thus a clear example of an ethnicizing discourse that ascribes material success to cultural forms of difference.

A good example of how these processes work in practice comes from the work of Stanton Wortham and his colleagues on the racial dynamics in an east coast American suburban community they call Marshall. A mixed-race neighbourhood, Marshall has seen tremendous growth in its Latino population over the past 20 years. During the time of their research, there was a string of "payday muggings": people robbed outside cheque-cashing stores on paydays. The researchers collected both media and in-person discussions of these crimes from a variety of Marshall residents, and they found that, through narratives of the events, people often imputed a range of racial identities, characteristics, and motives to others (Wortham et al. 2011). The stance any particular person took towards this issue was often a product of their own racial positioning.

White narrators, for instance, often used the crimes to comment on racial tensions in the community. The victims were nearly always described as undocumented Mexican migrants, using the cheque-cashing stores because they could not open a bank account. They were deemed helpless and vulnerable, "afraid" of reporting the mugging and "easy prey" for criminals. The perpetrators, on the other hand, were identified as Black, and the stories highlighted the callousness and brutality of their crimes. The muggers were called "crack heads" who attack their victims "like lions on lambs." These narrators also positioned themselves as concerned observers of the events through a type of grammatical construction called the "get-passive" ("he *got* mugged" instead of "he *was* mugged"), which highlights the victim's lack of control. In this way, Latinos were racialized as passive, victimized, and unwilling to stand up for themselves. Black people were racialized as violent drug addicts, savage, and dangerous.

In contrast, the stories told by Mexican narrators, using predominantly Spanish, altered many of these racial attributes. The motivation for the crimes was more likely to be ascribed to resentment towards Latinos by other minorities in the community ("they don't like Mexicans because they see us as really low") (Wortham et al. 2011, E70). They also took a more active stance, underlining how people resisted or fought back against the muggers. Two groups of narrators, white and Mexican, therefore used these stories of muggings to portray people as belonging to particular racial types: a summary of these can be found in Table 8.1. We can see how, through storytelling, the ostensible "facts" of these muggings became clear to members of the community (that they happen to Mexicans who are undocumented and cannot have bank accounts; that the criminals are violent gang members). People were slotted into varying racial types with certain attitudes, dispositions, and natures. Meanwhile, Mexican narrators also contested their own racialization as hapless victims, advancing an ethnicizing discourse of themselves as hardworking and family-oriented ("we came to work and to have a better future"). "These stories," the researchers write, "help Marshall residents make sense of each other at a time of rapid demographic change" (Wortham et al. 2011, E57). Racialization and ethnicization are twinned discursive processes through which races, cultures, and their languages become legible to people as a form of social knowledge.

Table 8.1 – Racializing Discourses Surrounding Payday Muggings

White Narrators		
Group	Narration	Social Type
Mexican	"people know that Mexicans can't have bank accounts, so they carry cash"	undocumented/illegal aliens, passive victims
Black	"It's like lions on lambs. Four to five African Americans on one Mexican"	violent, dangerous, greedy, gang members
White	get-passive: "they were getting their paychecks cashed and they were getting mugged"	normalized, detached observer, concern for the community
Mexican Narrators		
Group	Narration	Social Type
Mexican	"So we have to walk around carrying something like knives, gun or something"	proud, hardworking, resistant, assertive
Black	"they assault us in the streets whether its verbally or physically"	violent, unpredictable, greedy, racist
White	"Well for me Marshall isn't the best place to live."	indifferent, discriminatory, suspicious

AFRICAN AMERICAN LANGUAGE

Language also plays an important role in racial self-identification – if race is a social phenomenon, it is also one based on ideas of affinity and belonging among groups of people who are racially categorized in the same way. Working in Brazil, for instance, linguistic anthropologist Jennifer Roth-Gordon discusses what she calls "racial strategizing" in Rio de Janeiro, a city where more than half of residents identify themselves as non-white. Race is an enduring problem in Brazil, with many non-white people living in *favelas* or shanty towns, thus perpetuating both racial and economic inequalities: in the words of her informants, "poverty has a colour" (Roth-Gordon 2017, 7). Some choose to lean into a resurgent Black identity: drawing on hip-hop fashions from the United States, they dress in baggy clothes and style their hair in cornrows. Their speech is heavily influenced by *favela* slang. Others attempt to present *boa aparência* or "a good appearance" by dressing more conservatively and speaking more formally, styles associated with the white majority. These strategies demonstrate the malleability of race in the Brazilian context, as people use language, fashion, hairstyle, and so forth to position themselves in varying racial categories as the situation demands.

Language is a powerful component of this racial self-fashioning because language varieties are indexically tied to speech communities. Black people in North America share a form of English, often termed **African American Language** (AAL), that is remarkably consistent across the continent.[1] As linguist Geneva Smitherman writes,

AAL is "a style of speaking English words with Black flava – with Africanized semantic, grammatical, pronunciation and rhetorical patterns." She continues, "It was a language born in the crucible of Black economic oppression: tryna make a dolla outta fifteen cent… This coded language served as a mark of social identity and a linguistic bond between enslaved Africans of disparate socio-educational classes" (Smitherman 2006, 3–4).

One of the most obvious components of AAL is lexical: from "gangsta" to "wack," AAL possesses a range of unique words. Of course, many people who are not Black will use such words too – a great deal of AAL vocabulary and slang has been adopted into mainstream English, often in a way that deracializes its origins (people may call their partner "bae" without realizing the word originated in AAL). As linguist Chi Luu (2020) writes, "All along, while standard American English was busy convincing everyone that it was the superior dialect, it's Black English that's been a true cultural and linguistic force in contemporary society."

However, AAL is about more than just words; there is an entire grammatical system underlying this speech variety. In many settings, in both the United States and Canada, AAL is put down as slangy, unruly, and just a plain incorrect way to talk. People who are considered educated (often white people) are said to speak "proper English" with "proper grammar," and that implies Black people are just not trying very hard. Yet linguists recognize these are language ideologies, and while AAL does not employ the same grammatical system as Standard English, it is still very much a rule-bound system – the rules are just different.

BOX 8.3 – ZORA NEALE HURSTON (1891–1960)

Figure 8.2 – Zora Neale Hurston

Poet, author, playwright, film-maker, and anthropologist Zora Neale Hurston spent her life challenging stereotypes about Black people. Born in Alabama, a grandchild of slaves, Hurston attended Howard University and Barnard College (at the time, she was the only Black student enrolled). There she was influenced by Franz Boas and became one of his graduate students. Beginning in 1928, Hurston conducted fieldwork in Eatonville, Florida, and became a collector of Black folklore, stories, and narratives.

Although most publishers at the time avoided works on the Black experience in America, Hurston eventually published seven books. Her ethnographic studies of Black communities recounted the speech of her interlocutors as it was spoken, rather than in whitewashed Standard English. "What you mean, Zora," asked a former neighbour named B. Moseley when she told him she was going to record old stories, "them big old lies we tell when we're jus' sitting; around here on the store porch doin' nothin'?" (Hurston 1935, 8). Hurston also conducted extensive interviews with Cudjoe Lewis, one of the last survivors of the Atlantic slave trade; her refusal to revise his speech meant the text was not published until 2018 (Hurston 2018).

Hurston's approach to Black English provides us with a clear historical record of speech practices in early-twentieth-century Black communities. But in many ways, she also wrote as a Black author, pushing back against the objective conventions of scholarly writing: as she explains to her (presumably white) audience, "You see we are a polite people and we do not say to our questioner, 'Get out of here!' We smile and tell him or her something that satisfies the white person because, knowing so little about us, he doesn't know what he is missing" (Hurston 1935, 2).

Take *ain't* for example. In the song "Ain't Got No… I Got Life," the renowned Black musician Nina Simone sings:

Ain't got no home, ain't got no shoes
Ain't got no money, ain't got no class
Ain't got no skirts, ain't got no sweaters
Ain't got no perfume, ain't got no love

Prescriptivists would assert that it should properly be "I don't have a home, I don't have any shoes…" – is ain't even a word? Well first off, ain't makes perfect sense when you look at its development in context. Both "you're not" and "you aren't" are acceptable contractions for the same phrase in Standard English. But with the first-person pronoun, we only have "I'm not" and not "I amn't." Why? The *Oxford English Dictionary* attests several examples of amn't in various regional dialects of English in the seventeenth and eighteenth centuries, but with its two nasal consonants together, amn't is hard to pronounce. Over time, amn't underwent a sound change to become ain't. So if "ain't" ain't right, prescriptivists should also be telling people not to use "aren't" either.

There's one further aspect of Nina Simone's song, and ain't in general, that a lot of English speakers object to, and that's how ain't combines with "no." Both ain't and no are negative, goes the argument, and shouldn't two negatives make a positive, meaning that Simone does have a home and shoes and money? This is, however,

Table 8.2 – Temporal Reference in AAL

Past		Present	Future	
Distant	Immediate		Immediate	Distant
bin	dən	Ø	a-/finna	a-gonna

another example of a language ideology – there is no practical linguistic reason to think that two negations make a positive other than relying on a kind of mathematical metaphor. In fact, requiring the use of no after ain't is an example of negative concord, a grammatical rule in which negation must always be coordinated throughout a sentence (Labov 1972). It is part of Standard French (*je ne parle pas francais* means "I don't speak French," with the two negations underlined), along with other languages such as Portuguese, Greek, Welsh, and Finnish.

In other areas, AAL might even be said to be more detailed than Standard English. Think about how speakers of Standard English indicate the temporal form of actions: they can use the past tense (I walked), present tense (I walk), or future aspect (I will walk) to locate actions in time. Other languages, including AAL, have ways to differentiate the immediate past (meaning not too long ago) from the more distant past (meaning a while back), and the immediate future (soon) from the distant future (later). Lisa Green's (2002) grammar of AAL outlines this complex system (Table 8.2).

The Ø under Present tense means that it is usually not marked in AAL: you don't say "he walks to school" but instead "he walk to school" (using the bare form of the verb in the present tense can also be found in many other English dialects, including Newfoundland English). But note how *bin* (derived from the Standard English word "been") and *dən* (from the Standard English word "done") mark out two different time scales, one more distant and one more immediate (there is no absolute distinction here in terms of time; rather, it is the feeling that something happened either relatively long ago or more recently). The same is true of prefixing verbs with *a-* or *finna* (derived from the expression "fixing to") for things that will happen soon, and *a-gonna* for things that will happen later. Here are some examples:

1. He *bin* a preacher there for like seven years
2. I *dən* made it this far
3. See, I'm *a*-throw another random one out there
4. She's *finna* have a baby
5. That dam *a-gonna* break some day

When non-AAL speakers try to imitate AAL, they often just throw *a-* in front of verbs or randomly drop some consonants (like the *-g* in tryin'). But these structures show us that AAL is not sloppy or lazy English. Instead, it has a clear grammatical system – the rules may be different, but they are still rules (Laneheart 2021; Rickford 2000). Where, then, do our negative ideas about racialized language varieties (and their speakers) come from?

COVERT RACIST DISCOURSE

> "It's terrible! Gas now costs $3.85 a gallon. You know, it's cheaper to have illegal immigrants push your car than to fill your tank."

This is a joke from Jay Leno's *Late Show* monologue on April 27, 2006 (Santa Ana 2009). Is it racist? He did not say anything overtly derogatory or discriminatory about immigrants, yet most people would acknowledge that his comments were in bad taste. Linguistic anthropologist Jane Hill argues one of the dominant English language ideologies in the United States and Canada is something she calls "personalism." This is the idea that "each individual has an invisible interior self which is the site of beliefs and intentions and emotional states… Personalist ideology permits us to say that when a person speaks, he or she 'means' something" (Hill 2008, 88–9). Words are a window into our beliefs, and our beliefs become manifested in words. As a result, she argues, there is a predominant folk theory that identifies racism as a product of racists and their language; bigots who yell out obscenities or call people by derogatory terms.

Our ideas about race, however, often circulate in more obscure ways, like Jay Leno's joke. Hill argues that many racial stereotypes are manifested in what she calls **covert racist discourse**: forms of discourse in which racist ideologies are disseminated in a non-serious or humorous fashion, allowing the speaker to disavow any racist intention (such as by saying, "I was only joking") (see also Pérez 2013). Hill (2008, 42) gives an example of white middle-class speakers saying, "Let's get together and crack a few *cervezas*." Why would non-Spanish speakers pointedly use the Spanish word for beer in this invitation to informally socialize over a few drinks? Hill argues that the choice only makes sense in the context of widespread beliefs that Mexicans are relaxed and casual towards alcohol while white people are sober and formal. Without the stereotype, information about the proposed mood of the engagement would be unavailable to the speakers and the utterance would not make any sense. The performative effect of the joke is to refer back to the stereotype (and perpetuate it), without explicitly saying something racist like "Mexicans are drunkards."

What shared forms of racialized knowledge must we be able to draw upon to "get" Leno's joke about immigrants pushing your car? Sociolinguist Otto Santa Ana (2009) argues we have to know that some Spanish-speaking immigrants to the United States (but by no means even the majority) are undocumented. We must recognize that this lack of official immigration status traps them in a situation of precarious labour where they can be apprehended and deported. We have to realize that this precariousness means they must take on low-paying and marginalized work in order to remain in the United States. And we must understand that this labour is often exploited by American citizens who can hire that labour cheaply because of their marginalized status. All this information is referenced by the joke indirectly without having to say it out loud. Racism is therefore not simply a matter of holding racist beliefs and saying racist things; it is a structural issue that is created and sustained through acts of everyday discourse where "common knowledge" about different races is circulated through speech communities (Mullings 2005).

BOX 8.4 – THE RACIOLINGUISTIC POWER OF MOCKERY

Not all jokes about race are necessarily racist. They can also act as a strategy for what is known in comedy as "punching up" or using humour to make explicit otherwise unrecognized forms of inequality or privilege (Bhargava and Chilana 2023).

Keith Basso (1979) collected many examples of Apaches mocking white people during his fieldwork in Arizona: someone would straighten up their posture, adopt a sharp high-pitched voice and address others in the stereotypical speech of a white doctor or politician. The effect of these joking performances was to contrast an idealized Apache sense of personhood (self-aware, restrained, humble, and generous) with a white one that lacks these qualities (stereotypically self-important, overly talkative, and selfish). Much of the humour in these performances, Basso argues, comes from shared experiences that Apaches have in dealing with whites and the intrusions of outside social and political institutions into their homeland.

Similarly, Korean-American stand-up comedian Margaret Cho often explicitly draws upon stereotypes of Asians in her comedy, using stereotypically mock Asian voicings of various people to poke fun at her culture (Chun 2004). But she often does so in a way that turns the tables on her predominantly white audience as well, asking them to confront their own stereotypes and beliefs of Asian people. "Through this exaggerated style, Cho decontextualizes and critiques stereotypes of Asian women as idealizations of passive, petite, and self-sacrificing femininity" (Chun 2004, 283). Using a term from anthropologist James Scott's (1985) study of class antagonism in a Malaysian village, humour such as this has often been called, a "weapon of the weak," a way to reveal the nature of racial inequality and marginalization by laughing at it.

Another example of covert racist discourse can be found in what Hill calls **mock Spanish**, the use of ostensibly Spanish words and phrases, often in grammatically nonsensical ways, in the speech of non-Spanish speakers. Think of Arnold Schwarzenegger in the 1991 film *Terminator 2: Judgment Day* saying "hasta la vista baby," or an American advertising campaign for a Mexican beer that dubbed it "The Drinko for Cinco" (referring to the Mexican holiday of *Cinco de Mayo*). Much like the use of *cerveza* in the example above, the meaning of these phrases requires access to stereotypes of Latinos as, simultaneously, threatening and laid-back.

But the most revealing aspect of mock Spanish is the way it highlights racial markedness: white people can use mock Spanish in humorous ways, but the public use of Spanish by Latinos is often admonished as "un-American." In 2006, Latino musicians released a Spanish-language version of the US national anthem titled "Nuestro Himno." Unlike previous translations of the anthem into languages such as French and Yiddish, this particular composition provoked significant controversy. President George W. Bush even weighed into the debate, stating his belief that "people who want to be a citizen of this country ought to learn English and they ought to learn to sing the national anthem in English." Tellingly, Bush himself had sung the national anthem in Spanish while campaigning in Texas (Hill 2008, 125). In other words, mock Spanish reveals raciolinguistic ideologies pertaining to power over language: white English speakers can use Spanish in public without censure, while Hispanic people get called out for the same act. Recognizing the ways that racism is created through everyday conversation – and how we are all implicated in a system that perpetuates these ideologies – is really the first step towards dismantling it.

ENCOUNTERS ACROSS RACE AND LANGUAGE

Where these varying racializing and linguistic ideologies meet, interesting things can happen. Racially demarcated speech communities can manifest very different interactional patterns that do not always overlap with those of others. Benjamin Bailey (1997), for instance, looked at conversations between Korean convenience store owners and their customers in Los Angeles. These stores are often sites of interethnic tension, as they predominantly serve customers in Black neighbourhoods. Many of the store owners had been robbed, while customers often felt, in turn, that the stores exploited economically disadvantaged communities. Nevertheless, staff and customers attempted to relate to each other and build community together. In studying these service interactions, Bailey focused on the idea of "respect" and how Koreans and Black people communicated this to each other during their encounters. What is respect, and how does one offer it to others? Again, the specific strategies used are culturally specific.

Have a look at the lyrics from Lil' Wayne's 1999 track "Respect Us."

When I come through bustin'
Everybody on the block be runnin'
Weezy Wayne, Hot Boy I be thuggin'…
I hustle and slang slang
My block I hang hang
Who am I? Lil' Wayne, man

Through his rapping, Lil' Wayne communicates a particularly Black notion of respect. He notes his presence on the block, names himself and his boys, and describes how people react to him. Respect comes from knowing a person, their biography, and their public image, and by recognizing who they are and their place in the community. When Black people came to the store, their conversations were often highly personalized, asking for the Korean cashier's name, volunteering where they lived and what was happening in their lives.

CUSTOMER: Wow you guys moved a lot of things around
CASHIER: Hello, heh heh, how are you?
CUSTOMER: What's going on man? How've you been?
CASHIER: Sleeping
CUSTOMER: eh heh heh
CASHIER: That's it?
CUSTOMER: That's it.

(Bailey 1997, 340)

Notice how, in this interaction, the Black customer and the Korean cashier seem to be talking past each other. The customer makes several conversational openings that attempt to elicit comment from the cashier, such as by stating they have moved things around (and implying that he is therefore a regular customer) and asking how the cashier is doing. The cashier's responses are relatively short and curt, effectively declining to answer or providing only simple responses ("How've you been?" "Sleeping"), which effectively ends the encounter and minimizes further conversation.

Certainly this lack of an effusive response could be a product of the cashier's language abilities in English, but when the cashier interacted with Korean customers, his responses were relatively similar:

CASHIER: *Annyong haseyo*
Hello / How are you?
CUSTOMER: *Annyong haseyo. Tambae*
Hello / How are you? Cigarettes!

CASHIER: *Tambae turyoyo? Yogi issumnida*
You would like cigarettes? Here you are
[Customer turns to leave]
CASHIER: *Annyonghi kaseyo*
Good-bye
CUSTOMER: *Nye*
Okay

(Bailey 1997, 332)

Most interactions between the Korean cashier and Korean customers were minimal like this, even when the two people knew each other.

Bailey argues that the idea of respect in the Korean community is notably different. Respect comes from declining to impose on others, in maintaining a sense of restraint and social distance. Although both participants in the conversations (the Korean cashier and the Black customer) were trying to respect each other, they did so in ways that were interpreted as rude by the other party: Black customers saw these minimal responses as a refusal to engage with them and acknowledge their relationship, while Korean workers interpreted the customer's conversational probing as overly personal and intrusive. Racially marked communication patterns can therefore act as a source of conflict between populations.

In other contexts, however, raciolinguistic encounters can be positive, and even a tactic of solidarity between racial groups. In Britain, Ben Rampton (2009) has extensively studied a phenomenon called **crossing** whereby people adopt language patterns from racialized communities other than their own. This tends to occur in densely multicultural and multilingual settings where people of different backgrounds come together, such as schools. In one example, some middle school students of varying racial heritage – including Afro-Caribbean, South Asian, and white – were relaxing outside the school in a spot where they could not be seen by their teachers, when Colin lit a cigarette:

MASHUK (BANGLADESHI): You get the same t- <u>aah chaa me light it up man</u>
ADRIAN (AFRO-CARIBBEAN): Colin's behind you
ANDREW (AFRO-CARIBBEAN): Wh' Col- where's Colin man I can't-
where's Colin man where's Colin where's Colin?
[smile-voice] <u>aah dere you are</u>
Colin give me a pull please

(Rampton 2009, 159)

In this extract, the students switch back and forth between Standard English and racially marked Caribbean Creole words and pronunciation patterns (underlined above). These are employed both by Andrew, whose heritage is Afro-Caribbean, but also Mashuk, whose family is from South Asia. In other conversations, white students would use a South Asian accent when talking to Punjabi friends, non-white students would switch into posh British English or local Cockney, and all groups would teach each other swear words from their home languages. Rampton argues that these types of crossings work because the children involved are playing around with language in a conversational frame that includes multiple acts of joking and teasing. In other words, these were not performative claims to a particular racial identity, but speech acts that emphasize the students' familiarity and comfort with each other.

BOX 8.5 – THE ETHICS OF PLAYING AT RACE

Not all uses of another racial community's language patterns come from a place of camaraderie and respect. In fact, quite a few attempt to appropriate these language patterns for their symbolic or social value. This is important to point out because, even though people craft their racial identities through language, it does not mean a person can adopt any racial identity at will. That's because many racial communities are grappling with histories of exploitation, colonialism, and racism.

In 2015, the president of the Spokane, Washington, branch of a nationwide advocacy group for African Americans, Rachel Dolezal, resigned after it was revealed that she was not, in fact, Black as she claimed, but of European ancestry. Dolezal did everything Black: she styled her hair in box braids, wore African-patterned dresses, and peppered her social media posts with AAL tokens like "just-sayin." What is it about this case that is different from the speech acts of people of African American heritage?

As several commentators have noted, Dolezal did not just act Black, she co-opted the experiences of Black people, making up claims of racism and exploitation to further her own acceptance (Gaines 2017). Her privilege was that she felt free to racialize herself in ways that would be unavailable to most members of the Black community who cannot be unproblematically accepted as white whenever they want to. As the Black cultural commentator Jamelle Bouie (2015) writes, "She says she's black, but we don't know if she's always black. Is she black when she's purchasing a home? Talking to the police? Or is she black only when vying for a role where lived experience would help her odds?"

In Canada, there has been increasing recognition and criticism of "pretendians," white people who try to pass themselves off as Indigenous, from the scholar Carrie

Bourassa to singer Buffy Sainte-Marie (Kolopenuk 2023). This is a problem not simply of taking resources and opportunities away from actual Indigenous communities, but essentially claiming Indigenous experiences, heritage, and culture (including language) as one's own. Identity constitutes a moral claim to a people and a community, and it is not one that should be made under false pretences.

CONCLUSION

This chapter opened with two related ideologies about race and language: the notion that we can use language to identify a person's race, and that certain languages seem to naturally "belong" to certain types of racialized bodies. Neither of these has any basis in fact, but as we have seen, language and race often seem to constitute each other. We have also looked at the ways language is used to racialize various groups of people, and at the role of language in framing racialized speech communities.

One of the most significant contributions of raciolinguistics to linguistic anthropology is actually in critically analysing our own field. Recalling Frantz Fanon's quote at the opening of this chapter about his ambivalence towards French, Ryoku Kubota (2020) points out that many racialized scholars feel the same way about linguistics. Like anthropology, the field is rooted in colonial structures of knowledge that privilege certain types of scholars and certain types of approaches.

In linguistic anthropology more specifically, Wesley Leonard (2021, 219) challenges the field to be cognizant of "structures of white supremacy in the production, legitimization, and dissemination of anthropological knowledge." For all their liberalism, universities are still predominantly white institutions, and this biases scholars towards forms of knowledge detached from the communities "we" study. Indigenous concepts, in particular, are often treated as amateurish or unsophisticated. In other words, even in the university, racial structures of inequality are perpetuated through institutional means. This has led to some recent moves to de-centre European knowledge and philosophical traditions within disciplines like linguistic anthropology – but there is still a long way to go.

BOX 8.6 – RESEARCH SPOTLIGHT: STEVE BIALOSTOK AND MARCUS WATSON

Bialostok, Steve, and Marcus Watson. 2022. "Older Black Men Playing Dominoes: Talking Shit and Creating Black Place." *Transforming Anthropology* 30 (1): 34–47.

This chapter has dealt with some heavy issues: racism, conflict, ethnic mockery, and so forth. Sometimes it is valuable to read about quieter moments, such as groups of Black men at a community centre in Denver just sitting around a table playing dominoes. That is not to say nothing is going on underneath the surface – far from it, in fact. In this article, Steve Bialostok and Marcus Watson analyse the men's conversations for how they establish and reinforce a Black sense of space in a social world otherwise surrounded by white people. Denver has witnessed decades of redlining and gentrification that have pushed Black people out of the Northeast Park Hill area of the city where the community centre is located. The men, mostly retired seniors who still live in this historic Black community, spend their afternoons playing dominoes and – in their own words – "talking shit" with each other.

What is talking shit? "It generally entails humorous, insulting, entertaining, discursively clever rhetoric peppered with vulgarity. It comes across as frank and self-assertive, providing little to no innuendo and no apologies" (Bialostok and Watson 2022, 37). Although on its surface the talk can appear aggressive, like an attempt to humiliate its target, the authors argue this speech style has to be understood within Black rhetorical patterns that reframe it as a form of play. By pushing the envelope of good taste, the men not only deepen the bonds that link them together, but also carve out a space for themselves as Black men within a changing community.

This article is written in a straightforward style – there isn't a lot of theory or jargon to get bogged down in. Nevertheless, the authors' analysis draws on many of the concepts we have covered in this chapter. They argue that discourse is more than a communicative system; it is also expressive and essential for people crafting their racial identities. Those identities are embedded within the stylistic and grammatical structures of AAL, with ample examples throughout the article. And those conversational styles racialize the speakers as they try to "keep it real" within the spiritual rhythms of a Black existence.

Discussion

1. The only way to make generalizations about racialized language varieties is with good data, and fortunately we are starting to see ready access to data on AAL such as the Corpus of Regional African American Language (CORAAL). If you go to the CORAAL website (http://lingtools.uoregon.edu/coraal/explorer/), you can get access to over 100 hours of audio recordings and transcripts of Black people speaking from across the United States. You can either browse the corpus or search for particular words and features. Have a look through some of the files.

What recurring linguistic features do you see that are characteristic of speech in Black communities?

2. A list of trending words on Twitter from 2014 includes the following slang terms: bae, boolin, litt, rekt, senpai, shordy, and waifu (see Grieve, Nini, and Guo 2018 for a full list). Search the internet for the origins of these words: you might find information from slang archives and etymology sites, and online dictionaries often include dates and examples of early usage. Where do these terms come from? It is often not possible to trace back definitive origins, but you will probably notice a significant influence from AAL (and also Japanese). What accounts for the popular influence of these varieties, and why do you think the racial origins of these words are often erased in the popular imagination?
3. In 2017, the YouTuber Pewdiepie used the freelancing site Fiverr to pay two Indian men to hold up an anti-Semitic banner during a livestream. There was an understandable public uproar, and Pewdiepie ended up responding with he following statement: "I think it's important to say something and I want to make one thing clear: I am in no way supporting any kind of hateful attitudes. I make videos for my audience. I think of the content that I create as entertainment, and not a place for any serious political commentary." In other words, Pewdiepie says the stunt was not intended to be racist; it was a joke. Can you apply what we have learned in this chapter about racialization and covert racist discourse to this incident? How would you critique his response?
4. There is a recurring *Saturday Night Live* sketch called Black Jeopardy! which offers an African American take on the popular game show. Question categories include "Who's try'na" and "Oh snap," and there is usually one contestant who is completely out of their element. One of the interesting aspects of the sketch is the ways in which Black culture is presented, a kind of alternative self-racialization. There's the idea that steak is always cooked well done, people wear church clothes on Sunday, and duct tape is the best tool for fixing you car. In other words, the key linguistic and cultural elements of race are the things familiar to insiders, but which outsiders rarely comprehend. What else might go into such self-racializing discourses?

9
Multilingualism and Globalization

Topics

- Ideologies shaping multilingualism
- Characteristics of multilingual societies
- Languages created by colonialism and contact
- What multilingual speakers do with language

People move around. They travel, they migrate, they settle, sometimes in the next town over, sometimes on the other side of the globe. When they do so, they bring their languages (and all their beliefs, ideologies, and assumptions about language) with them (Blommaert 2010; Heller 2007). When I visited Toronto a few years back, I found you could get an incredible Vietnamese *bánh mì* sandwich, Chinese *huoguo* hotpot, and an amazing Afghan *firini* milk pudding for dessert all within a few blocks. You can also hear Vietnamese, Mandarin, and Pashto being spoken around you. Up to now, a lot of our discussion has assumed that people are speaking *one* language, but we have not looked specifically at how people use *multiple* languages in their daily lives. **Multilingualism** describes the practice of using more than one language on a regular basis. In North America and other English-speaking areas, monolingualism is typically considered the norm. In Canada, for instance, the 2021 census reported that 79 per cent of the population uses only one language at home (Statistics Canada 2023b). In the United States, 78 per cent of the population over the age of five uses only English at home (Dietrich and Hernandez 2022). On a global scale, however, speaking multiple languages is a common fact of life. François Grosjean, a leading French expert on bilingualism, estimates that about half of the global population can speak more than one language (Grosjean 2010, 13).

Indeed, in terms of human history, it is only relatively recently that being monolingual has become feasible – in the past, speech communities were generally more varied and diverse. Part of the development of nationalism in the last few centuries has been a process of language **standardization**, where various social institutions – such as schools, government offices, and publishers – work to define a single version of the language as the correct one. "Standardization allows for the shaping of a nation: by constructing a language to be shared by citizens, it becomes simultaneously possible to draw the nation's borders. Citizens are those who speak the language; noncitizens are those who do not" (Heller and McElhinny 2017, 104). In China, for instance, the government initiated a national language policy in 1956 that promoted the pronunciation, grammar, and writing of the Beijing dialect of Mandarin Chinese as the standard language of the nation (Tam 2017). Educational success and professional employment have all become dependent upon correct use of this national standard; consequently, other Chinese languages such as Cantonese and Shanghainese have declined in use to the point where they may soon be endangered in China (Xu 2021).

This is not to say that monolingualism, with each nation speaking a single language, is an inevitable development. Local forms of variation from the national standard almost always persist, such as Newfoundland English in Canada (Clarke 2010). In addition, patterns of migration in the past few decades have brought new groups of people into contact at an unprecedented scale. Many linguists have noted that traditional ideas of nations as monoethnic and monolingual states have started to break down. In cities like London or Toronto, citizens of diverse places of origin often live close together while new communication technologies connect people transnationally in a way that was not possible before. Anthropologists call this new intersection of transnational migration and global cosmopolitanism **superdiversity** (Vertovec 2007). The effects of these demographic changes on language use around the world have been profound (Blommaert 2013; Silverstein 2015).

BOX 9.1 – NEWFOUNDLAND ENGLISH

The island of Newfoundland, on the eastern coast of Canada, was settled in the eighteenth and nineteenth centuries by Europeans largely drawn from two areas: southwestern England and southeastern Ireland. Most of these migrants arrived to work in the cod fishery, settling in small fishing villages dotting the coastline. Newfoundland was a self-governing colony from 1854 to 1949, after which it became a province of Canada, now called Newfoundland and Labrador.

These conditions, including a common regional origin and relative social isolation, led to the retention of many dialectal features of the migrants' language, creating the distinctive Newfoundland English spoken today (Clarke 2010). Apart from some very noticeable features, such as the use of *b'y* as a term of address, other distinguishing aspects are:

- TH-stopping, which changes the *-th* in words like *with* and *this* into *-t* (*wit*) and *-d* (*dis*)
- Verbal s-marking, which adds an -s sound after present tense verbs, such as "We knows a lot of people out there"
- The after-perfect, as in "I'm after calling him," which is equivalent to "I have been calling him" in Standard English.

With that said, however, there is actually a great deal of regional variation throughout Newfoundland, and a particularly salient difference between urbanites (*townies*) and rural residents (*baymen*). Based on sociolinguistic research, Becky Childs and Gerard van Herk have shown that while some features of Newfoundland English are fading from use, others are resurging in popularity, particularly the s-marked "I loves it" (which acts as a kind of local shibboleth). They argue that Newfoundlanders, particularly townies, can shift in and out of Newfoundland English depending on the situation and whether they want to sound "Newfoundlandy" or differentiate themselves from baymen (Childs and van Herk 2014).

Nevertheless, multilingualism is not an easy phenomenon to pin down. Some children grow up in multilingual households and employ these languages fluently from an early age. Other people learn a second or third language in school, or later in life as an adult. They may live in a place that is suffused with multilingualism, or they may have only a limited circle of other speakers to use that language with. Multilingual speakers may possess varying levels of comfort and fluency in their various languages, sometimes only using them in particular places or for particular purposes. Our understanding of multilingualism must encompass all of these many experiences.

When we turn to the experiences of individual speakers, multilingualism is more than just knowing a multitude of separate languages. Because of standardization, we often think of languages as discrete wholes: *the* English language, for instance. In actual speech, multilingual people blend together a range of different registers, dialects, styles, and genres. Over a hundred years ago, the Soviet linguist Mikhail Bakhtin

Figure 9.1 – Sign outside a holistic animal store in Montreal

Source: Image courtesy of Patricia Lamarre

proposed the term **heteroglossia** to describe this quality of speech, directly opposed to the idea of standardization. "A unitary language," he wrote, "is not something given but is always in essence posited," meaning that the process of codifying and standardizing a language is always an ideological one (Bakhtin 1981, 270).

When people are exercising this creativity in their speech, linguists refer to it as **translanguaging**. Each person has access to a diverse range of linguistic resources, and translanguaging describes how they use them, combine them, and innovate with them as they speak. You can see some of the possibilities in how languages are combined with an example from Montreal where one store plays on the similarities between the English word "paw" and the French *pâtisserie* (pastry shop) in its name (Figure 9.1). As the sociolinguists Li Wei and Ofelia García (2022, 314) write, "the trans- in translanguaging connotes the transcendence of named languages, the going *beyond* named languages as have been socially constructed." This perspective focuses attention on multilingualism as a form of doing, with speakers drawing upon the full range of linguistic resources available to them in order to communicate with others.

In this chapter, we look at multilingualism from a variety of perspectives to understand how it shapes the linguistic and social environments we live in. We will start from a more social perspective, describing the characteristics of multilingual societies and considering the forces that drive speakers towards one or more languages. After that, we will turn to the experiences of individual multilingual speakers and what they do with languages.

COLONIALISM AND STANDARDIZATION

The language database *Ethnologue* estimates that there are 1.5 billion speakers of English worldwide (Ethnologue 2024). It is considered the global lingua franca of business, science, diplomacy, and pop culture (Pennycook 1994). To understand why certain languages, like Standard English or Standard Mandarin, get elevated to such paramount status, we have to go back and look at the role languages play in modern nationalism. Prior to the eighteenth century, most polities were segregated in a vertical fashion, with peasants tied to local officials or nobles, who were in turn tied to a monarch or ruler (Gellner 1983). Language variation was much more extensive and the idea of being the citizen of a nation just did not exist. However, the labour requirements of industrialization led to efforts by various states to develop a new kind of national consciousness, one that linked its members together. The historian Benedict Anderson (1983) calls the nation an **imagined community** in the sense that, even though two people from the same nation may never meet, they assume themselves to be part of a greater whole. A key technology of nationalism is language: "Modern mass nationalism goes beyond the objective, instrumental identification of community with language (i.e., with communication) to the identification of authenticity with a particular language which is experientially unique and, therefore, functional in a way that other languages cannot match" (Fishman 1972, 43).

In other words, language became a mark of one's identity, of belonging *to* a nation. Accompanying this was a growing linguistic homogenization through education and print technologies like the newspaper that standardized the form of national languages.

Despite their origins in Europe, such ideas were exported around the world during the colonial period (Hobsbawm 1990). With the need to administer vast new territories, colonizers looked for ways to systematize and regulate the languages of their new subjects. When Belgium asserted control over the Congo basin in central Africa, for instance, hundreds of languages were spoken throughout the region. The new rulers selected a widespread lingua franca, Kiswahili, as the language of colonial administration because it was not tied to any one ethnic group (Hillewaert 2021). A hundred years later, what was once a set of closely related vernaculars is now a standardized language spoken by millions throughout the region, and an official language in countries such as Tanzania, Rwanda, the Democratic Republic of the Congo, and Uganda (Mugane 2015).

Other colonies had European languages such as English imposed upon them, a practice often termed **linguistic imperialism** (Phillipson 1992). Those decisions have made certain languages, like English, global in scope, and often marginalize smaller languages and dialects. The power of English within these histories of conquest and colonialism is likely what led Mahatma Gandhi (1958, 5) to remark, at a time when India was still a British colony, "To give millions a knowledge of English is to enslave them." Nevertheless, after the end of colonialism India retained English as language that could both unify its linguistically diverse population and integrate them more easily into a global system – English is still the medium of schooling for the children of wealthy and upwardly mobile families today (LaDousa 2014).

BOX 9.2 – RUSSIAN COLONIALISM IN UKRAINE

Colonialism and imperialism are not confined to the distant past but remain potent forces affecting languages worldwide. Nowhere is this more evident today than in Russian President Vladimir Putin's policies in Ukraine. When Russian forces launched a full-scale invasion of Ukraine in 2022, Putin's goals were as much cultural as they were political. In a written statement justifying his invasion, Putin denied the legitimacy of Ukrainian, claiming it as a variety of Russian. Schools, businesses, and public offices in the occupied territories were instructed to switch to using Russian rather than Ukrainian, while libraries were emptied of Ukrainian-language books (Bilaniuk 2024).

The Ukrainian and Russian languages, although different, do share a great deal of vocabulary and the same basic grammatical structures. Since the independence from the Soviet Union in 1991, Ukrainian has gradually been transformed from a stigmatized vernacular to a valued national language, although most people are passively bilingual and can communicate in either. A mixed Russian–Ukrainian language called Surzhyk is also widely used (Bilaniuk 2006). Politics, however, has made people quite sensitive to the differences between them.

Ironically, Putin's invasion may have backfired in his attempts to eliminate the Ukrainian language. Many citizens are making active attempts to avoid Russian in their speech, while use of Ukrainian has become an act of resistance in Russian-occupied cities (Maxwell 2023). In the face of Putin's claim that the Ukrainian language (and by extension the Ukrainian people) does not exist, speaking it has become an act of defiance against Russian imperialism. As linguistic anthropologist Laada Bilaniuk (2024, 146) notes, the catchphrase *Dobroho vechora, my z Ukraïny* ("Good evening, we are from Ukraine"), stands as an assertion that Ukraine still exists, and will continue to exist, despite Putin's efforts to erase it.

In all of these cases, language variation was identified as a problem – if people speak differently, how can one manage and organize their labour, communicate orders, facilitate trade, and so forth? Nationalism almost always leads to the standardization of a privileged language as elites and institutions define what counts as acceptable or exemplary forms of language usage. For instance, the linguist Rosina Lippi-Green looks at the definition of Standard English in the United States from the Merriam-Webster dictionary: "Standard English: the English that with respect to spelling, grammar, pronunciation, and vocabulary is substantially uniform through not devoid of regional differences, that is well established by usage in the formal and informal speech and writing of the educated, and that is widely recognized as acceptable wherever English is spoken and understood" (quoted in Lippi-Green 1997, 53). She argues that this definition of a standard English contains a range of ideological assumptions about language:

- That the standard language is universal while non-standard ones are regional
- That "uneducated" people are using a language that is *not* standard
- That those not using the standard still recognize its superiority "wherever English is spoken and understood"

All of these assumptions position one particular form of English (that spoken by "educated," presumably upper- and upper-middle-class, speakers) as an objectively superior, clearer, more rational way of speaking than that used by others. These ideologies can become so ingrained in the public consciousness that non-standard ways of speaking are denigrated as "broken" or "unintelligible" and their speakers as "deficient" or "unintelligent" (Labov 1970; Silverstein 1996).

Such ideas make language competency a valuable currency in the global economy. Standardization makes possible the **commodification** of language, turning certain languages and language varieties into marketable skills and sources of value for their speakers (Duchêne and Heller 2012). Bilingual areas of Canada, for instance, are often favoured for call centres because speakers there can provide customer service in the two official languages of French and English; a practice which, of course, heightens the value of Standard English and Standard French at the expense of local speech practices (Comeau and King 2011; Roy 2004). Conversely, many countries in Asia now grant considerable value to English. South Korean workers in multinational corporations invest considerable time and effort in cultivating their English abilities. No matter their achievements, however, many find their careers stalled because they are non-native speakers of English (Park 2013). Whether in business, language teaching, tourism, translation, or other fields, standard languages act as marketable skills for workers and valuable human capital for corporations (Heller 2010). All of these forces drive people towards ideologies of monolingualism but, as we will see, variation remains part of the social reality of any diverse society.

MULTILINGUAL SOCIETIES

Although small communities may be linguistically homogeneous, larger ones are apt to have differences within them. These can be different languages spoken within the same area. In New York, for instance, Ana Celia Zentella (1997) has studied a Puerto

Rican neighbourhood called *el bloque* where Spanish-speaking immigrants mix with a historic Black community and middle-class white neighbours. Children growing up in this area therefore draw upon both Spanish and English during interactions with friends, family, and other community members. At home, they largely speak Spanish (and were duly chastised by parents if they did not); at school they have to speak English. With their friends, it is a mix of both.

Other communities combine different dialects of a language. In Beijing, for instance, long-time residents are familiar with both Standard Mandarin (used at work and in school), and Beijing dialect, a distinct variety of Mandarin native to the city. One of the most prominent features of Beijing dialect is *erhua*, a distinctive pronunciation that adds an 'r' sound to the end of many words: *bao* (bag) becomes *baor* and *wan* (play) becomes *wanr*.[1] People describe the Beijing dialect as "smooth" and "fluid" while Standard Mandarin comes off as "crisp" and overly formal (Zhang 2008). Speakers can therefore switch back and forth between Standard Mandarin and Beijing dialect depending on the circumstances: Beijing dialect if they want to be friendly with other locals, or Standard Mandarin when they need to be serious. The concept of **language variation** points to these differences within languages, and we speak of any particular pattern of language as a **language variety**.[2]

Notice how, in these examples, language choices are not random; people are instead motivated by where, when, and with whom they are speaking. In speech communities with multiple language varieties, each becomes mapped onto a particular domain. One language or variety might be used in the classroom with the teacher, but another in the schoolyard at recess with classmates. "The average educated person in Hyderabad," writes linguist Suzanne Romaine of the situation in India, "may use Telegu at home, Sanskrit at the temple, English at the university, Urdu in business, etc. He or she may also know other varieties of Telegu, or Kannada, Tamil, or Malayalam for reading, dealing with servants, or other specific purposes" (Romaine 2001, 517). In other contexts, especially informal ones, they might mix these languages together.

Canada: A Case Study in Multilingualism

In many ways Canada exemplifies how complicated multilingualism is when examined in detail. Histories of Canada frequently refer to two founding peoples, the French and the English, leading to the creation of a bilingual nation (Haque 2014; Heller et al. 2016). The *Charter of Rights and Freedoms*, part of the Canadian constitution adopted in 1982, states "English and French are the official languages of Canada and have equality of status and equal rights and privileges as to their use in all institutions of the Parliament and Government of Canada" (Canada 1982). The nation is also, at first glance, divided by a kind of linguistic geography, with French speakers (francophones) located in the province of Quebec, and English speakers (anglophones) located everywhere else.

As many scholars have pointed out, however, this story overly simplifies an often knotty history (Edwards 1998). Canada's Indigenous inhabitants spoke a range of languages before Europeans arrived and divided the lands into various territories. During the colonial era, French-speaking communities sprang up not only in Quebec but all across Canada, from Louisbourg in Nova Scotia to Maillardville in British Columbia (Mackey 1998). After a series of conflicts between France and Britain, the remaining French colonies in Canada were ceded to Britain in the eighteenth century, beginning a long process of assimilation that often either erased French-language heritage, or substantially curtailed its vitality in those communities. Meanwhile, in Quebec a parallel process occurred that reduced the public presence of English and emphasized the role of French in sustaining a distinct Quebecois identity (Oakes and Warren 2007). Neither are the English and French languages spoken across Canada entirely homogeneous – there are a range of dialectal and regional influences on the two official languages spoken throughout the country (Boberg 2010; Bouchard 2023).

Other languages have played, and continue to play, significant roles in Canada. At the time of Confederation in 1867, the third-largest language in Canada was Scottish Gaelic, distributed throughout the eastern Maritime provinces (Ó'Néill 2005). Many communities serving as ethnic enclaves for newly arriving immigrants have retained languages such as German, Ukrainian, Cantonese, and Italian right up to today. More recently, patterns of immigration have brought new groups of people, and new languages, to Canada, particularly in urban areas. The number of people who speak a non-official language at home increased from 2.9 million in 2001 to 4.7 million in 2021 (Statistics Canada 2024) (Figure 9.2). The generally accepted story of Canada as a bilingual nation composed of two distinct cultural populations therefore greatly simplifies a significant amount of complexity and variation.

French is a good case in point to illustrate this diversity. When people learn French in school, there is often the presumption of a unitary and cohesive language: everything in the dictionary or textbook is French, and anything else is *not* French. In practice, however, there are substantive differences between French spoken in France and French spoken elsewhere (Chevalier 2008). One online video, for instance, features speakers of French from France, Canada, and Belgium comparing their words for common things.[3] The French word for "beverage," for instance, is *boisson* in Belgium and *breuvage* in Quebec. In France, "handbag" is *sac à main* and in Quebec it is *sacoche*. Further differences exist at the levels of phonology and syntax. Of course, these differences mainly pertain to speech because, in written French, people often adhere to the European standard.

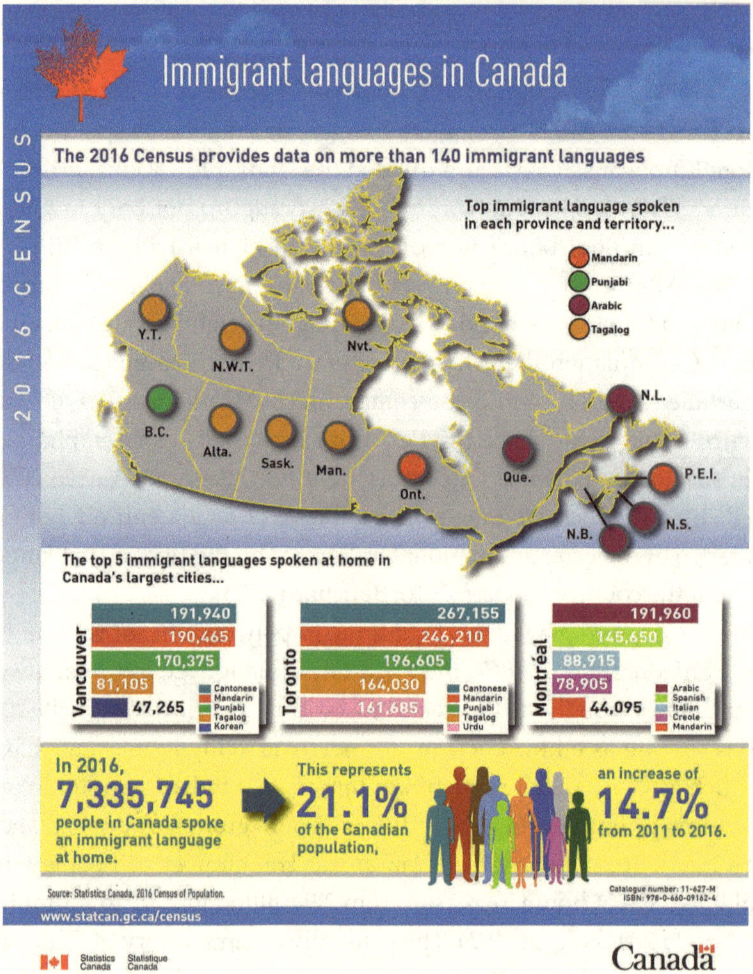

Figure 9.2 – Data from the 2016 census on immigrant languages in Canada

Source: Statistics Canada, 2016 Census: Immigrant Languages in Canada, August 2, 2017. Reproduced and distributed on an "as is" basis with the permission of Statistics Canada

BOX 9.3 – ACADIAN FRENCH

Les nations canadiennes-françaises et acadiennes sont des nations vigoureuses parce que nous avons conservé nos vieilles traditions, parce que nous avons gardé notre langue.

[The French-Canadian and Acadian nations are vigorous nations because we have preserved our old traditions, because we have preserved our language] (Tremblay 1973, 300).

This opinion, offered by an Acadian French speaker in 1919, highlights one of the central ideas surrounding this language variety in Canada, and is true even today. Acadians are the descendants of settlers from France who lived throughout the eastern Maritime provinces. After refusing to sign an oath of allegiance to the British Crown in 1755, the lieutenant governor of Nova Scotia conducted a massive deportation scheme now called *le grand dérangement* or the Acadian Expulsion. Acadians were scattered around the world: sent back to France, or to Britain, New England, the Caribbean, and New Orleans (where they became known as Cajuns) (Landry and Lang 2001). Those who escaped deportation, or eventually returned, found their lands given away to British settlers.

Despite this inherently diasporic character, language is one thing that binds Acadians together and sustains them as a transnational community (Heller et al. 2016). There are some significant differences between Acadian French and other French varieties (Dubois 2014):

- Unique words such as *hucher* (shout) and *mitaine* (mitten)
- Standard French no longer uses the /h/ sound, so the words *haler* (haul) and *aller* (go) are pronounced the same; Acadian French has retained this sound and pronounces those words differently
- The third-person plural verb ending is *-ont* or *-iont* (with the /t/ pronounced) rather than the *-ent* in Standard French (where the /t/ is silent)

Nevertheless, Acadian French speakers often experience a sense of insecurity and stigma due to the language's non-standard status. Shifting towards the more prestigious Standard French aligns speakers with a larger francophone world, creating links that can sustain their communities in an otherwise English-dominant society. At the same time, however, Acadian French contributes to a unique identity grounded in shared history, language, and culture (Boudreau and Dubois 2007; LeBlanc and Boudreau 2016).

Despite the diversity of language within Canada, we can see how multilingualism is subject to dominant language ideologies. People are often obliged to identify themselves as either anglophone or francophone in a variety of contexts, even if they are proficient in both languages. There are also social proscriptions against mixing the languages: in French educational contexts, for instance, students are often reminded "*parlez français* [speak French]!" on a regular basis to prevent the use of English in school. When bilingual politicians speak, they will typically use either one language or the other, rarely mixing them together. Linguistic anthropologist Monica Heller refers to this situation as "double monolingualism" (Heller 2001, 2002). Such ideologies constrain which languages are spoken, in which settings, and in what ways.

BOX 9.4 – SHOULD ENGLISH BE THE OFFICIAL LANGUAGE OF THE UNITED STATES?

Ideologies about the benefits of standard languages lie behind efforts in the United States to make English the official language. Although no language is granted special recognition in the constitution, there have been efforts at local, regional, and federal levels to pass "English-only" legislation, culminating in 2025 when President Donald Trump signed an executive order designating English as the official language of the United States. Proponents of such efforts argue that, without formal recognition of English as a national language, the United States will descend into linguistic chaos, with so many languages that no citizen will be able to comprehend another (González 2000). Other concerns prompting such legislation are that immigrant populations will refuse to assimilate or will be swayed by political misinformation from outside influences (Woolard 1989).

In reality, immigrant communities in the United States almost universally adopt English and there is no danger of the language going extinct. Ideologically, however, designating English as an official language draws upon the idea of language as a central pillar of a common national identity (Subtirelu 2013). The implication is that anyone who does not use English exclusively is opposed to that unity and a threat to the nation's harmony. As Roseann Dueñas González argues, "Over the past decade, the English Only movement has steadily intensified negative attitudes toward speakers of Spanish and other languages. Moreover, its ideology has nurtured a climate in which accents and other forms of variety in linguistic expression, including syntactic, lexical, or rhetorical varieties, are discriminated against or overtly ostracized" (González 2000, xxxii). Many linguistic anthropologists argue that the official language movement in the United States is less about elevating English and more about denigrating other languages that constitute the multicultural fabric of American society.

Ideologies also affect the values assigned to different language varieties. The many different French-speaking areas within Canada have developed unique varieties of French, but not all of them are treated equally. Speakers of Standard French are often accorded respect and prestige, while speakers of *joual* (the French spoken in Montreal) and other minority francophone varieties may be stigmatized for not speaking "good French" (Oakes and Warren 2007; Roy 2004). As linguistic anthropologist Mireille McLaughlin (2021, 97) writes, "At school and in the media of Canada's francophonie, [French] nationalist discourse shifted easily from the structural to the collective, and from the collective to the individual, urging students and minority francophones to show 'pride' by avoiding code-mixing and speaking French as often as possible, in as many contexts as possible, and in a form as close as possible to a standard… This discourse renders invisible the structural conditions of multilingualism that are part of the socialization of minority speakers in Canada."[4]

All of this shows us that, at the level of society, multilingualism is never just about using multiple languages. Issues of power, status, and class come to the fore as varieties are enregistered with distinct social value. The use of those varieties is then influenced by popular ideologies about how, when, and where they should be spoken.

Diglossia

A common phenomenon in many multilingual societies is **diglossia**, a term that describes speech communities with two or more languages that play very distinct and unequal roles (Ferguson 1959). One of these languages is a more formal **H-variety** and the other a more informal **L-variety** (the letters here derive from "high" and "low"). They differ not only in prestige but also function: H-variety is usually used for official or sacred contexts like government legislation, religious services, public speeches, university lectures, and so forth. The L-variety, in contrast, is used in more informal and mundane contexts, such as conversation among family, market transactions, and so-called lowbrow entertainment like comics and soap operas.

A paradigmatic case of diglossia can be found in Egypt, although it also exists in many other Arabic-speaking countries. The H-variety, in this case Standard Arabic, is derived from the classical language of the Qur'an and is used across the Arab world. It is the language of prayer, schooling, and government. Books, poetry, news broadcasts, and ritual or formal activities in Egypt are all performed in Standard Arabic (Haeri 2003). But Standard Arabic is not the language most people grow up speaking; that would be the L-variety, Egyptian Arabic, which is used in domestic settings, for entertainment programs on radio and television, and in conversation with friends and neighbours.

These languages are related, sharing much of their phonology, lexicon, and syntax, but there are significant differences in terms of grammar, word order, and style. For instance, Egyptian Arabic does not employ Standard Arabic's extensive case system (in much the same way Italian no longer uses the nominative or dative cases of Latin). People have varying abilities in Standard Arabic based on their level of education and

Figure 9.3 – Anti-Mubarak sign displayed during the Arab Spring protests in Egypt

Source: Photograph by Tarek (flikr.com). Creative Commons BY-ND 2.0

devoutness to Islam, but almost everyone agrees that Standard Arabic is more formal and refined, while Egyptian Arabic is "easy" (*sahl*) and "humorous" (*dammaha khafiif*). Nevertheless, the symbolic boundaries between these languages are strictly maintained; one teacher hearing his students speaking Egyptian Arabic in class exclaimed, "my ears do not allow the language of donkeys" (Haeri 2003, 117).

Some interesting issues arise when the public requirement for Standard Arabic is beyond a speaker's abilities. Hosni Mubarak, president of Egypt from 1981 to 2011, did not receive a classical education and thus spoke notoriously poor Standard Arabic. Linguistic anthropologist Niloofar Haeri (2003, 99) describes how, in media interviews, reporters would ask Mubarak questions in Standard Arabic to which he would respond in Egyptian Arabic. Overnight, translators would then render his responses into Standard Arabic to be published in newspapers the next day, often with the prefatory phrase, "And said the president…." Ironically, during the Arab Spring protests in 2011, ordinary Egyptian citizens exploited Mubarak's lack of Standard Arabic fluency to get their point across. One protest sign (Figure 9.3) plays on the difference between "go" in Standard Arabic (*irhal*) and Egyptian Arabic (*imshi*), reading "*Irhal* means *imshi*, in case you don't understand me." The implication is that, in saying "get lost," even a lowly protester's Standard Arabic was better than Mubarak's (Zimmer 2011).

Recent research has argued that, as a concept, diglossia tends to oversimplify multilingual settings and overstate the divide between languages (Snow 2013). Standard Arabic and Egyptian Arabic are not the only languages in Egypt, for example: these co-exist with Coptic, Berber, Nubian, and a range of Arabic dialects. There is also so much overlap between Egyptian and Standard Arabic that speech can span a range of levels from highly informal to highly formal (Owens 2001). Nevertheless, in the minds of most people these are ideologically marked varieties that should be kept separate.

Pidgins and Creoles

Some multilingual practices also arise from situations of contact between languages. The late nineteenth century witnessed the development of a plantation-based economy throughout the South Pacific, growing everything from cotton to sugar cane. Although lucrative for their owners, they required a major supply of human labour power often drawn from native populations in the area. These workers were recruited – or sometimes outright kidnapped – and transported to the plantations, often on three-year indentured contracts. From 1863 until 1907, more than 100,000 labour migrants were enlisted in this enterprise (Tryon and Charpentier 2004, 173).

One prominent source of such labour was Papua New Guinea, a remarkably diverse place in terms of languages. At present there are more than 1,300 spoken in the region, comprising about 40 different language families; that is roughly one-fifth of the world's total number of languages (Palmer 2018, 1). Despite coming from the same area, the Papuans who arrived on these plantations usually spoke very different languages from each other. A simplified jargon quickly emerged between the plantation owners and their indentured workers that adopted English vocabulary – including numbers, colours, and words like "go" and "him" – but used common grammatical patterns from Papuan languages. For instance, many Papuan languages include a suffix at the end of a verb to mark transitivity (whether a verb can take an object or not – the verb *throw* is transitive because you throw something, but *fall* is intransitive). So Papuans adapted the English word *him* for this purpose, creating sentences like "No one beat him that fellow" (Mühlhäusler, Dutton, and Romaine 2003, 37). Later, this would be shortened to *-im* and added to transitive verbs such as *tokim* ("talk to").

When the Papuan labourers returned home, they brought with them cash, commodities, and this new vernacular they called Tok Pisin. It not only connected them to the outside world but allowed them to communicate with other labourers from distant parts of New Guinea, creating networks of contacts between previously isolated settlements. In the developing cities, such as the capital Port Moresby, Tok Pisin became predominant. What started as a way for Europeans to communicate instructions to their workers developed into a way for Papuans to speak to each other (Mühlhäusler, Dutton, and Romaine 2003, 6). During the early twentieth century, Tok Pisin rapidly added new vocabulary and more complex grammatical patterns. By the 1930s, Tok Pisin had become a separate language in its own right – not English, but something entirely new.

The vernacular that developed between Papuan labourers and European plantation owners is an example of a **pidgin**, a relatively limited linguistic code that emerges in response to groups of people who have no shared language to communicate with each other. Pidgins are generally used only for certain purposes – trade, for instance – and comprise a very simplified vocabulary and syntax. But when this vernacular is more widely adopted within a community, is actively spoken by adults and learned by children as a first language, it becomes a full-fledged language in its own right, a **creole**.[5]

Now one of Papua New Guinea's official languages, Tok Pisin illustrates an important point about language evolution and development. We often think of languages evolving independently of each other: Ancient Greek becomes Modern Greek, and Old English becomes Middle English and then Modern English. In reality, languages are often the product of hybrid influences and extensive forms of contact and mixing (Mufwene 2023). Just as artistic or musical styles often blend a variety of cultural influences together, languages also draw upon multiple influences in terms of both their grammar and lexicon.

Compared to pidgins, creoles possess a more diverse lexicon and elaborate syntax, and exhibit all the hallmarks of a human language. Nevertheless, creoles are often treated, even by their own speakers, as illegitimate languages. Creole language ideologies have been shaped by histories of colonization and biases towards language mixing. They are often spoken in relatively impoverished countries that have long been exploited economically by developed nations, and so they get called "broken English" (for Jamaican and Nigerian Pidgin) or other pejorative terms (Gaudio 2011). Linguistic anthropologists Christine Jourdan and Johanne Angeli have written about the development of Solomon Islands Pijin under colonialism, particularly in the capital city of Honiara. British officials, for instance, often mocked this emerging language as a sign of native backwardness, or saw it as a transitional stage through which islanders would eventually acquire "real" English (Jourdan and Angeli 2014, 272).

Since the independence from Britain, however, attitudes towards Pijin in Honiara have begun to shift. Pijin is used in a range of everyday interactions, even formal ones such as speeches in Parliament. Many Solomon Islanders see Pijin as part of their local heritage and identity. As one student put it:

> *Mifala tritim dat iu should spikim Pijin nomoa kos mitufala semsem.* (…) *Iu should tok lo mi, olsem,* normal language *wea iumi iusim.*
>
> We consider that the other one should speak Pijin because we both are of the same kind. (…) You should talk to me in the normal language that we use. (Jourdan and Angeli 2014, 276)

As we can see, young people also feel comfortable mixing Pijin with English and other languages. "Thus the symbolic domination of English over Pijin has significantly shifted in meaning over the years, as young middle-class Honiarans now reinterpret those colonial readings of Pijin through the lens of nationalist and pragmatic linguistic ideologies" (Jourdan and Angeli 2014, 280). English may still hold tremendous prestige as a global language, but its superiority over Pijin is no longer assured.

BOX 9.5 – IS ENGLISH A CREOLE?

What if, far from being unusual, creoles are actually quite common, maybe even the norm? Is a language like English itself a creole? Consider the evidence: most words in Modern English do not come from Old English, but from other sources. Words like *money*, *judge*, and *music*? Those come from French. *Egg*, *ugly*, and *their*? Those are from Old Norse (see Hogg and Denison 2006). From the ninth to the eleventh centuries, England (and its speakers of many varieties of Old English) was invaded and settled by other groups. First were the Vikings, who took over substantial parts of several Anglo-Saxon kingdoms, ranging from London in the south to York in the north. Then in 1066, William of Normandy arrived from France and conquered most of what is known as England today.

For a time, English and French remained as distinct languages in England – a prime example of diglossia, where English was the marginalized language of peasants and French the prestige language of the nobility (Bergs 2010). By the thirteenth century, however, they had merged into what we now call Middle English. During this process, some grammatical features of Old English were simplified: English used to have grammatical gender (much like French does today) and specialized case inflections (like German). Other features were borrowed from French, such as the adoption of suffixes like *-age* and *-ity* (which can be found today in words like *passage* and *charity*) (Trotter 2010).

This prompted some linguists in the 1970s to argue that, like Tok Pisin or Jamaican Patois, contemporary English has its origins in a creole language. The assertion caused extensive academic debate, not just about the history of the English language but also about what distinguishes creoles from other languages. One of the problems with the theory is that we do not have any clear evidence of pidginization between English and French in the Norman period (Trotter 2010). Nevertheless, considering the many ways that the history of English parallels languages such as Haitian Creole guards against what Michel DeGraff (2003) terms **creole exceptionalism**, the ideology that creoles are somehow linguistically deficient or peculiar.

MIXING LANGUAGES TOGETHER

As the social study of language developed in the 1960s and 1970s, sociolinguists and linguistic anthropologists took notice of the ways people shifted between languages during a conversation, a phenomenon called **codeswitching**. While many early scholars saw such linguistic behaviour as a way to deal with gaps in a speaker's linguistic competence (essentially relying on another language as a crutch when they could not form a sentence), subsequent research has argued that codeswitching demonstrates a great deal of creativity and skill in both languages. A classic example is from the title of a paper by University of Ottawa sociolinguist Shana Poplack (1980): "Sometimes I'll start a sentence in Spanish *y termino en Español* [and finish in Spanish]." On the basis of ethnographic research with Puerto Rican Spanish speakers in New York City, Poplack argued that bilingual speakers incorporated the grammatical constraints of both languages into their switches. Moreover, it was the most proficient speakers of both languages who codeswitched the most often, and they tended to do so in settings, and with other speakers, where they felt most comfortable. Poplack concluded that codeswitching between English and Spanish constitutes a distinct discourse style that is acceptable, and even expected, in many contexts.

Codeswitching is not just random shifts between languages: there is a social dimension to codeswitching. When Jan-Petter Blom and John Gumperz (1972) studied codeswitching in northern Norway, for instance, they observed people shifting between a local dialect called Ranamål and the national language known as Bokmål. These languages were used for different purposes and with different people. When visiting the town hall, for instance, a person would conduct their official business in Bokmål but then switch into Ranamål to inquire about the clerk's family. And when Blom and Gumperz approached a group of local men casually speaking Ranamål, the group suddenly straightened up and began to speak Bokmål in response to the presence of the outsiders. These shifts were so natural that many of the speakers did not even realize they had switched between varieties. Linguistic anthropologists therefore argue that the choice of which code to use in any given situation might not always be conscious, but it is a socially meaningful one (Mendoza-Denton and Osborne 2009).

Choice of language may be a response to the context of a conversation, but it can also be used strategically by speakers. In Goma, a city in the eastern Democratic Republic of Congo, most people speak Kiswahili in their daily lives, while in the capital city of Kinshasa, far to the west, Lingala is the dominant language. Despite the fact that most Goma residents are not proficient in Lingala, the language is nevertheless associated with a Congolese national identity. When dealing with the police, citizens often switch to using whatever Lingala they know as a way of demonstrating their national belonging and insider status in order to avoid fines or harassment (Büscher, D'Hondt, and Meeuwis 2013). Or consider a story told to me by one of my own informants who returned home after many years living in southern China. After hearing his Standard Mandarin speech at the train station, a taxi driver quoted an exorbitant price to take him home, which started a fight: "So I'm shouting and we push each other and I'm hitting and the people around us just looking. Then the other taxi drivers, they like want to help their friend, so they start punching on me. And nobody helping! And I say it in the local accent, I scream, 'Hey, help me you bastards!' And then they stop the fight." In these examples, each language indexes a particular identity, and speakers choose among the various possibilities in their speech repertoires to represent themselves differently from situation to situation.

In places where language varieties have been in contact for some time and people are used to codeswitching, hybrid forms of speech may emerge (Auer 1999). Rather than just switching between languages, speakers mix and blend them together to the point the two become inseparable, a process called **codemixing**. In Yakutsk, linguistic anthropologist Jenanne Ferguson found that many ethnically Sakha people living in the city speak a blended language combining Russian and Sakha together. When teased that his girlfriend was arriving the next day, a young man named Kostya replied:

Che?? Huokh! ***Piatnitsa****gha manna tiijier dii!*
Yeah?? No! She gets here on Friday!

[Russian bolded, adapted from Ferguson 2019, 170]

In his response, Kostya uses the Russian word for Friday, *piatnitsa*, but adds the Sakha grammatical suffix *-gha* to the end. Moreover, he also pronounces the Sakha word "no" (*suokh*) using a prominent /h/, a sound found in some dialects of Sakha but not Russian, which implicitly distances him from monolingual Russian speakers. In other words, he does not switch between Sakha and Russian so much as he combines them together in a way that signals his own complex identity.

BOX 9.6 – CHIAC

The following advertisement was posted in 2012 to an online classified advertisement site:

> *Ouaille hallo back everyone, ces back joey light-hangner... jvoulai ink vou dire jhangnais back der christmas light st'anner...*
>
> [Yeah, hello again everyone, it's Joey the light-hanger again... I wanted to tell you that I'm hanging Christmas lights again this year...]

This is an example of **Chiac**, a French–English mixed linguistic variety used mainly in New Brunswick, particularly around the city of Moncton (Perrot 2014). The advertisement has many examples of dialectal Acadian French features, but note also how it borrows extensively from English, sometimes even combining English verbs (hang) with French verb conjugations (*-ais*). The meaning of some English words is different in Chiac as well, with "back" meaning "to repeat" or "do again" (King 2008).

There is some debate as to whether Chiac constitutes a fully hybridized language or whether it exhibits strategic forms of mixing by speakers from French and English (Papen 2014). Most speakers of Chiac are fully bilingual and can switch into either French or English as the situation requires, but they are apt to use Chiac in less formal contexts. However, if our focus is on what Chiac does in conversation, it is inherently local (the term Chiac itself probably derives from the community of Shédiac). While outside of this area Chiac appears to violate many of the norms of language usage (such as the taboo on mixing languages), with other locals it acts as a shibboleth of belonging, right beside local foods such as *poutines à trou* and rappie pie (Comeau and King 2011).

Another good example comes from the work of Sonia Das, who has examined Tamil heritage language teaching in Montreal. The Tamil community there is drawn from both southern India and from the neighbouring country of Sri Lanka, which leads to certain dialectal differences. In addition, there is a poetic classical Tamil that was used more than a thousand years ago and a formal literary Tamil that forms the basis for the standard language taught to the students. Das shows how the speech of language teachers blends these various codes together to add important moral lessons for students. In one class, the teacher summarized the point of a story as:

adāvadu tīya ceyalkalɛ pārkkātɛ, keṭṭadɛ pēcādɛ – pēcapaṭādu
Therefore you should try not to do bad things or speak badly – don't speak badly

While most of the lesson was in literary Tamil (shown in bold above), the teacher also adds colloquial endings to some of the words (/ɛ/ like the vowel in "bed") and a word from Sri Lankan Tamil (*paṭādu*) instead of the literary alternative. The pragmatic effect, Das argues, is to connect the students' diasporic experience today with their Tamil heritage. "These hybrid constructions, beginning in literary Tamil yet ending in colloquial [Sri Lankan] Jaffna, hint at the close… affinity of literary Tamil with its Sri Lankan descendent" (Das 2016, 133).

CONCLUSION

When I first moved to the east coast of Canada over a decade ago, I wrote a grant proposal that contrasted the multilingualism of northeastern China with what I characterized as the "predominant monolingualism" of Halifax. I wasn't totally wrong, but I've come to realize that language here is much more complex than I originally thought; scratch the surface a little, and you start to see and hear languages you would never expect (and a whole lot, like French, that I *should* have expected). Even I was taken in by the kinds of monolingual ideologies I mentioned earlier.

What do we find instead? As we've seen, Canada is a deeply multilingual space. Histories of settlement, colonization, and social mobility have brought together people from a range of backgrounds, not just the two founding languages that exist in many narratives of the nation's becoming. And the number of languages (and number of speakers of those languages) is increasing. It is a good reminder for linguistic anthropologists to not just accept terms like anglophone or francophone at face value, and to listen carefully to what people are actually saying (and what resources they are drawing on) when they speak. But we have also seen the ways in which multilingualism is structured by language ideologies about which languages are acceptable, in what places, and at what times. That is a story echoed in many places around the world.

You may have noticed that, at the beginning of this chapter, I used some statistics to represent the language situation in Canada and the United States. That is one way to approach the topic, and it is often used in studies of language policy and planning. But if you think about it, the various forms of complexity we have been talking about defy easy categorization. If our language is, as Bakhtin argued, heteroglossic, composed of a range of influences from different speech communities, it contests the very idea that there is one English or one French. Taken together, the examples in this chapter challenge some of our fundamental ideas about what a language is. In essence, Bakhtin would argue that we are always codemixing, every time we open our mouths.

BOX 9.7 – RESEARCH SPOTLIGHT: PATRICIA LAMARRE

Lamarre, Patricia. 2013. "Catching 'Montréal on the Move' and Challenging the Discourse of Unilingualism in Québec." *Anthropologica* 55 (1): 41–56.

A lot of research on multilingualism outside of linguistic anthropology takes the identities we have been talking about (francophone and anglophone, for instance) at face value in order to count the number of speakers and relative vitality of various languages. But as we have learned, speakers can draw on a range of linguistic resources in their everyday lives to communicate with others. A sociolinguist at the University of Montreal, Patricia Lamarre, sought to document the complex relationships people have to the languages they speak. How, she asks, do young people in the increasingly global city of Montreal use language in such complex ways in their everyday lives? She also looked at how these practices changed in different contexts: at home, at school, at work, and so forth.

To do this, Lamarre engaged in what she calls "an ethnography 'on the move'" (2013, 44). She recruited 15 multilingual young adults and interviewed them to learn more about their language background. They were all given digital recorders and asked to record some of their conversations. Afterwards, Lamarre analysed those conversations with the participants, asking them about the significance of their language choices: why did they use a particular language in each situation. How did they perceive the meaning of their choices for others?

A lot of these conversations show vibrant forms of language mixing. One Lebanese participant, for instance, would speak to her parents in Beirut using both French and Arabic, another dialect of Arabic when talking to her Egyptian boyfriend, English and French with her sister, and so on. She even had a Korean friend she met during an exchange program in Mexico with whom she communicated solely in Spanish. She could be unilingual when she wanted to be, speaking to the receptionist at her gym entirely in French, but that was more the exception than the rule. The interplay among various languages was so dense that Lamarre dubs her speech "*parler multilingue*." Ultimately, she argues that traditional approaches to identity, such as surveys, fail to capture the fluidity and hybridity of both speech and identity in Montreal.

Discussion Questions

1. Urban concentrations of foreign-language speakers have become a delight for linguists. Whereas a linguist might once have had to travel to the other side of the world to document an endangered language, speakers can now often be found

nearby. Tools like Languages of New York City (https://languagemap.nyc/) show us just how many languages can be found in densely populated cities. Have a look at this map – if you were a linguist studying endangered languages, where would you go in the city? Why do you think the languages show up where they do? Check out some of the video links on the site to more information about the speakers who live in New York.

2. For years, Disney dubbed its popular movies into Egyptian Arabic, but this changed in 2014 with *Frozen*, the story of the troubled relationship between two orphaned princesses, one of them with the power to control ice. Whether for reasons of cost or politics, *Frozen* was dubbed into Standard Arabic, meaning that lines such as "Let it go! Can't hold it back anymore" came off sounding more like "Discharge thy secret! I shall not bear the torment!" (Muhanna 2014). The lines were so stilted that Disney fans in Egypt started an online petition to restore the use of Egyptian Arabic. Have a look at that petition (it is easy to locate through a web search). Keeping in mind our discussion of Egyptian diglossia, how do the writers characterize these languages and the social roles they play?
3. Codeswitching and codemixing are behaviours that we often engage in without even being fully aware of. People notoriously misreport what they actually do, claiming to speak one language exclusively even when mixing in others. Look online for some examples of people codeswitching (a simple search of YouTube will bring up thousands of videos). What are people doing with their languages and how are they combining them? What social factors might be influencing the choices they make?
4. One creole language that has been experiencing a resurgence lately is Hawaiian Pidgin (and even though it is called Pidgin, it still qualifies as a creole language). The following text is from an article by a Pidgin activist talking about his experiences with students: "You kinda wondah how kids come out li'dis. Trying fo' write '[proper] english' but end up writing stuff dat no even make sense. Classic conditioning gotta be. From my experience, teachahs nevah sed, you're stupid if you talk in Pidgin; dey nevah sed 'em direck li'dat. Wuz mo' INSIDIOUS da way dey do 'em" (Tonouchi 2004, 76).

   We have discussed the idea that creole languages follow grammatical rules, even if they are different from the source languages. So what are the rules here? What differences do you notice between the way this author writes and what he calls "proper English" and what does that tell us about the linguistic structure of Pidgin?

10

Orality and Literacy

Topics

- What is a "text"?
- Verbal art and performance
- Literacy as a form of practice
- Multiliteracies: going beyond written texts

You are reading this right now. You are probably not listening to it, or having it dictated – you are reading it. And the fact that you can read it, that in your mind you are assigning sound values and meaning to these little marks on the paper, has profound implications for our understanding of language. For most of human history, language was not written but existed solely as transient sounds carried through the air. Roughly five thousand years ago, however, in the ancient Near East, people began using symbols to record language. In southern Mesopotamia, pictograms and symbols inscribed on clay tablets represented words, often through a process of sound similarity: a stylized depiction of an arrow (*ti*), for instance, became the basis of writing the Sumerian word for life (*til*) (Coulmas 1989, 77–8). A similar process fuelled the development of writing systems in Egypt, China, India, and Mesoamerica which, through centuries of adaptation and change, have shaped the many scripts in use today (Fischer 2001). Whether alphabetic or pictographic (or a combination of both), all of these writing systems have the capacity to graphically represent spoken language.

The development of writing was a revolution in human communication. No longer was language use limited to the immediate moment of speech or the space around the speaker. It enables the extensive development of historical records, legal codes, ritual texts, and even the notion of authorship itself (Ong 1982). Dictionaries preserve archaic vocabulary that in other settings would have faded from lack of use. The French philosopher Jacques Derrida (1974) has even argued that the very idea of a *language* – in the sense of a self-contained and structured system of signs – is the product of a written perspective. Within societies that are predominantly literate, the implications of text, and the ability of individuals to read and write them, are therefore pervasive.

For all this, however, we still talk, and while most languages do employ some kind of writing system, there are usually highly elaborate ideologies around discourse – how we talk, how we structure a conversation, and how we should interpret the speech of others.[1] Historically, many scholars analysed **orality**, or communication and expression through the medium of spoken language, as distinct from **literacy**, communication and expression through the medium of written language. More recent research has shown such a division is too broad: we can talk *and* write, and our engagements with texts are often mediated also by spoken discourse. In this chapter we will consider the differences between spoken and written discourse and try to understand their relationships – and entanglements – with each other.

SPOKEN AND WRITTEN TEXTS

Many written texts have their origins in speech. Plato's philosophy was often presented as a series of dialogues between his teacher, Socrates, and other scholars. Governments publish transcripts of speeches and debates by legislators. People may be quoted in the media, with their spoken words rendered into written form. On the other hand, a written text can be read out loud; that transcribed political speech was probably being read off a page or teleprompter. In southern India, men often gather in tea shops in the morning to drink tea and talk politics, reading out and discussing headlines from the morning papers. As linguistic anthropologist Francis Cody (2011, 248) writes, "the printed newspaper acts a textual generator of talk among readers and hearers alike." The question then is: what, if anything, separates written and spoken language?

Most linguistic anthropologists recognize the complexity in the ways writing and speech are tied together. Instead of limiting the idea to writing, a **text** is more generally defined by its coherence. William Hanks (1989, 95) defines a text as "any configuration of signs that is coherently interpretable by some community of users." When a student considers the best way to answer a question asked in class, or composes a written essay for their professor, these are both texts because they reflect an intentional effort to arrange and organize the words. Moreover, both of these texts are oriented outwards to an audience who will hear, interpret, and maybe even grade the person's textual production (Barber 2007).

There are some important differences between how oral and written texts are used, though. One is the way they encode social memory. In predominantly oral societies, genealogies, ritual practices, esoteric knowledge, and so on are often learned through extensive oral performance as people recite long stretches of information (Martindale, Shneiderman, and Turin 2018). For instance, in the 1920s, Bronislaw Malinowski (1954) recorded an epic oral myth cycle in the Trobriand Islands comprising hundreds of characters, lineages, events, and places that, in his opinion, rivalled the Greek and Roman traditions. In Senegal, Wolof orators known as *griots* can recount complicated kinship relations going back several generations (Irvine 1978). And in Fiji, dance-songs called *meke,* which can reach up to 20 pages of text if they are written out, are commissioned from a poet by important chiefs. The poet is inspired by gifts from the chief and then is given the words, music, and choreography of the *meke* in a vision (Finnegan 1988, 95). Upon waking, the poet must dictate the *meke* to a group of apprentices, who will memorize it and rehearse it with the performers, because once the poet communicates the *meke* to others, he promptly forgets it. It is only through the memory of others that the dance-song can be performed.

Often oral texts such as these employ various mnemonic devices, or memory aids, that allow the recall of extensive amounts of information. In the 1930s, the classicist Milman Parry (1930) argued that Homer's epic oral poems the *Iliad* and *Odyssey* exhibited a complex structure that facilitated memorization. These poems contain certain stock phrases and formulaic patterns, making it easier for the poet to recall large chunks of the text. In the Andes of South America, the Inca people used collections of knotted string called *khipu* for census records, accounts of tribute payments and economic output. The configuration of cords, knots, colours, and patterns allowed the organization of numerical data that could be carried across the Inca empire (Ascher and Ascher 1997). In many ways, *khipu* functioned like a modern spreadsheet, allowing the storage of far more numerical information than can be memorized directly.

BOX 10.1 – THE HINDU VEDAS AS ORAL LITERATURE

The Vedas are a collection of sacred oral texts and the basis for much Indian philosophy (Figure 10.1). But while written versions of these texts exist, the Vedas are meant to be spoken rather than read: in the *Mahabharata*, a classical Indian epic, people who write the Vedas down are condemned to hell. The reasons for this severity are rooted in a distinctly Indian sense of aesthetics towards language and the world. The Vedas are classified by Hindu scholars as *śruti*, meaning "learning by hearing"

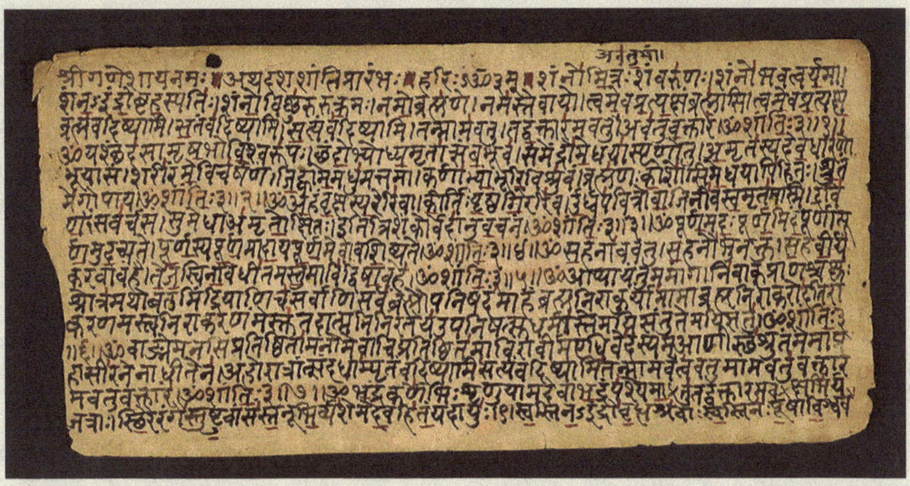

Figure 10.1 – Hindu mantra written in Sanskrit from 1829

Source: Kislak Center for Special Collections, University of Pennsylvania. Creative Commons PDM 1.0

(Coburn 1984), and the sacred content of these oral texts is tied to their pronunciation of the sounds acquired and spoken by holy sages after intense meditation. In Hindu tradition, great emphasis is therefore placed on correct recitation, particularly in the course of religious sacrifices and rituals, a skill that cannot be developed through reading alone. “Not only should the words or the order of words not be changed; even a single syllable wrongly pronounced or a single accent wrongly placed might bring ruin on the sacrificer and make his sacrifice futile” (Rocher 1994, 8).

The requirement that the Vedas and other classical Sanskrit texts be recited orally led to the development of complex mnemonics (ways of remembering) within the texts themselves. The Vedas are organized into verses called mantras that follow a very rigid and consistent poetic structure. For instance, the Bhagavadgita is organized into verses consisting of four lines of eight syllables. That poetic structure is itself then encoded into the text through lines that remind the orator what syllables and structures comprise the oration. Through these types of complex metrics, Indian priests can recite the entirety of the Bhagavadgita from memory, even those who do not understand the Sanskrit language in which it is written. The sacred truth of the Vedas is therefore not in the text itself, but in its sounds.

Predominantly literate cultures, on the other hand, rely more on written records, charts, and documents to record their histories. In Chinese lineage temples, for instance, genealogies are recorded in the form of bamboo or wooden tablets inscribed with the names of deceased ancestors. These ancestral tablets are both objects of worship and inscriptions of family history, charting back the lineage to its founding (Watson 1988, 13). Mayan scribes carved hieroglyphic texts onto shells and stone monuments that recount speeches by kings and other high officials. Along with a depiction of the event and the speaker were often "speech scrolls," lines of text that act like speech bubbles in comic books, quoting the exact words that were spoken as both a record and commemoration of the occasion (Law et al. 2013). In the following sections we will look at orality, then literacy, and finally how they are combined.

ORALITY AND VERBAL ART

The Boasian tradition that dominated anthropology in the early twentieth century made the collection of cultural texts (myths, stories, and songs) a key priority. These texts, written down by anthropologists wherever they did their research, were intended to provide grammatical information about the language, but also act as a kind of repository of cultural knowledge for future generations – Edward Sapir considered such texts to be sacrosanct (Darnell 2021, 148). For all their value as records, however, such texts are always partial. One thing that is lost when speech is written down is its prosody, the elements of intonation, stress, and pitch in a person's voice. These components allow the listener not only to infer a speaker's emotions (do they sound angry, sad, or cheerful?) but are a key component of interpreting the meaning of a sentence. A rising intonation turns a statement into a question ("Another test?"), while the literal meaning of a sentence can be inverted by saying it sarcastically ("That's just what I need").

During the 1970s, a group of linguistic anthropologists began trying to recapture the prosodic elements of ethnographic texts, to analyse them as they would have been spoken rather than as they were written down. Many of these texts were collected by folklorists and early anthropologists who attempted to preserve the songs, myths, legends, and stories of various groups, especially Indigenous peoples. This approach, called **ethnopoetics**, analyses the aesthetic patterns of narratives as forms of performance (Swann 1983; Tedlock 1977).

Compare two records of a Chinook myth about Grizzly Woman, a bear that has taken human form, and Water Bug. The first is a plain verbatim written account of the myth as told to the anthropologist Melville Jacobs.

> They are going, they turned to look, now she is pursuing them there. She curses Water Bug: "So that is why you came! You tell the people lies." She gets close to them, she took her snot, she threw it at them: their paddles broke.

Later, the linguistic anthropologist Dell Hymes (1981, 368) rearranged the text to reflect its poetic structure:

They are going,
  they turned to look,
    now she is pursuing them there.
She curses Water Bug:
  "So that is why you came!
  "You tell the people lies."
She gets close to them,
  she took her snot,
  she threw it at them:
    their paddles broke.

Hymes points out that organizing the text in this way highlights the many patterns of rhyme, metre, and rhythm that would have been present in the original spoken performance, such as alliteration of the pronoun "she" at the beginning of many lines. But there is also a deeper structure to this legend as well; in some parts, Grizzly Woman is given a grammatical prefix indicating that she is the agent of the action, while in others she is labelled as the passive recipient of action (even when she is the one doing things, like getting angry). The alternation between active and passive suggests the overall back-and-forth struggle between Grizzly Woman and Water Bug, as well as Grizzly Woman's own dual nature as both animal and human (Hymes 1981). These are far more than just incidental aspects of the narrative: instead, they elevate these stories to the status of **oral literature**, what Richard Bauman (1986, 9) describes as "the *artful* uses of oral language."

Another key component of oral texts is their situatedness, how they are rooted in specific acts of narration. A narrator is often recounting a past event (the narrative of what happened) to a current audience (the act of narration). These two events are in dialogue; the narrator tells the story for a reason, such as to comment on current events or impart some kind of lesson to the audience (Bakhtin 1981). A good example can be found in the work of Lila Abu-Lughod on Bedouin women's poetry. During a ceremony of reconciliation meant to bring together two lineages that had split, the wife of a tribal leader spontaneously offered Abu-Lughod the following verse:

yiksīhā dhbāb il-yās
il-'ēn wēn mā rāg jūhā…
A fog of despair shrouds
the eye, just when it starts to clear…

According to the women who interpreted it for her, the poem dramatizes the tension between the two groups and the poet's anxiety that the reconciliation will fail, but it also reflects back to the loss of her own son by violence many years before (Abu-Lughod 1986, 24–5). These poems therefore connect past and present while adding commentary on personal situations and relationships.

Performance

"Oral literature," writes Ruth Finnegan (2012, 4), "is by definition dependent on a performer who formulates it in words on a specific occasion – there is no other way in which it can be realized as a literary product." This performance includes the prosodic and poetic features discussed above, but we also need to appreciate how oral performers are in dialogue with their audiences, often in ways that are more direct than for authors of written texts. Performance is, in many ways, audience centric. Because the speaker is usually speaking *to* others – an audience that can hear and evaluate the quality of the speaker's performance – greater attention is paid to the mode of expression than in non-performance contexts.

Performances draw upon a particular shared model of language called a **genre**. A genre is a combination of features that structure a text and allow us to identify it as being of a particular type (Bauman 1999). This idea can be applied to both oral and written texts. Think of a fairy tale: it is usually a timeless tale involving enchantments, mythical creatures, and talking animals. It opens with the words "Once upon a time" and concludes with a happy ending and an overarching moral lesson for the audience. These elements were first explored by the Soviet folklorist Vladimir Propp (1968) in the 1920s. By following these conventions, the fairy tale text associates itself with other examples from the genre (like Cinderella or Rapunzel) and gives the audience a standard by which to evaluate the text: is it a good fairy tale? Or a bad one?

In a now-classic article called "Verbal Art as Performance," the linguistic anthropologist Richard Bauman (1975) argued that three major elements are constitutive of oral performance. The first are linguistic features that orient the audience towards what type of genre they can expect to hear. Bauman, borrowing a term from Erving Goffman (1974) calls these **keys**, and they include things such as stock phrases or conventional expressions, structural features like rhyme or parallelism, and patterns of tempo or stress. When an American president greets an audience with the words, "My fellow Americans…" we can expect a performance in the genre of a political speech. Hip-hop performances may include keying phrases such as "Yo, yo, yo," with a rising intonation on each syllable that secures the attention of the audience and reinforces the use of that particular style.

Second, performances are typically **patterned**, by which Bauman means they follow a set of cultural ground rules for how the performance *should* be done. These include things like the setting, the organization of the text, and the roles various people will take on in the performance. Stage magic performances typically feature a single performer (perhaps with an assistant), who stands on a stage facing the audience. Their illusions usually proceed from performing simple tricks to, ideally, ending with an unbelievable climax. And they employ light-hearted humour and persistent patter to distract the audience while sleight of hand is being performed (Jones 2011). If the performance does not follow these familiar patterns, the audience might feel lost (which, of course, is sometimes the point with performances that try to upend familiar genres).

Finally, Bauman argues that a performance is not purely scripted but shows **emergence** during the act of performance itself. In other words, despite the conventionalized patterns, the success or failure of any given performance is a product of the performer's creativity and ability to respond to the audience. In stand-up comedy, jokes may not always elicit laughter, and from there the comedian may alter how they tell the next joke, skip material they think is too similar, or even go off on a tangent and heckle the audience for not laughing. The audience's evaluation of the performance is always, therefore, dependent upon the performer's skill in adapting to the audience's feedback.

Cheryl Wharry's description of sermons in African American churches shows how all these aspects of performance come together. Based on research conducted across the United States, Wharry argues, first of all, that Black ministers are not the sole authors of their sermons: the audience plays a critical role in constructing worship as an interactive event. "Silence in traditional Black churches is generally not viewed as indicative of a mesmerized or attentive audience; instead, it typically carries negative connotations" (Wharry 2003, 205). Wharry describes preachers and congregants engaging in a complex call-and-response dialogue, with formulaic phrases offered by the preachers ("Lord have mercy") eliciting responses from members of the audience ("Amen!"). Preaching is therefore a joint production, making the audience active participants in the performance.

Wharry notes that congregants are keyed into the performance by a series of phrases that frame the sermon – where the preacher becomes animated by "the Spirit" – as separate from other parts of the church service. For instance, preachers punctuate their talk with formulaic expressions such as "Praise God" and "Say Amen." While preaching from the pulpit, these sermons are patterned through frequent use of repetition in lines such as "a spiritual restoration, a spiritual revival, a spiritual resurrection." Sermons also employ a certain "rhythmic intensity" that builds from quiet to loud and makes use of pauses and metred emphasis to build up the sermon's emotional and spiritual impact. Finally, Wharry demonstrates how Black preachers use these rhetorical strategies to encourage the audience to "go up in praise"; the performance is emergent as preachers build upon the emotional response of the audience in crafting their own speech.

In Chapter 1 we discussed the notion of performance outlined in Noam Chomsky's work on generative grammar, which he describes as the imperfect realization of a speaker's competence in the act of speaking. The work in this section, in contrast, highlights that **verbal performance** is about more than just talking or a simple way of getting a message across. Performers make use of the full potential offered by language, playing with rhythm, words, sentence structure, and style to create verbal art. These texts draw upon cultural scripts that connect speakers and audiences in shared artistic events (Bauman and Briggs 1990b).

BOX 10.2 – SIGNIFYIN' IN BLACK ENGLISH

Oral discourse styles are not universal but tied to particular speech communities and their collective histories. Specific strategies shape how people talk, but also how they interpret the talk of others. A good example of this is the role played by **signifyin'** (written with the 'g' intentionally dropped from the end of the word) in the speech of Black communities. Signifyin' has a know-it-when-you-hear-it quality to it, but it points to a kind of intentional misunderstanding over the interpretation of meaning. As Claudia Mitchell-Kernan, a pioneering Black linguistic anthropologist, puts it, "Complimentary remarks may be delivered in a left-handed fashion. A particular utterance may be an insult in one context and not in another. What pretends to be informative may intend to be persuasive" (Mitchell-Kernan 1972, 166).

Adrienne Washington provides an example from a speech by Therese Patricia Okoumou, an activist who climbed the base of the Statue of Liberty in 2018 to protest the detention and separation of immigrant families. After her arrest and arraignment, Okoumou spoke outside the courthouse and expressed her gratitude to several groups. "I also wanna thank the United States Park Police... they've been very very wonderful to me. Talking about respect, courtesy, professionalism: I think the NYPD [New York Police Department] can learn something or two from them" (Washington 2020, 369). This kind of "pointed indirectness" allows Okoumou to praise one group of police while implicitly criticizing another group for the use of excessive violence.

Signifyin' and other Black verbal strategies have become important elements of hip-hop performance and rhyming. H. Samy Alim (2006, 84) describes how The

Roots, during a concert for a predominantly white audience at Stanford University, shifted from their usual hip-hop to performing theme songs from 1980s Black sitcoms while the students sang along snapping their fingers, seemingly oblivious to the group's implicit taunting. We can therefore see how a verbal strategy like signifyin' acts to subtly criticize outsiders while also linking its users together in a shared social world. Understanding these types of complex verbal pragmatics are key to successfully navigating a speech community.

LITERACY

Historically, the development of writing and literacy constituted nothing less than a revolution in information technology – it expanded the horizons of communication, creating new forms of media and new social structures organized around textual production (Finnegan 1988). Nevertheless, there has always been a tendency to invest this invention with monumental significance for the development of "civilization" and human "progress." Literacy gets associated with literature, law, and religion rather than the everyday minutiae of shopping lists and commercial accounts. As the linguist Roy Harris remarks, when Ezra Pound offered advice for *writers*, it was not in how to hold a pen; it was in how to compose great works of art (Harris 2000, 10). The conceit is that those people who cannot read are less intelligent, and those societies without a written script for their language are less developed.

Early anthropological work on literacy subscribed implicitly to this ideology that equated writing with cultural superiority. The anthropologist Jack Goody (1977) called literacy a "technology of the intellect" that marked a "great divide" between modern and small-scale societies. In fairness, his assertion was largely in response to early scholars who had posited that "primitive" peoples were cognitively different from modern Westerners; Goody argued that our brains are the same, but that literacy had enabled new cultural patterns. Among these were analytical logic, complex mathematics, and a new sense of time and history. These were possible, he maintained, because written texts facilitate new social practices. Texts allow people to reflect on the meanings and uses of particular words; genealogies record kinship relations back in time; histories give people a sense of what conditions led to the present. In other words, literacy permits what Goody characterizes as "abstract" forms of thinking, as contrasted with pre-literate, "concrete" forms of thinking (see also Greenfield 1972).

Many of Goody's grandiose claims about literacy as a kind of revolution in human thought have been critiqued by other scholars (Halverson 1992; Street 1984). Literacy, for instance, is not an either-or state; in many of the societies Goody discusses, only a small proportion of the population could actually read and write, and those who can often act as brokers that facilitate textual interaction with non-literate others (Besnier 1995). Most languages today have some kind of written orthography, and even when they do not, people are still impacted by written languages all around them; the intrusion of colonialism was often mediated by texts such as treaties and contracts (Hermes and Uran 2006). And the notion that logic is a consequence of literacy is belied by the fact that literate people act illogically all the time; rationality is not a product of being able to read.

At the same time, the emergence of literacy has had important social effects. These are evident not just in the ability to read, but in the *significance* of the written word itself. In many societies, writing acts as a kind of sacred or authoritative practice (Keane 2013). On Rossel Island, off the coast of Papua New Guinea, anthropologist Stephen Levinson notes that mission schools have led to widespread literacy; nevertheless, there are limited opportunities to use these skills. When things are written down, it is often in ritual contexts. During celebrations, public exchanges of traditional wealth (such as axes and shell necklaces) take place. "A young man is pressed into service to note who donated which axe, or which high-ranking shell coin, and to whom it was entrusted for safe keeping – for within a generation or two it will flow back to the donors or their descendants" (Levinson 2020, 14). The record he scrawls out will not last long, as bugs and the elements will quickly destroy the paper, but it is the act of writing itself that gives these exchanges a stamp of authority.

BOX 10.3 – LOVE LETTERS

> Dear my derling,
>
> What situation you are in there. I hope you are 100% fine. At this moment, I hope, you are enjoying your life with your friends. and this time I have nothing much to say. but just to let you know I realy want to make friendship with you.

This is how Luke, a young Papuan man, opened a letter to a young woman he liked (Kulick 2019, 149). The goals of the missionaries and government officials who brought schooling to Luke's area were to enable people to read the Bible and participate in Papua New Guinea's economic growth. But Luke and other young people like him saw another possibility: romance. If literacy enables communication across time and space, it allows young people to court each other in ways that were hardly possible before. And this gave birth to a new Papuan literary genre, the love letter.

In Nepal, Laura Ahearn studied the impacts of literacy on marriage. She discovered that the expansion of schooling and literacy also prompted young people to compose love letters as a way of courting each other (Ahearn 2001). As a result, the former practice of arranged marriages declined while elopements soared, as young people gradually began to exert more control over their life choices. Although traditional gender roles in Nepal can be very hierarchical, Ahearn found that the increased use of love letters in courtship also placed greater emphasis on the woman's consent in marriage. Overall, the genre of love letters can reveal a great deal about what is going on in a speech community.

The broad claims of Goody and other scholars about the cognitive and social impacts of literacy therefore often ignore the very specific ways literacy is practised in a range of different places and the changes over time. Brian Street (1984) labels their framework an **autonomous model of literacy**, which he critiques as generalizing and overly reductionist. "What is taken in the 'autonomous' model to be qualities inherent to literacy are in fact conventions of literacy practice in particular societies" (Street 1984, 4). In opposition to this, he proposes an **ideological model of literacy** that accounts for the ways in which literacy itself is a product of social forces, institutions, technologies, and their respective impacts on people's lives; in other words, it does not regard literacy as an attribute that a person or a society either has or does not have, but as an ideologically constituted practice.

For instance, Street traces out two types of literacy present in a northern Iranian village he studied. In schools, children developed what he calls "Maktab literacy," meaning schooling in Arabic for the purpose of reading the Qur'an. But opportunities in fruit-cropping also led to "commercial literacy" as literate people turned their skills towards economic development. While Maktab literacy focused on recitation and reflected a sacred approach to texts, commercial literacy required growers and dealers to innovate new ways to organize texts to reflect contract agreements and economic transactions. Despite both of these types of literacy being mediated by the Arabic script, the relations each group had with texts were very different (Street 1984).

Literacy and Power

One thing Street learned from his research is that literacy is not just an individual skill; it is a social practice, and one often rooted in institutions that maintain relations of hierarchy and authority in a society. Literacy is, in other words, part of the exercise of power. In imperial China, for instance, entry into the elite ranks of government officials was limited to scholars who could score highly on civil examinations which tested their knowledge of classical Chinese texts and composition (Elman 2013).

Table 10.1 – Literacy Styles in Three Southeastern US Communities

Community	Maintown	Roadville	Trackton
Composition	White, middle-class	White, working-class	Black, working-class
Literacy Events	• Reading is interactive, combining stories with comments and questions about the text • Children collaborate with parents	• Reading limited to recitation of texts by parents • Children listen passively to parents	• Storytelling and narration are verbal; limited use of literacy skills • Children develop and employ rich verbal repertoires
Literacy Practice	Metaliteracy	Textual Literacy	Orality

Source: Adapted from Heath (1983)

Because such knowledge required years of schooling and preparation, literacy therefore reinforced power hierarchies in classical Chinese society between those families that could afford a rigorous education for their children and those families that could not. But literacy often excludes people in ways that are considerably more subtle.

Did anyone read you bedtime stories when you were a kid? When linguistic anthropologist Shirley Brice Heath (1983) wanted to understand why some types of students succeed in reading while others do not, she found that most studies at the time focused on what was going on in classrooms. Instead, Heath proposed looking at the ways children become literate at home. We are socialized to literacy – to a particular relationship with the written word – in much the same way that we are socialized to language as children (see Chapter 3 – Language Socialization). In particular, Heath argued that people are taught what a text is – how to use it, how to create a new one, and so forth – and that these ideas are perceived as natural ("Of course that's how you read") when in fact they are culturally specific.

To understand this, Heath decided to differentiate **literacy practices**, which are the cultural norms for using and understanding written texts, from **literacy events**, specific times and places when people are using texts (Barton and Hamilton 2000, 7–8). Heath argues that our cultural literacy practices are taught to children through literacy events like reading books together or pointing out words in the environment, and that researchers in turn can use literacy events to reveal common literacy practices. Therefore, she spent time in three different communities in the southeastern United States, stratified in terms of race and class, that she labels Maintown, Roadville, and Trackton, to see how the children learned to read (Table 10.1).

In Maintown, children were exposed to literacy at an early age through books and story times. Parents not only read to their children, they also asked questions as they read ("What does the doggie say? What colour is the ball?"). As the children got older, there were frequent instances of "book talk" as children were encouraged to talk about what they were reading, create stories based on those books, and use their imagination.

In essence, reading became an interactive activity as parents used books to direct their child's attention to the topic, structure, and organization of the text.

In Roadville, children were also exposed to books as infants, but in a slightly different manner. Book reading focused on the information in the books: letters, numbers, objects, and so forth. The book was rarely the stimulus for other discussions. As one parent, whose daughter was interrupting to ask a question, said: "Wendy, stop that, you be quiet when someone is reading to you. You listen; now sit still and be quiet" (Heath 1983, 60). Books, in other words, were intended to be consumed passively for the factual information they contain.

In contrast, books were rarely part of the lives of children in Trackton. Children grew up in an oral environment, surrounded by multiple people talking. They quickly learned to imitate those styles of talk, and adults responded positively to children who could speak engagingly and hold an audience's attention. Stories were opportunities to perform (as in the oral texts discussed above), often incorporating outrageous or inventive content, and children learned to engage in complex forms of narration. But they were rarely exposed to written texts until they got to school.

Heath argues that these three environments, with very different types of literacy event, constitute three distinct forms of literacy practice: Trackton is predominantly oral, Roadville features textual literacy, and Maintown – with its focus on a critical awareness of literacy itself – is what we might call metaliteracy. All of these children exhibited equal levels of intelligence, but in school Maintown children did better. They were far more likely to go on to study in university, while Roadville children were streamed into vocational schools and Trackton children often ended up dropping out.

Why? Heath argues that schools employ the very forms of metaliteracy that Maintown children learned at home. Teachers ask children to reflect on texts, discuss the lessons that can be learned from them, and use them as a springboard for students to create their own – that's exactly what the Maintown parents were doing with their children at bedtime. Roadville children had trouble seeing books as anything other than sources of information. When Roadville children were asked to narrate a story, they tended to tell one from a book they had read rather than create their own. Trackton children often had problems at school; they were labelled disruptive and uncooperative. Instead of sitting quietly at their desks, they would walk around, imitate the teacher, break out into their own stories while being read to ("That's like the time I went to church…"), and so on. Heath points out that if their oral narratives had been written out, they probably would have captured the attention of educators, but as it was the students often received very low grades. Therefore, despite the variety of literacy practices in these three communities, only one of them was rewarded, and the structure of literacy ends up reproducing the social class distinctions as Maintown children were the ones that went on to higher-paying jobs.

MULTILITERACIES

From our discussion so far, it is clear that there is no singular form of text, and no singular way of reading or writing texts. How we read a letter, for instance, is different from how we read a text on our phones. These ideas are further developed by the notion of **multiliteracies**, a scholarly approach that accounts for the variety of textual forms we use, and the ways those texts are entangled with other modalities such as speech, images, and objects (Budach, Patrick, and Mackay 2015; Cope and Kalantzis 2009). Part of this approach also recognizes that knowledge and information are not always encoded in ways that are readily apparent if we use books and other written texts as a model for literacy. Indigenous knowledge practices that incorporate landscape, myth, music, and dance can be "read" for meaning in ways that parallel – but are experientially different from – reading words on a page (Balanoff et al. 2009).

In one literacy project based in the Arctic territory of Nunavut, for instance, spoken and written proficiency in Inuktitut was fostered through Inuit elders teaching younger women sewing skills. "For a given sewing project, a participant might start by journalling her goal, or looking for ideas in magazines, or asking an Elder for ideas. She might then do a draft drawing of pattern pieces, write labels on the pieces (maybe with the help of an instructor), and then listen to instructions on how to put the pieces together, ask for clarification, write notes for herself, and finally file all of the above in her learner's portfolio" (Tulloch et al. 2017, 451).

Another study of an Inuit community centre in Ottawa contrasts conventional language-teaching programs, generally used to provide Inuit with employment skills, with an Aboriginal-centred one (Patrick, Budach, and Muckpaloo 2013). A significant challenge for Inuit families that have migrated to urban areas is not only the preponderance of other languages around them, but the physical distance from their Arctic homeland and environment. To foster youth literacy, rather than teaching Inuktitut solely from textbooks, the activists and elders leading this program incorporated songs, objects, and interactive activities into language instruction drawn from their heritage.

In one activity, urban Inuit children learned about fishing for sculpin, small bony fish common in Arctic environments. Through a *kanaijuq* (an Inuktitut chant), they learned to how to urge the fish to stay near shore and be caught. The children then constructed fishing rods using wood and *ulu* knives. These objects were not just learning aids, but necessary components of the song and the knowledge it was trying to teach: "divorcing the song from the object and the practice would not be appropriate – we need the rod!" (Patrick, Budach, and Muckpaloo 2013, 57). The activity then became the basis for collaborative stories written by the children and adults in Inuktitut. Recognizing the ways in which literacy is embedded in other material and narrative practices – from telling stories to holding a sewing needle – helps language learners develop connections to relevant cultural knowledge and heritage. Ultimately, it has a positive effect on the development of their overall language abilities, enabling them to pass this knowledge on to succeeding generations.

CONCLUSION

Literacy is about far more than just reading. As we have seen in this chapter, something as simple as opening a newspaper in a teashop or reading a bedtime story are practices charged with significance. They can incorporate forms of talk, such as in oral performance, and integrate them with the written word. These are not passive skills but modes of social action: we *do* things with texts.

Texts are also sites of power. Those who can read may control access to information for those who cannot, while institutions shape ideologies about how texts should be read, circulated, and interpreted.

As Dell Hymes showed in rearranging Chinook narratives into poetry, even the ways we write texts can impact our impressions of others. The other side of this is the immense creativity that authors can put into their texts, like Papuan or Nepali love letters. When used in oral performance, texts can stir emotions and call us to action. In the next chapter, we will consider how the digital revolution, which has moved so much of our textual communication online and is mediated by technological interfaces like phones and tablets, affects our use of language.

BOX 10.4 – RESEARCH SPOTLIGHT: JENANNE FERGUSON

Ferguson, Jenanne. 2021. How Words Make the World: Language Materialities and the Circulation of the Sakha Algys. *Multilingua* 40 (4): 433–61.

One of the key lessons of this chapter is that orality and literacy are not mutually exclusive – almost all societies employ both in communication. But as the ideological model of literacy posits, they are often used in different ways and for different purposes. In this article, MacEwan University linguistic anthropologist Jenanne Ferguson looks at *algys*, a traditional genre of spoken blessing among Sakha speakers of Siberia (Figure 10.2).

Algys are offered during rituals and ceremonies, from major events like the summer solstice celebration to everyday occasions such as weddings or a family meal. Important algys are the preserve of an *algyschyt*, a ritual orator or shaman, who composes a long

Figure 10.2 – An algyschyt (blessing-giver) makes an offering of food during an algys, summer solstice festival, Sakha Republic

Source: Image courtesy of Jenanne Ferguson

and original blessing while making offerings of mare's milk, food, and burnt herbs. The Sakha that Ferguson worked with characterize the spoken words of the algys as animated by the algyschyt's spiritual power. This gives language potency, the ability to influence the material world and bring desired conditions into reality.

Recently, various algys have been appearing as text, both in the form of books and magazines but also online, circulated and shared through social media (see Chapter 11 – Digital Language). Ferguson argues that the power of the spoken algys has been transformed in this new written format. Instead of embodying the spiritual power of the shaman, written texts spread the blessings widely to new audiences. As Ferguson argues, "writing is not powerful because it is uncommon in Sakha speakers' lives, but rather it is powerful for what it can do within the global sphere, partly in terms of bestowing prestige and legitimacy on the language and also what it can do for easing the continuous transmission of not only the Sakha language in general but for oral literary genres like algys" (Ferguson 2021, 453).

Ferguson's article is rich in ethnographic detail about the performance and reception of algys among urban Sakha. She contributes to an emerging field of research on **language materiality**, which essentially points to how language is often entangled with objects (like the fishing rod or *ulu* in the Inuktitut example above). Consider how, for instance, language is a key component of branding or advertising for various products. Or, in this case, think of the ways the algys is tied to ritual offerings and even the physicality of the paper on which it is now being recorded.

Sakha is a minority language within Russia, and during the Soviet period performing rituals – or even speaking Sakha – was devalued by the state. However, new technologies and the circulation of written algys through the internet constitute an emerging forum within which Sakha language and culture can be celebrated.

Discussion

1. Heath's research on bedtime stories that we discussed above is very poignant because it shows how something as simple as reading a bedtime story is actually tied into the reproduction of social class. Do you remember being read to? How did you engage with texts as a child? In her research, Heath says that teachers expect students to move from *what-explanations* (such as "what is the frog doing in this story?") to *reason-explanations* ("why is the frog doing that?"). Did the questions you were asked reflect this kind of progression?
2. Literacy events are times when people use written texts, and literacy practices are our general rules for using written texts. In other words, the way we do things is a reflection of a larger cultural framework, and anthropologists often see a connection between culture and practice. How does this compare to the competence/performance distinction discussed by Chomsky or to Saussure's *langue* and *parole* (discussed in Chapter 1)?
3. We generally think of oral performances as something done on stage: acting in a play or giving a speech. But the ideas we have discussed about oral performance can be applied to a range of different activities. Think about a typical class: how does your professor key the audience into the lecture? What patterns does that performance exhibit, and how is the performance emergent during the class itself?
4. Signifyin' is a typical verbal strategy in Black communities, but all speech communities have such oral discourse styles. Sometimes these can be highly formalized, like Robert's Rules of Order (where someone makes a motion, another seconds it, and then people vote). Or they can be less explicit, like teasing your friends. Think of a genre of talk you regularly use and see if you can express the full range of social rules behind it.

11

Digital Language

Topics

- New communication technologies
- Relationships between media
- Digital environments creating new forms of language

Suppose you are a university student who has been in a relationship for the last two months, but it isn't working out. Maybe you two have different schedules, or you argue too much about politics, or you've just come to the realization this person isn't your type. You want to break up. How do you do it?

Even just 30 years ago you had pretty much three choices: you could write the person a letter, give them a phone call, or tell them in person. Each of these had advantages and disadvantages. Telling someone in person was perceived as more considerate, but you might have to deal with some emotional fallout. Writing a letter had no such risk, but unless it was a long-distance relationship, it felt cold and impersonal. Doing it over the phone was somewhere in between.

Now, however, there are a lot of options. You can do it in person, over the phone, send a text, send a direct message, or leave a voice message. You can video chat, video message, or you could stop following them on social media, unfriend them, ghost them – meaning you stop responding to their messages – or, and this is probably the most extreme, block them altogether. Each of these options also has different implications. Is it all right to end a two-month relationship by text message? Or do you owe it to them to do it in person? What about how you do it: should you write out all your words, or can you use textspeak (omg!)? How long does it need to be? Are emoji okay?

These are the kinds of questions linguistic anthropologist Ilana Gershon sought to explore in her book *The Breakup 2.0: Disconnecting over New Media* (2010). One of the things she realized is that not only is the message itself a crucial concern for how people evaluate the nature of a breakup, but also the medium. In this context, a **medium** (from which we get the plural "media") is a particular channel of communication. Media can include conventional formats like books and television, but also voice, photography, music, social media platforms, and so forth. We already know about language ideologies; Gershon develops the notion of **media ideologies** to explain the sets of beliefs we have about different channels of communication. Those beliefs, in turn, shape how we engage with and use those technologies.

For instance, think about email. An email retains much of the structure and organization of printed letters: it has a salutation, full sentences, paragraphs, and a signature (a lot of workplaces even have standard digital signatures the same way they have a letterhead for official letters). That gives email a relatively formal feel; it is a medium for official or formal correspondence. Students told Gershon that they used email with professors, parents, bosses, and other people in authority – but they would *never* send an email to a friend about meeting up for dinner. These media ideologies shape how we use and interpret a message sent by email. Yet Gershon also points out that not everyone agrees on how different media should be used; some people think it is fine to break up with a text, others would disagree. As with any speech community, the norms and ideologies surrounding the choice of various media are a product of practice, of people using those technologies and figuring them out as they go.

BOX 11.1 – DIGITAL SPEECH COMMUNITIES

In Chapter 1 we discussed the concept of a speech community, defined as a group of people with a shared set of language practices and ideas about their use. As we saw, the presumption of a speech community is that it is based around people talking to each other. But digital technologies and social media raise the possibility of online speech communities which are effectively "deterritorialized"; they exist in virtual, rather than physical, space.

Many people imagine that our lives will gradually move online until we exist primarily in virtual worlds; this belief led Facebook chairman Mark Zuckerberg to invest billions of dollars in the attempt to develop an immersive augmented reality called the metaverse (it did not go well). Online communities such as Second Life, Decentraland, and Habbo thrive on the promise of being able to do anything virtually that you can do in real life while participating in a shared community of other users (Boellstorff 2008).

Despite this, as Marco Jacquemet (2019, 41) writes, people in digital speech communities maintain "simultaneous presence in a multiplicity of sites and by participating in elective networks spread over transnational territories." In other words, we just can't seem to give up on non-virtual interaction.

Even people whose lives are deeply interwoven with the virtual connectivity of online life still often celebrate the opportunity for in-person connections. When Gabriella Coleman studied hacker conferences – events catering to hardcore computer programmers – she found a celebration of the chance to socialize in real life by people who normally interact with each other virtually. Conferences allowed hackers to "collectively enact, make visible, and subsequently celebrate many elements of their quotidian technological lifeworld, whether it is by laying down cable, setting up a server, giving talks about technology or hacking up some new source code" (Coleman 2010, 5). Coleman therefore argues that we should not think of online connectivity as displacing physical interaction. Indeed, as most of us found out during the COVID-19 pandemic, talking to others in person after long periods of virtual interaction can be intensely emotional and cathartic.

The ways we communicate, the languages we communicate with, and the implications of all those choices have changed considerably in the last few decades. Many of you will conduct the majority of your communication with others online, through social media and other apps, which was hardly possible before the invention of smartphones. A lot of people see these as merely technological changes – faster computers, better Wi-Fi, new apps – but they are also profoundly cultural. Remember, if culture is a way of *doing*, then the culture of staying in touch and interacting with others has been transformed by how we *use* technologies. It's a brave new world, and the implications for language and how we communicate with each other are profound.

NEW COMMUNICATION TECHNOLOGIES

The modern telephone was invented in 1876, and by 1930 there were nearly 20 million telephones in the United States, with 42 per cent of American households having one (Fischer 1992, 53). Nevertheless, telephones were rarely marketed as social tools; they were originally envisioned as a way for businesses to connect with customers. Marketing for telephone services in the 1910s, for instance, stressed that businesses could save time with telephones by sending messages more quickly than by using mail, while customers could call to book appointments, order goods, or retain services when urgently needed (Fischer 1992, 67). Despite those efforts, by the 1920s, most people were using telephones socially to check in with friends and relatives, share news, or let someone know if they were going to be late.

Adopting the telephone required a process of socialization as people worked out the norms and etiquette of this new technology. What should one say when making or answering a call? The AT&T company notoriously viewed saying "hello" as vulgar, encouraging customers to formally introduce themselves and state the name of the person they sought to speak with (Fischer 1992, 71). Many households at the time had shared telephone lines, and questions were raised about whether it was rude to listen in on the conversations of others, how long conversations should last, and in what circumstances someone could interrupt a conversation to make their own call. The telephone also became a key medium for creating and managing romantic relationships, leading to questions about proper and respectable usage: "An etiquette column in 1930 warned 'Patty' that to ensure that her boyfriend would 'respect and admire her, she does not call him up during business or working hours… [and at home] she should not hold him up to the ridicule of his family by holding an absurdly long telephone conversation'" (Fischer 1992, 234). In other words, the introduction of the telephone as a new communicative technology led to discussions between its inventors, service providers, and customers negotiating the ways it should be used.

One of the early scholars who considered the impact of new communication technologies was Marshall McLuhan. Writing in 1964, he coined the very popular, but somewhat enigmatic, phrase, "the medium is the message" (McLuhan 1964, 23). McLuhan's point was that the content of any message (a phone call, for instance) is of secondary importance to the nature of the medium itself (the telephone) and its power to reshape our lives and understandings. Even at a time when not every household had one, the telephone changed how people spread news, did business, designed their living spaces, cultivated relationships, and projected their voices out into the world. These changes were provoked by the capabilities the new technology offered. The possibilities and constraints of any communication technology are known as **affordances**, and they shape how communities use media (boyd 2010).

When new media technologies are introduced, they are often initially used in ways similar to pre-existing technologies, but what follows is a period of rapid acculturation and adaptation to new possibilities. The first television shows were shot like stage plays, but as creators got used to the medium, the camera became more mobile and actors learned to speak directly to the viewing audience through it. The developers of the social media platform Twitter (now called X) at first believed their software would be used like other social media. As Evan Williams, one of its creators, has noted, "With Twitter, it wasn't clear what it was. They called it a social network, they called it microblogging, but it was hard to define, because it didn't replace anything. There was this

Figure 11.1 – Two tweets that share the same hashtag but are used for very different pragmatic effects

path of discovery with something like that, where over time you figure out what it is" (Lapowsky 2013). Twitter provided unique technological affordances that other social media lacked. People could use hashtags (like #linganth) to mark their tweets, allowing users to conduct searches of related conversations and retweet them to others. As people interacted with the platform, Twitter became less a means of updating others about one's life and more of a distributed conversation through which people engage and debate with each other.

In 2014, an unarmed Black teenager named Michael Brown was shot and killed by police in the city of Ferguson, Missouri. Anthropologists Yarimar Bonilla and Jonathan Rosa (2015) note that, in the aftermath, eight million tweets were tagged with #Ferguson. On its surface, #Ferguson appears to fulfill the organizational function of hashtags that the platform's designers intended. Users were able to use #Ferguson to share information, find eyewitness accounts, and register their opinions about the event. But Bonilla and Rosa argue that hashtags also have a broader pragmatic function for people commenting on the shooting and subsequent protests.

> Hashtags allow users to not simply "file" their comments but to performatively frame what these comments are "really about," thereby enabling users to indicate a meaning that might not be otherwise apparent. Hence, someone could write, "Decades of racial tension and increasing suburban poverty boiled to the surface last night" followed by the text "#Ferguson," as a way of creating a particular interpretive frame. (Bonilla and Rosa 2015, 5)

Nevertheless, hashtags can be deployed in different ways in different contexts and for different audiences, as the two tweets in Figure 11.1 make clear. The first merely tags the tweet with #InternationalWomensDay to associate itself with that movement. The second inverts the meaning of #InternationalWomensDay to make a sexist commentary on politics.

Despite the similarities to the adoption of the telephone and television in the twentieth century, today's new communication technologies do differ in important ways from prior ones. Unlike television and radio, where audiences are mainly passive recipients, new media are more likely to be interactive and participatory, where users contribute to the medium through posting, commenting, or "liking" various forms of content (Tagg 2015, 6). Let's look at what effects these new communicative technologies have on the way language is used.

INTERDISCURSIVITY

Discourse is not confined to one medium; it circulates among them. Part of the inherent creativity of people using language is the ability to link language used in one medium with that used in another. The term for this is **interdiscursivity** (Silverstein 2005). In an early study of this phenomenon, Debra Spitulnik (1996) considered the ways that radio language in Zambia circulated into everyday discourse. For instance, when a broadcaster on Zambian radio turns to a live reporter outside the studio, they often check that the connection is successful with the phrase "*Mwaikata* line?" This phrase blends ChiBemba, the most widely spoken national language, with English, and means, "Do you have the line?" Young Zambians have appropriated this phrase in everyday conversation, using the less formal "*Waikata* line?" to mean "Do you get me?"

Once the broadcaster has confirmed the reporter is on the line, they might signal for them to start with the phrase "*Ofata yu*," which is "over to you" assimilated to ChiBemba phonology. At a marriage preparation ceremony, where women take turns leading each other in song, Spitulnik watched as elder women used "*Ofata yu*" to hand responsibility for the next song over to other groups of women (Spitulnik 1996). In other words, discourse relevant to one medium (radio) was imported over into another (conversation) while still retaining its indexical values of cosmopolitanism and sophistication.

Interdiscursivity exists wherever messages are linked across multiple communicative channels, not just ones where the form of the message is the same. In fact, when similar messages are expressed differently *because* of the different media used, they can reveal information about the media ideologies governing each channel. The choice of which medium to use is significant because such channels do not exist in isolation; people always have a choice. The interdependency of different communicative channels is called **remediation**. For instance, texting – as not just a technology but a social practice – shares the same purpose as email: sending written messages to another person. But the affordances of texting are very different from the affordances of email, and the channels are therefore used in different ways. Email is more long-form and formal, texting short and concise. These differences exist because texting and email are linked together as related communicative technologies.

When Freddy MacKee (2016) studied how gay men in the United Kingdom use hook-up apps, he discovered that two of the most popular are Tinder and Grindr. Both are apps that allow users to connect with people they might be interested in dating. The difference, though, is that Tinder is a general-use dating app, whereas Grindr is marketed specifically to gay people. Tinder works by matching people through mutual attraction (swiping right to indicate interest), while Grindr shows profiles in order of proximity. The varying nature of these two different platforms leads to important differences in how gay men portray themselves. Profiles on Grindr tended to be more sexually explicit: users identified their sexual preferences ("top" or "bottom") and posted more sexually provocative pictures. Profiles on Tinder tended to focus on hobbies, interests, and type of employment (Figure 11.2).

When MacKee interviewed gay men using these apps, he learned that the remediation of these two channels was discussed in terms of their purpose. Grindr was deemed suitable for hookups and casual sex, while Tinder was a place to look for deeper and more long-term relationships. As one of his informants put it, "You should just assume that people logging on to Grindr are looking for sex" (MacKee 2016, 4). MacKee argues that this dynamic is not just due to Tinder being a predominantly heterosexual environment (where gay men feel the need to sanitize their sexuality in public), but to the app's design as well – Tinder automatically links the user's dating profile to their Facebook account. Since Facebook is frequently perceived to be a curated version of one's public self, Tinder profiles feel like a more formal, more public side of a person's identity.

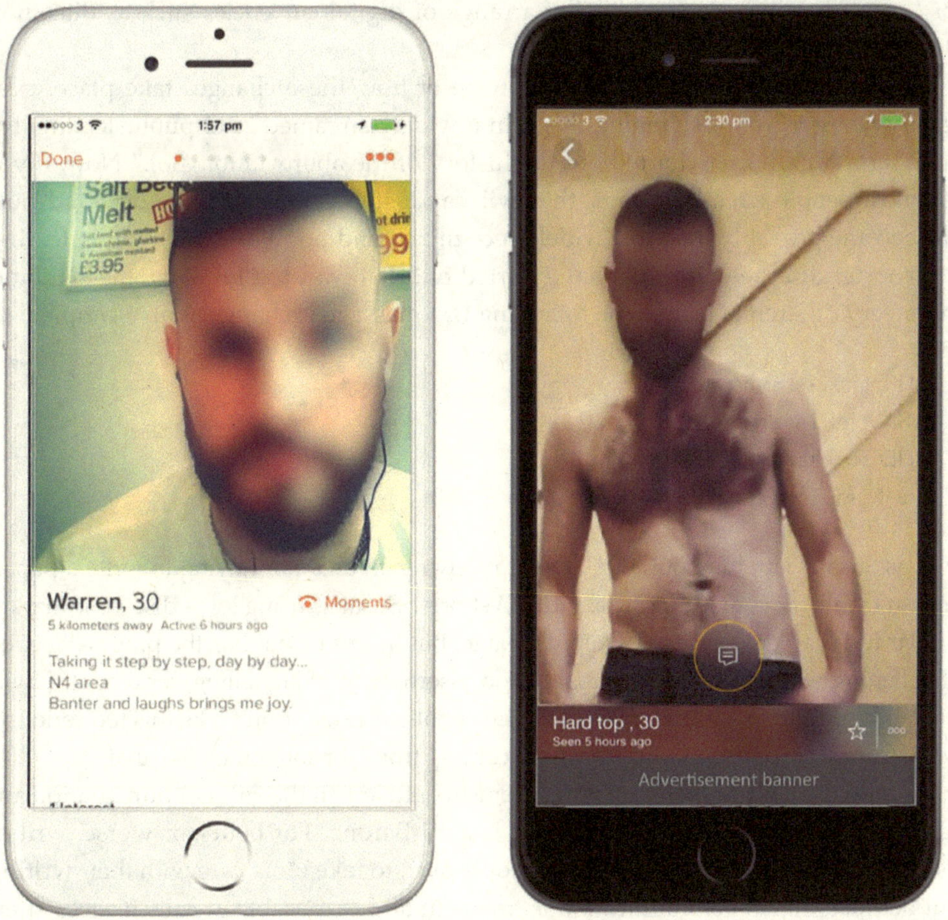

Figure 11.2 – Two dating profiles created by the same person. Tinder is on the left, Grindr on the right

Source: Reproduced by permission from MacKee (2016)

TEXTING LOL!

New communicative channels are not just different ways of using language; they can also change language itself and how it is used as a means of expression. Looking at any list of new words added to dictionaries shows that a significant number of them are related to new technologies: deepfake, influencer, and deplatform, for instance. These can also alter the meaning or interpretation of existing words. The prefix crypto- is attested as early as 1798 to convey a sense of something being concealed or not readily apparent (with "crypto-Catholic" and "crypto-Royalist" being early examples). Today, however, the term is most well-known as an abbreviation for "cryptocurrency," encompassing a range of digital currencies such as Bitcoin or Dogecoin.

We are often not even completely aware of how these changes take place, even when we are the ones changing them. In a widely streamed 2013 public lecture, linguist John McWhorter charted out the history of the abbreviation "lol." Now, if you ask most people what lol means, they will say it stands for "laughing out loud" and has become probably the most widely recognized and popular expression in texting. McWhorter disagrees; it might have started out that way, but lol today means something very different. He uses the following text message exchange as an example:

> JULIE: I just sent you an email
> SUSAN: lol, I see it
> JULIE: So what's up?
> SUSAN: lol, I have to write a 10 page paper

Why is Susan "laughing out loud" about receiving an email or having to write a paper? She isn't really, of course. According to McWhorter, Susan is using lol as discourse marker, similar to "um" or "hey" in spoken language, but in this case it has the pragmatic effect of softening what could come across as too assertive, or of signalling her empathy with the other speaker (McWhorter 2013). Lol essentially means, "don't take this too seriously, we're friends, I understand where you're coming from" or something like that.

People often get upset that texting seems to jettison all the rules of punctuation and capitalization. In the words of linguist Naomi Baron, "For better or worse, writing used to be different." She argues that people used to take more care with their writing, but because digital communication is transient and disposable, it calls for less attention from the author. "As a result, our standards as readers, writers, and even publishers are becoming less discerning" (Baron 2008, 166). However, McWhorter pushes back against the idea that texting is killing language. The technological affordances of text messaging, he argues, make the medium far more like speaking than writing: "Now we can write the way we talk" (McWhorter 2013). Formal writing and literature still exist, but they are more likely to emerge from the author using a keyboard on a computer, not from typing on a phone.

Texting therefore signals a monumental shift in communicative practices as we draw upon new media channels with new technological affordances that exist in new relationships of remediation with other channels. Those shifts, however, can play out in different forms in different settings; we should not assume that the effects of texting on language in North America or Europe will be identical to what is happening elsewhere in the world.

BOX 11.2 – EMOJI 🤔 😉 😆

In 1999, digital designer Shigetaka Kurita, building upon other image-based character sets, released a set of 176 pictograms for use with mobile phones in Japan (Danesi 2017). These **emoji** proved tremendously popular and have become standard on smartphones around the world. But what do these little pictures do and how are they used in communication?

Some people talk about emoji as a new kind of language. In 2010, Fred Benenson crowdfunded the translation of Herman Melville's novel *Moby Dick* into emoji and published it as *Emoji Dick; Or,* 🐳 (Benenson 2010). Keeping in mind the linguistic feature of perfect translatability (Chapter 2 – What Is Language?), this would seem to indicate that emoji, like any other language, have clear meanings that allow us to render any sentence in any language into emoji. That is not, however, the case. Lisa Gitelman, a professor of English at New York University, pointed out in a blog post that a reader already needs to be familiar with Melville's original (and the English text is provided in *Emoji Dick* along with the emoji) to understand Benenson's version. "Rare are the communications – within *Emoji Dick* or abroad in the world – in which emoji have syntactic utility" (Gitelman 2018). Would you be able to read 👎🔫❌👍➡😊👌 and derive meaning from it? (That is a translation of the line, "This is my substitute for pistol and ball.")

If not language, what are emoji and what do they do? First of all, it is worth pointing out that humans have been encoding narrative into images for thousands of years, even in early cave paintings (Nowell 2019). Pictographic representations are nothing new. Secondly, emoji are cultural artefacts rather than transparently meaningful signs. Marcel Danesi points out that 🤓 (nerd) and 🖖 (live long and prosper) make no sense outside of a Western cultural setting (and rely on a heady dose of pop culture). Rather, emoji provide nuance to a substantively textual medium. "They reinforce, expand, and annotate the meaning of a written communication, usually by enhancing the friendliness of the tone, or else by adding humorous tinges to it" (Danesi 2017, 15).

Like winks, nods, smirks, and other gestures, emoji supply multimodal information about our mood, intention, and the preferred interpretations of our discourse, but in a medium that is otherwise textual. That is probably why the most commonly used emoji are representations of human bodies (faces 😃, hands 🙏, and features like eyes 👀). They allow us to append subtle commentary to our words such as "that was a joke," "I am being sincere," or "that makes me sad."

In Papua New Guinea, for instance, Courtney Handman (2013) observed that texting is the main medium driving the spread of "cool" forms of speech. In particular, young people have taken to shortening and adding new sounds to words for people and places: the neighbourhoods of Sabama and Hohola in Port Moresby, for instance, become Sabs and Hox, respectively. That is significant, she argues, because Tok Pisin does not usually feature consonant clusters (like /bs/ and /ks/ in these examples). This shows that youth speech is being influenced by English (a language with many consonant clusters and one of the original sources for Tok Pisin) even though many traditionalists emphasize their language's autonomy from English. "Text messaging in Tok Pisin brings into focus… a re-imagination of the ways in which Papua New Guineans confront Western models of modernist transformation" (Handman 2013, 281).

Meanwhile, when linguistic anthropologist Janet McIntosh (2010) studied texting at her research site of Malindi, Kenya, she found it was transforming communication in very different ways. Members of the Giriama ethnic group are typically conversant in three different languages: their first language, Kigiriama; the national language, Kiswahili; and the colonial language of English. In speech, people tend to stick to Kigiriama or would occasionally use Kiswahili in professional settings and English in church. But on their phones, McIntosh noticed Giriama draw upon and blend all three languages together. Here, for instance, is a text from one Giriama woman to her sister, with Kigiriama italicized, Kiswahili in bold, and English in plain text:

> *Nikirira* pliz **bila kukosa**, the rent is neede,tell thom.
> *Come by*, please, **without fail**; the rent is needed. Tell them.

In this example, Giriama texters also draw upon the shorthands and acronyms of Western English texting (such as using "pliz" for "please").

McIntosh argues that while choice of spoken language is tied to conversational context, texting is a technology that transcends a sense of place by letting language "fly" between users. Giriama are therefore far more likely to blend languages together in texting than in speech. At the same time, the choice of which language to use in any particular message conveyed important information about the context and the user in terms of their social identity. The use of Kirigiama performatively marks a message with seriousness and weight, such as when people text their elders or discuss family issues and traditional healing rituals. English, on the other hand, is "associated with a hypothetical outside world of possibility, experimentation, and freedom. English offers the self-fashioning texter the opportunity to shuck off the weight and, perhaps, the stigma associated with Giriamaness, to create a persona who can instead flit between letters and numbers, shedding vowels and inventing shorthand, while demonstrating command over the highest status, most 'modern' language" (McIntosh

2010, 343). In a study of Facebook practices in another part of Kenya, Sarah Hillewaert (2015, 199) similarly argues that users are "consciously styling the self" through their online heteroglossic language choices that blend English with standard and vernacular forms of Swahili.

Is texting turning us into a herd of linguistic imbeciles unable to string together more than a few words or express ourselves clearly without resorting to textspeak abbreviations? srsly ppl, like wtf? Linguistic anthropologists – especially those of us of a certain age – might roll our eyes in private, but we also tend to look at the creative and transformational possibilities of texting. As with any new medium, people adapt it – and their language – to their needs, and that can teach us quite a bit about how societies engage with technology as a whole.

CONCLUSION

Ready to upload your consciousness to the cloud yet? Probably not, but as we have seen in this chapter, there are very real changes taking place in how we communicate. And I don't just mean new technologies – the ways we engage with emerging media are cultural, and therefore the norms around how we communicate, using which channel, with whom, and in which ways are in a constant state of development. Meanwhile, the language practices spawned in one medium are apt to bleed into others. I've even heard people hashtag their words in speech. Rather than existing in isolation, textual genres cross boundaries from digital platforms to speech and vice versa.

Apologies if anything written in this chapter feels corny and outdated. In my defence, most of you reading this book will have grown up with these technologies all around you, habituated to them from a young age, while for me they still feel unfamiliar and strange. But if there is a silver lining for me, it is this: change is going to continue happening. The sad truth is that it will be largely driven by the people who follow you, your younger siblings, cousins, and eventually children. Sorry, but if you're reading this now, you're about to be old like me.

BOX 11.3 – RESEARCH SPOTLIGHT: KAREN PENNESI

Pennesi, Karen. 2021. "What Does a Pandemic Sound Like? The Emergence of COVID Verbal Art." *Anthropologica* 63 (1): 1–15.

Do you remember that moment in March 2020? The one where our lives were suddenly disrupted and we had to learn how to Zoom and configure our webcams? I do – my students had a test scheduled for the next day and were emailing me in a panic about what this all meant. It is incredible to think in how short a span our lives were changed: teaching moved online, social distancing became the norm, and we turned to little rituals like banging pots outside in the evenings to support healthcare workers.

A linguistic anthropologist at Western University, Karen Pennesi, found refuge during that time in silly parody videos, songs, poems, and comedic sketches. Chris Mann's "My Corona," sung to the tune of The Knack's "My Sharona," declared, "I'm out of toilet paper, it's my Corona!" She argues, however, that these are not just trivial performances. "In response to the isolation, boredom, fear, uncertainty and upheaval brought on by the pandemic, people were turning to art to help make sense of the changing world around them, and to release some of their anxiety" (2021, 2).

People have always turned to art during troubled times, but Pennesi argues that the technological affordances of platforms like YouTube and TikTok lend COVID art a greater immediacy. If anti-war protest music of the 1960s was about a world living in peace, COVID songs made reference to more specific experiences such as face masks, hand sanitizer, and elbow bumping. Audiences can feel more engaged with these performances, leaving comments or replying to those of others, sometimes even with the artists responding themselves.

As much of the world returns to a kind of pre-pandemic normal, Pennesi reminds us that these digital performances act as an archive of the thoughts, feelings, and emotions that were part of the shared experience of quarantine. Hopefully the camaraderie of artists singing together with their audiences, making drums out of buckets and reflecting together on the challenges of isolation will remain one artefact of that moment when everything changed.

Discussion

1. As noted above, texting and email perform the same overall communicative function, but in very different ways. The remediation of these channels is evident in the genres and styles of the language used. You can actually compare them yourself: open the sent folder in your email and compare one of the messages there to the texts you have sent. Look at the style of the language, level of formality, organization and structure of the message, and so forth. How do they compare?

2. John McWhorter's lecture on texting is a masterpiece of linguistic storytelling but also raises some interesting questions. You might remember his name from Chapter 4 – Linguistic Relativity when we discussed his stance on linguistic relativity. Remember, he argues that the world looks the same in any language. How does his argument about texting – that this technology is fundamentally altering the way we communicate – connect with linguistic relativity?
3. New communication technologies beget new language ideologies and practices as we learn to use them on a regular basis. For instance, what does it mean to "like" someone's social media post? Is it different when you know the person well than when it is a relative stranger? Is it friendly? Flirty? And what about if you make a post and someone you are close to reads it but does not "like" it? Make a list of the conventions of using social media and how you navigate the significance of these new styles of interaction.
4. People have been annoying each other for as long as humans had speech, but the pragmatics of digital interaction are bringing new concepts and practices into being. For instance, consider the practice of trolling, instances where people attempt to provoke arguments and hijack online conversations. How do you understand the nature of trolling and how is this online practice different from what we do with speech? How do you respond to acts of trolling and what does that say about the conversational norms on digital platforms?

12

Researching Language in Society

Topics

- Research ethics
- Doing interviews
- Visual studies of language around us
- Mapping regional variation

Congratulations! If you've read everything in the book to this point, you have a solid grounding in the field of linguistic anthropology. Now just take some advanced courses, do a few years of graduate school, write a research proposal, apply for grants, and you're ready to go do your own research.

At least that's the path most students who are aiming to become linguistic anthropologists follow. But there is no reason you cannot apply what you have learned so far to interesting questions about language all around you. Perhaps your instructor will assign you some kind of research project for this class, or maybe you'd like to write an undergraduate thesis on a topic related to language. Or you could just do it for fun. In this chapter, we will be looking at the questions, methods, data, and research strategies that undergraduate students can use.

ETHICS

Before you start collecting data, you need to think about ethics. Most universities today have an office that reviews and clears research under one or more sets of ethics guidelines; these can be called Research Ethics Boards (REBs) or Institutional Review

Boards (IRBs). Ethics approval is normally required any time a person (either student or faculty) does research on living human beings.

There are a range of legal and policy guidelines governing ethical practices of research. In the United States these may operate at the state, institutional, or disciplinary level. For instance, the American Anthropological Association has published a set of *Principles of Professional Responsibility* that are intended to guide how anthropologists do their research. "In a field of such complex rights, responsibilities, and involvements, it is inevitable that misunderstandings, conflicts, and the need to make difficult choices will arise. Anthropologists are responsible for grappling with such difficulties and struggling to resolve them in ways compatible with the principles stated here" (AAA 2012). Research on human subjects in Canada is covered by guidelines created by three major funding bodies called the *Tri-Council Policy Statement* (CIHR, NSERC, and SSHRC 2018). If any of the research you undertake as a student involves working with people, you should consult your professor for advice on how to comply with the regulations of your university or college.

These policy frameworks can be very complex, and many linguistic anthropologists argue that because they were created with biomedical and psychological research methods in mind, they are largely unsuited to the types of ethnographic fieldwork pursued in our discipline. Psychology experiments, for instance, often employ practices of deception where the researchers do not inform participants why they are doing an experiment, because doing so might bias their results; deception is almost never practised in anthropological fieldwork. Nevertheless, there are some core principles found in all these documents that social science researchers should keep in mind.

1. **Do no harm** – This does not just mean physical harm (although you should definitely avoid that too) but includes social harm to the reputations or relationships of people as members of a community, harm to someone's mental health, harm to their sense of physical security, and harm to their sense of privacy.
2. **Informed consent** – People who participate in your research should know what they are getting into and what your methods and goals will be. Only once they understand what you are doing and why you are doing it can they make a reasonable choice about whether they will participate or not.
3. **Transparency and accessibility** – Back in the day, scholars who did research on language would write up a paper or thesis and it would get filed in the basement of a library, never to be seen again. Now that theses are digitized, it has become easier to access that research, but how often do people go looking for it? Increasingly, researchers are encouraged to share their findings with the public, particularly the people who contributed to it. This can be done through community presentations, blogs, websites, and social media.

Common practices to fulfill these principles include avoiding the publication of information that could identify individual participants (instead, we almost always use pseudonyms for people and places); obtaining permission from community leaders and elders before starting a research project; and treating our participants as meaningful collaborators rather than mere sources of data. Despite the straightforward nature of these principles, however, linguistic anthropological research is often characterized by multiple competing ethical obligations.

BOX 12.1 – ETHICS CASE STUDIES

One way of teaching ethical standards of research is to ask people to consider real or hypothetical ethical dilemmas. These are called **case studies** and encourage us to think about how we would respond to various predicaments, conflicts of interest, or uncomfortable situations during our research. The American Anthropological Association has posted several of these as part of an effort to communicate ethical principles to its membership (https://americananthro.org/learn-teach/handbook-on-ethical-issues-in-anthropology/).

- Is it okay to give and accept gifts from participants in our research? Gift-giving can be an important part of belonging to a community, and the relationships between anthropologists and research participants usually extend into the areas of friendship and collaboration. What to do, then, if the gifts given are illicit (like drugs) or were stolen?
- Although anthropologists usually use pseudonyms for their research participants, what if they want themselves to be identified in publications? How should one balance the obligation to protect the identities and private information of participants with their own agency and desire to be named?
- If an anthropologist witnesses a crime, are they obligated to report it to the authorities? What if the community has its own practices of dispute resolution that are typically followed to avoid conflicts spiralling out of control? What if the police directly question the anthropologist about the event – should we lie to them?

Not everyone will agree on how to resolve these dilemmas, not even professional anthropologists, who might offer competing perspectives. The point is not to find the "correct" course of action, but to consider how to fulfill our professional responsibilities in the best manner possible.

At this point, you might be wondering, "isn't this overthinking things a bit? How can doing research on *language*, of all things, be an ethically complicated undertaking?" But linguistic anthropologists confront ethical dilemmas all the time. For instance, who "owns" the research a linguistic anthropologist does on a language (particularly an endangered language)? What responsibilities does the researcher have to the community or the individuals who are the sources of language data? Is there information in the data that should be kept private or confidential, such as participation in criminal activity or immoral behaviour? In the 1980s, Mayan activists objected to linguistic research that appeared to legitimize Quechua borrowings from Spanish. Although such borrowings were widely used by Quechua speakers, documenting them as "Quechua" words could undermine efforts to assert their cultural distinctiveness and political autonomy (England 1992). None of these issues are easy to resolve, and they often emerge in practice because anthropologists may not be familiar with all the relationships, ideologies, and conflicts within a community at the outset of their research, no matter how good their planning going in.

Ethics education is becoming more widespread in graduate-level training for ethnographers and linguists. The point is to not simply avoid acting unethically, but to grapple with the various situations we might face and apply the principles of ethical research appropriately. A key part of this is recognizing that any kind of research does not take place in a vacuum where we can simply answer questions objectively. We always operate within complex political and social environments that require us to balance the rights and obligations of multiple stakeholders (the public, the community, funding organizations, and even ourselves) in the conduct of research.

INTERVIEWING: LEARNING HOW TO ASK, LEARNING HOW TO LISTEN

As we learned in Chapter 1 – Talking About Talk, most linguistic anthropologists engage in a long period of ethnographic fieldwork to gather their data. We do this because sociocultural phenomena, like language, are emergent; they are not fixed or predetermined, but the product of ongoing and complex interactions among people, ideologies, institutions, and social structures (we used this term to talk about the outcomes of performance too in Chapter 10 – Orality and Literacy). We may not even recognize a social pattern as a pattern until we have encountered it several times, talked about it, reflected on it with others, and so on. Long-term ethnography supports a nuanced appreciation of social action by undergoing a constant practice of learning, understanding, and revision by the researcher (Blommaert and Dong 2020). In other words, we really don't know what it is we are studying until we get somewhere and actually start studying it.

That is, however, not usually a viable strategy for undergraduate students who have classes, jobs, deadlines, and probably a mountain of student debt to worry about. If you can tackle a full ethnographic research project, that's great; but even if you cannot, or can only undertake a very limited ethnographic engagement with a question, there are other methods linguistic anthropologists draw on to inform their understandings. Some of these are **quantitative**; they involve identifying and counting things, such as how often a person uses a particular variable in their speech. Others are **qualitative**; they involve describing and interpreting things to understand causes and connections. Many combine both approaches to some degree or another (Johnstone 2000). I will talk more about linguistic landscape and dialect survey methods later, but let's start with interviewing.

If ethnography is a bit unplanned and relies upon things happening to the ethnographer (or the ethnographer putting themselves in *situations* where things happen to them), interviews provide a way of collecting data without waiting around for it. Some interviews, called unstructured interviews, are unguided; they are open-ended with no overarching plan or goal. Many have argued that ethnography itself is just one long unstructured interview. Other interviews, called structured interviews, are tightly controlled: think of a job interview where a person asks you a list of questions and records your answers. But in social science research, the most common type is the **semi-structured interview**. This method includes an overall plan and structure to the interview, but also recognizes the intersubjective nature of the interaction, with the flexibility to explore new questions, concepts, and ideas as the interview proceeds (Galletta 2013). While in a structured interview the emphasis is on comparability (seeing how each person answers a single question differently), in a semi-structured interview it is on collecting a person's ideas and interpretations, and then refining your understanding of them as you go.

Students of mine have interviewed Gaelic heritage language learners to understand their motivations, urban Acadian French speakers to determine how they build a connection to the rural areas where the language is more commonly spoken, and multiple pronoun users to comprehend what the practice says about their identities. We should be wary, however, of just treating an interview as a transparently objective way of gathering data. As Charles Briggs (1986, 2) has written, "because the interview is an accepted speech event in our own native speech communities, we take for granted that we know what it is and what it produces." In other words, we are so familiar with interviews (for jobs, to get into university, or on the news) that we tend to see the whole process as natural, even banal. But as linguistic anthropologists, we need to see the interview as a textual genre or framework just like any other interaction.

For instance, when I was doing fieldwork in China on the teaching of English, I would frequently sit for interviews with teachers and school administrators. These were obviously more formal to the participants, as the questions and answers were the focus of our interaction (instead of a complement to other things going on around us), and I would frequently record the interview to have a transcript of exactly what was said later. In the back of my notebook I had a plan, a list of topics I wanted to cover, including the person's background, pedagogy, relations with students, and so forth. Most of the time we did cover those topics. Eventually. But I was always struck by the sheer number of questions people were asking me: what is life abroad like, how does China compare to my home country, and what English teaching methods did I think were best? At first, I resisted answering these since *they* were the ones who were supposed to be giving *me* information. But over time, I realized just how productive these conversations were, as they challenged me to revise some of the assumptions I had brought into the field with me. We can call this a process of "learning how to listen," as we take the social world of the people we do research with seriously rather than trying to impose our own structures of understanding upon it.

Briggs's own interviews with Mexican-American carvers were initially very terse, as establishing a framework in which he was an outside researcher asking questions violated Mexicano cultural norms in which elders ask questions and novices answer. Briggs instead advocates for a period of reflection and accommodation where researchers first develop communicative competence in local language practices so that they can phrase their questions in a culturally appropriate manner (what he calls "learning how to ask") (Briggs 1986). In his own case, it was only when he took a more passive role and allowed the people he was working with to ask the questions that community members began taking it upon themselves to educate him in everything he needed to know.

Asking good questions is probably the most important thing linguistic anthropologists can do to gather data on language practices. But recent years have also seen the development of other techniques that can be used supplement what people "say" they do with language and can viably form the basis of the smaller research projects students undertake.

LINGUISTIC LANDSCAPE

In a landmark study, the Canadian scholars Rodrigue Landry and Richard Bourhis (1997) proposed documenting the **linguistic landscape** of any given territory by examining the presence (or absence) of various languages on signs such as advertising billboards, commercial shop signs, road signs, and place names. While their purpose was part of an effort to regulate language usage (they hypothesized that increasing signage in a particular language would increase the vitality of its speech community), many linguists have now turned our attention to documenting the ways language exists in social space.

Landry and Bourhis argued there are several types of signs around us that tell us different things about the environment. For instance, **public signage** is authorized by local authorities, such as in schools, government offices, on monuments, or in public announcements. **Private signage**, in contrast, is created by people or businesses, including advertising, retail signage, and unofficial messages like graffiti. Examining the diversity of languages included in these different types of signage has two functions:

- An **informational function** that tells us (and the people who live there) what languages are present in the community, their distribution, and what role they play
- A **symbolic function** that represents the identity, vitality, and relative status of the speech communities that use those languages in a particular area.

Private signage is more likely to serve the informational function: if there are lots of signs in Chinese script, for instance, as in the many Chinatowns throughout North America, it tells us something about the ethnic composition of the neighbourhood. Public signage, in contrast, is often symbolic, in that it represents official language policies and a view of what the community *should* look like. Public signs that include minority languages, for instance, affirm the validity of minority language speakers as rightful members of that community.

This is not to say that some signs (whether public or private) cannot perform both functions. Figure 12.1 is an image of public art painted on a wall in the Basque region of Spain. Although the Basque language, Euskara, is recognized as an official language at the local level, it has no official status at the national level (Cenoz and Gorter 2006). Up until the 1960s Euskara was stigmatized by outsiders and actively discouraged by Spain's leaders. Despite Euskara not being included in most public signage created by the national government, here we see an example of private signage created by Euskara speakers. It shows three athletes jumping hurdles labelled "integrity" (*osotasuna*), "right to decide" (*erabakitze eskubidea*), and "it's in our hands" (*gure esku dago*). That last phrase is also the name of organization advocating for a referendum on the Basque region's political status. This message shows us that Euskara is present in the area and valued by local speakers, but it would be difficult to comprehend without the background knowledge of Euskara and its history of marginalization. Linguistic landscapes therefore highlight the many ways in which language is political.

Conducting linguistic landscape research consists of two related processes: one is identifying the region to be investigated, along with examining its demographic and

Figure 12.1 – Mural in Euskara from Deba, Spain

Source: Image courtesy of Joakim Lilljegren

sociolinguistic characteristics. The other involves documenting the signage within that region. These two processes are inseparable because, as with discourse, visual signs of language are always embedded within a sociohistorical context (Blommaert 2013). For instance, to investigate the linguistic situation in Montreal – a city that is officially monolingual French, unofficially French–English bilingual, and, with large immigrant populations, increasingly multilingual – Jakob Leimgruber (2020) chose to document signage on Saint Catherine Street as it runs from one end of the city to the other. He travelled the entire length of the street, taking pictures of one sign within each city block. These images were geolocated and then added to a map indicating the distribution of each language in space (Figure 12.2).

Leimgruber noticed that public signs did not feature any languages other than English and French. Private signs included a mix of different languages, often with French and/or English combined with Arabic, Chinese, German, Hebrew, Spanish, and so forth. In the majority of cases, as a result of provincial language policies, the French text came first or was larger than that of other languages. The distribution of the signs was also significant. Monolingual English signs were mostly found in the western part

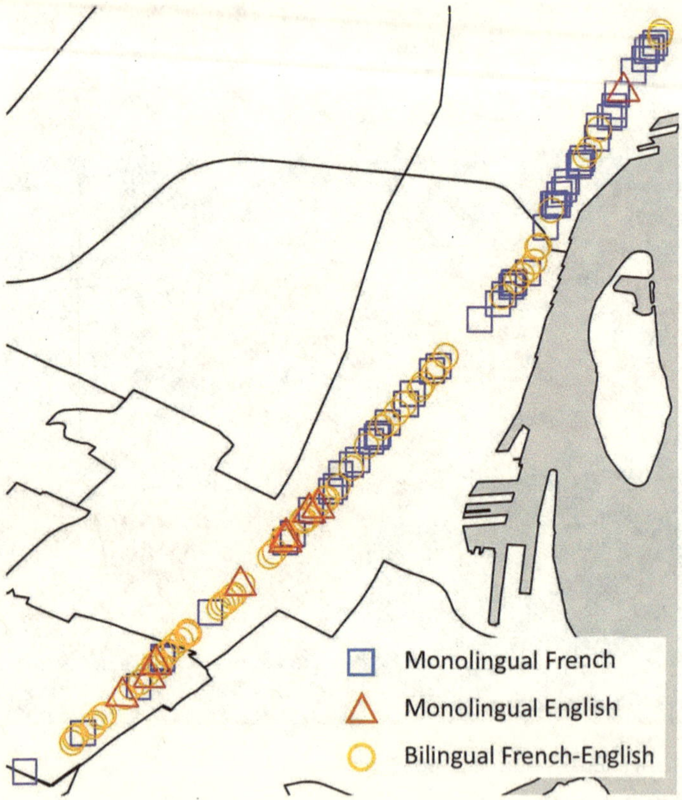

Figure 12.2 – Location of signs on Saint Catherine Street in Montreal categorized by language
Source: Image courtesy of Jakob Leimgruber

of the city, while monolingual French ones were concentrated in the east. Bilingual French–English signs were distributed throughout the whole street, but with their highest density in tourist areas. Languages other than French and English were only present in neighbourhoods with a traditionally ethnic character or the downtown commercial zone. This placement of signs reflects the demographic character of Montreal, with a traditionally anglophone population in the west and a francophone population in the east. As Leimgruber concludes, "The languages visible on Saint Catherine Street are, therefore, a multilayered reflection of the demographic distribution of speakers on the ground, of a complex policy environment, of local actors utilizing non-local linguistic resources, and of linguistic resources being used for indexical, symbolic functions" (2020, 12–13).

To do a linguistic landscape study, therefore, requires nothing more than a camera and a keen understanding of the communities inhabiting urban environments.

The software tools to compile and organize the data are mostly free and easy to use. Information on each photograph can be contained in a database or spreadsheet, with the location, language(s), text translation, and other relevant data. Most map applications (such as Google Maps) allow users to create their own personal maps and upload images to them, tagged to the places where the images were taken. There is also a free linguistic landscape app called Lingscape (https://lingscape.uni.lu/) that automatically tags and integrates the images taken on a smartphone with digital maps.

Many of my own students have completed projects such as these. In one of my classes, students collect images of non-English-language signage in Halifax as they travel throughout the city, which are then uploaded to a shared map. This allows us to see how non-English languages are distributed and what purposes they serve. We have found, for instance, that most non-English languages are found on private commercial signs for restaurants and businesses. The exception is French, which tends to only be found on public signage (such as plaques at tourist sites).

We also compare how certain languages are used in and around our province. In Truro, a mid-size city about an hour's drive north of Halifax, Chinese script can be found on Chinese restaurants, but it tends to be highly stylized and limited to the restaurant's name, often found on the building itself or at the top of menus. In contrast, Chinese script in Halifax Chinese restaurants is more likely to be intended for reading, with a legible font and sometimes even without English translation (as in a list of specials written on a whiteboard by the entrance). These two examples show the same language intended for two different audiences: the first lends a sense of exotic charm and authenticity to largely English-speaking customers, the other provides communicative clarity for a presumably Chinese-speaking clientele.

DIALECT SURVEYS

Shortly after I started teaching on the east coast, I told one of my classes we would take up the test during our next class. Two hundred students looked at me in confusion. A couple came up after the class ended and asked what I meant: did I mean they had to go somewhere and pick up their test papers? I was confused too – why couldn't they understand what I meant, that we would go over the correct responses together? I had inadvertently hit upon a dialect difference between central and eastern Canada. The phrase "take up the test" means something where I grew up and went to school, but it is not used outside that region.

How can we detect and understand dialect differences like these, particularly when people often are not consciously aware of those differences unless they run into a situation like mine? Another practical research strategy that anyone can undertake is a **dialect survey**. This approach asks people about their speech and, with a large enough sample size, allows us to make generalizations about the variety of language used in a particular area (Dollinger 2015). One of the most extensive of these surveys has been the North American Regional Vocabulary Survey (NARVS), which asks 53 questions about the words used in different English dialects (Boberg 2005). When combined with other methods (such as interviewing or ethnography), dialect surveys can also give us a sense of the attitudes and ideologies towards local speech practices in a community. I also put together a dialect survey with students in one of my classes, and we administer it to research the characteristics of the local dialect.

Most dialect survey questions elicit lexical information: what the word for something is. For instance:

> What do you call the sweet creamy layer on top of a cake?

The two most common answers are "frosting" and "icing"; studies have shown that these are geographically distinct, with icing being most common in Canada and the southern United States, and frosting throughout the rest of North America (Boberg 2005).

Other types of questions may examine pronunciation patterns:

> Does the word NEWS sound like *nooze* or *nyooze*?

Speakers of British English tend to choose the latter, while speakers of Canadian and American English choose the former (a phenomenon called yod-dropping). The exception is English speakers in Quebec who still retain the *nyooze* pronunciation as a prestige form from British English (Pi 2006).

By asking a range of these types of questions, we can begin to see how dialect differences are organized geographically. For instance, while Canadian English has been heavily influenced by American English in terms of both vocabulary and pronunciation, there are still some distinct differences between them. Dialect surveys like NARVS have shown that Canadians still predominantly use the British *tap* rather than American *faucet*, British *chocolate bar* rather than American *candy bar*, and British *cutlery* rather than American *silverware* (Boberg 2010, 111). The unique form of Canadian English sustains the sense of a distinct Canadian identity.

Another line of analysis offered by dialect surveys is the correlation of speech differences to demographic differences. Most dialect surveys collect some basic information from respondents in terms of gender, age, and place where the person grew up. That's because our natural speech styles are generally developed when we are young and resist changes as we grow up; seeing how older people speak is therefore like looking at a time capsule of what language was like when they were young. You know that long, upholstered piece of furniture in your living room? When the linguist Jack Chambers asked Canadians for this word, people in their seventies and eighties tended to call it a *chesterfield* (derived from British English). No one in their twenties used the word, however, with almost all of them calling it a *couch* or *sofa* (Chambers 1998). That is because *chesterfield* was a prestigious term in the 1940s and 1950s but sounds quaint and outdated to young people today.

The first step in putting together a dialect survey requires a bit of brainstorming: what words, phrases, and pronunciations are different or unique to the area you are studying? This information can come from both in-group members (who may have travelled outside the region and realized some of these differences) and out-group members (who may have travelled into this region and done the same). Once, when my son was playing outside with a neighbour's child, the father called out, "Don't *biff* the ball at your friend!" Bingo! In Nova Scotia, biff means to throw something really hard, and that became one item on our dialect survey ("what word means throwing something really hard?"). Once these have been collected, you need to come up with a list of questions designed to elicit those words, such as the ones above, or see the list of questions used in NARVS (Boberg 2005). One key idea to communicate to survey participants is that you are not looking for the "correct" or "accepted" term (doing so just collects information on the standard language) but rather what people actually use.

Next is conducting the survey itself. There are a range of methodological issues to consider in that regard. Posting a dialect survey online, for instance, will generally net more responses, but responses to surveys administered in person are generally considered more valid because the researcher makes sure questions are answered conscientiously. Note that too many questions will leave respondents bored and exhausted; most dialect surveys feature between 20 and 50 questions. Those questions should also avoid guiding people to an answer: there are lots of words for sports shoes, such as *runners, running shoes, gym shoes,* and *sneakers,* but if you ask people what shoes they run in, it will bias the results to the former answers (NARVS uses the question, "what is the word for athletic shoes worn with jeans as casual footwear?"). The exact number of respondents needed depends on the method used and total number of questions, but generally scholars stress that a representative sample of the speech community (with a range of ages, locations, genders, education levels, and so on) is more important than sheer numbers.

Finally, once the data are collected, there are a range of statistical and graphical techniques for analysing and representing them. Many dialectologists perform sophisticated multivariate analyses on their data, such as correlating lexical choices to factors such as age, gender, social class, or education level (Dollinger 2015). This

Table 12.1 – Chart Recording Responses to a Dialect Survey

Q2.1	Q2.2	Q2.3	Q2.5	Q3.1	Q3.3	Q3.4	Q3.6
Birth Decade	Country	Province/ State	Hometown	What's the word for any sweet carbonated drink?	What do you call the stuff you put out each week to be taken to the dump?	What do you call a pizza with all the toppings on it?	What do you call the sweet creamy layer on top of a cake?
1960s	Canada	NS	Dartmouth	pop	garbage	the works	icing
1970s	Canada	BC	Comox	pop	garbage	loaded	icing
1930s	Canada	MB	The Pas	soda	garbage	the works	icing
1960s	Canada	NL	Goose Bay	pop	garbage	the works	icing
1990s	United States	MD	Baltimore	soda	trash	supreme	frosting

might be beyond the level of undergraduate research, but organizing responses by age allows the representation of language change in the form of a chart, such as Table 12.1. Another common means of presenting dialect data is in the form of heat maps, where the density of particular responses can be overlaid onto their geographical location.

CONCLUSION

One of the great things about studying language is that it is all around us: in the words people use, in how we communicate, in the signs that populate our environment. When I started my job as a professor, they asked me what resources I needed to do my research. The answer was pretty much a pen and paper, a digital recorder, and a plane ticket (that was the expensive part).

There is often a bit of mysticism surrounding academia, with all those fancy graduation gowns and higher degrees. But a lot of the research tools we use are straightforward – they just require a bit of initiative and practice. And these research practices have utility outside the university too – interviewing and linguistic landscape methods have been employed in market research, community engagement projects, political outreach, and more.

If you are the kind of person who likes studying language, hopefully this chapter has given you some ideas. It's not rocket science! All you need are some basic tools, a good ear, an open mind, and the right questions. Good luck!

BOX 12.2 – RESEARCH SPOTLIGHT: LISA SCHLEGL AND SALI TAGLIAMONTE

Schlegl, Lisa, and Sali Tagliamonte. 2021. "'How Do You Get to Tim Hortons?' Direction-Giving in Ontario Dialects." *Canadian Journal of Linguistics/Revue canadienne de linguistique* 66 (1): 1–30.

There's a popular chain of coffee and doughnut franchises in Canada called Tim Hortons; seriously, you're never very far away from one almost anywhere in the country. If you ask a random person how to get to one, they could employ a range of different verbal strategies. They might reference a landmark ("drive past the mall") or a direction ("drive north"). They could use specific names of streets ("go up Bloor") or generic terms ("go up this road"). Even the verb can vary: "turn left" or "make a left."

Sali Tagliamonte is a sociolinguist at the University of Toronto and, in collaboration with students like Lisa Schlegl, has been conducting a research project throughout the province on direction-giving. Although that is a very broad and complicated topic, their research methodology is surprisingly simple. Students were dropped off in a variety of places, from small towns to metropolitan cities, with a single task: approach people in public places and ask them how to get to Tim Hortons. Then they audio-recorded the responses.

Sociolinguists often incorporate more quantitative methods in their research, so Tagliamonte and colleagues have spent a lot of time coding and analysing the data. But even a cursory look at what they collected reveals some surprising patterns that show clear dialect differences between the more rural northern Ontario and densely populated southern Ontario groups. Speakers from Toronto, a major city, used landmarks and cardinal directions in their responses twice as often as people from rural areas. There were also regional differences in verb use: "In Northern Ontario, use of *turn* far surpassed any of the other variants, while in Toronto *make* was nearly as frequent as *turn*" (Schlegl and Tagliamonte 2021, 18–19).

What are we to make of these differences? Schlegl and Tagliamonte propose that rural speakers tend to take a more cooperative first-person perspective – they imagine themselves following the route with the listener – while urban speakers adopt a more top-down mental map of landmarks and cardinal directions for the listener to follow. But just by asking for directions, they also show that urban and rural populations in Ontario do not speak exactly alike – there are clear differences between them that sustain divergent forms of social identity; you just have to know how to ask about them.

Discussion

1. In this chapter, we talked about case studies as one way to grapple with ethical dilemmas in research. I put together one such case study for a class I teach on fieldwork methods in linguistic anthropology about the ethics of drawing on real languages and communities in popular fiction and media, based on the television show *Game of Thrones*. Have a look at the scenario detailed in the following text and think about how you would address the situation (https://tinyurl.com/2e3exp6s). This works well as a group exercise, and you can compare your own approach with others in the class. Ask your instructor what they would have done in that situation.
2. During the pandemic, researchers and students had to shift to new methods as social distancing rules and quarantines came into effect. A lot of us moved our research online. As we discussed in Chapter 11 – Digital Language, there are differences in the ideologies surrounding each channel, such as online or in-person communication. What would you need to change about your research strategy to conduct the types of projects we discussed above online? How would doing so affect your data or the conclusions you reach?
3. A linguistic landscape exercise does not have to have a huge dataset; just considering the histories, ideologies, and geographies of individual images can be an illuminating exercise in itself. If you are working in a group, have each person bring in an image, taken on their phone or with a camera, of a sign in the environment that stands out as unique or different. What do we need to know about the place to understand the informational and/or symbolic function of each sign?
4. What's unique about the dialect of the place you're living right now? Are there words or phrases that are different, that people outside of your area might not understand? Take a brief survey in the class – you can use the NARVS questions or ones you come up with on your own. What do you find?

Notes

1. Talking About Talk: Key Terms and Concepts

1 In linguistics, sentences that are incorrect in a grammatical sense are usually marked with an asterisk (*).

2. What Is Language?

1 My thanks to users on the Klingon Language Institute discord channel for assistance with this translation.

2 Dell Hymes (1974) developed an acronym to encompass all of the information about social context relevant to a conversation called the SPEAKING model. This includes setting, participants, and goals (which he called "ends") but also social norms, genre conventions, act sequences and so forth. I have only identified the most important components of this model here.

3 Deaf is capitalized to refer to the culture and community of people who all share an audiological disability, rather than the physical condition of deafness.

3. Language Socialization

1 There is an entire literature, particularly in the fields of psychology and sociology, on how general theories of cognition, development, and behaviour are based on research with people who are WEIRD (Western, educated, industrialized, rich, and democratic). The use of white middle-class households in this example is meant to highlight the differences with those in other parts of the world and to "de-naturalize" their presumed universality. Research on Black households, lower-class households, or even rural households in North America would likely lead to different findings.

4. Linguistic Relativity

1 Whorf's approach, which argued that Mayan glyphs were a form of phonetic representation, did not turn out to be correct: they are, in fact, largely syllabic. The consensus among scholars today is generally that while Whorf was wrong, his ideas moved interpretation of the script away from a predominantly symbolic model to a linguistic one (see, for instance, Lee 1996, 6).

2 In contrast, many field linguists, those who spend years learning and analysing a language with the people who speak it, often endorse linguistic relativity in some form (see many of the essays in Newman and Ratliff 2001).

3 It probably doesn't help that Whorf usually wrote for a popular audience and, consequently, tried to play up the more romantic and exotic parts of his ideas about language. He does label Hopi a "timeless" language, although he never says Hopi are a timeless people.

5. Indigenous Languages and Revitalization

1 This example is from the Inuktitut language resource https://tusaalanga.ca.

2 Boas was writing before the creation of Qaliujaaqpait, a standard system for writing Inuktitut in English. For instance, the Inuktitut language resource Tusaalanga writes the North Baffin word for snowdrift as *qimugjuk*.

3 Waldie (2012, 93–7) argues that not all of the obligatory verb suffixes in Nuu-chah-nulth declaratives are evidentials, notably the indicative and mirative, which mark personal experience and surprise, respectively. Basically, he argues that because these can be combined with other evidentials, they do not qualify as evidentials in their own right. It's a fairly technical argument, but for our purposes I simply want to highlight the obligatoriness of marking the source of knowledge.

6. Social Identity and Performativity

1 There is some debate about whether Vološinov's book was not actually written by his colleague Mikhail Bakhtin. It is certain they discussed and assisted each other with their works, so the content and style of their writing is often similar. Vološinov died very young after a serious illness, and some suspect that Bakhtin published his work under Vološinov's name to avoid stirring up political trouble for himself (Clark and Holquist 1984). Whatever the case, the book itself is a landmark study that highlighted language as a social phenomenon.

2 Ludwig Wittgenstein is probably the only philosopher in history who became famous for saying something, and then even more famous for saying the complete opposite. His *Tractatus Logico-Philosophicus* (1922) argued that language is a logical projection of the mind that we use to describe reality. Thirty years later, his *Philosophical Investigations* (1958) instead contended that our sense of reality is actually a product of how we use of language. Bertrand Russell hated the latter work, but it is far more in line with contemporary approaches in linguistic anthropology.

8. Raciolinguistics

1 The name given to this language variety has not been consistent over the years. Early studies called it Negro English or Black Street English, which inadvertently stigmatized the dialect. Although the most prevalent term is African American Vernacular English (AAVE), as Sharese King (2020) points out, it incorrectly presumes a uniformity to this set of language practices. I therefore follow her in calling this African American Language (AAL). However, even this term is a bit imprecise because it also describes varieties of Black English outside the United States (see Poplack and Tagliamonte 1991).

9. Multilingualism and Globalization

1 Technically this is a retroflex approximant denoted by the IPA symbol /ɻ/.
2 *Language variety* is more commonly used in sociolinguistics and focuses on the linguistic pattern, while *register* is more common in linguistic anthropology and focuses on the socially recognized nature of these patterns. Linguistic anthropologists and sociolinguists have started moving away from using the term *dialect* because it presumes a regional language variety is just part of a larger standard language. Thus, Canadian French is sometimes referred to as a dialect of French, implying it is subordinate to this larger category. In reality, though, Parisian French and Canadian French are equally expressive and complete linguistic systems.
3 The video, "Word Differences Between French Language Countries!! (France, Belgium, Canada)" by the channel World Friends can be found at: https://youtu.be/n_3ROTieRgs.
4 My thanks to Mireille McLaughlin for assistance with the translation of this passage.
5 Note that many creoles are still popularly called pidgins, such as Hawaiian Pidgin or Solomon Islands Pijin, even though these are actually creole languages.

10. Orality and Literacy

1 Despite the focus on orality in this chapter and the uses of words like "talk" and "speak," we do have to keep in mind that sign languages are also fundamentally "oral" as opposed to written forms of language, and should be included anytime we discuss orality.

Glossary

absolute spatial reference a linguistic system for referring to space that employs fixed directions such as "north" and "south." See *relative spatial reference*.

affordances the possibilities and constraints offered by a communicative *medium*.

African American Language a variety of language historically associated with African American communities.

animator in a speech event, the person physically forming the words and uttering them for others (one of three potential roles of a speaker). See *author, principal*.

arbitrariness the idea that there is no natural link between the meaning of a word and its sounds. See *sign*.

author in a speech event, the person who has selected the ideas that will be expressed and chosen the words to express them (one of three potential roles of a speaker). See *animator, principal*.

autonomous model of literacy a theory of literacy that focuses on the universal impacts of literacy on human societies. See *ideological model of literacy*.

backstage a setting for social action that is relatively private. See *frontstage*.

Canadian raising a phonetic feature of Canadian speech varieties in which certain vowels (evident in the word "house") are pronounced higher in the mouth than other dialects.

case study a pedagogical method in teaching ethics that involves considering a real or hypothetical ethical dilemma.

Chiac a regional variety of French spoken in eastern Canada with extensive borrowings from English.

child-raising a characteristic of North American *language socialization* in which infants are addressed as if they can already talk. See *protoconversation, self-lowering*.

closed system a communication system that is relatively fixed and resistant to the creation of new messages (i.e., animal communication). See *open system*.

codemixing the practice of blending languages together in conversation. See *codeswitching*.

codeswitching the practice of switching between languages in conversation. See *codemixing*.

commodification the process of turning certain languages and language varieties into marketable skills and sources of value for their speakers.

communicative competence knowledge of the sociocultural rules governing language use.

competence the intuitive, cognitive knowledge of language structure developed during *language acquisition*. See *performance*.

conlang abbreviation of "constructed language," a language intentionally created by people for a particular purpose.

covert racist discourse forms of discourse in which racist ideologies are disseminated in a non-serious or humorous fashion.

creole a language that develops from the contact between other languages. See *pidgin*.

creole exceptionalism a *language ideology* asserting that creoles are linguistically deficient or peculiar. See *creole*.

critical period the period between birth and the age of about six when children are most capable of acquiring language. See *language acquisition*.

crossing the practice of adopting language patterns from racialized communities other than the speaker's own.

culture the set of beliefs, ideas, and practices shared by members of a society.

decolonization the process of dismantling the colonial structures of settler outsiders imposed on Indigenous peoples.

deixis language whose meaning is relative to the context of a conversation. See *spatial deixis, social deixis*.

descriptivism the idea that we should describe how people actually use language in practice. See *prescriptivism*.

design features features shared by all human languages.

diachronic an approach to language that studies the change and development of the system over time. See *synchronic*.

dialect a regional variety of a language.

dialect survey a research method that asks people questions about their speech to investigate dialect patterns.

difference model a model of gender that highlights the ways men and women are socialized to different communication styles. See *dominance model, rapport-talk, report-talk*.

diglossia a *speech community* with two or more languages that play very distinct and unequal roles. See *H-variety, L-variety.*

direct indexicality forms of language that directly refer to the gender of a person, such as pronouns or address terms. See *indexicality, indirect indexicality.*

discourse language as it is embedded in *social context.*

domain a commonly recognized setting of conversation such as a school, workplace, or home.

dominance model a model of gender that highlights the ways society uses language to control and subordinate women. See *difference model.*

emergence a quality of *verbal performance* in which its outcome is a product of the performer's creativity and ability to respond to the audience.

emergent vitalities the creative ways endangered *speech communities* engage with and sustain their languages. See *language reclamation.*

emoji pictograms used in texting and other forms of digital communication.

enregisterment the process through which the *indexical* values of a *register* are established.

entextualization borrowing *discourse,* and its *indexical* values, from one context and using it in another.

ethnicity a way of classifying people on the basis of perceived cultural differences. See *ethnicization, race.*

ethnicization the process of projecting *ethnicity* onto groups of people based on such things as language and cultural practices.

ethnography a long-term research method in anthropology of engaging with a group of people and immersing oneself in their cultural lives.

ethnopoetics a method of analysing ethnographic texts as they would have been spoken rather than as they were written down, intended to recapture their aesthetic patterns.

ethnosemantics the study of how various languages classify the world.

evidential a grammatical element that indicates the source of knowledge being expressed in a sentence. See *evidentiality.*

evidentiality ways of indicating the source of knowledge being expressed in a sentence. See *evidential.*

felicity conditions criteria that must be satisfied for a *speech act* to be effective. See *performative.*

footing a person's social position or stance within a conversation.

four-field anthropology a tradition of anthropology that combines archaeology, biological anthropology, sociocultural anthropology, and linguistic anthropology.

frontstage a setting for social action that is relatively public. See *backstage.*

generative grammar a theory of language which posits that the basic structures of syntax allow us to generate an infinite variety of sentences.

gender the socially constructed nature of "men" and "women," along with ideas of masculinity and femininity.

genre categories of discourse (such as a fairy tale or sermon) that structure and organize a text. See *performance*.

habitus an approach to *culture* that describes how common forms of action develop shared understandings between people.

heteroglossia the idea that speech is always a blend of different registers, dialects, styles, and genres. See *standardization*.

homesigns idiosyncratic gestures that Deaf children in hearing households develop on their own.

H-variety the more formal and prestigious language variety in a *diglossic speech community*. See *L-variety*.

icon a *sign* in which the relationship between *signifier* and *signified* is based on a physical resemblance or likeness. See *semiotics*.

identity a person's sense of self and social position based on similarities and differences with others.

ideological model of literacy a theory of literacy that focuses on the particular relationship of literacy in a society to its social context, institutions, and technologies. See *autonomous model of literacy*.

illocution in a *speech act*, the action that the *performative* performs, such as betting, congratulating, announcing, appointing, etc. See *locution, perlocution*.

imagined community an idea in nationalism that even though two people from the same nation may never meet, they assume themselves to be part of a greater whole.

index a *sign* in which the relationship between *signifier* and *signified* is based on a logical or causal connection. See *semiotics*.

indexicality the capacity for forms of language to *index*, or point to, various concepts, contexts, and social identities.

indirect indexicality forms of language that indirectly point to the gender of a person, such as vocal pitch or assertive speech. See *direct indexicality, indexicality*.

informational function the ability of signs in the *linguistic landscape* to show what languages are present in the community, their distribution, and what role they play. See *symbolic function*.

interdiscursivity the ability to link language used in one *medium* with that used in another.

intergenerational transmission the acquisition of language from the older generation by children, a key measure of a language's vitality. See *language endangerment*.

International Phonetic Alphabet a writing system for representing the full range of sounds in human languages. See *phoneme*.

kabary a stereotypically masculine speech genre from Madagascar that employs elaborate politeness formulae, indirect allusion, and excessive deference.

keys in *verbal performances,* linguistic features that orient the audience towards what type of *genre* they can expect to hear.

kros A stereotypically feminine speech genre from Papua New Guinea that employs elaborate swearing and belligerence.

languaculture the idea that language and culture are inseparably linked together.

language acquisition the process of learning language as a cognitive system, especially its *phonology, morphology,* and *syntax*. See *language socialization.*

language death a situation in which no living speakers of a language remain. See *language endangerment, sleeping language.*

language endangerment a situation in which the number of people using a language is declining. See *language death, language shift.*

language family a group of languages that share a common ancestor. See *language isolate.*

language ideologies common ideas and assumptions in a *speech community* about language and how it is (or should be) used.

language isolate a language that does not appear to be related to any others. See *language family.*

language materiality a scholarly approach that looks at how language is entangled with objects and the physical world, and in turn how language becomes objectified. See *commodification.*

language policy and planning the practices, regulations, and actions taken by states, communities, and institutions towards language.

language reclamation the practice of reversing *language shift* by empowering *speech communities* to take control of the project of *language revitalization* and addressing the social factors that cause *language endangerment.*

language revitalization the process of halting the decline of a language and reversing *language shift* within a *speech community*. See *language reclamation.*

language shift a change in the balance of languages in a *speech community,* typically as a local language is gradually replaced by a national or global language. See *language death, language endangerment.*

language socialization the process of learning a language in tandem with learning the sociocultural knowledge of how to use it. See *communicative competence, language acquisition.*

language variation the principle that languages are never coherent wholes but exhibit differences in how they are spoken by different groups of people or in different settings. See *language variety.*

language variety any particular pattern of language. See *dialect, language variation, register.*

langue the shared, psychological component of language. See *parole.*

linguistic anthropology a field of study that investigates the role of language in framing, interpreting, and creating our social worlds. See *sociolinguistics*.

linguistic imperialism the imposition of languages on *speech communities* by external social forces and institutions, often in the context of colonialism or militarism.

linguistic landscape a research method that examines the presence (or absence) of various languages on signs such as advertising billboards, commercial shop signs, road signs, and place names in a given location.

linguistic relativity a principle that language, culture, and thought are linked together in a dynamic and interactive process. See *Sapir–Whorf hypothesis*.

linguistics the study of language.

literacy communication and expression through the medium of written language. See *literacy event, literacy practice, orality*.

literacy event specific times and places when people are using written *texts*. See *literacy, literacy practice*.

literacy practice the cultural norms for using and understanding written *texts*. See *literacy, literacy event*.

locution in a *speech act*, the words that a person utters as a *performative*. See *illocution, perlocution*.

L-variety the more informal language variety in a *diglossic speech community*. See *H-variety*.

marked forms of language that are noticeable, different, or stand out in some way. See *markedness, unmarked*.

markedness the differentiation of forms of language as either normative or irregular. See *marked, unmarked*.

media ideologies common ideas and beliefs we have about different channels of communication. See *ideology, medium, remediation*.

medium a particular channel of communication.

metaphor a linguistic form that allows one thing to represent or stand in for another. See *semiotics*.

metapragmatic discourse discourse that assess or comments on the speech of others.

mock Spanish the use of ostensibly Spanish words and phrases, often in grammatically nonsensical ways, in the speech of non-Spanish speakers.

morpheme in linguistics, the smallest unit of meaning. See *morphology*.

morphology the study of the formation and structure of *morphemes*.

multilingualism the practice of using more than one language on a regular basis.

multiliteracies a scholarly approach that studies the variety of *texts* we use, and the ways those texts are entangled with other modalities such as speech, images, and objects.

multimodality the idea that our communication is not limited to language but involves a range of other channels such as gesture, tone, and text that affect how participants interpret the situation. See *prosody*.

multispecies ethnography an approach that expands the scope of *ethnography* beyond the human to include other species.

natural language processing a branch of computing focused on software that can understand and generate naturalistic human language.

open system a communication system that is relatively flexible and allows for the deliberate creation of new messages (i.e., human language). See *closed system*.

oral literature the artful use of oral *texts*. See *orality*.

orality communication and expression through the medium of spoken language. See *literacy*.

parole the physiological act of speaking. See *langue*.

performance the fragmentary and imperfect expression of linguistic competence by a person in the act of speaking. See *competence*.

performative an utterance that is also an action, such as blessing, cursing, betting, or apologizing. See *performativity, speech act*.

performativity the idea that our identities are produced through the ways we talk. See *performative, speech act*.

perlocution in a *speech act*, the social consequences of the *performative* on the speaker or others. See *locution, illocution*.

perspectivism an idea, common in many Amazonian cultures, that our perceptions of others are dependent upon our perspective as humans, animals, or spirits.

philology the study of language through the interpretation and understanding of canonical *texts*, primarily in literary languages.

phoneme a unit of sound in spoken languages. See *phonology*.

phonetics the study of how the human vocal tract produces sounds and how our brains interpret them. See *phoneme, phonology*.

phonology the study of the use of sounds in human languages to create meaning. See *phoneme, phonetics*.

pidgin a relatively limited linguistic code that emerges in response to contact between other languages. See *creole*.

polysynthesis a *morphological* structure, common to many North American Indigenous languages, that modifies a root verb with a range of affixes to build sentences.

pragmatics the study of the relationship between linguistic meaning and social context.

prescriptivism an idea that there is one correct form of a language that people should use. See *descriptivism*.

principal in a speech event, the person whose position or identity is represented through the speech (one of three potential roles of a speaker). See *animator, author*.

private signage in a *linguistic landscape*, signage that is created by people or businesses, including advertising, retail signage, and unofficial messages like graffiti. See *public signage.*

prosody the non-linguistic elements of speech, including intonation, tempo, volume, and pitch. See *multimodality.*

protoconversation A one-sided conversation in which parents talk to infants as if they could already speak and interpret their sounds as meaningful responses. See *child-raising, language socialization.*

public signage in a *linguistic landscape*, signage that is authorized by local authorities, such as in schools, government offices, on monuments, or in public announcements. See *private signage.*

qualitative research methods that involve describing and interpreting things to understand causes and connections. See *quantitative.*

quantitative research methods that involve identifying and counting things. See *qualitative.*

race a way of classifying people on the basis of perceived biological differences. See *ethnicity, racialization.*

racialization the process of projecting racial categories onto groups of people.

raciolinguistics a scholarly approach that attempts to destabilize common ideologies around language and *race.*

rapport-talk a feminine speech style focused on establishing connections and negotiating relationships. See *difference model, report-talk.*

reconciliation a process of healing relationships between settler and Indigenous peoples that requires public truth sharing, apology, and commemoration that acknowledges and redresses past harms.

register any particular socially recognized pattern of language such as a regional dialect or professional code (e.g., "lawyer talk"). See *language variety.*

relative spatial reference a linguistic system for referring to space that employs directions relative to the speaker such as "right" and "left." See *absolute spatial reference.*

remediation the interdependency of different communicative channels and the ways they relate to each other. See *media ideology, medium.*

report-talk a masculine speech style focused on preserving independence and maintaining social status. See *difference model, rapport-talk.*

salvage ethnography the practice of making a record of cultures and languages before they disappear. See *language death.*

Sapir–Whorf hypothesis the idea that our view of the world is built upon the structures of our language and our habits of speaking. See *linguistic relativity.*

self-lowering a characteristic of North American *language socialization* in which adults adopt a grammatically simplified speech style (also called babytalk or child-directed speech). See *child-raising.*

semantics the study of how meaning is created and interpreted in a language.

semiotics the study of *signs* and meaning. See *icon, index, symbol.*

semi-speakers speakers who have only a restricted knowledge of a language due to *language shift*. See *language endangerment.*

semi-structured interview an interviewing method that includes an overall plan and structure but has the flexibility to explore new questions, concepts, and ideas as the interview proceeds. See *qualitative.*

shibboleths language forms, such as a word choice or pronunciation, that are emblematic of a person's membership in a *speech community*.

sign the link between a set of sounds or letters and a concept. See *semiotics, signified, signifier.*

sign language any language performed in three-dimensional space using movements of the body rather than speech.

signified the concept or idea that acts as one component of a *sign*. See *semiotics, signifier.*

signifier the set of sounds or letters that acts as one component of a *sign*. See *semiotics, signified.*

signifyin' a discourse style common in African American communities involving intentional misunderstanding over the interpretation of a sentence's meaning.

sleeping language a language that is no longer actively used but has sufficient documentation that it can be reclaimed later by its community. See *language reclamation, salvage ethnography.*

social context the social environment within which any *discourse* is embedded, including the setting, goals, and participants of a conversation.

social deixis language that encodes the roles and relationships of conversational participants, such as words like "sir" or "darling." See *deixis.*

sociolinguistics the study of the social dimensions of language in use. See *linguistic anthropology.*

spatial deixis language that describes and labels the space around us, such as words like "here" or "below." See *deixis.*

speech act the action accomplished as a result of using a *performative*. See *felicity conditions, performativity.*

speech community any human aggregate characterized by regular and frequent interaction by means of a shared body of verbal *signs* and set off from similar aggregates by significant differences in language usage.

standardization a process in which various social institutions – such as schools, government offices, and publishers – work to define a single version of the language as the correct one. See *heteroglossia, prescriptivism.*

superdiversity the pattern of increasing transnational migration and global cosmopolitanism that characterizes the contemporary world.

symbol a *sign* in which the relationship between *signifier* and *signified* is arbitrary and based on convention or culture. See *semiotics*.

symbolic function the ability of signs in the *linguistic landscape* to represent the identity, vitality, and relative status of the different *speech communities* in a particular area. See *informational function*.

synchronic an approach to language that studies the relationship between all elements of the system at a single point in time. See *diachronic.*

syntax the rules and principles through which meaningful sentences are generated in a language.

text any configuration of *signs* that is coherently interpretable by some community of users.

transcription a way of representing discourse in textual form that highlights its *prosody*.

translanguaging the practice of using a diverse range of linguistic resources, combining and innovating with them as a person speaks.

translatability the principle that anything said in one human language can be translated into any other language.

unmarked forms of language that are generally considered normal and pass without much notice. See *marked, markedness.*

verbal hygiene when everyday speech is critically examined and regulated by others.

verbal performance a speaker's use of the full potential offered by language, playing with rhythm, words, sentence structure, and style to create verbal art. See *performance.*

vocal fry a low-pitched vibration of the larynx during speech often associated with feminine speech styles.

References

AAA (American Anthropological Association). 2012. "AAA Statement on Ethics: Principles of Professional Responsibility." https://americananthro.org/about/policies/statement-on-ethics/

Absolon, Kathleen. 2011. *Kaandossiwin: How We Come to Know.* Halifax: Fernwood Press.

Abu-Lughod, Lila. 1986. *Veiled Sentiments: Honor and Poetry in a Bedouin Society.* Berkeley: University of California Press.

Agar, Michael. 1994. *Language Shock: Understanding the Culture of Conversation.* New York: William Morrow.

Agha, Asif. 2005. "Voice, Footing, Enregisterment." *Journal of Linguistic Anthropology* 15 (1): 38–59. https://doi.org/10.1525/jlin.2005.15.1.38

——— 2007. *Language and Social Relations.* Cambridge: Cambridge University Press.

Ahearn, Laura. 2001. *Invitations to Love: Literacy, Love Letters, and Social Change in Nepal.* Ann Arbor: University of Michigan Press.

Aikhenvald, Alexandra. 2004. *Evidentiality.* Oxford: Oxford University Press.

Alim, H. Samy. 2006. *Roc the Mic Right: The Language of Hip Hop Culture.* New York: Routledge.

Alim, H. Samy, John Rickford, and Arnetha Ball, eds. 2016. *Raciolinguistics: How Language Shapes Our Ideas About Race.* Oxford: Oxford University Press.

Alim, H. Samy, and Geneva Smitherman. 2012. *Articulate While Black: Barack Obama, Language, and Race in the U.S.* Oxford: Oxford University Press.

AMA (American Management Association). 2023. "Assertiveness Training for Women in Business." www.amanet.org/assertiveness-training-for-women-in-business/

Anderson, Benedict. 1983. *Imagined Communities: Reflections on the Origin and Spread of Nationalism.* London: Verso.

Anderson, Rindy, Casey Klofstad, William Mayew, and Mohan Venkatachalam. 2014. "Vocal Fry May Undermine the Success of Young Women in the Labor Market." *PLoS One* 9 (5): e97506. https://doi.org/10.1371/journal.pone.0097506

Anderson, Stephen. 2010 "How Many Languages Are There in the World?" *Linguistic Society of America.* https://rom.uga.edu/sites/default/files/inline-files/how-many-languages.pdf

Ardener, Edwin. 2007. *The Voice of Prophecy and Other Essays*. New York: Berghahn.

Ascher, Marcia, and Robert Ascher. 1997. *Mathematics of the Incas: Code of the Quipu*. New York: Dover.

Auer, Peter. 1999. "From Codeswitching via Language Mixing to Fused Lects: Toward a Dynamic Typology of Bilingual Speech." *International Journal of Bilingualism* 3 (4): 309–32. https://doi.org/10.1177/13670069990030040101

Austin, J.L. 1962. *How to Do Things with Words*. Cambridge: Harvard University Press.

Bailey, Benjamin. 1997. "Communication of Respect in Interethnic Service Encounters." *Language in Society* 26 (3): 327–56. https://doi.org/10.1017/S0047404500019497

Bakhtin, Mikhail. 1981. *The Dialogic Imagination: Four Essays*. Austin: University of Texas Press.

Balanoff, Helen, Emily Kudlak, Alice Kaodloak, and Cynthia Chambers. 2009. "'This Is the Way We Were Told…': Multiple Literacies in Ulukhaktok, Northwest Territories." In *Orality in the 21st Century: Inuit Discourse and Practices. Proceedings of the 15th Inuit Studies Conference*, edited by Béatrice Collignon and Michèle Therrien. Paris: Inalco.

Barber, Karin. 2007. *The Anthropology of Texts, Persons and Publics*. Cambridge: Cambridge University Press.

Baron, Naomi. 2008. *Always On: Language in an Online and Mobile World*. Oxford: Oxford University Press.

Barrett, Rusty. 2017. *From Drag Queens to Leathermen: Language, Gender, and Gay Male Subcultures*. Oxford: Oxford University Press.

Barth, Frederik. 1969. "Introduction." In *Ethnic Groups and Boundaries: The Social Organization of Culture Difference*, edited by Frederik Barth, 9–38. London: George Allen & Unwin.

Barton, David, and Mary Hamilton. 2000. "Literacy Practices." In *Situated Literacies: Theorising Reading and Writing in Context*, edited by David Barton and Mary Hamilton, 7–14. New York: Routledge.

Basso, Keith. 1979. *Portraits of "The Whiteman": Linguistic Play and Cultural Symbols Among the Western Apache*. Cambridge: Cambridge University Press.

——— 1996. *Wisdom Sits in Places: Landscape and Language among the Western Apache*. Albuquerque: University of New Mexico Press.

Bastien, Betty. 2004. *Blackfoot Ways of Knowing*. Calgary: University of Calgary Press.

Battiste, Marie. 2013. *Decolonizing Education: Nourishing the Learning Spirit*. Saskatoon: Purich Publishing.

Bauman, Richard. 1975. "Verbal Art as Performance." *American Anthropologist* 77 (2): 290–311. https://doi.org/10.1525/aa.1975.77.2.02a00030

——— 1986. *Story, Performance, and Event: Contextual Studies of Oral Narrative*. Cambridge: Cambridge University Press.

——— 1999. "Genre." *Journal of Linguistic Anthropology* 9 (1/2): 84–7. https://doi.org/10.1525/jlin.1999.9.1-2.84

Bauman, Richard, and Charles Briggs. 1990a. "'The Foundation of All Future Researches': Franz Boas, George Hunt, Native American Texts, and the Construction of Modernity." *American Quarterly* 51 (3): 429–528. https://doi.org/10.1353/aq.1999.0036

——— 1990b. "Poetics and Performance as Critical Perspectives on Language and Social Life." *Annual Review of Anthropology* 19: 59–88. https://doi.org/10.1146/annurev.an.19.100190.000423

Beauvoir, Simone de. 2011 [1949]. *The Second Sex*. New York: Vintage.

Benedict, Ruth. 1934. *Patterns of Culture*. Boston: Houghton Mifflin.

Benenson, Fred. 2010. *Emoji Dick*. Morrisville: Lulu Press.

Bergs, Alexander. 2010. "Sociolinguistics." In *The History of English, Vol. 3: Middle English*, edited by Laurel Brinton and Alexander Bergs, 239–60. Berlin: De Gruyter Mouton.

Berlin, Brent, and Paul Kay. 1969. *Basic Color Terms*. Berkeley: University of California Press.

Berman, Elise. 2019. *Talking Like Children: Language and the Production of Age in the Marshall Islands*. Oxford: Oxford University Press.

Bernardini, Wesley, Stewart Koyiyumptewa, Gregson Schachner, and Leigh Kuwanwisiwma. 2021. *Becoming Hopi: A History*. Tucson: University of Arizona Press.

Berreby, David. 2012. "Obese? Smoker? No Retirement Savings? Perhaps It's Because of the Language You Speak." *BigThink*. https://bigthink.com/articles/obese-smoker-no-retirement-savings-perhaps-its-because-of-the-language-you-speak/

Besnier, Niko. 1995. *Literacy, Emotion, and Authority: Reading and Writing on a Polynesian Atoll*. Cambridge: Cambridge University Press.

Bhargava, Rashi, and Richa Chilana, eds. 2023. *Punching Up in Stand-Up Comedy: Speaking Truth to Power*. New York: Routledge.

Bialostok, Steve, and Marcus Watson. 2022. "Older Black Men Playing Dominoes: Talking Shit and Creating Black Place." *Transforming Anthropology* 30 (1): 34–47. https://doi.org/10.1111/traa.12227

Bilaniuk, Laada. 2006. *Contested Tongues: Language Politics and Cultural Correction in Ukraine*. Ithaca: Cornell University Press.

——— 2024. "Memes as Antibodies: Creativity and Resilience in the Face of Russia's War." In *Dispossession: Anthropological Perspectives on Russia's War Against Ukraine*, edited by Catherine Wanner, 143–66. New York: Routledge.

Billings, Sabrina. 2009. "Speaking Beauties: Linguistic Posturing, Language Inequality, and the Construction of a Tanzanian Beauty Queen." *Language in Society* 38 (5): 581–606. https://doi.org/10.1017/S0047404509990443

Blackburn, Carole. 2007. "Producing Legitimacy: Reconciliation and the Negotiation of Aboriginal Rights in Canada." *Journal of the Royal Anthropological Institute* 13 (3): 621–38. https://doi.org/10.1111/j.1467-9655.2007.00447.x

Blom, Jan-Petter, and John Gumperz. 1972. "Social Meaning in Linguistic Structure: Code-Switching in Norway." In *Directions in Sociolinguistics: The Ethnography of Communication*, edited by Dell Hymes and John J. Gumperz, 407–34. New York: Holt, Rinehart and Winston.

Blommaert, Jan. 2001. "Investigating Narrative Inequality: African Asylum Seekers' Stories in Belgium." *Discourse & Society* 12 (4): 413–49. https://doi.org/10.1177/0957926501012004002

——— 2010. *The Sociolinguistics of Globalization*. Cambridge: Cambridge University Press.

——— 2013. *Ethnography, Superdiversity and Linguistic Landscapes: Chronicles of Complexity*. Bristol: Multilingual Matters.

——— 2015. "Meaning as a Nonlinear Effect: The Birth of Cool." *AILA Review* 28 (1): 7–27. https://doi.org/10.1075/aila.28.01blo

Blommaert, Jan, and Dong Jie. 2020. *Ethnographic Fieldwork: A Beginner's Guide*, 2nd ed. Bristol: Multilingual Matters.

Blum, Susan. 1997. "Naming Practices and the Power of Words in China." *Language in Society* 26 (3): 357–79. https://doi.org/10.1017/S0047404500019503

Boas, Franz. 1911. *Handbook of American Indian Languages*. Washington, DC: Government Printing Office.

——— 1940. *Race, Language and Culture*. New York: Macmillan.

Boberg, Charles. 2005. "The North American Regional Vocabulary Survey: New Variables and Methods in the Study of North American English." *American Speech* 80 (1): 22–60. https://doi.org/10.1215/00031283-80-1-22

——— 2010. *The English Language in Canada: Status, History and Comparative Analysis*. Cambridge: Cambridge University Press.

Boellstorff, Tom. 2008. *Coming of Age in Second Life: An Anthropologist Explores the Virtually Human*. Princeton: Princeton University Press.

Bohnemeyer, Jürgen. 2020. "Linguistic Relativity: From Whorf to Now." In *The Blackwell Companion to Semantics*, edited by Daniel Gutzmann, Lisa Matthewson, Cécile Meier, Hotze Rullmann, and Thomas E. Zimmermann, 1–33. London: Blackwell.

Bonilla, Yarimar, and Jonathan Rosa. 2015. "#Ferguson: Digital Protest, Hashtag Ethnography, and the Racial Politics of Social Media in the United States." *American Ethnologist* 42 (1): 4–17. https://doi.org/10.1111/amet.12112

Boltokova, Daria. 2017. "'Will the Real Semi-Speaker Please Stand Up?' Language Vitality, Semi-Speakers, and Problems of Enumeration in the Canadian North." *Anthropologica* 59 (1): 12–27. https://doi.org/10.3138/anth.591.T03

Bouchard, Marie-Eve. 2023. "The Hierarchization of French Varieties in an English-Dominant Context of Canada." *Canadian Modern Language Review* 79 (4): 322–51. https://doi.org/10.3138/cmlr-2022-0062

Boudreau, Annette, and Lise Dubois. 2007. "Français, Acadien, Acadjonne: Competing Discourses on Language Preservation along the Shores of the Baie Sainte-Marie." In *Discourses of Endangerment: Ideology and Interest in Defense of Languages*, edited by Alexandre Duchêne and Monica Heller, 99–120. London: Continuum.

Bouie, Jamelle. 2015. "Is Rachel Dolezal Black Just Because She Says She Is?" *Slate Magazine*. https://slate.com/news-and-politics/2015/06/rachel-dolezal-claims-to-be-black-the-naacp-official-was-part-of-the-african-american-community-but-did-she-accept-the-racial-hardships-too.html

Bourdieu, Pierre. 1977. *Outline of a Theory of Practice*. Cambridge: Cambridge University Press.

boyd, danah. 2010. "Social Network Sites as Networked Publics: Affordances, Dynamics, and Implications." In *A Networked Self: Identity, Community, and Culture on Social Network Sites*, edited by Zizi Papacharissi, 39–58. New York: Routledge.

Bradley, David, and Maya Bradley. 2019. *Language Endangerment*. Cambridge: Cambridge University Press.

Brenneis, Donald. 1994. "Discourse and Discipline at the National Research Council: A Bureaucratic *Bildungsroman*." *Cultural Anthropology* 9 (1): 23–36. https://doi.org/10.1525/can.1994.9.1.02a00020

Briggs, Charles. 1986. *Learning How to Ask: A Sociolinguistic Appraisal of the Role of the Interview in Social Science Research*. Cambridge: Cambridge University Press.

Brown, Lucien. 2011. *Korean Honorifics and Politeness in Second Language Learning*. Amsterdam: John Benjamins.

Brown, Penelope, and Stephen Levinson. 1993 "'Uphill' and 'Downhill' in Tzeltal." *Journal of Linguistic Anthropology* 3 (1): 46–74. https://doi.org/10.1525/jlin.1993.3.1.46

Brown, Roger, and Eric Lenneberg. 1954. "A Study in Language and Cognition." *Journal of Abnormal and Social Psychology* 49 (3): 454–62. https://doi.org/10.1037/h0057814

Bruchac, Margaret. 2018. *Savage Kin: Indigenous Informants and American Anthropologists.* Tucson: University of Arizona Press.

Bucholtz, Mary. 2009. "Styles and Stereotypes: Laotian American Girls' Linguistic Negotiation of Identity." In *Beyond Yellow English: Toward a Linguistic Anthropology of Asian Pacific America*, edited by Angela Reyes and Adrienne Lo, 21–42. Oxford: Oxford University Press.

——— 2011. *White Kids: Language, Race, and Styles of Youth Identity.* Cambridge: Cambridge University Press.

Bucholtz, Mary, and Kira Hall. 2005. "Identity and Interaction: A Sociocultural Linguistic Approach." *Discourse Studies* 7 (4–5): 585–614. https://doi.org/10.1177/1461445605054407

Bucholtz, Mary, Elena Skapoulli, Brendan Barnwell, and Jung-Eun Janie Lee. 2011. "Entextualized Humor in the Formation of Scientist Identities among U.S. Undergraduates." *Anthropology & Education Quarterly* 42 (3): 177–92. https://doi.org/10.1111/j.1548-1492.2011.01126.x

Budach, Gabriele, Donna Patrick, and Teevi Mackay. 2015. "'Talk around Objects': Designing Trajectories of Belonging in an Urban Inuit Community." *Social Semiotics* 25 (4): 446–64. https://doi.org/10.1080/10350330.2015.1059575

Bulag, Uradyn E. 2003. "Mongolian Ethnicity and Linguistic Anxiety in China." *American Anthropologist* 105 (4): 753–63. https://doi.org/10.1525/aa.2003.105.4.753

Burenhult, Niclas, and Asifa Majid. 2011. "Olfaction in Aslian Ideology and Language." *The Senses & Society* 6 (1): 19–29. https://doi.org/10.2752/174589311X12893982233597

Büscher, Karen, Sigurd D'Hondt, and Michael Meeuwis. 2013. "Recruiting a Nonlocal Language for Performing Local Identity: Indexical Appropriations of Lingala in the Congolese Border Town Goma." *Language in Society* 42: 527–56. https://doi.org/10.1017/S0047404513000651

Butler, Judith. 2007. *Gender Trouble: Feminism and the Subversion of Identity.* New York: Routledge.

Byler, Darren. 2021. "Anti-Colonial Friendship: Contemporary Police Violence, Storytelling, and Uyghur Masculinity." *American Ethnologist* 48 (2): 153–66. https://doi.org/10.1111/amet.13020

Bylund, Emanuel, Panos Athanasopoulos, and Marcelyn Oostendorp. 2013. "Motion Event Cognition and Grammatical Aspect: Evidence from Afrikaans." *Linguistics* 51 (5): 929–55. https://doi.org/10.1515/ling-2013-0033

Cameron, Deborah. 1995. *Verbal Hygiene.* London: Routledge.

——— 1997. Performing Gender Identity: Young Men's Talk and the Construction of Heterosexual Masculinity." In *Language and Masculinity*, edited by Sally Johnson and Ulrike Meinhof, 47–64. Oxford: Blackwell.

——— 2006. *On Language and Sexual Politics.* New York: Routledge.

——— 2016. "On Banter, Bonding and Donald Trump." *Language: A Feminist Guide.* https://debuk.wordpress.com/2016/10/09/on-banter-bonding-and-donald-trump/

Canada. 1982. *Constitution Act.* https://laws-lois.justice.gc.ca/eng/const/page-12.html

Canadian Language Museum. 2019. *Indigenous Languages in Canada*. Toronto: Canadian Language Museum.

Carrithers, Michael, Steven Collins, and Steven Lukes, eds. 1985. *The Category of the Person: Anthropology, Philosophy, History*. Cambridge: Cambridge University Press.

Cenoz, Jasone, and Durk Gorter. 2006. "Linguistic Landscape and Minority Languages." *International Journal of Multilingualism* 3 (1): 67–80. https://doi.org/10.1080/14790710608668386

Chambers, J.K 1998. "Social Embedding of Changes in Progress." *Journal of English Linguistics* 26 (1): 5–36. https://doi.org/10.1177/007542429802600102

——— 2006. "Canadian Raising: Retrospect and Prospect." *Canadian Journal of Linguistics /Revue canadienne de linguistique* 51 (2–3): 105–18. https://doi.org/10.1017/S000841310000400X

Chao, Monika, and Julia Bursten. 2021. "Girl Talk: Understanding Negative Reactions to Female Vocal Fry." *Hypatia* 2021: 1–18. https://doi.org/10.1017/hyp.2020.55

Chen, M. Keith. 2013. "The Effect of Language on Economic Behavior: Evidence from Savings Rates, Health Behaviors, and Retirement Assets." *American Economic Review* 103 (2): 690–731. https://doi.org/10.1257/aer.103.2.690

Chernela, Janet. 2023. "The Great Pirahã Brouhaha: Linguistic Diversity and Cognitive Universality." *Annual Review of Anthropology* 52: 137–49. https://doi.org/10.1146/annurev-anthro-052721-091031

Chevalier, Gisèle. 2008. "Les français du Canada: faits linguistiques, faits de langue." *Alternative Francophone* 1 (1): 80–97. https://doi.org/10.29173/af4139

Chiblow, Susan, and Paul Meighan. 2022. "Language Is Land, Land Is Language: The Importance of Indigenous Languages." *Human Geography* 15 (2): 206–10. https://doi.org/10.1177/19427786211022899

Childs, Becky, and Gerard van Herk. 2014. "Work That –s!: Drag Queens, Gender, Identity, and Traditional Newfoundland English." *Journal of Sociolinguistics* 18 (5): 634–57. https://doi.org/10.1111/josl.12094

Choe, Hanwool. 2019. "Eating Together Multimodally: Collaborative Eating in *Mukbang*, a Korean Livestream of Eating." *Language in Society* 48 (2): 171–208. https://doi.org/10.1017/S0047404518001355

Chomsky, Noam. 1959. "Review – Verbal Behavior, by B.F. Skinner." *Language* 35 (1): 26–58. https://doi.org/10.2307/411334

——— 1965. *Aspects of the Theory of Syntax*. Cambridge: MIT Press.

Chua, Amy. 2011. *Battle Hymn of the Tiger Mother*. London: Bloomsbury.

Chun, Elaine. 2004. "Ideologies of Legitimate Mockery: Margaret Cho's Revoicings of Mock Asian." *Pragmatics* 14 (2/3): 263–89. https://doi.org/10.1075/prag.14.2-3.10chu

CIHR (Canadian Institutes of Health Research), NSERC (Natural Sciences and Engineering Research Council), and SSHRC (Social Sciences and Humanities Research Council. 2018. "Tri-Council Policy Statement: Ethical Conduct for Research Involving Humans." https://ethics.gc.ca/eng/policy-politique_tcps2-eptc2_2018.html

Clark, Katerina, and Michael Holquist. 1984. *Mikhail Bakhtin*. Cambridge: Harvard University Press.

Clarke, Sandra. 2010. *Newfoundland and Labrador English*. Edinburgh: Edinburgh University Press.

Clemetson, Lynette. 2007. "The Racial Politics of Speaking Well." *The New York Times*, February 4. www.nytimes.com/2007/02/04/weekinreview/04clemetson.html

Coates, Jennifer. 2013. "The Discursive Production of Everyday Heterosexualities." *Discourse & Society* 24 (5): 536–52. https://doi.org/10.1177/0957926513486070

Coburn, Thomas. 1984. "'Scripture' in India: Towards a Typology of the Word in Hindu Life." *Journal of the American Academy or Religion* 52 (3): 435–59. https://doi.org/10.1093/jaarel/52.3.435

Cody, Francis. 2011. "Echoes of the Teashop in a Tamil Newspaper." *Language & Communication* 31: 241–54. https://doi.org/10.1016/j.langcom.2011.02.005

Cohn, Carol. 1987. "Sex and Death in the Rational World of Defense Intellectuals." *Signs: The Journal of Women in Culture and Society* 12 (4): 687–718. https://doi.org/10.1086/494362

Coleman, Gabriella. 2010. "The Hacker Conference: A Ritual Condensation and Celebration of a Lifeworld." *Anthropological Quarterly* 83 (1): 47–72. https://doi.org/10.1353/anq.0.0112

Comeau, Philip and Ruth King. 2011. "Media Representations of Minority French: Valorization, Identity, and the *Acadieman* Phenomenon." *Canadian Journal of Linguistics* 56 (2): 179–202. https://doi.org/10.1017/S0008413100003133

Conklin, Harold. 1955. "Hanunóo Color Categories." *Southwestern Journal of Anthropology* 11 (4): 339–44. https://doi.org/10.1086/soutjanth.11.4.3628909

Cope, Bill, and Mary Kalantzis. 2009. "'Multiliteracies': New Literacies, New Learning." *Pedagogies: An International Journal* 4 (3): 164–95. https://doi.org/10.1080/15544800903076044

Coulmas, Florian. 1989. *The Writing Systems of the World*. Oxford: Basil Blackwell.

Craft, Aimée, and Paulette Regan, eds. 2020. *Pathways of Reconciliation: Indigenous and Settler Approaches to Implementing the TRC's Calls to Action*. Winnipeg: University of Manitoba Press.

Crystal, David. 2000. *Language Death*. Cambridge: Cambridge University Press.

——— 2014. "The Tongue that Shakespeare Really Spoke." *Babel: The Language Magazine* 7: 14–18.

Danesi, Marcel. 2017. *The Semiotics of Emoji: The Rise of Visual Language in the Age of the Internet*. London: Bloomsbury.

Darnell, Regna. 1990. *Edward Sapir: Linguist, Anthropologist, Humanist*. Berkeley: University of California Press.

——— 2021. *The History of Anthropology: A Critical Window on the Discipline in North America*. Lincoln: University of Nebraska Press.

Das, Sonia. 2016. *Linguistic Rivalries: Tamil Migrants and Anglo-Franco Conflicts*. Oxford: Oxford University Press.

Davidson, Deanna. 2007. "East Spaces in West Times: Deictic Reference and Political Self-Positioning in a Post-Socialist East German Chronotope." *Language & Communication* 27 (3): 212–26. https://doi.org/10.1016/j.langcom.2007.01.002

Davies, Dai. 2014. "Coming Out: A Rite of Passage Toward the Creation of Lesbian, Gay, and Bisexual Identities." Undergraduate Thesis. Halifax: Saint Mary's University.

Davis, Jenny. 2017. "Resisting Rhetorics of Language Endangerment: Reclamation Through Indigenous Language Survivance." *Language Documentation and Description* 14: 37–58. https://doi.org/10.25894/ldd147

De Vos, Connie. 2014. "Absolute Spatial Deixis and Proto-Toponyms in Kata Kolok." *NUSA: Linguistic Studies in and Around Indonesia* 56: 3–26.

DeGraff, Michel. 2003. Against Creole Exceptionalism. *Language* 79 (2): 391–410. https://doi.org/10.1353/lan.2003.0114

Derrida, Jacques. 1974. *Of Grammatology.* Baltimore: Johns Hopkins University Press.

Dietrich, Sandy, and Erik Hernandez. 2022. "Language Use in the United States: 2019." www.census.gov/content/dam/Census/library/publications/2022/acs/acs-50.pdf.

Dikötter, Frank. 2015. *The Discourse of Race in Modern China*, 2nd ed. Oxford: Oxford University Press.

DiNova, Joanne, and Lila Pine. 2015. "Sight Unseen: Imag(in)ing Indigeneity in English." *AlterNative: An International Journal of Indigenous Peoples* 11 (4): 363–75. https://doi.org/10.1177/117718011501100404

Dollinger, Stefan. 2015. *The Written Questionnaire in Social Dialectology: History, Theory, Practice.* Amsterdam: John Benjamins.

Dorais, Louis-Jacques. 2010. *The Language of the Inuit: Syntax, Semantics, and Society in the Arctic.* Montreal: McGill-Queen's University Press.

Dorian, Nancy. 1977. "The Problem of the Semi-Speaker in Language Death." *Linguistics* 15 (191): 23–32. https://doi.org/10.1515/ling.1977.15.191.23

Dryer, Matthew, and Martin Haspelmath, eds. 2013. "WALS Online (v2020.3)." https://wals.info

Dubois, Lise. 2014. "Le français en Acadie des Maritimes." In *Le français en Amérique du Nord: État present*, edited by Albert Valdman, Julie Auger, and Deborah Piston-Hatlen, 81–98. Quebec: Presses de l'Université Laval.

Dubreuil, Benoît, and Christopher Stuart Henshilwood. 2013. "Archaeology and the Language-Ready Brain." *Language and Cognition* 5 (2–3): 251–60. https://doi.org/10.1515/langcog-2013-0018

Duchêne, Alexandre, and Monica Heller, eds. 2007. *Discourses of Endangerment.* London: Continuum.

——— 2012. *Language in Late Capitalism: Pride and Profit.* New York: Routledge.

Duranti, Alessandro. 1994. *From Grammar to Politics: Linguistic Anthropology in a Western Samoan Village.* Berkeley: University of California Press.

——— 2003. "Language as Culture in U.S. Anthropology: Three Paradigms." *Current Anthropology* 44 (3): 321–450. https://doi.org/10.1086/368118

——— 2006. "Narrating the Political Self in a Campaign for U.S. Congress." *Language in Society* 35 (4): 467–97. https://doi.org/10.1017/S0047404506060222

Eberhard, David, Gary Simons, and Charles Fennig, eds. 2022. *Ethnologue: Languages of the World*, 25th ed. Dallas: SIL International.

Eckert, Penelope. 1989. *Jocks and Burnouts: Social Categories and Identity in the High School.* New York: Teachers College Press.

——— 2012. "Three Waves of Variation Study: The Emergence of Meaning in the Study of Sociolinguistic Variation." *Annual Review of Anthropology* 41: 87–100. https://doi.org/10.1146/annurev-anthro-092611-145828

———. 2019. "The Limits of Meaning: Social Indexicality, Variation, and the Cline of Interiority." *Language* 95 (4): 751–76. https://doi.org/10.1353/lan.2019.0072

Edwards, John, ed. 1998. *Language in Canada.* Cambridge: Cambridge University Press.

Eliot, Lise, Adnan Ahmed, Hiba Khan, and Julie Patel. 2021. "Dump the 'Dimorphism': Comprehensive Synthesis of Human Brain Studies Reveals Few Male-Female Differences

Beyond Size." *Neuroscience and Biobehavioral Reviews* 125: 667–97. https://doi.org/10.1016/j.neubiorev.2021.02.026

Elman, Benjamin. 2013. *Civil Examinations and Meritocracy in Late Imperial China*. Cambridge: Harvard University Press.

Enfield, N.J. 2015. "Linguistic Relativity from Reference to Agency." *Annual Review of Anthropology* 44: 207–24. https://doi.org/10.1146/annurev-anthro-102214-014053

England, Nora. 1992. "Doing Mayan Linguistics in Guatemala." *Language* 68 (1): 29–35. https://doi.org/10.1353/lan.1992.0073

Eriksen, Thomas Hylland and Finn Sivert Nielsen. 2013. *A History of Anthropology*. London: Pluto Press.

Errington, Joseph. 2008. *Linguistics in a Colonial World: A Story of Language, Meaning, and Power*. Oxford: Blackwell.

Ethnologue. 2024. "What Are the Top 200 Most Spoken Languages?" www.ethnologue.com/insights/ethnologue200/

Everett, Daniel. 2005. "Cultural Constraints on Grammar and Cognition in Pirahã: Another Look at the Design Features of Human Language." *Current Anthropology* 46 (4): 621–46. https://doi.org/10.1086/431525

——— 2012. *Language: The Cultural Tool*. New York: Vintage.

Fanon, Frantz. 1967. *Black Skin, White Masks*, translated by Richard Philcox. New York: Grove Press.

Fausto-Sterling, Anne. 2012. *Sex/Gender: Biology in a Social World*. New York: Routledge.

Ferguson, Charles. 1959. "Diglossia." *Word* 15 (2): 325–40. https://doi.org/10.1080/00437956.1959.11659702

——— 1983. "Sports Announcer Talk: Syntactic Aspects of Register Variation." *Language in Society* 12 (2): 153–72. https://doi.org/10.1017/S0047404500009787

Ferguson, Jenanne. 2019. *Words Like Birds: Sakha Language Discourses and Practices in the City*. Lincoln: University of Nebraska Press.

——— 2021. "How Words Make the World: Language Materialities and the Circulation of the Sakha Algys." *Multilingua* 40 (4): 433–61. https://doi.org/10.1515/multi-2020-0075

Fields, Jessica. 2001. "Normal Queers: Straight Parents Respond to Their Children's 'Coming Out.'" *Symbolic Interaction* 24 (2): 165–87. https://doi.org/10.1525/si.2001.24.2.165

Finnegan, Ruth. 1988. *Literacy and Orality: Studies in the Technology of Communication*. Oxford: Blackwell.

——— 2012. *Oral Literature in Africa*. Cambridge: Open Book Publishers.

Fischer, Claude. 1992. *America Calling: A Social History of the Telephone to 1940*. Berkeley: University of California Press.

Fischer, Steven. 2001. *A History of Writing*. London: Reaktion.

Fishman, Joshua. 1972. *Language and Nationalism: Two Integrative Essays*. Rowley: Newbury House.

——— 1991. *Reversing Language Shift: Theoretical and Empirical Foundations of Assistance to Threatened Languages*. Clevedon: Multilingual Matters.

Fouts, Roger. 1975. "Capacities for Language in Great Apes." In *Socioecology and Psychology of Primates*, edited by Russell Tuttle, 371–90. The Hague: De Gruyter Mouton.

Fox, Robin. 1967. *Kinship and Marriage: An Anthropological Perspective*. Cambridge: Cambridge University Press.

Frake, Charles. 1970. "The Ethnographic Study of Cognitive Systems." In *Readings in the Sociology of Language*, edited by Joshua Fishman, 434–46. The Hague: De Gruyter Mouton.

Fuentes, Augustin. 2012. *Race, Monogamy, and Other Lies They Told You: Busting Myths About Human Nature*. Berkeley: University of California Press.

Gaines, Alisha. 2017. *Black for a Day: White Fantasies of Race and Empathy*. Chapel Hill: University of North Carolina Press.

Gal, Susan. 1995. "Language, Gender, and Power: An Anthropological Review." In *Gender Articulated: Language and the Socially Constructed Self*, edited by Kira Hall and Mary Bucholtz, 169–82. New York: Routledge.

Galletta, Anne. 2013. *Mastering the Semi-Structured Interview and Beyond: From Research Design to Analysis and Publication*. New York: New York University Press.

Gandhi, Mahatma. 1958. *Evil Wrought by the English Medium*. Ahmedabad: Navajivan.

Gardner, R.A., and B.T. Gardner. 1975. "Early Signs of Language in Child and Chimpanzee." *Science* 187 (4178): 752–53. https://doi.org/10.1126/science.187.4178.752

Gates, Hill. 1996. *China's Motor: A Thousand Years of Petty Capitalism*. Ithaca: Cornell University Press.

Gaudio, Rudolf. 2003. "Coffeetalk: Starbucks™ and the Commercialization of Casual Conversation." *Language in Society* 32 (5): 659–91. https://doi.org/10.1017/s0047404503325035

——— 2011. "The Blackness of 'Broken English'." *Journal of Linguistic Anthropology* 21 (2): 230–46. https://doi.org/10.1111/j.1548-1395.2011.01108.x

Gaudry, Adam, and Danielle Lorenz. 2018. "Indigenization as Inclusion, Reconciliation, and Decolonization: Navigating the Different Visions for Indigenizing the Canadian Academy." *AlterNative: An International Journal of Indigenous Peoples* 14 (3): 218–27. https://doi.org/10.1177/1177180118785382

Gellner, Ernest. 1983. *Nations and Nationalism*. Ithaca: Cornell University Press.

Gershon, Ilana. 2010. *The Breakup 2.0: Disconnecting over New Media*. Ithaca: Cornell University Press.

Gitelman, Lisa. 2018. "Emoji Dick and the Eponymous Whale, An Essay in Four Parts." *Post45*. https://post45.org/2018/07/emoji-dick-and-the-eponymous-whale-an-essay-in-four-parts/

Glass, Aaron. 2009. "A Cannibal in the Archive: Performance, Materiality, and (In)Visibility in Unpublished Edward Curtis Photographs of the Kwakwa̱ka̱'wakw Hamat'sa." *Visual Anthropology Review* 25 (2): 128–49. https://doi.org/10.1111/j.1548-7458.2009.01038.x

Goffman, Erving. 1953. "Communication Conduct in an Island Community." Doctoral Dissertation, University of Chicago.

——— 1959. *The Presentation of Self in Everyday Life*. New York: Doubleday.

——— 1974. *Frame Analysis*. Cambridge: Havard University Press.

——— 1981. *Forms of Talk*. Philadelphia: University of Pennsylvania Press.

——— 1983. "Felicity's Condition." *American Journal of Sociology* 89 (1): 1–53. https://doi.org/10.1086/227833

Gomashie, Grace. 2019. "Kanien'keha/Mohawk Indigenous Language Revitalization Efforts in Canada." *McGill Journal of Education* 54 (1): 151–71. https://mje.mcgill.ca/article/view/9472

González, Roseann Dueñas. 2000. "Introduction." In *Language Ideologies: Critical Perspectives on the Official English Movement, Vol. 1*, edited by Roseann Dueñas González and Ildikó Melis, xxvii–xlvii. Mahwah: Lawrence Erlbaum.

Goodwin, Marjorie Harness. 2008. *The Hidden Life of Girls: Games of Stance, Status, and Exclusion*. Malden: Wiley-Blackwell.

Goody, Jack. 1977. *The Domestication of the Savage Mind*. Cambridge: Cambridge University Press.

Gordon, Peter. 2003. "Numerical Cognition without Words: Evidence from Amazonia." *Science* 306 (5695): 496–99. https://doi.org/10.1126/science.1094492

Gould, Stephen Jay. 1981. *The Mismeasure of Man*. New York: W.W. Norton.

Gray, John. 1992. *Men Are from Mars, Women Are from Venus*. New York: Harper Collins.

Green, Lisa. 2002. *African American English: A Linguistic Introduction*. Cambridge: Cambridge University Press.

Greenfield, Patricia. 1972. "Oral or Written Language: The Consequences for Cognitive Development in Africa." *Language and Speech* 15 (2): 169–78. https://doi.org/10.1177/002383097201500207

Grieve, Jack, Andrea Nini, and Diansheng Guo. 2018. "Mapping Lexical Innovation on American Social Media." *Journal of English Linguistics* 46 (4): 293–319. https://doi.org/10.1177/0075424218793191

Groat, Cody, and Kim Anderson. 2021. "Holding Place: Resistance, Reframing, and Relationality in the Representation of Indigenous History." *Canadian Historical Review* 102 (3): 465–84. https://doi.org/10.3138/chr-2020-0045

Grosjean, François. 2010. *Bilingual: Life and Reality*. Cambridge: Harvard University Press.

Guardado, Martin. 2009. "Speaking Spanish Like a Boy Scout: Language Socialization, Resistance, and Reproduction in a Heritage Language Scout Troop." *Canadian Modern Language Review* 66 (1): 101–29. https://doi.org/10.3138/cmlr.66.1.101

Gumperz, John. 1968. "The Speech Community." In *International Encyclopedia of the Social Sciences*, 381–6. New York: Macmillan.

Gumperz, John, and Jenny Cook-Gumperz. 2008. "Studying Language, Culture, and Society: Sociolinguistics or Linguistic Anthropology?" *Journal of Sociolinguistics* 12 (4): 532–45. https://doi.org/10.1111/j.1467-9841.2008.00378.x

Gupta, Akhil, and James Ferguson. 1997. "Beyond 'Culture': Space, Identity, and the Politics of Difference." In *Culture, Power, Place: Explorations in Critical Ethnography*, edited by Akhil Gupta and James Ferguson, 33–51. Durham: Duke University Press.

Gusterson, Hugh. 1996. *Nuclear Rites: A Weapons Laboratory at the End of the Cold War*. Berkeley: University of California Press.

Haeri, Niloofar. 2003. *Sacred Language, Ordinary People: Dilemmas of Culture and Politics in Egypt*. New York: Palgrave Macmillan.

Hall, Kira. 1995. "Lip Service on the Fantasy Lines." In *Gender Articulated: Language and the Socially Constructed Self*, edited by Kira Hall and Mary Bucholtz, 183–216. New York: Routledge.

Halverson, John. 1992. "Goody and the Implosion of the Literacy Thesis." *Man* 27 (2): 301–17. https://doi.org/10.2307/2804055

Hammarström, Harald, Robert Forkel, Martin Haspelmath, and Sebastian Bank. 2022. "Glottolog 4.7." http://glottolog.org.

Handman, Courtney. 2013. "Text Messaging in Tok Pisin: Etymologies and Orthographies in Cosmopolitan Papua New Guinea." *Culture, Theory and Critique* 54 (3): 265–84. https://doi.org/10.1080/14735784.2013.818288

Hanks, William. 1989. "Text and Textuality." *Annual Review of Anthropology* 18: 95–127. https://doi.org/10.1146/annurev.anthro.18.1.95

———. 2005. "Explorations in the Deictic Field." *Cultural Anthropology* 46 (2): 191–220. https://doi.org/10.1086/427120

Haque, Eve. 2014. "Multiculturalism within a Bilingual Framework: A Retrospective." *Canadian Ethnic Studies* 46 (2): 119–25. https://doi.org/10.1353/ces.2014.0034

Haque, Eve, and Donna Patrick. 2015. "Indigenous Languages and the Racial Hierarchisation of Language Policy in Canada." *Journal of Multilingual and Multicultural Development* 36 (1): 27–41. https://doi.org/10.1080/01434632.2014.892499

Harris, Roy. 2000. *Rethinking Writing*. London: Athlone.

Harrison, Faye. 1995. "The Persistent Power of 'Race' in the Cultural and Political Economy of Racism." *Annual Review of Anthropology* 24: 47–74. https://doi.org/10.1146/annurev.anthro.24.1.47

Harrison, K. David. 2007. *When Languages Die: The Extinction of the World's Languages and the Erosion of Human Knowledge*. Oxford: Oxford University Press.

Haviland, John. 1998. "Gugu Yimithirr Cardinal Directions." *Ethos* 26 (1): 25–47. https://doi.org/10.1525/eth.1998.26.1.25

Heath, Shirley Brice. 1983. *Ways with Words: Language, Life, and Work in Communities and Classrooms*. Cambridge: Cambridge University Press.

Heller, Monica. 2001. "Legitimate Language in a Multilingual School." In *Voices of Authority: Education and Linguistic Difference*, edited by Marilyn Martin-Jones and Monica Heller, 381–402. Westport: Ablex.

——— 2002. "Globalization and the Commodification of Bilingualism in Canada." In *Globalization and Language Teaching*, edited by Deborah Cameron and David Block, 47–63. New York: Routledge.

——— ed. 2007. *Bilingualism: A Social Approach*. Basingstoke: Palgrave Macmillan.

——— 2010. "The Commodification of Language." *Annual Review of Anthropology* 39: 101–14. https://doi.org/10.1146/annurev.anthro.012809.104951

Heller, Monica, and Bonnie McElhinny. 2017. *Language, Capitalism, Colonialism: Toward a Critical History*. Toronto: University of Toronto Press.

Heller, Monica, Lindsay Bell, Michelle Daveluy, Mireille McLaughlin, and Hubert Noël. 2016. *Sustaining the Nation: The Making and Moving of Language and Nation*. Oxford: Oxford University Press.

Henry, Eric. 2021a. *The Future Conditional: Building an English-Speaking Society in Northeast China*. Ithaca: Cornell University Press.

——— 2021b. "Narrating the Future Self: Strategic Stylization and Cosmopolitan Desire in Chinese IELTS Preparation Classes." In *Unpacking Discourses on Chineseness: The Cultural Politics of Language and Identity in Globalizing China*, edited by Shuang Gao and Xuan Wang, 106–25. Bristol: Multilingual Matters.

Hermes, Mary, and Chad Uran. 2006. "Treaties That Dominate and Literacy That Empowers? I Wish It Was All in Ojibwemowin." *Anthropology and Education Quarterly* 37 (4): 393–98. https://doi.org/10.1525/aeq.2006.37.4.393

Herschensohn, Julia. 2007. *Language Development and Age*. Cambridge: Cambridge University Press.

Hill, Jane. 2002. "'Expert Rhetorics' in Advocacy for Endangered Languages: Who Is Listening, and What Do They Hear?" *Journal of Linguistic Anthropology* 12 (2): 119–33. https://doi.org/10.1525/jlin.2002.12.2.119

——— 2008. *The Everyday Language of White Racism*. Oxford: Wiley-Blackwell.

Hill, Jane, and Bruce Mannheim. 1992. "Language and Worldview." *Annual Review of Anthropology* 21: 381–404. https://doi.org/10.1146/annurev.anthro.21.1.381

Hillewaert, Sarah. 2015. "Writing with an Accent: Orthographic Practice, Emblems, and Traces on Facebook." *Journal of Linguistic Anthropology* 25 (2): 195–214. https://doi.org/10.1111/jola.12079

——— 2021. "Reimagining Linguistic Heritage: Or How Mother Tongue Speakers Re-Create Their Language." *Journal of Linguistic Anthropology* 31 (3): 396–411. https://doi.org/10.1111/jola.12338

Hinton, Leanne, Leena Huss, and Gerald Roche. 2018. "Introduction: Language Revitalization as a Growing Field of Study and Practice." In *The Routledge Handbook of Language Revitalization*, edited by Leanne Hinton, Leena Huss, and Gerald Roche, xxi–xxx. New York: Routledge.

Hobsbawm, E.J. 1990. *Nations and Nationalism Since 1780: Programme, Myth, Reality.* Cambridge: Cambridge University Press.

Hockett, Charles. 1963. "The Problem of Universals in Language." In *Universals of Language*, edited by Joseph Greenberg, 1–22. Cambridge: MIT Press.

Hogg, Richard, and David Denison, eds. 2006. *A History of the English Language.* Cambridge: Cambridge University Press.

Howe, Cymene, and Dominic Boyer. 2024. "The Okjökull Memorial and Geohuman Relations." *Social Anthropology* 32 (1): 30–45. https://doi.org/10.3167/saas.2024.320104

Humboldt, Wilhelm von. 1988. *On Language: The Diversity of Human Language-Structure and Its Influence on the Mental Development of Mankind*, translated by Peter Heath. Cambridge: Cambridge University Press.

Hurston, Zora Neale. 1935. *Mules and Men*. New York: Harper & Row.

——— 2018. "Barracoon: The Story of the Last." In *Black Cargo*, edited by Deborah Plant. New York: HarperCollins.

Hwang, Kwang-Kuo. 1987. "Face and Favor: The Chinese Power Game." *American Journal of Sociology* 92 (4): 944–74. https://doi.org/10.1086/228588

Hymes, Dell. 1972. "On Communicative Competence." In *Sociolinguistics: Selected Readings*, edited by John Pride and Janet Holmes, 269–93. Harmondsworth: Penguin.

——— 1974. *Foundations in Sociolinguistics: An Ethnographic Approach*. Philadelphia: University of Pennsylvania Press.

——— 1981. "In Vain I Tried to Tell You." In*Essays in Native American Ethnopoetics.* Philadelphia: University of Pennsylvania Press.

Ignatiev, Noel. 1995. *How the Irish Became White.* New York: Routledge.

Inoue, Miyako. 2006. *Vicarious Language: Gender and Linguistic Modernity in Japan*. Berkeley: University of California Press.

Irvine, Judith. T. 1978. "When Is Genealogy History? Wolof Genealogies in Comparative Perspective." *American Ethnologist* 5 (4): 651–74. https://doi.org/10.1525/ae.1978.5.4.02a00020

——— 1979. "Formality and Informality in Communicative Events." *American Anthropologist* 81 (4): 773–90. https://doi.org/10.1525/aa.1979.81.4.02a00020

Jacknis, Ira. 2019. "No Object Without Its Story: Franz Boas, George Hunt, and the Creation of a Native Material Anthropology." In *Disruptive Voices and the Singularity of Histories*, edited by Regna Darnell and Frederic Gleach, 231–52. Lincoln: University of Nebraska Press.

Jacquemet, Marco. 2019. "Beyond the Speech Community: On Belonging to a Multilingual, Diasporic, and Digital Social Network." *Language & Communication* 68: 46–56. https://doi.org/10.1016/j.langcom.2018.10.010

Jaffe, Alexandra. 1999. *Ideologies in Action: Language Politics on Corsica*. Berlin: De Gruyter Mouton.

Joe, Rita. 1996. *Song of Rita Joe: Autobiography of a Mi'kmaq Poet*. Lincoln: University of Nebraska Press.

Johnstone, Barbara. 2000. *Qualitative Methods in Sociolinguistics*. Oxford: Oxford University Press.

——— 2015. *Speaking Pittsburghese: The Story of a Dialect*. Oxford: Oxford University Press.

Jones, Graham. 2011. *Trade of the Tricks: Inside the Magician's Craft*. Berkeley: University of California Press.

Joseph, R. 2000. "The Evolution of Sex Differences in Language, Sexuality, and Visual–Spatial Skills." *Archives of Sexual Behavior* 29 (1): 35–66. https://doi.org/10.1023/a:1001834404611

Jourdan, Christine, and Johanne Angeli. 2014. "Pijin and Shifting Language Ideologies in Urban Solomon Islands." *Language in Society* 43 (3): 265–85. https://doi.org/10.1017/s0047404514000190

Kay, Paul, and Willett Kempton. 1984. "What Is the Sapir–Whorf Hypothesis?" *American Anthropologist* 86 (1): 65–79. https://doi.org/10.1525/aa.1984.86.1.02a00050

Keane, Webb. 2013. "On Spirit Writing: Materialities of Language and the Religious Work of Transduction." *Journal of the Royal Anthropological Institute* 19: 1–17. https://doi.org/10.1111/1467-9655.12000

Keenan [Ochs], Elinor. 1974. "Norm-Makers, Norm-Breakers: Uses of Speech by Men and Women in a Malagasy Community." In *Explorations in the Ethnography of Speaking*, edited by Richard Bauman and Joel Sherzer, 125–43. Cambridge: Cambridge University Press.

Kegl, Judy, Ann Senghas, and Marie Coppola. 1999. "Creation Through Contact: Sign Language Emergence and Sign Language Change in Nicaragua." In *Language Creation and Language Change: Creolization, Diachrony, and Development*, edited by Michel DeGraff, 179–238. Cambridge: MIT Press.

Kiesling, Scott. 2004. "Dude." *American Speech* 79 (3): 281–305. https://doi.org/10.1215/00031283-79-3-281

——— 2007. "Men, Masculinities, and Language." *Language and Linguistics Compass* 1 (6): 653–73. https://doi.org/10.1111/j.1749-818x.2007.00035.x

King, Ruth. 2008. "Chiac in Context: Overview and Evaluation of Acadie's Joual." In *Social Lives in Language – Sociolinguistics and Multilingual Speech Communities: Celebrating the Work of Gillian Sankoff*, edited by Miriam Meyerhoff and Naomi Nagy, 137–78. Amsterdam: John Benjamins.

King, Sharese. 2020. "From African American Vernacular English to African American Language: Rethinking the Study of Race and Language in African Americans' Speech." *Annual Review of Linguistics* 6: 285–300. https://doi.org/10.1146/annurev-linguistics-011619-030556

Kipnis, Andrew. 1997. *Producing Guanxi: Sentiment, Self, and Subculture in a North China Village*. Durham: Duke University Press.

Kirkness, Alan. 2006. "Lexicography." In *The Handbook of Applied Linguistics*, edited by Alan Davies and Catherine Elder, 54–81. Malden: Blackwell.

Kirksey, S. Eben, and Stefan Helmreich. 2010. "The Emergence of Multispecies Ethnography." *Cultural Anthropology* 25 (4): 545–76. https://doi.org/10.1111/j.1548-1360.2010.01069.x

Klemperer, Victor. 2013. *The Language of the Third Reich*, translated by Martin Brady. London: Bloomsbury.

Kockelman, Paul. 2010. *Language, Culture, and Mind: Natural Constructions and Social Kinds.* Cambridge: Cambridge University Press.

——— 2013. "Huckleberry Finn Takes the Turing Test: The Transformation of Ontologies and the Virtuality of Kinds." *Language & Communication* 33: 150–54. https://doi.org/10.1016/j.langcom.2013.03.002

Kohn, Eduardo. 2007. "How Dogs Dream: Amazonian Natures and the Politics of Transspecies Engagement." *American Ethnologist* 34 (1): 3–24. https://doi.org/10.1525/ae.2007.34.1.3

Kolopenuk, Jessica. 2023. "The Pretendian Problem." *Canadian Journal of Political Science/Revue canadienne de science politique* 56 (2): 468–73. https://doi.org/10.1017/S0008423923000239

Krauss, Michael. 1992. "The World's Languages in Crisis." *Language* 68 (1): 4–10. https://doi.org/10.1353/lan.1992.0075

Krupnik, Igor, and Ludger Müller-Wille. 2010. "Franz Boas and Inuktitut Terminology for Ice and Snow: From the Emergence of the Field to the 'Great Eskimo Vocabulary Hoax.'" In *SIKU: Knowing Our Ice: Documenting Inuit Sea Ice Knowledge and Use*, edited by Igor Krupnik, Claudio Aporta, Shari Gearheard, Gita Laidler, and Lene Kielsen Holm, 377–400. Dordrecht: Springer.

Kubota, Ryuko. 2020. "Confronting Epistemological Racism, Decolonizing Scholarly Knowledge: Race and Gender in Applied Linguistics." *Applied Linguistics* 41 (5): 712–32. https://doi.org/10.1093/applin/amz033

Kulick, Don. 1992. *Language Shift and Cultural Reproduction: Socialization, Self, and Syncretism in a Papua New Guinean Village.* Cambridge: Cambridge University Press.

——— 1993. "Speaking as a Woman: Structure and Gender in Domestic Arguments in a New Guinea Village." *Cultural Anthropology* 8 (4): 510–41. https://doi.org/10.1525/can.1993.8.4.02a00050

——— 2003. "No." *Language & Communication* 23 (2): 139–51. https://doi.org/10.1016/s0271-5309(02)00043-5

——— 2019. *A Death in the Rainforest: How a Language and a Way of Life Came to an End in Papua New Guinea.* Chapel Hill: Algonquin Books.

Labov, William. 1963. "The Social Motivation of a Sound Change." *Word* 19 (3): 273–309. https://doi.org/10.1080/00437956.1963.11659799

——— 1970. "The Logic of Nonstandard English." In *Language and Poverty: Perspectives on a Theme*, edited by Frederick Williams, 153–89. Chicago: Markham.

——— 1972. "Negative Attraction and Negative Concord in English Grammar." *Language* 48 (4): 773–818. https://doi.org/10.2307/411989

LaDousa, Chaise. 2014. *Hindi Is Our Ground, English Is Our Sky: Education, Language, and Social Class in Contemporary India.* New York: Berghahn.

Lakoff, George, and Mark Johnson. 1980. *Metaphors We Live By.* Chicago: University of Chicago Press.

Lakoff, Robin. 1975. *Language and Woman's Place.* New York: Harper & Row.

Lamarre, Patricia. 2013. "Catching 'Montréal on the Move' and Challenging the Discourse of Unilingualism in Québec." *Anthropologica* 55 (1): 41–56.

Landry, Nicolas, and Nicole Lang. 2001. *Histoire de l'acadie*. Sillery: Septentrion.

Landry, Rodrigue, and Richard Bourhis. 1997. "Linguistic Landscape and Ethnolinguistic Vitality: An Empirical Study." *Journal of Language and Social Psychology* 16 (1): 23–49. https://doi.org/10.1177/0261927x970161002

Laneheart, Sonja. 2021. *Language in African American Communities*. New York: Routledge.

Lapowsky, Issie. 2013. "Ev Williams on Twitter's Early Years." *Inc.*, October 4. www.inc.com/issie-lapowsky/ev-williams-twitter-early-years.html

Law, Danny, Stephen Houston, Nicholas Carter, Marc Zender, and David Stuart. 2013. "Reading in Context: The Interpretation of Personal Reference in Ancient Maya Hieroglyphic Texts." *Journal of Linguistic Anthropology* 23 (2): E23–E47. https://doi.org/10.1111/jola.12008

Leavitt, John. 2011. *Linguistic Relativities: Language Diversity and Modern Thought*. Cambridge: Cambridge University Press.

LeBlanc, Mélanie, and Annette Boudreau. 2016. "Discourses, Legitimization, and the Construction of Acadianité." *Signs and Society* 4 (1): 80–108. https://doi.org/10.1086/685436

Lee, Penny. 1996. *The Whorf Theory Complex: A Critical Reconstruction*. Amsterdam: John Benjamins.

Lefebvre, Henri. 1991. *The Production of Space*. Oxford: Blackwell.

Leimgruber, Jakob. 2020. "Global Multilingualism, Local Bilingualism, Official Monolingualism: The Linguistic Landscape of Montreal's St. Catherine Street." *International Journal of Bilingual Education and Bilingualism* 23 (6): 708–23. https://doi.org/10.1080/13670050.2017.1401974

Leonard, Wesley. 2008. "When Is an 'Extinct Language' Not Extinct? Miami, a Formerly Sleeping Language." In *Sustaining Linguistic Diversity: Endangered and Minority Languages and Language Varieties*, edited by Kendall King, Natalie Schilling-Estes, Lyn Fogle, Jia Jackie Lou, and Barbara Soukup, 23–34. Washington, DC: Georgetown University Press.

——— 2012. "Reframing Language Reclamation Programmes for Everybody's Empowerment." *Gender and Language* 6 (2): 339–67. https://doi.org/10.1558/genl.v6i2.339

——— 2021. "Toward an Anti-Racist Linguistic Anthropology: An Indigenous Response to White Supremacy." *Journal of Linguistic Anthropology* 31 (2): 218–37. https://doi.org/10.1111/jola.12319

Levinson, Stephen. 1997. "Language and Cognition: The Cognitive Consequences of Spatial Description in Guugu Yimithirr." *Journal of Linguistic Anthropology* 7 (1): 98–131. https://doi.org/10.1525/jlin.1997.7.1.98

——— 2020. "On 'Technologies of the Intellect'." In *Goody Lecture 2020*. Halle: Max Planck Institute for Social Anthropology.

Li, Wei, and Ofelia García. 2022. "Not a First Language but One Repertoire: Translanguaging as a Decolonizing Project." *RELC Journal* 53 (2): 313–24. https://doi.org/10.1177/00336882221092841

Liddell, Scott. 2003. *Grammar, Gesture, and Meaning in American Sign Language*. Cambridge: Cambridge University Press.

Liebersohn, Harry. 2008. "Anthropology Before Anthropology." In *A New History of Anthropology*, edited by Henrika Kuklick, 17–32. Oxford: Blackwell.

Lippi-Green, Rosina. 1997. *English with an Accent: Language, Ideology, and Discrimination in the United States*. London: Routledge.

Lo Bianco, Joseph. 2010. "Language Policy and Planning." In *New Perspectives on Language and Education*, edited by Nancy Hornberger and Sandra McKay, 143–76. Clevedon: Multilingual Matters.

Lucy, John. 1992. *Language Diversity and Thought: A Reformulation of the Linguistic Relativity Hypothesis*. Cambridge: Cambridge University Press.

Lust, Barbara. 2006. *Child Language: Acquisition and Growth*. Cambridge: Cambridge University Press.

Luu, Chi. 2020. "Black English Matters." *Lingua Obscura*. https://daily.jstor.org/black-english-matters/

MacKee, Freddy. 2016. "Social Media in Gay London: Tinder as an Alternative to Hook-Up Apps." *Social Media + Society* 2 (3): 1–10. https://doi.org/10.1177/2056305116662186

Mackey, William. 1998. "The Foundations." In *Language in Canada*, edited by John Edwards, 13–35. Cambridge: Cambridge University Press.

Malinowski, Bronislaw. 1923. "The Problem of Meaning in Primitive Languages." In *The Meaning of Meaning*, edited by C.K. Ogden and I.A. Richards, 296–336. New York: Harcourt Brace.

——— 1954. *Magic, Science and Religion and Other Essays*. New York: Doubleday Anchor.

Malotki, Ekkehart. 1983. *Hopi Time: A Linguistic Analysis of the Temporal Concepts in the Hopi Language*. Berlin: De Gruyter Mouton.

Manning, Paul. 2008. "Barista Rants About Stupid Customers at Starbucks: What Imaginary Conversations Can Teach Us about Real Ones." *Language & Communication* 28 (2): 101–26. https://doi.org/10.1016/j.langcom.2008.02.004

Manning, Philip. 1992. *Erving Goffman and Modern Sociology*. Malden: Polity.

Marks, Jonathan. 2017. *Is Science Racist?* Malden: Polity.

Martin, Emily. 1991. "The Egg and the Sperm: How Science Has Constructed a Romance Based on Stereotypical Male–Female Roles." *Signs: Journal of Women in Culture and Society* 16 (3): 485–501. https://doi.org/10.1086/494680

Martin, Laura. 1986. "'Eskimo Words for Snow': A Case Study in the Genesis and Decay of an Anthropological Example." *American Anthropologist* 88 (2): 418–23. https://doi.org/10.1525/aa.1986.88.2.02a00080

Martindale, Andrew, Sara Shneiderman, and Mark Turin. 2018. "Time, Oral Tradition, and Technology." In *Memory*, edited by Philippe Tortell, Mark Turin, and Margot Young, 197–206. Vancouver: Peter Wall Institute.

Maxwell, Olga. 2023. "In Russia's War against Ukraine, One of the Battlegrounds Is Language Itself." *The Conversation*. https://theconversation.com/in-russias-war-against-ukraine-one-of-the-battlegrounds-is-language-itself-201170

McCarty, Teresa. 2016. "Policy and Politics of Language Revitalization in the USA and Canada." In *Indigenous Language Revitalization in the Americas*, edited by Serafín Coronel-Molina and Teresa McCarty, 15–34. New York: Routledge.

McCarty, Teresa, Sheilah Nicholas, Kari Chew, Natalie Diaz, Wesley Leonard, and Louellyn White. 2018. "Hear Our Languages, Hear Our Voices: Storywork as Theory and Praxis in Indigenous-Language Reclamation." *Dædalus* 147 (2): 160–72. https://doi.org/10.1162/DAED_a_00499

McElgunn, Hanna. 2021. "Intertextual Politics: Presence, Erasure, and the Hopi Language." *American Ethnologist* 48 (4): 432–45. https://doi.org/10.1111/amet.13038

McElhinny, Bonnie. 2003. "Fearful, Forceful Agents of the Law: Ideologies About Language and Gender in Police Officers' Narratives About the Use of Physical Force." *Pragmatics* 13 (2): 253–84. https://doi.org/10.1075/prag.13.2.03elh

McIntosh, Janet. 2010. "Mobile Phones and Mipoho's Prophecy: The Powers and Dangers of Flying Language." *American Ethnologist* 37 (2): 337–53. https://doi .org/10.1111/j.1548-1425.2010.01259.x

McLaughlin, Mireille. 2021. "L'insécurité linguistique à travers le prisme des questions de classe sociale: le cas de l'Acadie." In *Retour en Acadie: Penser les langues et la sociolinguistique à partir des Marges: Textes en hommage à Annette Boudreau*, edited by Laurence Arrighi and Émilie Urbain, 87–107. Quebec: Presses de l'Université Laval.

McLemore, Cynthia. 1991. "The Interpretation of L*H in English." *Texas Linguistic Forum: Discourse* 32: 127–47. https://languagelog.ldc.upenn.edu/myl/ldc/llog/CAM_ Interpretation.pdf

McLuhan, Marshall. 1964. *Understanding Media: The Extensions of Man*. London: Routledge & Kegan Paul.

McWhorter, John. 2013. "Txtng Is Killing Language. JK!!!" *TED*. www.ted.com/talks /john_mcwhorter_txtng_is_killing_language_jk

——— 2014. *The Language Hoax: Why the World Looks the Same in Any Language*. Oxford: Oxford University Press.

Meek, Barbra. 2010. *We Are Our Language: An Ethnography of Language Revitalization in a Northern Athabascan Community*. Tucson: University of Arizona Press.

——— 2017. "Native American Languages and Linguistic Anthropology: From the Legacy of Salvage Anthropology to the Promise of Linguistic Self-Determination." In *Engaging Native American Publics: Linguistic Anthropology in a Collaborative Key*, edited by Paul Kroskrity and Barbra Meek, 3–24. New York: Routledge.

Mendoza-Denton, Norma. 2008. *Homegirls: Language and Cultural Practice among Latina Youth Gangs*. Oxford: Blackwell.

——— 2011. "The Semiotic Hitchhiker's Guide to Creaky Voice: Circulation and Gendered Hardcore in a Chicana/o Gang Persona." *Journal of Linguistic Anthropology* 21 (2): 261–80. https://doi.org/10.1111/j.1548-1395.2011.01110.x

Mendoza-Denton, Norma, and Dana Osborne. 2009. "Two Languages, Two Identities?" In *Language and Identities*, edited by Carmen Llamas and Dominic Watt, 113–22. Edinburgh: Edinburgh University Press.

Mertz, Elizabeth. 2007. *The Language of Law School: Learning to "Think Like a Lawyer."* Oxford: Oxford University Press.

Mertz, Elizabeth, and Richard Parmentier, eds. 1985. *Semiotic Mediation: Sociocultural and Psychological Perspectives*. Orlando: Academic Press.

Metcalf, Allan. 2000. *How We Talk: American Regional English Today*. Boston: Houghton Mifflin.

Meyerhoff, Miriam, and Susan Ehrlich. 2019. "Language, Gender, and Sexuality." *Annual Review of Linguistics* 5: 455–75. https://doi.org/10.1146/annurev-linguistics-052418-094326

Miller, Laura. 2008. "Those Naughty Teenage Girls: Japanese Kogals, Slang, and Media Assessments." *Journal of Linguistic Anthropology* 14 (2): 225–47. https://doi.org/10.1525 /jlin.2004.14.2.225

Mitchell-Kernan, Claudia. 1972. "Signifying and Marking: Two Afro-American Speech Acts." In *Directions in Sociolinguistics: The Ethnography of Communication*, edited by John Gumperz and Dell Hymes, pp. 161–79. New York: Holt, Rinehart and Winston.

Mithun, Marianne. 1999. *The Languages of Native North America*. Cambridge: Cambridge University Press.

Miyazaki, Hiro. 2013. *Arbitraging Japan: Dreams of Capitalism at the End of Finance*. Berkeley: University of California Press.

Momma, Haruko. 2013. *From Philology to English Studies: Language and Culture in the Nineteenth Century*. Cambridge: Cambridge University Press.

Morgan, Marcyliena. 2014. *Speech Communities*. Cambridge: Cambridge University Press.

Morris, Brian. 1994. *Anthropology of the Self: The Individual in Cultural Perspective*. London: Pluto Press.

Muehlmann, Shaylih. 2012. "Von Humboldt's Parrot and the Countdown of Last Speakers in the Colorado Delta." *Language & Communication* 32 (2): 160–68. https://doi.org/10.1016/j.langcom.2011.05.001

Mufwene, Salikoko. 2023 "Linguistic Hybridization in the Emergence of Creoles." *Cambridge Journal of Postcolonial Literary Inquiry* 10 (1): 74–89. https://doi.org/10.1017/pli.2022.32

Mugane, John. 2015. *The Story of Swahili*. Athens: Ohio University Press.

Muhanna, Elias. 2014. "Translating 'Frozen' into Arabic." *New York Times*, May 30.

Mühlhäusler, Peter, Thomas Dutton, and Suzanne Romaine. 2003. *Tok Pisin Texts: From the Beginning to the Present*. Amsterdam: John Benjamins.

Mullings, Leith. 2005. "Interrogating Racism: Toward an Antiracist Anthropology." *Annual Review of Anthropology* 34: 667–93. https://doi.org/10.1146/annurev.anthro.32.061002.093435

Nash, Joshua. 2013. "Response and Rejoinder to Perley's 'Zombie Linguistics': It Is Easier for a Camel to Pass Through the Eye of a Needle Than a Linguist to Pass Through the 'Perley Gates': A Response to Perley's 'Zombie Linguistics.'" *Anthropological Forum* 23 (1): 107–13. https://doi.org/10.1080/00664677.2012.752717

Nettle, Daniel, and Suzanne Romaine. 2000. *Vanishing Voices: The Extinction of the World's Languages*. Oxford: Oxford University Press.

Newell, Sasha. 2012. *The Modernity Bluff: Crime, Consumption, and Citizenship in Côte d'Ivoire*. Chicago: Chicago University Press.

Newman, Paul, and Martha Susan Ratliff, eds. 2001. *Linguistic Fieldwork*. Cambridge: Cambridge University Press.

Ngai, Mae. 2004. *Impossible Subjects: Illegal Aliens and the Making of Modern America*. Princeton: Princeton University Press.

Nowell, April. 2019. *Growing Up in the Ice Age: Fossil and Archaeological Evidence of the Lived Lives of Plio-Pleistocene Children*. Oxford: Oxbow.

Nuckolls, Janis. 1993. "The Semantics of Certainty in Quechua and Its Implications for a Cultural Epistemology." *Language in Society* 22: 235–55. https://doi.org/10.1017/S0047404500017127

——— 2008. "Deictic Selves and Others in Pastaza Quichua Evidential Usage." *Anthropological Linguistics* 50 (1): 67–89. http://www.jstor.org/stable/27667625

Ó Néill, Diarmuid. 2005. "Reversing Language Shift – Gaelic in Nova Scotia." In *Rebuilding the Celtic Languages*, edited by Diarmuid Ó Néill, 366–81. Talybont: Y Lolfa.

Oakes, Leigh, and Jane Warren. 2007. *Language, Citizenship and Identity in Quebec*. Houndmills: Palgrave Macmillan.

Ochs, Elinor. 1992. "Indexing Gender." In *Rethinking Context: Language as an Interactive Phenomenon*, edited by Alessandro Duranti and Charles Goodwin, 335–58. Cambridge: Cambridge University Press.

Ochs, Elinor, and Bambi Schieffelin. 1984. "Language Acquisition and Socialization: Three Developmental Stories and Their Implications." In *Culture Theory: Essays on Mind, Self and Emotion*, edited by Richard Shweder and Robert Levine, pp. 276–320. Cambridge: Cambridge University Press.

Ochs, Elinor, and Carolyn Taylor. 1992. "Family Narrative as Political Activity." *Discourse & Society* 3 (3): 301–40. https://doi.org/10.1177/0957926592003003003

——— 1995. "The 'Father Knows Best' Dynamic in Dinnertime Narratives." In *Gender Articulated: Language and the Socially Constructed Self*, edited by Kira Hall and Mary Bucholtz, pp. 99–122. New York: Routledge.

Ohnuki-Tierney, Emiko. 1993. *Rice as Self: Japanese Identities Through Time*. Princeton: Princeton University Press.

Okamoto, Shigeko. 1995. "'Tasteless' Japanese: Less 'Feminine' Speech Among Young Japanese Women." In *Gender Articulated: Language and the Socially Constructed Self*, edited by Kira Hall and Mary Bucholtz, pp. 297–325. New York: Routledge.

Okrent, Arika. 2015. "9 Reasons We Adore This Little Girl's Sign Language Version of 'Twas the Night Before Christmas.'" *The Week*. https://theweek.com/articles/453784/9-reasons-adore-little-girls-sign-language-version-twas-night-before-christmas

Omi, Michael, and Howard Winant. 1986. *Racial Formation in the United States: From the 1960s to the 1980s*. New York: Routledge.

Ong, Walter. 1982. *Orality and Literacy: The Technologizing of the Word*. New Accents. London: Methuen.

Orwell, George. 1949. *Nineteen Eighty-Four: A Novel*. Hammondsworth: Penguin.

Ostler, Nicholas. 2005. *Empires of the Word: A Language History of the World*. New York: HarperCollins.

Owens, Jonathan. 2001. "Arabic Sociolinguistics." *Arabica* 48 (4): 419–69. https://doi.org/10.1163/157005801323163816

Palmer, Andie. 2005. *Maps of Experience: The Anchoring of Land to Story in Secwepemc Discourse*. Toronto: University of Toronto Press.

Palmer, Bill. 2018. *The Languages and Linguistics of the New Guinea Area: A Comprehensive Guide*. Berlin: De Gruyter Mouton.

Papen, Robert. 2014. "Hybrid Languages in Canada Involving French: The Case of Michif and Chiac." *Journal of Language Contact* 7 (1): 154–83. https://doi.org/10.1163/19552629-00701007

Park, Joseph Sung-Yul. 2013. "Metadiscursive Regimes of Diversity in a Multinational Corporation." *Language in Society* 42 (5): 557–77. https://doi.org/10.1017/S0047404513000663

Parry, Milman. 1930. "Studies in the Epic Technique of Oral Verse-Making. I. Homer and Homeric Style." *Harvard Studies in Classical Philology* 41: 73–147. https://doi.org/10.2307/310626

Pasch, Timothy. 2010. "Starting Fire with Gunpowder Revisited: Inuktitut New Media Content Creation in the Canadian Arctic." *Études/Inuit/Studies* 34 (2): 61–80. https://doi.org/10.7202/1004071ar

Patrick, Donna, Gabriele Budach, and Iga Muckpaloo. 2013. "Multiliteracies and Family Language Policy in an Urban Inuit Community." *Language Policy* 12: 47–62. https://doi.org/10.1007/s10993-012-9258-3

Paz, Alejandro. 2016. "Speaking Like a Citizen: Biopolitics and Public Opinion in Recognizing Non-Citizen Children in Israel." *Language & Communication* 48: 18–27. https://doi.org/10.1016/j.langcom.2016.01.002

Pennesi, Karen. 2021. "What Does a Pandemic Sound Like? The Emergence of COVID Verbal Art." *Anthropologica* 63 (1): 1–15. https://doi.org/10.18357/anthropologica6312021229

Pennycook, Alistair. 1994. *The Cultural Politics of English as an International Language*. London: Routledge.

Pérez, Raúl. 2013. "Learning to Make Racism Funny in the 'Color-Blind' Era: Stand-Up Comedy Students, Performance Strategies, and the (Re)Production of Racist Jokes in Public." *Discourse & Society* 24 (4): 478–503. https://doi.org/10.1177/0957926513482066

Perley, Bernard. 2011. *Defying Maliseet Language Death – Emergent Vitalities of Language, Culture, and Identity in Eastern Canada*. Lincoln: University of Nebraska Press.

——— 2012. "Zombie Linguistics: Experts, Endangered Languages and the Curse of Undead Voices." *Anthropological Forum* 22 (2): 133–49. https://doi.org/10.1080/00664677.2012.694170

——— 2013. "'Emergent Vitalities' as Antidote to 'Zombie Linguistics': A Rejoinder to Joshua Nash." *Anthropological Forum* 23 (1): 114–19. https://doi.org/10.1080/00664677.2012.750234

Perrot, Marie-Ève. 2014. "Le trajet linguistique des emprunts dans le chiac de Moncton: quelques observations." *Minorités linguistiques et société* 4: 200–18. https://doi.org/10.7202/1024698ar

Phillipson, Robert. 1992. *Linguistic Imperialism*. Oxford: Oxford University Press.

Phillipson, Robert, and Tove Skutnabb-Kangas. 1995. "Linguistic Rights and Wrongs." *Applied Linguistics* 16 (4): 483–504. https://doi.org/10.1093/applin/16.4.483

Pi, Chia-Yi Tony. 2006. "Beyond the Isogloss: Isographs in Dialect Topography." *Canadian Journal of Linguistics/La revue canadienne de linguistique* 51 (2/3): 177–84. https://doi.org/10.1017/S0008413100004059

Pinker, Steven. 2007. *The Stuff of Thought: Language as a Window onto Human Nature*. New York: Viking.

Poplack, Shana. 1980. "Sometimes I'll Start a Sentence in Spanish Y TERMINO EN ESPAÑOL: Toward a Typology of Code-Switching." *Linguistics* 18: 581–618. https://doi.org/10.1515/ling.1980.18.7-8.581

Poplack, Shana, and Sali Tagliamonte. 1991. "African American English in the Diaspora: Evidence from Old-Line Nova Scotians." *Language Variation and Change* 3 (3): 301–39. https://doi.org/10.1017/S0954394500000594

Propp, Vladimir. 1968. *Morphology of the Folktale*. Austin: University of Texas Press.

Quay, Suzanne. 2008. "Dinner Conversations with a Trilingual Two-Year-Old: Language Socialization in a Multilingual Context." *First Language* 28 (1): 5–33. https://doi.org/10.1177/0142723707083557

Radice, Martha. 2021. "Creativity, Sociability, Solidarity: New-Wave Carnival Krewes' Responses to COVID-19 in New Orleans." *Anthropologica* 63 (1): 1–27. https://doi.org/10.18357/anthropologica6312021230

Rampton, Ben. 2009. "Interaction Ritual and Not Just Artful Performance in Crossing and Stylization." *Language in Society* 38 (2): 149–76. https://doi.org/10.1017/S0047404509090319

Rettberg, Jill Walker. 2022. "ChatGPT Is Multilingual but Monocultural, and It's Learning Your Values." *jill/txt*, December 6. https://jilltxt.net/right-now-chatgpt-is-multilingual-but-monocultural-but-its-learning-your-values/

Reyes, Angela, and Adrienne Lo, eds. 2009. *Beyond Yellow English: Toward a Linguistic Anthropology of Asian Pacific America.* Oxford: Oxford University Press.

Rickford, John. 2000. *Spoken Soul: The Story of Black English.* New York: Wiley.

Riley, Kathleen. 2009. "Who Made the Soup? Socializing the Researcher and Shaping Her Data." *Language & Communication* 29 (3): 254–70. https://doi.org/10.1016/j.langcom.2009.02.007

Robertson, Jennifer. 2018. *Robo Sapiens Japanicus: Robots, Gender, Family and the Japanese Nation.* Berkeley: University of California Press.

Roche, Gerald. 2022. "The Necropolitics of Language Oppression." *Annual Review of Anthropology* 51: 31–47. https://doi.org/10.1146/annurev-anthro-041420-102158

Rocher, Ludo. 1994. "Orality and Textuality in the Indian Context." *Sino-Platonic Papers* 49: 1–28. https://www.sino-platonic.org/complete/spp049_india_oral_transmission.pdf

Romaine, Suzanne. 2001. "Multilingualism." In *The Handbook of Linguistics,* edited by Mark Aronoff and Janie Rees-Miller, 512–32. Oxford: Blackwell.

Rosa, Jonathan. 2019. *Looking Like a Language, Sounding Like a Race: Raciolinguistic Ideologies and the Learning of Latinidad.* Oxford: Oxford University Press.

Rosa, Jonathan, and Nelson Flores. 2017. "Unsettling Race and Language: Toward a Raciolinguistic Perspective." *Language in Society* 46 (5): 621–47. https://doi.org/10.1017/S0047404517000562

Rosaldo, Renato. 1986. "Illongot Hunting as Story and Experience." In *The Anthropology of Experience,* edited by Victor Turner and Edward Bruner, 97–138. Urbana: University of Illinois Press.

Roth-Gordon, Jennifer. 2017. *Race and the Brazilian Body: Blackness, Whiteness, and Everyday Language in Rio de Janeiro.* Berkeley: University of California Press.

Roy, Sylvie. 2004. "Language Varieties as Social Practices: Evidence from Two Minority Francophone Communities in Canada." *Canadian Journal of Linguistics/Revue Canadienne de linguistique* 49 (3/4): 353–73. https://doi.org/10.1353/cjl.2006.0007

Russell, Bertrand. 1940. *An Inquiry into Meaning and Truth.* London: Allen & Unwin.

Sable, Trudy, and Bernie Francis. 2012. *The Language of This Land, Mi'kma'ki.* Sydney: Cape Breton University Press.

San Roque, Lila. 2019. "Evidentiality." *Annual Review of Anthropology* 48 (1): 353–70. https://doi.org/10.1146/annurev-anthro-102218-011243

Santa Ana, Otto. 2009. "Did You Call in Mexican? The Racial Politics of Jay Leno Immigrant Jokes." *Language in Society* 38 (1): 23–45. https://doi.org/10.1017/S0047404508090027

Sapir, Edward. 1921. *Language: An Introduction to the Study of Speech.* New York: Harcourt Brace.

——— 1924. "The Grammarian and His Language." *American Mercury* 1 (2): 149–55.

——— 1929a. "The Status of Linguistics as a Science." *Language* 5 (4): 207–14. https://doi.org/10.2307/409588

——— 1929b. "The Unconscious Patterning of Behavior in Society" In *The Unconscious: A Symposium,* edited by E.S. Dummer, 114–42. New York: Knopf.

Saunders, Barbara. 2000. "Revisiting Basic Color Terms." *Journal of the Royal Anthropological Institute* 6 (1): 81–99. https://doi.org/10.1111/1467-9655.00005

Saussure, Ferdinand de. 1959. *Course in General Linguistics*, edited by Charles Bally, Albert Sechehaye, and Albert Riedlinger, translated by Wade Baskin. New York: McGraw-Hill.

Schieffelin, Bambi. 1990. *The Give and Take of Everyday Life: Language Socialization of Kaluli Children*. Cambridge: Cambridge University Press.

Schiffrin, Deborah. 1996. "Narrative as Self-Portrait: Sociolinguistic Constructions of Identity." *Language in Society* 25 (2): 167–203. https://doi.org/10.1017/s0047404500020601

Schlegl, Lisa, and Sali Tagliamonte. 2021. "'How Do You Get to Tim Hortons?' Direction-Giving in Ontario Dialects." *Canadian Journal of Linguistics/Revue canadienne de linguistique* 66 (1): 1–30. https://doi.org/10.1017/cnj.2020.34

Schreyer, Christine. 2018. "Media, Information Technology, and Language Planning: What Can Endangered Language Communities Learn from Created Language Communities?" *Current Issues in Language Planning* 12 (3): 403–25. https://doi.org/10.1080/14664208.2011.604965

Schürch, Roger, Keiran Zwirner, Bethany Yambrick, Tiffanie Pirault, James Wilson, and Margaret J. Couvillon. 2019. "Dismantling Babel: Creation of a Universal Calibration for Honey Bee Waggle Dance Decoding." *Animal Behaviour* 150: 139–45. https://doi.org/10.1016/j.anbehav.2019.01.016

Schwartz, Saul. 2019. "The Boas Plan: A View From the Margins." In *Disruptive Voices and the Singularity of Histories*, edited by Regna Darnell and Frederic Gleach, 281–317. Lincoln: University of Nebraska Press.

Scott, James. 1985. *Weapons of the Weak: Everyday Forms of Peasant Resistance*. New Haven: Yale University Press.

Seargeant, Philip. 2011. "Lexicography as a Philosophy of Language." *Language Sciences* 33: 1–10. https://doi.org/10.1016/j.langsci.2010.06.002

Segerdahl, Pär, William Fields, and Sue Savage-Rumbaugh. 2005. *Kanzi's Primal Language: The Cultural Initiation of Primates into Language*. Houndmills: Palgrave Macmillan.

Senghas, Ann, Sotaro Kita, and Asli Özyürek. 2004. "Children Creating Core Properties of Language: Evidence from an Emerging Sign Language in Nicaragua." *Science* 305: 1779–82. https://doi.org/10.1126/science.1100199

Senghas, Richard. 2003. "New Ways to Be Deaf in Nicaragua: Changes in Language, Personhood, and Community." In *Many Ways to Be Deaf: International Variation in Deaf Communities*, edited by Leila Monaghan, Constanze Schmaling, Karen Nakamura, and Graham Turner, 260–82. Washington, DC: Gallaudet University Press.

Seyfarth, Robert, Dorothy Cheney, and Peter Marler. 1980. "Monkey Responses to Three Different Alarm Calls: Evidence of Predator Classification and Semantic Communication." *Science* 210 (4471): 801–3. https://doi.org/10.1126/science.7433999

Shohet, Merav. 2021. *Silence and Sacrifice: Family Stories of Care and the Limits of Love in Vietnam*. Berkeley: University of California Press.

Shulist, Sarah. 2018. *Transforming Indigeneity: Urbanization and Language Revitalization in the Brazilian Amazon*. Toronto: University of Toronto Press.

Sidnell, Jack, and N.J. Enfield. 2012. "Language Diversity and Social Action: A Third Locus of Linguistic Relativity." *Current Anthropology* 53 (3): 302–33. https://doi.org/10.1086/665697

Silverstein, Michael. 1976. "Shifters, Linguistic Categories, and Cultural Description." In *Meaning in Anthropology*, edited by Keith Basso and Henry Selby, 11–55. Albuquerque: University of New Mexico Press.

——— 1996. "Monoglot 'Standard' in America: Standardization and Metaphors of Linguistic Hegemony." In *The Matrix of Language: Contemporary Linguistic Anthropology*, edited by Ronald Macaulay and Donald Brenneis, 284–306. Boulder: Westview.

——— 2005. "Axes of Evals." *Journal of Linguistic Anthropology* 15 (1): 6–22. https://doi.org/10.1525/jlin.2005.15.1.6

——— 2015. "How Language Communities Intersect: Is 'Superdiversity' an Incremental or Transformative Condition?" *Language & Communication* 44: 7–18. https://doi.org/10.1016/j.langcom.2014.10.015

Sium, Aman, Chadni Desai, and Eric Ritskes. 2012. "Towards the 'Tangible Unknown': Decolonization and the Indigenous Future." *Decolonization: Indigeneity, Education & Society* 1 (1): x–xiii.

Skinner, B.F. 1957. *Verbal Behavior*. Englewood Cliffs: Prentice-Hall.

Slocombe, Katie, and Thom Scott-Phillips. 2017. "Communication and Language." In *Chimpanzees and Human Evolution*, edited by Martin Muller, Richard Wrangham, and David Pilbeam, 791–823. Cambridge: Belknap.

Slocum, Sally. 1975. "Woman the Gatherer: Male Bias in Anthropology." In *Toward an Anthropology of Women*, edited by Rayna Reiter, 36–50. New York: Monthly Review Press.

Smitherman, Geneva. 2006. *Word from the Mother: Language and African Americans*. New York: Routledge.

Smith-Hefner, Nancy J. 2007. "Youth Language, Gaul Sociability, and the New Indonesian Middle Class." *Journal of Linguistic Anthropology* 17 (2): 184–203. https://doi.org/10.1525/jlin.2007.17.2.184

Snow, Don. 2013. "Revisiting Ferguson's Defining Cases of Diglossia."*Journal of Multilingual and Multicultural Development* 34 (1): 61–76. https://doi.org/10.1080/01434632.2012.699531

Soderstrom, Melanie. 2007. "Beyond Babytalk: Re-Evaluating the Nature and Content of Speech Input to Preverbal Infants." *Developmental Review* 27 (4): 501–32. https://doi.org/10.1016/j.dr.2007.06.002

Sökefeld, Martin. 1999. "Debating Self, Identity, and Culture in Anthropology." *Current Anthropology* 40 (4): 417–48. https://doi.org/10.1086/200042

Song, Juyoung. 2019. "Language Socialization and Code-Switching: A Case Study of a Korean-English Bilingual Child in a Korean Transnational Family." *International Journal of Bilingual Education and Bilingualism* 22 (2): 91–106. https://doi.org/10.1080/13670050.2016.1231165

Spitulnik, Debra. 1996. "The Social Circulation of Media Discourse and the Mediation of Communities." *Journal of Linguistic Anthropology* 6 (2): 161–87. https://doi.org/10.1525/jlin.1996.6.2.161

Statistics Canada. 2023a. "Indigenous Languages Across Canada." https://www12.statcan.gc.ca/census-recensement/2021/as-sa/98-200-X/2021012/98-200-X2021012-eng.cfm

——— 2023b. "Multilingualism of Canadian Households." https://www12.statcan.gc.ca/census-recensement/2021/as-sa/98-200-X/2021014/98-200-X2021014-eng.cfm

——— 2024. "Language Indicators Over Time." https://www150.statcan.gc.ca/n1/pub/71-607-x/71-607-x2024014-eng.htm

Stern, Pamela. 2014. "*Super Shamou Versus Captain Al Cohol*: Inuit Cultural Productions and the Discourses of Inuit Drinkers." *Topia: Canadian Journal of Cultural Studies* 32: 67–91. https://doi.org/10.3138/topia.32.67

Sterzuk, Andrea, and Russell Fayant. 2016. "Towards Reconciliation Through Language Planning for Indigenous Languages in Canadian Universities." *Current Issues in Language Planning* 17 (3/4): 332–50. https://doi.org/10.1080/14664208.2016.1201239

Street, Brian. 1984. *Literacy in Theory and Practice*. Cambridge: Cambridge University Press.

Subtirelu, Nicholas Close. 2013. "'English… It's Part of Our Blood': Ideologies of Language and Nation in United States Congressional Discourse." *Journal of Sociolinguistics* 17 (3): 37–65. https://doi.org/10.1111/josl.12016

Swann, Brian, ed. 1983. *Smoothing the Ground: Essays on Native American Oral Literature*. Berkeley: University of California Press.

Tagg, Caroline. 2015. *Exploring Digital Communication: Language in Action*. New York: Routledge.

Tagliamonte, Sali. 2005. "So Who? Like How? Just What? Discourse Markers in the Conversations of Young Canadians." *Journal of Pragmatics* 37: 1896–915. https://doi.org/10.1016/j.pragma.2005.02.017

Takahashi, Daisuke. 2012. "The Distributional Effect of the Rice Policy in Japan, 1986–2010." *Food Policy* 37 (6): 679–89. https://doi.org/10.1016/j.foodpol.2012.07.008

TallBear, Kim. 2013. "Genomic Articulations of Indigeneity." *Social Studies of Science* 43 (4): 509–33. https://doi.org/10.1177/0306312713483893

Tam, Gina Anne. 2017. "'Orbiting the Core': Politics and the Meaning of Dialect in Chinese Linguistics, 1927–1957." *Twentieth-Century China* 41 (3): 280–303. https://doi.org/10.1080/15215385.2016.1205791

Tannen, Deborah. 1990. *You Just Don't Understand: Women and Men in Conversation*. New York: Morrow.

Tattersall, Ian. 2018. "Language Origins: An Evolutionary Framework." *Topoi* 37: 289–96. https://doi.org/10.1007/s11245-016-9368-1

Tedlock, Dennis. 1977. "Toward an Oral Poetics." *New Literary History* 8 (3): 507–19. https://doi.org/10.2307/468297

Terrace, Herbert. 2019. *Why Chimpanzees Can't Learn Language and Only Humans Can*. New York: Columbia University Press.

Todd, Zoe. 2016. "An Indigenous Feminist's Take on the Ontological Turn: 'Ontology' Is Just Another Word for Colonialism." *Journal of Historical Sociology* 29 (1): 4–22. https://doi.org/10.1111/johs.12124

Tonouchi, Lee. 2004. "Da State of Pidgin Address." *College English* 67 (1): 75–82. https://doi.org/10.2307/4140726

Tremblay, Marc-Adélard. 1973. "Les sentiments acadiens." In *Communautés et culture: Éléments pour une ethnologie du Canada français*, edited by Marc-Adélard Tremblay and Gérald-Louis Gold, 294–318. Montreal: Éditions HRW.

Trotter, David. 2010. "Middle English Creolization." In *The History of English, Vol. 3: Middle English*, edited by Laurel Brinton and Alexander Bergs, 224–38. Berlin: De Gruyter Mouton.

Trouillot, Michel-Rolph. 2003. *Global Transformations: Anthropology and the Modern World*. New York: Palgrave Macmillan.

Trudgill, Peter. 1972. "Sex, Covert Prestige and Linguistic Change in the Urban British English of Norwich." *Language in Society* 1 (2): 179–95. https://doi.org/10.1017/s0047404500000488

Truth and Reconciliation Commission. 2015a. "Canada's Residential Schools: The History, Part 1 Origins to 1939." https://ehprnh2mwo3.exactdn.com/wp-content/uploads/2021/01/Volume_1_History_Part_1_English_Web.pdf

——— 2015b. "The Survivors Speak: A Report of the Truth and Reconciliation Commission of Canada." https://ehprnh2mwo3.exactdn.com/wp-content/uploads/2021/01/Survivors_Speak_English_Web.pdf

——— 2015c. "What We Have Learned: Principles of Truth and Reconciliation." https://ehprnh2mwo3.exactdn.com/wp-content/uploads/2021/01/Principles_English_Web.pdf

Tryon, Darrell, and Jean-Michel Charpentier. 2004. *Pacific Pidgins and Creoles: Origins, Growth and Development*. Berlin: De Gruyter Mouton.

Tuck, Eve, and K. Wayne Yang. 2012. "Decolonization Is Not a Metaphor." *Decolonization: Indigeneity, Education & Society* 1 (1): 1–40.

Tulloch, Shelley, Adriana Kusugak, Cayla Chenier, Quluaq Pilakapsi, Gloria Uluqsi, and Fiona Walton. 2017. "Transformational Bilingual Learning: Re-Engaging Marginalized Learners through Language, Culture, Community, and Identity." *Canadian Modern Language Review* 73 (4): 438–62. https://doi.org/10.3138/cmlr.4052

Turing, Alan. 1950. "Computing Machinery and Intelligence." *Mind* 49: 433–60. https://doi.org/10.1093/mind/lix.236.433

Tylor, Edward. 1874. *Primitive Culture: Researches into the Development of Mythology, Philosophy, Religion, Language, Art, and Custom, Vol. 1*. Boston: Estes & Lauriat.

United Nations. 2020. "Resolution 74/135 Rights of Indigenous Peoples." https://documents.un.org/doc/undoc/gen/n19/426/26/pdf/n1942626.pdf

Urciuoli, Bonnie. 1996. *Exposing Prejudice: Puerto Rican Experiences of Language, Race, and Class*. Boulder: Westview.

Vakoch, Douglas, and Jeffrey Punske, eds. 2023. *Xenolinguistics: Towards a Science of Extraterrestrial Language*. London: Routledge.

Vertovec, Steven. 2007. Super-Diversity and Its Implications." *Ethnic and Racial Studies* 30 (6): 1024–54. https://doi.org/10.1080/01419870701599465

Vigouroux, Cécile. 2017. "The Discursive Pathway of Two Centuries of Raciolinguistic Stereotyping: 'Africans as Incapable of Speaking French.'" *Language in Society* 46 (1): 5–21. https://doi.org/10.1017/S0047404516000804

Viveiros de Castro, Eduardo. 1998. "Cosmological Deixis and Amerindian Perspectivism." *Journal of the Royal Anthropological Institute* 4 (3): 469–88. https://doi.org/10.2307/3034157

Vološinov, Valentin. 1986. *Marxism and the Philosophy of Language*, translated by Ladislav Metejka and I. R. Titunik. Cambridge: Harvard University Press.

Waldie, Ryan James. 2012. "Evidentiality in Nuu-chah-nulth." PhD thesis, University of British Columbia. http://hdl.handle.net/2429/43754

Ward, Shannon. 2022. "Spatializing Kinship: The Grammar of Belonging in Amdo, Tibet." *Pragmatics* 32 (3): 452–87. https://doi.org/10.1075/prag.20039.war

Washington, Adrienne Ronee. 2020. "'Reclaiming My Time': Signifying, Reclamation and the Activist Strategies of Black Women's Language." *Gender and Language* 14 (4): 358–85. https://doi.org/10.1558/genl.41607

Watson, James. 1988. "The Structure of Chinese Funerary Rites: Elementary Forms, Ritual Sequence, and the Primacy of Performance." In *Death Ritual in Late Imperial and Modern*

China, edited by James Watson and Evelyn Rawski, 3–19. Berkeley: University of California Press.

Wharry, Cheryl. 2003. "Amen and Hallelujah Preaching: Discourse Functions in African American Sermons." *Language in Society* 32 (2): 203–25. https://doi.org/10.1017/S0047404503322031

White, Lydia, and Fred Genesee. 1996. "How Native Is Near-Native? The Issue of Ultimate Attainment in Adult Second Language Acquisition." *Second Language Research* 12 (3): 233–65. https://doi.org/10.1177/026765839601200301

Whorf, Benjamin Lee. 1956. *Language, Thought, and Reality: Selected Writings of Benjamin Lee Whorf.* Edited by John Carroll. Cambridge: MIT Press.

Winawer, Jonathan, Nathan Witthoft, Michael Frank, Lisa Wu, Alex Wade, and Lera Boroditsky. 2007. "Russian Blues Reveal Effects of Language on Color Discrimination." *Proceedings of the National Academy of Sciences* 104 (19): 7780–85. https://doi.org/10.1073/pnas.0701644104

Wittgenstein, Ludwig. 1922. *Tractatus Logico-Philosophicus*. London: Kegan Paul.

——— 1958. *Philosophical Investigations*. Oxford: Blackwell.

Wolf, Naomi. 2015. "Young Women, Give Up the Vocal Fry and Reclaim Your Strong Female Voice." *The Guardian*, July 24. www.theguardian.com/commentisfree/2015/jul/24/vocal-fry-strong-female-voice

Woll, Bencie, Rachel Sutton-Spence, and Frances Elton. 2004. "Multilingualism: The Global Approach to Sign Languages." In *The Sociolinguistics of Sign Languages*, edited by Cecil Lucas, 8–32. Cambridge: Cambridge University Press.

Woolard, Kathryn. 1989. "Sentences in the Language Prison: The Rhetorical Structuring of an American Language Policy Debate." *American Ethnologist* 16 (2): 268–78. https://doi.org/10.1525/ae.1989.16.2.02a00050

——— 2008. "Why Dat Now? Linguistic-Anthropological Contributions to the Explanation of Sociolinguistic Icons and Change." *Journal of Sociolinguistics* 12 (4): 432–52. https://doi.org/10.1111/j.1467-9841.2008.00375.x

Wortham, Stanton, Elaine Allard, Kathy Lee, and Katherine Mortimer. 2011. "Racialization in Payday Mugging Narratives." *Journal of Linguistic Anthropology* 21 (s1): E56–75. https://doi.org/10.1111/j.1548-1395.2011.001097.x

Xu, Fang. 2021. *Silencing Shanghai: Language and Identity in Urban China.* Lanham: Lexington Books.

Yang, Jie. 2007. "Zuiqian 'Deficient Mouth': Discourse, Gender and Domestic Violence in Urban China." *Gender and Language* 1 (1): 107–18. https://doi.org/10.1558/genl.2007.1.1.107

Yang, Mayfair Mei-Hui. 1994. *Gifts, Favors, and Banquets: The Art of Social Relationships in China.* Ithaca: Cornell University Press.

Yingling, Julie. 2004. *A Lifetime of Communication: Transformations Through Relational Dialogues.* Mahwah: Lawrence Erlbaum.

Yuasa, Ikuko Patricia. 2010. "Creaky Voice: A New Feminine Voice Quality for Young Urban-Oriented Upwardly Mobile American Women." *American Speech* 85 (3): 315–37. https://doi.org/10.1215/00031283-2010-018

Zentella, Ana Celia. 1997. *Growing Up Bilingual: Puerto Rican Children in New York.* Malden: Blackwell.

Zhang, Qing. 2008. "Rhotacization and the 'Beijing Smooth Operator': The Social Meaning of a Linguistic Variable." *Journal of Sociolinguistics* 12 (2): 201–22. https://doi.org/10.1111/j.1467-9841.2008.00362.x

Zimman, Lal. 2009. "'The Other Kind of Coming Out': Transgender People and the Coming Out Narrative Genre." *Gender and Language* 3 (1): 53–80. https://doi.org/10.1558/genl.v3i1.53

——— 2018. "Transgender Voices: Insights on Identity, Embodiment, and the Gender of the Voice." *Language and Linguistics Compass* 12 (8): e12284. https://doi.org/10.1111/lnc3.12284

Zimmer, Ben. 2011. "How Mubarak Was Told to Go, in Many Languages." *Language Log*, February 13. https://languagelog.ldc.upenn.edu/nll/?p=2964.

Index

absolute spatial reference, 79–80, 237
Abu-Lughod, Lila, 191–2
affordances, 207, 237
  technological, 208, 210, 212, 216
African American Language, 237
  appropriation of, 153–4, 159, 162
  structure and use of, 150–3, 161, 235n1
Agar, Michael, 60–2
Agha, Asif, 117–18
Akkadians, 95
algys (Sakha speaker blessing), 201–3
American Management Association women's assertiveness workshop, 140
American Sign Language (ASL), 38–9, 44, 80
  ape studies using, 27–8
Anderson, Benedict, 167
animal communication, 44, 192, 243
  ape studies on, 26–8
  bees, 26, 28–30
  differences with human communication, 28–32, 238
  dogs/cats and, 12, 25, 29–30, 33, 42
animator, 37, 237
Anishinaabemowin, 65, 106
Anishininiimowin (Oji-Cree), 84
Apache (Western), 94–5, 155
Arabic, 95, 184, 197, 225
  Standard versus Egyptian, 175–7, 185
Arab Spring protests, 176–7
arbitrariness, 38–9
  signifier versus signified meaning, 11, 20, 33, 237, 246
Arrival (science fiction film), 64, 83
artificial intelligence (AI), 30, 35–7
Asian people, 169
  assumptions/stereotypes about, 144, 148, 155
  interethnic relations, 156–9
Austin, J.L., 111–13, 123
author(s), 37, 237
autonomous model of literacy, 197, 237
Avíla Runa, 29

backstage, 115, 237
Bailey, Benjamin, 156–8
Bakhtin, Mikhail, 165–6, 183, 234n1
baristas, 57
Baron, Naomi, 212
Barrett, Rusty, 129
Basso, Keith, 94–5, 155
Baumann, Richard, 191–2

Bedouin women's poetry, 191–2
Benedict, Ruth, 115
Berlin, Paul, 68, 73
Berman, Elise, 56–7
Bialostock, Steve, 18, 160–1
Biden, Joe, 144
Bilaniuk, Laada, 168
Billings, Sabrina, 122–3
Black Jeopardy! (*Saturday Night Live*), 162
Black people/communities, 170, 198, 208
  church sermons in, 193–5
  identity associations, 116–17, 129, 143–4, 146–50, 159
  interethnic tensions, 156–8
  linguistic features of, 150, 161–2
  "talking shit," 18, 160–1
  See also African American Language; signifyin'
Blommaert, Jan, 118–20
Blum, Susan, 75
Boas, Franz, 65, 84–6, 90, 146, 190, 234n2
  students of, 31, 101, 151
Boltokova, Daria, 102
Bonilla, Yarimar, 208–9
Bouie, Jamelle, 159
Bourassa, Carrie, 159–60
Bourdieu, Pierre, 5
Bourhis, Richard, 223–4
Brazil, 74, 102, 126, 150
breakups, relationship, 204–5
Brenneis, Don, 58
Briggs, Charles, 222–3
British Columbia, 21–2, 93–4, 97, 171
Brown, Michael, 208–9
Bucholtz, Mary, 60–1, 116, 126, 144
bureaucrats, 58
Burenhult, Niclas, 82
Butler, Judith, 113, 129
Byler, Darren, 140

Cameron, Deborah, 125–6, 132, 139
Canadian raising, 8, 237
capitalism, 6, 52, 72, 169
Capps, Walter, 116, 120
case studies, 38, 220, 237
Changhyun (*mukbang* streamer), 43
ChatGPT, 36. *See also* artificial intelligence
Chen, Keith, 72
Chernela, Janet, 74
Chiac, 182, 237
child-raising, 48, 50, 237
China
  author experiences/research in, 4, 6, 38, 53, 222–3
  cultural features in, 60, 69, 71–3, 75
  English use/multilingualism in, 55, 59, 116, 145, 183
  giving face in, 6–7
  guanxi in, 75–6
  interethnic tensions in, 99, 140, 146
  Mandarin (language) in (*see* Mandarin Chinese)
  speech communities in, 17, 99
  writing and literacy development in, 186, 198, 197–8
Chinese, 224
  Mandarin (*see* Mandarin Chinese)
  signage in, 148, 225, 227
  terms/phrases in, 2, 44, 141
Chiwere, 101
Cho, Margaret, 155
Choe, Hanwool, 42–3
Chomsky, Noam, 11, 15, 23, 42
  on competence/performance, 12–13, 46–7, 203
  on generative grammar, 12, 74, 194
Chua, Amy, 148
Clemetson, Lynette, 144
closed system, 29, 238
codemixing, 181, 183, 185, 238
codeswitching, 180–1, 185, 238
Cohn, Carol, 78
Coleman, Gabriella, 206

colonialism
  anthropology/linguistics histories of, 5, 160
  cultural embeddedness in, 3, 5–6, 146, 196
  decolonial/racialized struggles against, 86–7, 159, 238
  Indigenous language eradication as goal of, 86, 107, 171
  language associations with/ideologies of, 17, 167–8, 171, 178–9, 214
  See also linguistic imperialism
colour classification, 68, 70, 73–5, 81–2
coming out, 112–13
commodification, language, 169, 238
communicative competence, 47, 51, 60, 223, 238
competence, 135, 180, 238
  communicative (*see* communicative competence)
  performance and, 12–13, 46–7, 194, 203, 243
Congo, Democratic Republic of, 167, 181
Conklin, Harold, 68
conlangs, 97, 238
Corsica, 97
Côte d'Ivoire, 118–19
covert racist discourse, 154–6, 238
COVID-19 pandemic, 123, 206, 215–16, 232
creole, 158, 185, 235n5
  concept of, 178, 238
  English as, 179–80
  exceptionalism, 180, 238
critical period, 46, 56, 96, 238
crossing, 158–9, 238
Crystal, David, 9, 95
Cucapá, 102
culture, 240
  anthropological/linguistic study of, 2–3, 38, 71–3, 81, 101, 244
  definitions of, 4–6, 238, 242
  as doing, 22, 38, 46–7, 64, 73, 206
  language as embedded in, 15, 20, 26, 33, 64–7, 73–7
  socialization into, 46, 51, 56, 58, 78, 115–16
  See also languaculture
Deaf people/communities, 39–40, 233n3, 240
de Beauvoir, Simone, 126
decolonization, 87, 106, 238
DeGraff, Michel, 180
deixis
  concept of, 78–9, 238
  social, 80, 245
  spatial, 79, 82, 245
Derrida, Jacques, 187
descriptivism, 7–8, 19, 24, 238
design features, language, 32–3, 38–9, 41, 238
determinism, 31, 133
  linguistic, 72, 74
diachronic approach, 11, 238
dialect(s), 113, 240
  Beijing, 164, 170
  Canada's, 90, 97, 164–5, 171, 237
  Chinese, 4, 15, 17
  concept of, 21, 238
  English, 107, 114, 151–3, 165–7, 235nn1,2
  language mixing, 177, 180–2, 184
  observing local, 4, 17, 52–3, 118, 180, 244
  surveys (*see* dialect surveys)
dialect surveys, 222, 227–31, 238
Diaz, Natalie, 87
difference model, 128–9, 238
diglossia, 179, 185
  concept of, 175–7, 239
diglossic speech communities, 175, 240, 242
DiNova, Joanne, 106–7
direct indexicality. *See* indexicality
discourse(s), 74, 175, 225
  concept of, 34–5, 37, 209–10, 239
  differences in cultural, 50, 78, 102, 242

discourse(s) (*continued*)
examples of complexity of, 36–7, 43, 61, 180, 187
gendered, 127, 137–9, 141
legal/professional, 59, 117
oral/written/digital, 187, 194, 203, 212–13, 239–40
racist/racializing, 148–50, 154–6, 161–2, 238, 245
socialization via, 59, 61, 118
See also covert racist discourse; interdiscursivity
Dolezal, Rachel, 159
domains of language use, 96–9, 138, 170, 239
dominance model, 127–9, 239
Dorian, Nancy, 98
drag queens, 129
Duranti, Alessandro, 23–4, 116

Eckert, Penelope, 109–10
El Grupo Scout Vistas, 51–2
emailing, 204–5, 210–12, 216
emergence, 193, 239
emergent vitalities, 103–5
emoji, 204, 213, 239
English (language), 18, 116
African American Language and, 150–4, 194–5, 235n1
American/British versus Canadian, 159, 228–9
blending of other languages with, 84, 170, 177–9, 182, 209, 214–15
as creole, 178–80
cultural differences with other languages, 55–6, 65–70, 72–6, 79–83
French use in Canada versus, 170–1, 173, 225–7
grammatical rules/customs of, 7–9, 14–15, 20, 90, 132
Indigenous languages versus, 84–6, 89–94, 99–107, 234n2
Newfoundland, 21, 153, 164–5
perceived dominance/opportunity of, 4, 16–17, 36, 59–60, 163, 166–9, 174
philological influence on grammar, 7–8, 11
racialization through use of, 144, 147, 156, 158–9
Received Pronunciation, 117–18
relatively rare/weird features of, 88–9
Standard, 151–3, 158, 165–9
teaching, 4, 222–3
using other languages versus, 30–4, 39, 51–5, 120–2, 170
enregisterment, 117–21, 175, 239
entextualization, 60–1, 239
ethics, 59, 75, 159
case studies and, 220, 232, 237
core principles and common practices, 219–20
research guidelines and policies, 218–21
ethnicity
concept of, 147, 239
speech communities and, 18, 109
ethnicization, concept/contestations of, 148–9, 239
ethnography, 85, 219, 228
concept of, 16, 239
linguistic, 7, 23, 109–10, 120, 190, 221–2
multispecies, 29, 243
practice of, 141, 152, 180, 184, 203
salvage, 101, 244
Ethnologue (language database), 15, 166
ethnopoetics, 190, 239
ethnosemantics, 67, 151, 239
euskara (Basque), 89, 224–5
Everett, Daniel, 74
evidentiality, 71, 91–3, 234n3, 239

Facebook, 205, 210, 215
Fanon, Frantz, 143–4, 160
felicity conditions, 113, 119, 123, 239
femininity

biological differences and, 77, 113, 142, 240
critiques of dominant notions of, 135–6, 155
gendered performances of, 129, 133, 135–7
speech/voice styles and, 129–33, 136, 241, 244, 246
feminist movement, 140
critiques by, 78, 131–2
growth within linguistics, 126–8
scholarship, 78, 126–7, 131
Ferguson, Jenanne, 181, 201–3
Ferguson, Missouri, 208–9
Fiji, meke dance-songs, 188
Finnegan, Ruth, 192
Finnish (language), 33, 81, 88, 153
Fishman, Joshua, 96
footing, 43, 239
four-field anthropology, 3, 239
Frake, Charles, 67–8
francophones, 173, 183–4, 225–6
Acadian, 171–3, 182, 222
assumptions about, 21–2, 174–5, 183–4
Quebecois, 21–2, 170–1
French (language), 156, 179
assumptions about, 19, 143–4, 171, 179
colonial dominance of/racism in, 84, 97, 100, 143–4, 160, 170–1
learning, 3, 171, 173
signs, 225–7
specifying gender/formality in, 14–15, 65
Standard, 22, 152, 169, 173–4
terms/words used in, 1, 11, 33, 143–4, 166
theoreticians, 5, 52, 126, 163, 187
variations of, 22, 118, 153, 171, 235n2
See also Chiac; francophones
frontstage, 115, 239

Gaelic, 171, 222
Gal, Susan, 131
García, Ofelia, 166
Gaudry, Adam, 87
gay men, 129
coming out, 112–13
dating apps, 210–11
derision/stigma facing, 125, 138
gender(ed)
binary notions of, 117, 125–6, 128
communication/differences, 124–7, 228, 238
concept of, 125–6, 240
doing/performing, 6, 22, 125–6, 129
identities, 5–6, 109, 112–13, 116, 121
ideologies, 127, 129, 132, 139–42
indexing, 20–2, 125–6, 132, 137–40
inequities/power, 128, 131, 135, 239
language, 126–8, 132, 139–40
linguistic marking of, 65, 71, 117, 137, 144, 179
norms/socialization, 53–5, 77, 127–8, 137–40, 197, 238
reading, 125–6
speech communities and, 18–19, 109, 229
stereotypes, 21, 36, 125
violence, 141
voices, 132–4
See also transgender people
generative grammar, 12, 74, 194, 239
genre(s), 13
blending/switching of, 59, 165, 193, 215
concept of, 192, 240
global literary/textual, 196–7, 201–2, 215–16, 222
language conventions of, 48, 59, 233n2, 241
German(y), 171, 225
cultural/political change and language in, 52, 63
words/grammar in, 31, 65, 89, 179
Gershon, Ilana, 205
Giriama (Kenya), 214–15
Goffman, Erving, 37–8, 115, 121, 192
Gomashie, Grace, 100
González, Rosann Dueñas, 174

Goodwin, Marjorie, 33–4, 44
Goody, Jack, 195, 197
gossiping, gendered notions of, 125, 128, 141
Graded Intergenerational Disruption Scale (GIDS), 96
Greek (language), 7–9, 71, 89, 153, 178
Grindr, 210–11
Grizzly Woman and Water Bug (Chinook myth), 190–1, 201
Grosjean, François, 163
Guardado, Martin, 51–2
Gumperz, John 109, 180
Guugu Yimithirr, 80

habitus, 5, 240
hacker conferences, 206
Halifax, 4, 80, 183, 227
Hall, Kira, 116, 136
Hamill, Mark, 36–7
Hanks, William, 79, 187
Hanunóo, 68
Harrison, K. David, 95
hashtags, 208–9, 215
Heath, Shirley Brice, 198–9, 203
Heller, Monica, 174
heteroglossia, 166, 183, 215, 240
Hill, Jane, 102, 154
Hindu Vedas, 188–9
Hockett, Charles, 32, 38, 41
Homer, 7, 188
homesigns, 40, 42, 240
Hopi, 66–7, 70–3, 234n3
Humboldt, Wilhelm von, 64–5
Hurston, Zora Neale, 151–2
H-variety, 175, 240
Hymes, Dell, 47, 109, 191, 201, 233n2

icon(s), 20, 39–41, 76, 240
identity, 224
  assumptions about, 48, 129, 143–50, 159
  concepts of, 114–15, 240
  five characteristics of, 116–17
  francophone/Quebecois, 171, 173, 184
  gender(ed), 5–6, 109, 112–13, 116, 121
  indexing of, 21, 23, 116–18, 121, 144, 150, 181, 210
  language use and, 8, 37, 67, 100, 119–23, 167, 214
  national/regional, 118, 174–5, 179, 181, 228, 231
  race and, 116–17, 129, 146–51, 159–61
  sharing of, 18, 77, 123, 158–9, 174, 179–81
  speech act impacts on, 112–14, 116, 119–21, 159
  varied concepts of, 5–6, 114–15
  waves of research on, 109–10
ideological model of literacy, 197, 201, 240
illocution, 111–12, 123, 240
imagined community, 167, 240
immigrants, 194
  arrival in North America, 3, 114, 164–5, 171
  racist perceptions of, 148–9, 154, 174
indexicality, 226
  concept of, 21–3, 116, 240
  direct, 132, 239
  indirect, 132, 137, 240
index(ing), 61, 76
  concept of, 20–1, 240
  of identities, 116–18, 121, 144, 150, 181, 210
Indigeneity, 103, 106, 159
Indigenous communities (*people*)
  autonomy/self-determination of, 106, 190, 221
  colonial assimilation/discrimination facing, 86, 100–2, 238
  language importance to, 88, 94, 97–8, 102–3
  reconciliation and, 87, 106, 191–2, 244
  See also Indigenous languages
Indigenous languages
  anthropological/linguistic study of, 31, 66, 84–6, 101
  colonial attempts to eradicate, 86, 107, 171

discrimination for speaking, 86, 106–7, 160
endangerment of, 86, 95–6, 100, 105–7
English versus, 84–6, 88–94, 99–107, 243
language revitalization, 86, 97, 100, 102–6
linguistic relativity, 91–3
as tied to the land, 93–5, 102, 107
Indonesia, 18, 71
informational function, 224, 232, 240
Inoue, Miyako, 135–6
interdiscursivity, 209–10, 240
intergenerational transmission, 96, 99, 240
International Phonetic Alphabet (IPA), 9–10, 240
interviewing, 228, 230
examples of researcher, 59, 120, 141, 152, 184, 210
semi-structured, 222–3, 245
Inuit Broadcasting Corporation (IBC), 103, 105
Inuktitut, 107
increasingly common use of, 21, 86, 105
learning resources and standardization, 103, 105, 200–1, 234n2
specific terms/words, 31–2, 89–91, 203
Israel, 120–1

Jacquemet, Marco, 206
Jaffe, Alexandra, 97
Japan(ese), 55, 88, 162, 213
significance of rice in, 77
teyo dawa speech/kogals in, 135–6
Jocks and Burnouts, 109–10
Joe, Rita, 100–1
Johnson, Mark, 76–7, 83
jokes (*humour*), 193, 213
gender and, 128–9
human versus computer differentiation of, 35–7, 42
identity/socialization functions of, 18, 60–1, 116, 123, 158–9
racism and covertly racist, 154–6, 161–2, 238

kabary, 130–1, 241
Kaluli (Papua New Guinea), 47–51
Kanien'keha, 100
Kaska language revitalization, 86–7, 99
Kay, Brent, 68, 73
Key, Keegan-Michael, 147
keys, 192–3, 241
Kiesling, Scott, 138
kinship
Chinese names for differentiating, 69, 73, 75–6
encoding of, 188, 195
understandings of relationality via terms for, 53, 81, 93, 115
Kiswahili, 122, 167, 181, 214
Klemperer, Victor, 63
Klingon (language), 30–1, 97–8, 233n1
Kohn, Eduardo, 29
Korea(ns), 15, 55, 79, 169, 184
convenience store owners, 156–8
mukbang, 42–3
kros, 130–1, 241
Kubota, Ryoku, 160
Kulick, Don, 17, 130–1
Kuwanwisiwma, Leigh, 67
Kwak'wala, 65, 85–6

Labov, William, 108–9, 117
Lakoff, George, 76–7, 83
Lakoff, Robin, 127–30, 132, 136–7
Lamarre, Patricia, 184
Landry, Rodrigue, 223–4
languaculture, 60, 241
language(s), 234n2
as biological organism, 102
as communication codes, 2, 12–13, 182
as cultural system, 2, 13–15, 22, 34, 60–4, 81
debates about, 31, 169, 183
design features of, 32–3, 38–9, 41, 238
global number of, 15–16, 86, 95

language(s) (*continued*)
as interactive/relational process, 28, 110, 203, 209, 241
making identity/the world via, 22, 52, 73, 87, 109–10, 117
as patterned/classificatory, 11, 67, 73, 75–6
as political, 131, 145, 224
as social, 1–6, 11, 14, 81, 42, 111
as symbolic/ideological, 19–20, 26, 94, 100, 111, 166
language acquisition, 60, 178
concept of, 46–7, 241
socialization and, 55–6, 95–6, 98–9, 238, 240
theories of, 12, 42, 46–7
language death, 95, 102, 241
language endangerment, 164, 221, 245
attempts to resist, 101–2, 239, 241
Canada's Indigenous peoples', 86, 95–6, 100, 105–7
process of/measuring, 95–7, 101–2, 184, 241
language family, 89, 177, 241
language ideologies
communication technologies and, 205, 217
concept of, 19, 241
implicit/explicit, 19, 55, 122, 181, 195
multilingual/creole, 173, 178, 183, 238
racial/gendered, 141, 144, 151–4
socialization into, 51, 55, 75
speech community understanding of, 22, 35, 51
language isolates, 89, 241
language materiality, 203, 241
language policy and planning, 100–2, 164, 183, 226, 241
language reclamation, 101, 103, 106, 241, 245
language revitalization, 107
approaches to, 66–7, 86, 96, 99–101
concept/process of, 98–9, 241
Indigenous movements for, 97, 100, 102–6
studies of, 87, 97, 100
language shift, 95, 99, 103, 241, 245
three main elements of, 96–8
language socialization
children's, 48–50, 55–6, 96, 198, 237, 244
concept of, 46–7, 241
ongoing/adult, 55–61
varying processes of, 47–50, 53, 60
language variation, 81, 101, 108–9, 167–9
concept of, 170, 241
language variety, 181
commodification of, 169, 238
concept of, 170, 241
formal/informal, 240, 242
racialized, 150, 154, 161, 235nn1,2
regional, 18, 173–4
langue, 8, 12, 172, 203, 241
Latin, 8–9, 30, 80, 175
Latino community, 15, 51, 156
assumptions about identity of, 62, 137, 144, 148–9
lawyers, talking/thinking like, 58–9, 244
Lefebvre, Henri, 52
Leimgruber, Jakob, 225–6
Leno, Jay, 154
Leonard, Wesley, 87, 101, 160
Levinson, Stephen, 196
Lil' Wayne, 157
linguistic anthropologists
focus areas/approaches of, 19–23, 31–2, 84, 109–10, 205
holistic approach of, 2–3, 7–8, 129, 187
linguistic relativity of (*see* linguistic relativity)
(socio)linguists versus, 7–8, 13–16, 33, 109, 180–1, 235n2
studies/research by, 57–60, 95–7, 113–15, 190–2, 214–15
viewpoints/beliefs of, 13–15, 45–7, 64, 121–3, 146, 160

linguistic anthropology
basic concepts of, 20–3, 43, 183
definition, 3, 242
methods/practices, 15–18, 44, 101, 106, 222–3, 232
principles guiding, 2, 33–5, 87, 99–100, 107, 218–21
shifts in, 23–4, 67, 87, 110
linguistic imperialism, 167–8, 242
linguistic landscape(s), 242
methods/tools for, 226–7, 230, 232
signage in, 223–4, 240, 244, 246
linguistic relativity, 70
approaches/research of, 76–8, 80, 217, 234n2
concept of, 64, 73–4, 81, 242
Indigenous languages and, 91–3
linguistics, 242
debates within, 35, 56, 64, 74, 179
development of, 7–8, 11, 106–7, 126–7
focus areas of, 22–3, 40, 160
language/grammar ideologies in, 72, 137, 151, 164, 233n1, 242
research in, 8, 65, 88, 184
zombie, 103, 107
linguists
on animal versus human communication, 25, 28, 30, 42, 46, 166
focus areas/perspectives of, 2, 89, 13, 20–3, 71, 85, 221
studies/research of, 7, 14–16, 81, 101–2, 224
Lippi-Green, Rosina, 168–9
literacy
concept of, 187, 201, 242
Maktab versus commercial, 197
meta-, 198–9
misconceptions about, 195–7, 200
models of, 197, 201, 237, 240
orality versus, 187, 201–2, 235n1
power and, 197–8, 201
socialization into, 197–9
See also literacy practices; multiliteracies
literacy events, 198–9, 203, 242
literacy practices, 198–201, 242
Li Wei, 166
locution, 111–12, 242
L-variety, 175, 242
Lynch, Allyson, 103–4

MacKee, Freddy, 210–11
Madagascar, 130–1, 241
Majid, Asifa, 82
Malinowski, Bronislaw, 2, 188
Maliseet, 103
Mamakwa, Sol, 84, 86
Mandarin Chinese
Beijing dialect of, 164, 170
learning/knowledge of, 4, 30, 56
Standard, 4, 167, 170, 181
terms/grammar of, 1, 44, 60, 69, 71–2
use versus other languages, 16–17, 55, 82–3, 140, 163–4
Manning, Paul, 57
markedness, language, 177
concept of, 132, 137, 242
examples of, 40, 91, 144
racial/ethnic, 148, 153, 156–9
unmarked versus, 132, 148, 153, 246
Marsh, Gordon, 101
Marshall, perspectives on muggings in, 148–50
Martha's Vineyard, 108–9, 117
Martin, Emily, 77
Martin, Laura, 90
masculinity
biological differences and, 77, 113, 142, 240
critiques of dominant notions of, 135–6, 140
heterosexual norms of, 138–9
policing and, 139
speech/voice styles and, 129–30, 132–3, 137, 241, 244
Maya(n) (people/language), 65, 190, 221, 234n1
Yucatec, 79

McElgunn, Hannah, 67
McElhinny, Bonnie, 139
McIntosh, Janet, 214–15
McLaughlin, Mireille, 175
McLemore, Cynthia, 138
McLuhan, Marshall, 207
McWhorter, John, 71, 73, 212, 217
media ideologies, 205, 210, 242
medium (media)
  choice of, 209–10, 213–15, 237
  concept of, 205, 242
  interdiscursivity and, 209–10, 240
  language dominance as expressive, 65, 167
  as message, 207
  oral versus written language, 38, 187, 242–3
  technological/textual, 205, 207, 209, 212–14
Men Are From Mars, Women Are From Venus (Gray), 124, 127
Mendoza-Denton, Norma, 15
Meek, Barbra, 87, 99
Mertz, Elizabeth, 58–9
metaphors
  concept of, 76, 242
  examples of cultural, 71, 76–8, 83, 115
  language extinction/revitalization, 87, 102
metapragmatic discourse, 141, 242
Mexico/Mexicans, 184, 223
  Indigenous communities in, 79, 102
  racist stereotypes of, 149–50, 154–6
migrants
  multilingual cities of, 177, 225
  speech communities of, 17, 164–5, 170–2
  undocumented, 120, 149, 154–5
Mi'kmaw (language/people), 91, 93, 100, 106–7
Miller, Laura, 136
mock Spanish, 156, 242
Mongolian (language), 99
monolingualism, 169, 181
  variations in Canada, 163–4, 173–4, 183, 225–6
Montreal, 80, 174
  linguistic landscape in, 166, 225–6
  multilingualism in, 182, 184
morphemes, 14, 32, 66, 90, 92, 242
morphology, 19, 241
  concept of, 14, 242
  polysynthesis as structure of, 89, 243
  study of, 15–16, 71
Mubarak, Hosni, 176–7
Muehlmann, Shaylih, 102
mukbang, 43
multilingualism
  artificial intelligence and, 36
  concept of, 163, 165–6, 242
  ideologies of, 173, 175
  language domains and, 96, 98, 102–3, 158, 175–7
  research on, 170, 183–4
  socialization and, 55
  speech communities and, 18, 22, 225
multiliteracies, 200–1, 242
multimodal(ities), 34, 43, 213, 243
multispecies ethnography, 29, 243

nationalism, 118, 175, 179, 240
  language standardization and, 164, 167–8
National Science Foundation (US) reviewers, 58
natural language processing, 35, 243
Nazis, 63
Nicaragua, 38, 40–2
Nineteen Eighty-four (novel), 63–4
North American Regional Vocabulary Survey (NARVS), 228–9, 232
nouchi, 118–19
Nucholls, Janis, 92–3
nuclear weapons, metaphors for, 77–8
"Nuestro Himno," 156
Nuu-cha-nulth, 31, 92, 234n3

Ochs, Elinor
  on gender and language, 20–1, 53–5, 130–2, 142
  on language socialization, 47–9, 54–5
Ohnuki-Tierney, Emiko, 77
Ontario, 3, 22, 84
  direction giving in, 231
open systems of communication, 29–30, 33, 243
orality, 187, 198, 201, 235n1, 243
oral literature, 188–92, 202, 243
Orwell, George, 63–4
Ozaki Koyo, 135

Palmer, Andie, 93
Papua New Guinea, 16–17
  language development in/near, 47–50, 97, 130, 177–8, 241
  love letter writing in, 196, 201
  Tok Pisin (*see* Tok Pisin)
parole, 8, 12, 203, 243
Paz, Alejandro, 120–1
Peele, Jordan, 147
Peirce, Charles Sanders, 20
Pennesi, Karen, 215–16
performance
  as audience centric, 192–3
  gender, 6, 22, 125–6, 129
  oral literature and, 192–4, 203
  three elements of oral, 192–4
  verbal (*see* verbal performance)
performative utterances, 243
performativity, 110–12, 120, 129, 243
Perley, Bernard, 99, 103, 107
perlocution, 111–13, 243
perspectivism, 92, 243
Pewdiepie (YouTuber), 162
philology, 23, 31
  concept of, 7–8, 11, 243
phonemes, 14, 32, 68, 243
phone sex operators, 136–7
phonetics, 14–15, 108, 234n1, 243. *See also* International Phonetic Alphabet
phonology, 24, 209
  approaches to analysing, 64, 71, 88, 109
  concept of, 14, 243
  cultural rules and, 47, 117–18, 241
  language relatedness and difference, 171, 175
pidgins, 178, 180, 185, 235n5, 243
Pine, Lila, 106–7
Pirahã, 74
Pittsburgh, 114, 139
police, 159, 181, 194, 220
  masculinity and, 139
  racist violence by, 62, 140, 208
polysynthesis, 89–92, 243
Poplack, Shana, 180
power relations
  gendered, 128, 131, 135–6, 239
  language reflecting, 19, 106, 141
  literacy and, 197–8, 201
  multilingualism and, 167, 175, 177
  racial, 155–6
pragmatic(s), 179, 195
  concept of, 14, 243
  effects, 19–20, 81, 127, 183
  interdiscursivity and, 208–9, 212, 217
  See also metapragmatic discourse
prescriptivism, 7, 24, 152–3, 243
pretendians, 159–60
principal, 37, 243
private signage, 224–5, 227, 244
prosody, 34, 129, 190, 192, 244
protoconversation, 48–9, 61, 244
public signage, 224–7, 230, 232, 244
Puerto Ricans, 147, 180
Putin, Vladimir, 168

qualitative research methods, 222, 244
quantitative research methods, 109, 119, 222, 231, 244
Quechua/Quichua, 92–3, 221

race, 59
  discourse/comedy about, 147, 154–5, 162, 209
  as identity characteristic, 116–17, 129, 150, 159–61
  language ideologies on, 19, 31, 143–5, 156–60
  literacy and, 198–9
  as socially constructed category, 144–8, 150, 244
racialization
  concept of, 146–7, 244
  cultural belonging and, 5, 128, 144, 150–1, 156–60
  ethnicization versus, 147–8
  language and, 150–1, 154–62, 238
  stereotypes/biases based on, 36, 129, 147–50, 154–5
raciolinguistics, 145, 155–8, 160, 244
racism
  in discourse, 148–50, 154–6, 161–2, 238, 245
  in humour, 154–6, 161–2, 238
  immigrants facing, 148–9, 154, 174
  Latinos/Mexicans facing, 149–50, 154–6
  in police violence, 62, 140, 208
  zombie, 147
Rampton, Ben, 158–9
rapport-talk, 128, 244
Received Pronunciation (RP), 117–19
reconciliation, 87, 106, 191–2, 244
recursion, 28, 74
refugees, 120
registers, 71, 165, 208, 239–40
  concept of, 117–19, 123, 235n2, 244
relative spatial reference, 79, 244
remediation, 210, 212, 216, 244
report-talk, 128, 244
residential schools, 86–7, 100–1
Rettberg, Jill Walker, 36
Romaine, Suzanne, 170
Rosa, Jonathan, 145, 208–9
Roth-Gordon, Jennifer, 150
Russell, Bertrand, 110–11
Russia(n), 89, 146, 203
  colonial expansion in Ukraine, 168
  language features in, 68–72
  use of language, 168, 181

Sakha, 181, 201–3
salvage ethnography, 101, 244
Sanskrit, 8, 30, 170, 189
Santa Ana, Otto, 154–5
Sapir, Edward, 31, 65, 71, 190
Sapir-Whorf hypothesis, 74
  concept of, 64, 67, 244
  evaluations/critiques of, 70–3
Saussure, Ferdinand de, 8, 11–12, 20, 23, 111, 203
Schieffelin, Bambi, 47–8, 50, 55
Schiffrin, Deborah, 115–16
Schlegl, Lisa, 231
Schreyer, Christine, 97–8
Secwepemc, 93
self-lowering, 48, 50, 244
semanticity, 32–3
semantics, 20, 27–8, 66
  concept of, 14, 245
  ethno- (*see* ethnosemantics)
semiotics, 19–20, 76, 245
semi-speakers, 98, 102, 245
semi-structured interviews, 222, 245
Senghas, Ann, 40–2
sexism, 125, 131, 209
shibboleths, 114, 123, 165, 182, 245
Shohet, Merav, 45–6, 50
Shulist, Sarah, 102–3
signified, 11, 19–20, 240, 245–6
signifier, 11, 19–20, 240, 245–6
signifyin', 194–5, 203, 245
sign language, 245
  absolute spatial reference system in, 80
  American (*see* American Sign Language)
  in Nicaragua, 38, 40–2
  as real language, 38–42, 235n1

sign(s), 9
  concept/types of, 11, 20, 240, 245–6
  functions of, 223–4, 232, 240
  home- (*see* homesigns)
  human language production of, 32, 187, 213
  language (*see* sign language)
  private (*see* private signage)
  public (*see* public signage)
  speech communities and, 17, 223, 245
  study of, 19–20, 223–4, 232, 242, 245
Siksiká, 91, 103
Simone, Nina, 152
Skinner, B.F., 12
sleeping language, 101, 245
Smitherman, Geneva, 150–1
social class
  grammar/language use and, 109, 117–19, 135, 154, 169–70
  maintenance of distinctions in, 18, 135, 198–9, 203
  societal worldview integration of, 76, 111, 115
  theorist analysis of, 38, 179, 229–30
social context, 240
  discourse and, 33–5, 239, 245
  understanding language meaning via, 14, 20, 233n2, 243
social deixis, 80, 245
social media, 159, 162, 202
  affordances through, 207–8, 216, 219
  profile styling on, 210–11, 215
  public commentary/reactions via, 18, 36, 142, 217
  speech communities via, 205–6
sociolinguistics, 7, 133, 154, 235n2
  concept and waves of, 109–10, 245
  research in, 115, 118, 165–6, 180, 184, 224–5, 231
Solomon Islands pidgin, 178–9, 235n5
Spain, 146, 224–5
Spanish, 225
  discrimination for use of, 155–6, 174
  language borrowing/switching from, 29, 154–6, 180, 184, 221
  mock, 155–6, 242
  perspectives on reality in, 71, 149
  speech communities, 40, 51–2, 62, 147, 170
  words/phrasing, 33, 155–6
spatial deixis, 79, 82, 245
speech act(s), 137
  concept of, 111, 245
  felicity conditions and, 113, 119, 123, 239
  identities and consequences of, 112–13, 116, 119–21, 159
  parts of, 111, 240, 242–3
speech communities, 35, 197
  complex concepts of, 16–19, 245
  cultural socialization in, 46, 51, 56, 58, 73, 78
  digital, 205–6
  endangerment/revitalization of, 67, 95, 98–100, 107, 239–42
  gendered, 130
  language ideologies of, 18–19, 22, 42, 194, 241
  multilingual/diglossia, 164, 170, 175, 183, 239–42
  racialized, 150, 155–6, 160, 194–5, 203
  signs for, 222–3, 246
  theorizing/research on, 13, 23, 107–10, 229
Spitulnik, Debra, 209–10
standardization, language, 98, 164–9, 245
stereotypes, 2, 36
  gendered, 125, 129–31, 138, 141, 241
  language ideologies and, 19, 119, 241
  racial, 147–8, 151, 154–6
  regional, 21–2
Street, Brian, 197
Sumerian (language), 95, 186
superdiversity, 164, 245

symbol(s), 68, 176
  concept of, 20, 246
  first recorded language use of, 186
  gendered, 20, 133
  language as based on, 20, 26, 76, 103
  semiotic approach to, 20, 234n1
  sign language visual, 26, 28
  See also International Phonetic Alphabet
symbolic function, 224, 226, 232, 246
synchronic approach, 11, 246
syntax, 60
  concept of, 14, 246
  language development/forms in, 98, 132, 178, 241
  language differences in, 92, 144, 171
  linguistic study/elements of, 14, 16, 19, 64, 71, 88, 239
  sign language development of, 28, 39–40

Tagliamonte, Sali, 231
TallBear, Kim, 146
Tamil, 72, 170, 182–3
Tannen, Deborah, 127–8, 130
Tanzania, 122–3, 167
telephone(s), 227, 232
  communication via, 200, 204, 212–14
  fantasy line operators, 136–7
  invention and social adoption of, 206–7, 209
  personal use/allowances via, 35, 200–1, 209
  See also texting
Teller, Edward, 78
texting
  affordances via, 209–10, 212–13, 217
  breaking up via, 204–5
  email versus, 210, 215–16
  emoji in, 204, 213, 239
  lol, 211–12, 215
  multiliteracies and, 200, 214, 242
text(s), 243
  AI/computer analysis of, 35–6
  anthropological/linguistic study of, 7, 11–13, 16, 190–1, 239
  canonical, 58, 65, 186–7, 202, 243
  concept of, 187–8, 195, 246
  early documentation of Indigenous, 85, 101
  examples of oral, 37, 185, 188–91, 243
  genres of, 192, 240
  literacy and power, 195–8, 200–1, 203, 242
  oral versus written, 187–92, 195–6, 199–202
  performing, 192–4
  See also literacy practices; transcription
Tibet(an), 52–4
Tiger Mother phenomenon, 148
Tim Hortons, 231
Tinder, 210–11
Tok Pisin, 16–17, 131, 177–9, 214
transcription, 44, 58, 187, 190, 223
  concept of, 34, 246
transgender people, 126, 133
translanguaging, 166, 246
translatability, 31–2, 71, 213, 246
Trouillot, Michel-Rolph, 2–3
Trump, Donald, 36–7, 139, 174
Turing Test, 35
Twitter (X), 36, 162, 18, 207–8
Tylor, Edward, 4–6

unmarked language, 132, 148, 246
uptalk, 127, 138
Urciuoli, Bonnie, 146–8
Uyghur men, 140

verbal hygiene, 132, 138, 246
verbal performance, 128, 130, 239, 241
  concept of, 194, 246
Vietnam(ese), 11, 45–7, 50, 163
Vigouroux, Cécile B., 143
violence, 191
  anti-Black stereotypes of, 149–50

gendered/domestic, 131, 141
police, 62, 139–40, 194, 208
vocal fry, 134–6, 138, 246
Vološinov, Valentin, 111–12, 234n1

Ward, Shannon, 52–4
Watson, Marcus, 18, 160–1
Wharry, Cheryl, 193–4
white supremacy, contesting, 145, 160
Whorf, Benjamin Lee, 65–7, 70, 72–3, 234nn1,3
Williams, Evan, 207–8
Wittgenstein, Ludwig, 111–12, 234n2
Wolf, Naomi, 131–2, 134
women
dialect/regional language use by, 17, 109, 191–2
gendered ways of speaking, 124, 126–30, 133–8
marginalization of, 17, 19, 127, 131–2, 239
objectification of, 122–3, 138–9
social/familial relations, 48–9, 115, 124, 200, 209–10
stereotypes about, 19, 113, 124–5, 135–6, 140–2, 155
violence against, 139, 141
See also femininity; gender(ed)
Wortham, Stanton, 148–9
writing, 204, 212
anthropological, 4, 101, 111, 152, 234n2
complex ties to speech, 187–8, 200–1, 240
development of, 26, 186–7, 195–6, 207
Indigenous/ancient, 65, 95, 186
non-human, 36, 64
societal power and, 164, 169, 185, 198, 202
See also text(s)

Y'a bon (French phrase), 143–4
Yang, Jie, 141
Yoruba, 72, 88

Zambia, 209–10
Zimman, Lal, 133
zombie(s)
linguistics, 103, 107
racist, 147